6/21/93

To Patty

with whom I go back to
Kindergarten

Warmest Remembrances.

Bob

The Philadelphia Lawyer
A History, 1735-1945

The Philadelphia Lawyer
A History, 1735-1945

Robert R. Bell

SUP

Selinsgrove: Susquehanna University Press
London and Toronto: Associated University Presses

Associated University Presses
440 Forsgate Drive
Cranbury, NJ 08512

Associated University Presses
25 Sicilian Avenue
London WC1A 2QH, England

Associated University Presses
P.O. Box 39, Clarkson Pstl. Stn.
Mississauga, Ontario,
L5J 3X9 Canada

The paper used in this publication meets the requirements
of the American National Standard for Permanence of Paper
for Printed Library Materials Z39.48-1984.

Library of Congress Cataloging-in-Publication Data

Bell, Robert R., 1924-
    The Philadelphia lawyer: a history, 1735-1945/Robert R. Bell.
        p.   cm.
    Includes bibliographical references and index.
    ISBN 0-945636-26-1 (alk. paper)
    1. Lawyers—Pennsylvania—Philadelphia—History.   2. Lawyers—
Pennsylvania—Philadelphia—Biography.   I. Title.
KFP78.B45   1992
349.748'11'092—dc20
[347.48110092]   91-50194
                                                                                CIP

PRINTED IN THE UNITED STATES OF AMERICA

To my wife,
Wendy Lutkins Bell,
a Philadelphia lawyer

Contents

8 CONTENTS

Preface

One focus of attention in this book is to look at the interrelationship between the old Philadelphia upper class and the legal profession. Basically the upper class refers to a group of old Philadelphia families whose members were descendants of successful individuals. Occasionally they are of one, but far more often of two or more generations; those families have been at the top of the Philadelphia social class hierarchy. The individuals have typically grown up together, been socialized in the same schools, were friends and often intermarried. They have traditionally maintained a style of life socially restricted to those like themselves. They have had as a major value a commitment to privacy. Therefore much about their lives is unknown to the public.

There have been many attempts by sociologists to define social class. Our definition of the Philadelphia upper class is similar to that of E. Digby Baltzell in that we use listing in the *Social Register*[1] to define membership. In the first Philadelphia Social Register[2] in 1898 there were 1939 families, but by 1940 the number of families had increased to 5,150. Before its first publication in 1900 there was nothing similar to be used to establish upper-class membership. The method used has been to trace back from the *Social Register* the families and assign upper class status to their ancestors. Many of the early upper class families clearly had descendants listed in 1900. It has also been helpful, when possible, to use references from the Assembly Balls and membership in the *Philadelphia Club*. Both of those are clearly recognized upper class institutions. Of course this method is subjective and undoubtably has some error. It is the most accurate measurement of old Philadelphia status possible to devise, however. The interest in defining the upper class is to show the influence the old families had on law and how intimately intertwined the Philadelphia lawyer has been with the upper class.

In each chapter, for a historical period, an examination is made of the emerging American legal system, and the training and practice of law. Before the revolutionary war most American law was British law. After the Revolution there was often bitter struggles over the continued use of British common law. There was never any really serious alternative to the common law, however. Rapidly the British common law became modified to become American common law and that was the major focus of law up until the Civil War. Following the Civil War and well into the twentieth century the major thrust of law was that related to business, industrialization, and especially

9

corporations. By the 1930s there was an increasing focus of federal commissions and statute law.

During the decades the training of lawyers underwent change. Until into the twentieth century most lawyers were trained in law offices, and it was only slowly that law schools became the accepted means of legal training. For most of American history lawyers practiced alone and often appeared in court as advocates where their forensic skills were highly valued. For the various historical eras, when materials are available, the attempt is to show how Philadelphia lawyers lived, some of their values, how they learned to become lawyers, and how they practiced law. Anecdotal material is used to illustrate those points whenever possible. Forty-two Philadelphia lawyers were interviewed. They were mostly persons who entered the bar in the 1920s and 1930s. Some of their recollections and insights are presented, and for their help I am most appreciative.

Following each chapter there is a profile of a Philadelphia lawyer from that period. Most of the profiles are of outstanding lawyers not only in their time but throughout the history of great Philadelphia lawyers. The profiles attempt to show what was important to their legal careers and what made them outstanding lawyers.

This book could not have been researched without the professional help of Professor John M. Lindsey and his staff of the Temple University Law Library. Of equal importance for their great help was Professor Regina Smith and her staff at the Jenkins Law Library of the Philadelphia Bar Association. I would also like to thank Martindale-Hubbell Inc, publisher of the *Law Directory*, for their assistance.

In preparing the epilogue I spent several hours talking with each of the following Philadelphia lawyers: Wendy Lutkins Bell, Leonard Dubin, Milton Feldman, Thomas Hyndman, Kathleen M. Shay, and Harold P. Starr. I thank them for their many valuable insights. A special thanks to my stepdaughter, Bonnie Scott Jones, a Yale University law student, for sharing her knowledge about the Law School Admission Test (LSAT) and what it takes to do well on it.

The Philadelphia Lawyer
A History, 1735-1945

1

Early Colonies: 1682 to 1750

The lawyers, all, both great and small
  Come here to cheat the people
For be it known that justice's flown
  And perches on the steeple
                    —New York City Hall, mid-1700s

Pennsylvania was founded in 1682, about fifty years after the first settlement in Massachusetts. In 1683, sixty ships landed at Philadelphia, and brought thousands of settlers to expand the new town and to settle the interior land of Pennsylvania. Fifteen years after the city was first settled it had grown to a population of five thousand, and was equal to New York in wealth and trade.

The development of a legal system came about in the colonies because the social forces in America were based on the old European patterns, especially English ones. There were no social institutions transported to America intact. The emerging institutions were a combination of the old and the new. Of course, all social institutions in the modern world are based on laws, and the American society could never have come about without a legal system.

The system of trade and commerce that developed in Philadelphia was firmly rooted in the English system. In the new world, however, there were many unique factors that highly influenced trade. One factor was in being thousands of miles away from Britain and that meant that Philadelphia, as the other colonies, had to develop many of their own commercial markets. Problems emerged because England usually treated the trade of each colony as if that colony were only a few miles away from London. The commercial law that developed in America concerned with trade had to be changed from the laws used in England. Ultimately the refusal by England to modify their trade rules was a basic disagreement that contributed greatly to the American Revolution. From the beginning America developed a legal system increasingly unique and special to the new conditions and needs of the colonies.

In modern society law begins with lawyers and through them the conducting of transactions, of determining causes, and of advising parties as to legal questions. As law over time became more complex it passed into the hands of specialists in law. Justice according to the law is always justice administered by lawyers where lawyers as judges are aided by lawyers as advocates. The

13

legal system of seventeenth century England was not systematic, but rather was based on old traditions and often historical peculiarities. For example, in the seventeenth century the ancient Courts of the Shire were still very active in England.

In England land was the basis of wealth and social status, and land law was the heart of the royal common law. By the eighteenth century land in England was already a scare commodity. In contrast, the colonies had no shortage of land. Rather, their shortages were people, livestock, and hard money. This difference meant that the legal and social system that emerged in America was not fixed to estates of land as it was in England.

In some colonies land passed from person to person in a relatively free way, whereas in other colonies the informal means of conveyance operated alongside the classic forms. For example, in early Maryland, conveyances of land were often made by written agreement on the back of original patents, like the endorsement on a check. One of the first American legal inventions was the registration and recording of land titles.

In Europe when a man died his property was typically divided according to two different rules. The common law rules and courts controlled his land, whereas the church laws and courts controlled his personal property. If he left no will the common law gave the oldest son the land, and the church courts would divide his material goods in equal shares among his children. The colonies greatly modified the legal inheritance of land. In Europe primogeniture was the rule, but in the northern American colonies, remote from English law and upper class English society, there was little interest in primogeniture. In Pennsylvania it was rejected in favor of a double portion for the oldest son. In classic English law, the widow's share of her husband's land, her dowry, was a life interest in a third of her husband's land. Colonial law was much less rigid, however. For example, in Massachusetts, magistrates had the discretion to modify the wife's share according to her needs as well as the standards set by the community.[1]

In Penn's land, before the English colonization, there had been Indians and Swedes with some legal systems, but no remains have survived. There have been some influences handed down from the Dutch laws. For example, the office of district attorney may have been of Dutch origin. Possibly most important, was that the commonwealth courts of justice were first established by the Swedes in 1642. Along the eastern seaboard there were as many legal systems as there were colonies. Each colony had been founded at a different time and was isolated from others by distance and the limits of transportation. A hundred years separated the beginnings of Massachusetts from the beginnings of Georgia, and during that century European law underwent change. Therefore different colonies began at different stages in European historical influence. Whatever the period, however, the colonies depended overwhelmingly on

English law because that was the law they brought with them. In general the northern colonies deviated less from standard English law than did the southern colonies.

Two decades before the American Revolution, Blackstone wrote what he believed to be the essence of the Royal common law, and his *Commentaries* became a best seller. That work was not available in the colonies before the 1750s, however. The English legal system stood apart from most European systems because the law in France and Germany was statutory, whereas the English common law was the unwritten law—although not literally; the ultimate, highest source of law was not through enactment but rather through "general custom" as reflected in the decisions of English common law judges. Those judges had been the "depositories of the laws," the men of wisdom, who had to decide according to the law of the land.

Common law was the law made by judges. In practice, the judges relied on their own past actions, which they modified under the influence of changing times and changing patterns of litigation. Therefore common law adhered to precedent as a general rule, and precedent became one of the basic concepts of common law. Yet, from the beginning, American judges always took for themselves the right to overrule an earlier case if they considered it wrong. For many years American judges looked at statutes with some suspicion because they often saw them as intrusions on the common law. Unlike the statutory law the common law does not concern itself with the hypothetical or future case. Rather, it confines itself to actual disputes; if no one brings up a new matter, it will not be decided. The common law was often not only slow but incapable of bringing about many of the changes needed in the colonies.

The early American lawyers probably never heard of colonial cases and statutes because *Law Reports* did not become accessible until well after the Revolution. In the period from early settlement to the Revolution many legal needs in America became very different from those of England. Furthermore, the legal needs of a small colony in Massachusetts that was run by clergymen were different from what rapidly became the busy commercial center of Philadelphia. In the early years, colonial laws were seen as irrelevant by the British. The British assumption was that if the common law system could meet the needs of the most powerful nation of the time it could certainly define the conditions of the colonies.

The laws of each colony evolved as a loose collection of related traditions, some English and some local. The colonies began with simple, undifferentiated structures that over time became increasingly complex. England, in the mid-eighteenth century had a collection of highly specialized courts that were frequently overlapping and often counterproductive. There were more than a hundred courts ranging from the royal courts with general jurisdiction to such specialized courts as the Stannarce, concerned with tin mines and tin mine workers in Cornwell and Devon.[2] The courts of England had evolved to meet highly specialized vested interests, but in the colonies they had to meet the more general problems of a developing society.

The laws laid down in the early days of the colonies by the British were like military orders that were to be obeyed without question. In the beginning, judicial business generally was not separated from public business. The same people who made the laws enforced them. The people who decided cases were also the business and religious leaders of the community. The court system grew and subdivided as the population increased. The expanding population also led to many new legal problems as new land was being settled westward.

By 1600, the English lawyers had become a professional group of men educated specifically in the area of law. Because they came out of the Inns of Court they had no connection with English universities and therefore had no exposure to Roman law. Their legal training was primarily practical rather than jurisprudential, and their training was in the common law. At that time common law concentrated almost entirely on two general topics. Those were the formal legal processes and the law relating to land. Common law was essentially the law of the royal central courts and for the most part those courts handled the legal problems of a very few people. Those were the lords and ladies, landed gentry, high-ranking clergy, and wealthy merchants. The common law was for and of the gentry and the nobility, whereas the great mass of the population was hardly touched by the system and was only indirectly under its rule. Law books were written at the seat of power, and they dealt with the king's kind of law. The day-by-day law of the lower order was barely chronicled.[3]

In England there were two contradictory systems of civil law that coexisted, but not always peacefully. Those were the common law and equity. In some ways common law and equity complemented each other. The common law could proclaim duties and rights, but it could not compel any kind of performance, other than the payment of money. Equity, conversely, had a range of other solutions. For example, the injunction, an order commanding a person to do some specific act or to forebear from something he had been or might be doing. It was enforceable because, "if the defendant disobeyed, the chancellor could declare him in contempt and put him in jail. Early equity in England had power over persons, not things."[4]

In New England, the Puritan clergy and Puritan magistrates exercised great control over the community. Many colonists believed that the magistrates and clergy, and they alone, had all the knowledge and experience necessary for good government. The common law of England was in general to be observed entirely because it was a declaration of divine law as understood by the clergy. Those early courts often heard arguments as to whether an opinion allegedly voiced by Moses or the prophets counted infinitely more than a decision of the king's court chancellor.

The English common law was very unpopular among most of the early settlers because they distrusted its formalism and technical language. They also believed that the ideas fitted the medieval society they had left behind rather than the new society they were creating. Thomas Powell once said to Ben Franklin that the colonials being English carried with them the laws of the land, and therefore the common law of England was at all times the law of the colonies. Franklin's response was that the settlers carried with them a right to such parts of the laws of land as they judged advantageous. They also had the right to make such other laws as they felt necessary, however, so long as they did not infringe on the general rights of England.

The English common law came to be of major importance to the developing colonies in their struggle against England. During the eighteenth century in England the common law had been a powerful weapon in Parliament's struggle against an absolute monarchy. It was in that context that the common law began to be taken over as a colonial weapon in America's struggle for freedom. The great arguments against the Writs of Assistance, delivered in 1761 before the English judges in a Massachusetts Court by James Otis, were arguments taken directly out of the common law tradition and the parliamentary struggles. As the political use of the common law became important to the colonist, the law itself began to gain wider acceptance. "In effect, those who examined the British legal thinkers to find arguments for freedom remained to absorb the British approach to law."[5]

In Philadelphia the early hostility to the common law was strong and lasting. The Quakers, including William Penn, had many bitter experiences with English laws, English courts, and English lawyers. They saw the profession of law as a malevolent form of conflict, and viewed the legal profession as by definition evil and completely in opposition to their values of good fellowship. They also had a zealous belief that rejected all forms of strife and controversy. Certainly the early Quakers slowed down the initial development of a systematic body of law as well as a true legal profession.

William Penn was a seventeenth-century Royalist and aristocrat. He was intolerant of those, like lawyers, who might challenge his rights, and he was arrogant toward those he felt might try to deny him. The Quakers strongly believed in order, however, and knew it was necessary to have laws to govern themselves. Penn provided the colony with a set of laws written in a language that would be understandable to all. First, every man was allowed to plead his case. The first English courts in Pennsylvania were the Courts of Assizes, which had both legislative and judicial functions. There were also the Courts of Session, but because the Quakers refused to participate in legal controversies those courts initially had their judicial positions filled by laymen. The practice of referring litigation to peacemakers or referees became popular, and a large share of the administration of justice was entrusted to them.

The question of Quakers taking oaths with reference to law came up early.

In 1700, in the court of Quarter Sessions, William Penn was present after his return from England. The Justices of Peace disputed about their willingness to be sworn into their new commissions. Some alleged they could not in conscience take an oath and others insisted it was their duty. "Finally the dilemma was settled by the Governor, in substituting new names in the place of those who demurred, and then all were sworn."[6]

"The first organization of the Courts was admirable for its simplicity and convenience. The County Court was made the ground work of the edifice. It was composed of the Justices of Peace of the several counties, with an appeal to the Provincial or Supreme Court." The Provincial Court varied from three to five judges, who went on their circuits every fall and spring to each county. They dealt with the higher criminal offenses and all appeals from the County Courts, both in law and in equity. "To complete the structure were added the Quarter Sessions and Orphan's Court, and the Admiralty."[7]

Hostility to the chancery was common in the eighteenth century because it was closely associated with executive power. With equity there were no juries, and so there were no controls against the use of those courts to carry out royal policy. Equity courts also usually sat only in the capital, and unlike the common law those equity courts were not brought to all citizens. In America land transactions had shifted from status to contract so that land rights were no longer matters of family, birth, and tradition. Land had become a commodity traded on the open market.

Early Pennsylvania laws had the proscription that all officers and commissioners should profess a belief in Jesus Christ as the Son of God and the Savior of the world. The effect was that it excluded Jews but not Catholics. There were also legal stipulations that all children would be given the opportunity to learn to write and read the Scriptures by twelve years of age. Punishment was provided for those guilty of swearing and cursing, for sexual crimes, for those who sold liquor to the Indians, engaged in dueling, or who were "Clamorous, Scolding and Railing with the Tongues." Because of the Quaker aversion to anything that suggested self-indulgence they were against all forms of pleasure. There were Philadelphia laws that forbade all the creature comforts: "Prizes, Stage-plays, Masques, Revels, Bull-baiting, Cock-fighting, Cards, Dice, Lotteries, or such like enticing, vain and evil Sports and Games."[8]

In 1830 John F. Watson wrote a book that included antidotes about early Philadelphia. One of the earliest court trials he found to have taken place was in 1685. John Rambo was indicted in answer to the charge brought by Peter Cock for his having had criminal intercourse with his daughter Bridget. The witnesses testified that about the time of Christmas 1684, the said John Rambo came at midnight to the hosue of the father, and "by pulling off a plank of the house, in the loft, near the chamber, he jumped down to the floor, and directly after got into the bed wherein said Bridget and her two sisters (aged

16 and 19) were also laying." Rambo said that "he was resolved to be the husband of Bridgett (even as his brother had before taking another sister) and must therefore lie there. Whereupon, there being a crowded place, the two sisters, with strange submission, withdrew and lay upon the floor all night in a cold December! The court after a verdict of the jury, adjudged John Rambo to marry Bridgett before she delivered, or then maintain the child. Both to be fined £10 each."[9]

In the year 1705, men were fined by law 20 shillings for laboring on the Sabbath-day, and 10 shillings for being found tippling in a tavern on that day. Also in 1705 there was made an act against fornication and adultery. For adultery the parties received 21 lashes and hard labor for one year. For a second offence seven years imprisonment. For fornication, 21 lashes or pay £10 fine each.[10]

Although the early Quaker influences were anti-intellectual and antilitigation there were also other strong forces in the world of ideas. In the early colonies, including Pennsylvania, there were political writers who were among the ablest and best educated minds in the New World. Those men were greatly influenced by the ideas from abroad that they believed to fit their own experiences. One of the most important ideas was the doctrine of natural rights from John Locke's *Two Treatises of Civil Government*, published in 1690. That work helped to destroy the divine right theory of kingship. The Lockean view was that when men accepted government they entered into a "social contract" with their rulers. In return for security and protection, they accepted the ruler's authority. If the ruler violated his part of the bargain, however, the people were no longer bound by the contract. They then had the right to overthrow the government and establish a new one. Those were very exciting ideas and therefore attractive to the people of the colonies as their political obedience to England continued to be weakened and eventually broken.

In business, contractual relationships were becoming increasingly common. The common law rights of free-born Englishmen were closely identified with the natural rights of man. Those legal rights were sustained by the two English authorities who were immensely influential in America, Sir William Blackstone and Sir Edward Coke. Clearly the ideas about natural rights were influential long before the Declaration of Independence was written.

The body of early Pennsylvania laws consisted of laws agreed in England in 1682. Those were the Great Law, enacted at Chester in 1682, the Act of Settlement enacted in Philadelphia, 1683, eighty chapters of statutes passed in 1683, the Frame of Government enacted in 1683 and 1696, and the Charter of Privileges and statutes of 1701. The early laws were so arbitrary in their legal proceedings that the first governor, Benjamin Fletcher, informed the assembly that some of the laws were simply repugnant to the law of England and, hence, invalid. In the early courts no lawyer or attorney was permitted to appear before them. In 1682 the first chief justice, Dr. Nicholas More, a physician by training was appointed until 1743. With only a few exceptions, the most important judicial position in Pennsylvania was held by laymen. Almost all the people engaged in the administration of justice during the early years of the colony were "distinguished rather for their purity than their learning, for their high standing in the community, and their general capacity more than their legal attainment."[11]

In those early days the judiciary was not seen as an important branch of government. During the seventeenth century the most significant theoretical problem in political thinking was as to the rights of the individual citizen with respect to the Crown. There had to develop a clearer understanding of the nature of civil rights before the question as to the role of courts in administering those rights was examined to any great extent.

After Penn's arrival, appellate review was conducted by the provincial council, a body that performed both executive and judicial functions. Those men were elected by the citizens of Pennsylvania. Until the Revolution, however, the ultimate appeal from a Pennsylvania judgment was to the Crown.

The system where the council performed a judicial function in addition to its executive function was not entirely successful. The work load was too heavy, and because the council met only in Philadelphia, appeals were usually inconvenient and expensive when persons had to travel to Philadelphia to pursue their cases. As a result, in 1684 an act was passed creating a provincial court that consisted of five judges and was appointed by the governor. In addition to sitting twice a year in Philadelphia two of the judges rode a circuit. That Court was the predecessor of the present Supreme Court and had jurisdiction over appeals "as well as all civil and criminal cases of first impression over which there was no jurisdiction in the local district courts."[12]

It was in the hands of the upper class that the government of Philadelphia and the province rested in so far as it was not controlled by the proprieter or his representatives. It was the wealthy merchants and professional men who made up the membership of the provincial council, the assembly, the city council, and the magistracy. They constituted a small oligarchy of leading citizens. The same men constantly met in the various offices, and again in the social clubs and the philanthropic organizations for which Philadelphia was becoming famous. "Local society and government were not less an aristocracy because there was no royal court, no dominant church, and no semi-feudal body of land holders."[13]

The power to elect courts of justice and to appoint all judicial officers in and for the province of Pennsylvania was by express terms of the charter conferred by the proprietary. The county courts were vested with criminal jurisdiction in all except "cases of heinous and enormous crimes." Trials for larceny, swearing and maiming the prosecutor's hogs, unduly encouraging drunkenness, selling rum to the Indians, and offenses against public morality and decency constituted the bulk of the criminal business. "Lying in conversation was fined half a crown, drinking health (toasts) which might provoke people to unnecessary and excessive drinking" was fined five shillings. No person could "smoke tobacco on the streets of Philadelphia on penalty of a fine of 12 pence to be applied to the purchase of leather buckets and other instruments against fire." Any person "convicted of playing cards, dice, lotteries or other such like enticing, vain, or evil sports and games" was to be fined five shillings or to be imprisoned five days at hard labor.[14]

In criminal law there was the frequent use of physical punishments, like public whippings on the pillory or being placed in the stocks. Public opinion and shame were important instruments of punishment. In neither theory or practice, however, was colonial punishment especially bloodthirsty for the time. The colonies had fewer capital crimes on the books than were found in England, and the death penalty was not as often used. There are records of a total of forty executions in the colonies before 1660. Fifteen were in Massachusetts during that period; four for murder, two for infanticide, two for adultery, two for witchcraft, and one for "buggery." There were also four Quakers who were put to death. They went to Massachusetts and insisted on being martyrs, and the Puritans obliged them.[15]

The early court procedures were that on the day set for a trial or a hearing the parties appeared in person, or were represented by friends, to assert or defend their rights. If the defendant failed to appear a judgment was entered against him for default. If both parties were present the defendant was asked to answer the charge. Two witnesses were needed to establish the plaintiff's case. In general the judicial proceedings were designed to discourage litigation as much as possible. In criminal cases the prisoner was simply brought before the justices on their warrant and tried without either indictment or pleas. The whipping post, the pillory, and the imposition of fines were usually resorted to as punishment rather than long terms of imprisonment. Able-bodied men were too important to the community to lock them away in prison. Furthermore, no one wanted to pay taxes to support prisons.

From the first days of English settlement in Pennsylvania the primitive courts and legal procedures were in operation. From the very beginning the court was the most important social institution for providing social contact and control over the lives of the settlers. Those courts often touched individual lives through the legal process, writs, subpoenas, and orders that were enforced by constables and sheriffs. On the days when the courts were in session they were a popular gathering place. Court days and market days were often the same, making those days something of a holiday. The demands of work were so great that days off were few, and any day away from drudgery, whatever the occasion, was a welcome relief.

Those early courts established title to land and made it possible for the individual to collect any debts due him. In return the courts imposed obligations in the manner of taxes, levies, and jury service. Those early courts also regulated the liquor trade and the manufacture of such products as bread, flour, and leather goods. They were regulating hunting and fishing and the operation of ferries, registering cattle brands, and offering bounties for wolves. The courts were also naturalizing immigrants and licensing peddlers. They had the responsibility to protect those who were unable to protect themselves—the poor, the insane, the Indians, the blacks, the illegitimate children, and the indentured servants. In the end they administered the estates of those who died. In those early days the magistrate court gave almost all the legal structure and protection in the new country. Those courts, or some legal equivalent, were an absolute necessity for the development of the new colonies.[16]

Serving on the provincial council in Philadelphia were the most influential and prominent men of the community. They represented the most conservative and aristocratic element of society. The council was designed to impose checks and controls over the hasty and sometimes ill-advised actions of the assembly. The council's duties were executive, legislative, and judicial. There were also municipal regulations controlling behavior. For example, in 1693 in Philadelphia constables were empowered to arrest black men and women whom "they should find gadding abroad on the first days of the week, without a ticket from their Mr. and Mrs. and to carry them to gaol, there to remain the night and that without drink or meat and to cause them to be publicly whipt next morning with thirty-nine lashes, well laid ones, on their backs."[17]

The colonial laws punishing gaming, idleness, drunkenness, lying, and disobedient children were not idle threats. Those laws were taken and applied very seriously. Rules about personal conduct and about sexual morality fell most on the poorer people because of the belief that the public nature of punishment was to "reteach and retouch the erring soul." One Pennsylvania law of 1700 (disallowed five years later) was aimed at persons "clamorous with their tongues"; it gave the magistrate discretion to sentence the offending to be gagged and stood in public place." Other laws said if an indentured servant refused to serve his term, he was punished with extra years of service. That too was usually the fate of servant women who gave birth to illegitimate children. Fines were believed to be useless against the poor, and imprisonment would punish the master by depriving him of the servant's labor. Extra service was seen as the most effective punishment.[18]

Margaret Mattson was tried before the proprietary court in 1683. The evidence against her was that several witnesses declared they had been told by others that she bewitched their cattle. One swore that while boiling the heart of a calf, which he supposed had died by witchcraft, the prisoner came into his house and was "visibly disposed by him doing so." Another witness declared that a few nights before, his wife had waked him in great fright, alleging that she had seen a great light and an old woman with a knife in her hand at "Bedd's feet." Margaret Mattson conducted her own defense with great ability and presence of mind. She denied the allegations and forcefully pointed out that every particle of evidence against her was hearsay. The verdict was "guilty of having the common fame of a witch, but not guilty in manner and form as she stands indicted." She was released.[19]

Almost up to the time of the Revolution, because of expediency as well as scarcity of trained lawyers, the judges were usually not familiar with the law. That was most often found in lower courts, but even the higher courts had their share of incompetent laymen serving as judges. The first settlers mostly came from segments of the English population with no contact with the common law courts at Westminster and the kinds of laws those courts administered. When they were in England the colonists had experienced law through the minor lower courts of local attorneys or solicitors. With little experience in the king's court the colonial courts often were not guided by English law and procedure in the administration of justice. As a result colonial law was constantly changing and marked by uncertainty.

During those early years the lawyer in Philadelphia was often given high status for their learning and their high standing in the community rather than because of any great legal achievements. Most of the lawyer's cases were simple in principle, readily understandable, and easy to process. Nevertheless, the legal profession was often viewed with distrust and dislike. The law profession was seen as opposed to the views of peaceful good fellowship that the Quaker beliefs had taught them to value as an essential part of the true Christian character. In 1698 Gabriel Thomas said: "Of lawyers and Physicians I shall say nothing, because this Country is very Peaceable and Healthy; long may it so continue and never have occasion for the Tongue of the one, or the Pen of the other, both equally destructive to men's Estates and Lives."[20]

In 1683, the first gentlemen were admitted to practice, as attorneys-at-law in the County Courts of the city and county of Philadelphia. They were Francis Pastorius, Charles Pickering and John White. Over the next three years also admitted were Samuel Husent, Samuel Jenings, John Jones, Edward Lord, Dr. Nicholas More and Patrick Robinson. By 1735 about 35 lawyers had been admitted to the Philadelphia bar.[21]

Chief Justice Tilghman, was the grandson of Tench Frances, who was attorney general in 1745. Tilghman was connected by marriage and association with the most eminent families of the bar and according to Horace Binney was most knowledgeable about the "primitive" Philadelphia bar. Binney wrote that "from what I have been able to learn of the early history of Pennsylvania, it was a long time before she passed any lawyers of eminence. There was never wanting men of strong minds, very well able to conduct the business of the courts. Such was Andrew Hamilton, the immediate predecessor of Tench Francis. Francis appears to have been the first of our lawyers who mastered to technical difficulties of the profession."[22]

In 1699 Thomas Story arrived in Philadelphia and became a leader in the community. In 1701 Judge Guest was the first trained lawyer to sit on the bench in Pennsylvania. By 1709, twenty-eight years after the founding of Philadelphia, there were possibly five or six trained lawyers in the city. The first two practicing lawyers were John Moore and David Lloyd. Moore was a descendent of a titled English family and settled in Philadelphia as a lawyer. In 1698 he was appointed advocate of the admiralty and later became register general.

David Lloyd was described as a fiery Welshman and was the most outstanding of the very early Philadelphia lawyers. Between 1683 and 1686 Lloyd had done legal work for William Penn in London. In 1686, Pennsylvania was threatened with the loss of its charter because of reported disturbances among the settlers and alleged tendencies toward "political autonomy." Penn saw that as a serious threat so he appointed Lloyd as his attorney general in 1686. Two years after arriving, however, Lloyd left the proprietary government and became a leading political figure in early Pennsylvania. In 1688 he openly turned against the proprietary rule and in some respects may be seen as the first American revolutionary lawyer.[23]

Lloyd also became very involved in plans for judicial reform, and most of the important court laws that were passed during his lifetime were either directly a result of his efforts or were strongly influenced by his thinking. In 1718 he was appointed the chief justice of Pennsylvania. Lloyd, as the first of the great Philadelphia lawyers, was less a great lawyer in the practice of law than in the politics of law. Politics would continue to be the path of greatest legal achievement in Philadelphia up to and through the Revolution.

During the early eighteenth century much of the hostility toward lawyers was because they were identified with the upper class. Because they were trained in the Inns of Court they had to have considerable wealth, and they brought much of the English class thinking and behavior to America with them. From the beginning lawyers were generally viewed by Americans as the tools of the rich. As the law became more rational and professional the substantive nature of law became increasingly confusing and remote to merchants and businessmen.

Lawyers—like shopkeepers, money lenders, and lower-level bureaucrats—were basically middlemen. As a result they often served as lightning rods that drew rage during the ever-increasing political storms. Ultimately, however, lawyers came to be viewed by many as at least a necessary evil because they were necessary to the survival of society. As Chroust observes, as soon as any settled society poses problems for which lawyers have an expertise or at least a skill, the lawyers will thrive despite the hostility. In the early literature there was constant complaint against unauthorized lawyers, pettifoggers, shysters, and low lifes—unprincipled men who were constantly stirring up unprincipled litigation. "Lawyers were criticized both for incompetence and wrongful competence."[24]

Women and Practice of Law

During the colonial period many people either handled their own legal affairs or appointed someone with no specialized training. Sometimes women were permitted to act as attorneys-in-fact, as agents, or procurators. In keeping with a well-established English rule, a wife could be her husband's lawful attorney or agent. There were a few instances when the American courts made special concessions for those women attorneys. In *William v. Tallent*, argued in 1689, the court did not find the defendant in default but held that "the defendants wyfe appearing in Court but producing no letter from her husband, with both parties consent, the action is continued." John Bland, a prosperous London merchant who owned a large amount of property in Virginia sent his wife Sarah to the colony in 1678 to look after his interests. He authorized her by power of attorney to act as "his true and lawful attorney . . . and to his use to call to an account all persons whatsoever in Virginia his debtors . . . also to enter into and take into his custodie . . . the several plantations . . . & estates whatever due . . . & receive of the widow, Executors, Administrators, foods or estate of Theodore Bland . . . a merchant deceased . . . and all the said Plantation Lands . . . & estate whatsoever . . . and to grate bargains sell . . . at such rates & prices . . . as his wife & attorney shall find convenient."[25] Later she conveyed some property to a William Arlett and also instigated legal proceedings against a Colonel Codd.

Edith Craford of Salem personally sued and was sued in connection with certain bargains made by her husband Morecai Craford. In 1662 she acknowledged a debt of her husband to Edmont Batter that she promised to pay. In 1666, in the case of *Craford v. Savage* she argued before the Essex Quarterly Court and successfully alleged that in 1661 there was "delivered to Captain Savage by me & my husband at Mr. Oliver's dock in Boston, fish at money price."

Whenever the absence of the husband prevented the wife from protecting her own interests or those of her husband, she could petition the court to grant her full power of attorney. Such powers were granted to Sussanah Cooper of Virginia who after her husband's desertion was permitted by the court "the free disposition of her estate . . . to make contracts in her name, & to sue and be sued as though unmarried." Women also acted as attorneys-in-fact and attorneys-at-law for persons to whom they were in no way related. Gertrude James of Maryland, the widow of Reverent Cartwright James, was attorney for William Claiborne in 1650. Rebecca Heathersall of Virginia, a widow, in 1682 became the attorney of Anthony Hall who had taken up residence in England. In his letter of attorney he had made her his "trusty" and ordained that she "recover & receive of all & and every such person & persons which are indebted to me all monies owing to me."[26]

The most professional and most successful female attorney in all of colonial America was Margaret Brent of Maryland, a spinster. Her forensic performances and legal abilities were equal to any colonial lawyer of her time. Between 1642 and 1650 her name appeared 124 times in the records of the courts of Maryland. Governor Leonard Calvert constantly consulted her on political and legal matters, and after his death she became his executrix and residency legatee. The courts not only granted her letters of administration but decided that in all matters she should be received as his "Lordship's Attorney." She was empowered to dispose of all claims against his estate as well as initiate proceedings to collect outstanding debts. As the executrix and attorney for Lord Calvert, as attorney for Lord Baltimore, and as a lawyer acting on her own behalf, she became involved in more lawsuits than any other colonial lawyer during her lifetime. "She was held in universal respect for her thorough knowledge of the law, her high professional standards and great political acumen."[27]

The only reference found regarding a woman serving as an attorney in Pennsylvania was during the period from 1712 to 1718 when Hannah Penn represented her husband, William Penn, after he suffered a stroke. In Pennsylvania the early Quaker women had some equality with men in their religion, but not in matters of the meetings. There the decisions for women were made by the men. As men saw the practice of law as more important, they thought women incapable of participating in the legal profession; by the 1720s women had no rights to practice law in any form. It would be more than 150 years before women were found among Philadelphia lawyers.

As Philadelphia rapidly expanded during the early decades of the eighteenth century, the reputation of its lawyers became great. After 1735 the idea of the Philadelphia lawyer came to be the epitome of the outstanding colonial lawyer. That was brought about by the great achievements of Andrew Hamilton. At that time there may have been no more than one hundred qualified lawyers in the colonies.

Profile 1: Andrew Hamilton (1676–1741)

In 1735, at the age of fifty-nine and in poor health, Andrew Hamilton went from Philadelphia to New York to defend John Peter Zenger against the charge of libel. The reason for Hamilton's concern about Zenger and his New York *Weekly Journal* was because of the actions of the Royal Governor William Cosby and his attempt to control the New York courts. Cosby had fired Chief Justice Lewis Morris and replaced him with Delancy, who was more in sympathy with the governor. After Morris had been dropped as chief justice he, along with his son, Lewis, Jr., and lawyers James Alexander and William Smith tried to stir up the citizens about the governor's high-handed behavior. They attempted to do that by persuading John Peter Zenger, a partner of William Bradford of the *Gazette* to start a new paper, the *Weekly Journal*. In that new paper Morris and his associates attack the governor and his administration in a series of unsigned articles. Hamilton went to New York to participate in far more than simply a trial—it was really a revolt against the royal government by many New York citizens.

After Zenger's arrest he had hired as his counsels James Alexander and William Smith who were the two most eminent lawyers at the time in New York City. They were also two of the men who were writing the anonymous articles in Zenger's newspaper for which the action against him was being brought. The royal judges struck Alexander and Lewis from the list of acceptable attorneys. They did that on the grounds that the two lawyers had put in exceptions in Zenger's name to the Information, which the Judges asserted denied the legality of their judges' commissions. The result was there were no qualified lawyers in New York to take the case. The defense had to go out of town for help, and Hamilton was clearly the first and the best choice. Before describing the Zenger case it is of interest to look briefly at Andrew Hamilton's background.

Andrew Hamilton was a Scotsman, apparently from a respected clan. He had a very good education for the time through his attendance at three Scotch universities. Hamilton was born in 1676 but little is known of his early life. One story suggested he had to leave Scotland because he had killed an important person in a duel. The more likely explanation, however, was that he had been involved in some political difficulties during the reign of King William. Whatever the reason it was necessary for him to use an assumed name when he came to America and for several years he went under the name of Trent. Any danger

27

Andrew Hamilton, 1676–1741. Courtesy of the Historical Society of Pennsylvania.

he felt appears to have passed by the reign of Queen Anne when he began to use his name, Hamilton, once again.

When he first arrived in the colonies he lived on the eastern shore of Virginia, and a few years later moved to Kent County, Maryland. For several years he managed an estate and also appears to have run a classical school. He married a woman with a substantial fortune, Anne Brown, a widow who was related to some of the first families of Maryland. Hamilton was one of several educated Englishmen and Scotsmen who came to the colonies, worked hard, and amassed fortunes. The fortunes were often helped along by marrying wealthy widows. There was in colonial America very strong pressures on wealthy widows to remarry because as women they were held to be unable to manage their finances. Very quickly after marriage the new husband came to view the wealth as his own. Hamilton appears to have been no exception.

It appears that the early legal studies of Andrew Hamilton were completed in Maryland. There were, among the officials of the royal government, several men of high legal stature with whom he could have apprenticed. In those early days the position of the colonial lawyer depended on the favor of a license granted by the local authorities. If one could receive a call to the English Bar, as a member of one of the Inns of Court, that was highly prized because it gave rank and independence before the colonial judges who were English and themselves trained at the inns. When Hamilton felt it was safe to return to England he had the wealth to do so. At thirty-six years of age, and already a very successful lawyer, he sailed for England in 1712. He was admitted to Gray's Inn on 27 January, 1712 and was registered as Mr. Andrew Hamilton of Maryland. In only two weeks he was called to the bar, without keeping the usual terms. In those two weeks he probably displayed his good character and his learning in law. The inns were not educational institutions but rather granting agencies to practice law. After paying his fees and other costs he was admitted to the practice of law in England. He quickly returned to Maryland and was regarded with even greater respect than before. On his plantation Hamilton lived for several years and as his legal fame spread he practiced law as far north as Philadelphia. Because of his fame he was retained by the agents of William Penn in a suit against Berkeley Codd, Esq. of Sussex County, Delaware, who had disputed some of Penn's rights under the grant of the Duke of York.[1]

Hamilton's legal work for Penn was successful and led him to move to Philadelphia in that same year. Within a very short time he was the most eminent lawyer in the city and was appointed a member of the provincial council of Pennsylvania. He accepted it on the condition that his attendance would not interfere with his legal practice, and it appears that he rarely ever took his seat in that body. In 1727 he received from Governor Gordon the very lucrative post of prothonotary. He was given that position not only for his legal qualifications, but also for "the considerable service he had done to Proprietors in this Province and country." In 1728 he was made recorder of the city, and in 1737 (after the Zenger trial) he was appointed judge of vice-admiralty.

Many honors were bestowed on Hamilton and along with his political offices he was also appointed a trustee of the loan office and given the responsibility for the building of the State House (later renamed Independence Hall). His politics were described as "singularly independent." He was vigorous and determined in his opposition to "encroachments" by governors. However, he did not align himself with the Anti Proprietary Party, and throughout his career he retained the confidence and respect of the proprietary (Penn) family. His generally independent attitude kept him from formal adherence to any religious denomination. In Philadelphia, from the beginning, there was a freedom of religion, which included the freedom not to belong to any organized religion.[2]

Hamilton believed in a democracy run by those at the top of society. There was for him "none of the kind of ignorant democracy from below, which is often as provincial and undemocratic as the ordinary aristocrat."[3] He was described as intelligent, broad, and having a comprehensive outlook. He respected all individuals as well as class rights, and believed that for many persons there were limitations because of birth and training. He strongly believed that to lead all persons was an obligation of intellectual leadership. He always tried to avoid provincialism in religion, government, social life, education, and wealth. "This was the root of his brilliant diplomacy, honesty and modesty—a sincerity easy to be recognized by all."[4]

In 1735, when Andrew Hamilton arrived in New York he was approaching old age and had reached his high position in law through many outstanding achievements. His success in the Zenger case would be the capstone of his career, but even without the fame of the Zenger case he would have undoubtedly been considered the most distinguished colonial lawyer of that era. Certainly after the Zenger victory there was never any question as to who was the greatest lawyer in the colonies.

Zenger Case and Trial

It appears that many of the people of New York had welcomed Zenger's *Weekly Journal* as a voice against the unacceptable actions of their governor's administration. During that era the royal government used any available legal technicalities to make any public opposition to the governor be defined as lawlessness. On 17 November, 1734, by order of the government, Zenger had been imprisoned in the county jail, with all communication forbidden. Some of his friends on 20 November had brought habeas corpus proceedings and Zenger's counsels, Alexander and Smith, had objected to the illegality and the extremely high bail. It was not until April 1735 that the court refused a hearing, and the chief justice said to Zenger's lawyers "either we must go from the bench or you from the bar," whereupon he disbarred Alexander and Smith.

The chief justice said the two lawyers were speaking against "the being" of the court, and they were therefore guilty of questioning the legal existence of the court.

Zenger asked for counsel, and John Chambers was appointed. He pleaded "not guilty" for his client and ask for a "struck jury," a list that would be honored permanently, instead of simply a jury list. The chief justice sat on 4 August, 1735 and considered the choice of jury. A week before that time the clerk had presented a list of forty-eight names, nearly all of whom would not be able to serve. Chambers appealed to the court, and the chief Justice agreed to a struck jury. Attorney General Richard Bradley at once began the case and presented the "Information," containing some of the published matter in the libel charge. It was at this point that Andrew Hamilton was brought in and took over the case from John Chambers.

The issue at stake was in a very real sense the freedom of the press as the only available orderly means to resist an arbitrary and unscrupulous executive. At that time, the law of libel and the regular court procedure in such cases limited the function of the jury to determine simply the fact of publication. The libelous character of the words as a question of law was left totally to the judges. The libel laws were the same in all the colonies, and in effect the result was that if any governor was criticized it had to be by innuendo and could not be done directly. The only hope of success for Hamilton was to persuade the jury, at possible peril to themselves, to render a "general verdict" on both law and facts.

Hamilton offered the unheard of defense at that time that the articles the government complained about were the truth. Chief Justice De Lancey rejected that contention and insisted on the English common law rule that the greater the truth, the greater the libel. Hamilton countered with a passionate appeal to the jury declaring that the entire cause of English liberty was at stake. Hamilton succeeded through a masterful command of the techniques of advocacy and by a speech that was described as "the greatest oratorical triumph won in the colonies prior to the speech of James Otis against writs of assistance." The following are some of the high points in Hamilton's presentation.[5]

I was in hopes, as that terrible court, where those dreadful judgments were given referring to an earlier libel case in England, and that law established, which Mr. Attorney had produced for authorities to support this cause, was long ago laid aside, as the most dangerous court to the liberties of the people of England that ever was known in the Kingdom; that, Mr. Attorney, knowing this would have attempted to set up a star chamber here, nor to make their judgments a precedent to us; for it is well known, that what would have been judged treason in those days for a man to speak, I think, has since not only been practiced as lawful, but the contrary doctrine has been held to the law.

. . . what is good law at one time, and in one place, is not so at another time and in another place; so that I think the law seems to expect, that in these parts of the world, men should take care, by a good fence, to preserve their property from the injury of unruly beasts. And perhaps there may be as good reason why men should take the same care to make an honest and upright conduct a fence and security against the injury of unruly tongues.

. . . could Mr. Attorney support such an information by any precedent in the English law? No, the falsehood makes the scandal, and both make the libel. And to show the Court that I am in good ernest [sic], and to save the Court's time, and Mr. Attorney's trouble, I will agree, that if he can prove the facts charged upon us to be false, I'll recognize them to be scandalous, and a libel.

Mr. Attorney then held that whether they were false or true did not matter; they were still libel. Hamilton replied as follows:

I did not expect to hear that a negative can not be proved; but everybody knows there are many exceptions to the general rule; for if a man is charged with killing another, or stealing his neighbor's horse; if he is innocent in the one case, he may prove the man said to be killed is alive; and the horse said to be stolen, never to have been out of his master's stable—this I think is proving the negative. But we will save Mr. Attorney the trouble of proving a negative, and take the *onus probandi* upon ourselves, and prove those very papers that are called libels to be true.

Later the following exchange occurred regarding some of the earlier cases that had been referred to. Hamilton said: "These are Star Chamber cases, and I was in hopes that practice had been dead with the Court." The chief justice than reprimanded Hamilton for being unmannerly. Hamilton responded: "With submission, I have seen the practice in very great Courts, and never heard it deemed unmannerly to . . . ." The chief justice persisted and Hamilton said: "I will say no more at this time: the Court, I see is against us in this point." The chief justice told Hamilton if he would be mannerly, he would be given every reasonable liberty.
     Hamilton said:

I thank your honor. Then gentlemen of the jury, it is to you we must appeal, for witnesses to the truth of the facts we have offered, and are denied the liberty to prove; and let it not seem strange, that I apply myself to you in this manner; I am warranted so to do, both by law and reason.

He went on to say:

were you to find a verdict against my client, you must take upon you to say, the papers referred to in the information, and which we acknowledge we printed and published, are false, scandalous and seditious; but of this I can have no apprehension. You are citizens of New York; you are really, what the law supposes to be, honest and lawful men; and accordingly to my brief, the facts which we offer to prove were not committed in a corner; they are notoriously known to be true; and therefore in your justice lies out safely. And as we are denied the liberty of giving evidence, to prove the truth of what we have published, will beg leave to lay it down as a standing rule in such cases, that the suppressing of evidence ought always to be taken as the strongest evidence; and I hope it will have that weight with you.

Later Hamilton addressed the fears that the jury might have regarding their actions.

> . . . the judges, how great so ever they be, have no right to fine, imprison, or punish a jury, for not finding a verdict according to the direction of the Court. And this, I hope, is sufficient to prove, that jurymen are to see with their own eyes, to hear with their own ears, and to make use of their own consciences and understandings in judging of the lives, liberties, or estates of their fellow subjects.

As Hamilton moved toward his conclusion he said:

> If a libel is understood in the large and unlimited sense urged by Mr. Attorney, there is scare a writing I know that may not be called a libel, or scarce any person safe from being called to account as a libeler: for Moses, much as he was, libelled Cain; and who is it that has not libelled the Devil? For according to Mr. Attorney, it is not justification to say one has a bad name. Echard had libelled our good King William; Burnett has libelled, among others, King Charles and King James; and Rapin has libelled them all.

Hamilton ended with:

> I hope to be pardoned, Sir, for my zeal upon this occasion; it is an old and wise caution, "That when our neighbor's house is on fire, we ought to take care of our own." For though, blessed by God, I live in a government where liberty is well understood and freely enjoyed; yet experience has shown us all, that a bad precedent in one government, is soon set up for an authority in another; and therefore I cannot but think it mine and every honest man's duty, that, (while we pay all due obedience to men in authority), we ought at the same time to be upon our guard against power, whenever we apprehend that it may affect ourselves or our fellow subjects.
>
> I am truly unequal to such an undertaking on many accounts. And you see I labor under the weight of many years, and am with great infirmities of body; yet, old and weak as I am, I should think it my duty, if required, to go to the utmost part of the land, where my service could be of any use, in assisting to quench the flame of prosecutions upon information, set on foot by the government, to deprive a people of the right of remonstrating (and complaining too) of the arbitrary attempts of men in power. Men who injure and oppress the people under their administration, provoke them to cry out and complain; and then make that very complaint the foundation for new oppressions and prosecutions. I wish I could say there were no instances of this kind. But, to conclude: the question before the Court, and you, gentlemen of the jury, is not of small nor private concern; it is not the cause of a poor printer, nor of New York alone, which you are now trying. No! It may, in its consequence, effect [sic] every freeman that lives under a British government on the main of America. It is the best cause; it is the cause of liberty; and I make no doubt but your upright conduct, this day, will not only entitle you to love and esteem of your fellow citizens; but every man, who prefers freedom, to a life of slavery, will bless and honor you, as men who have baffled the attempt of tyranny.

When Andrew Hamilton concluded his argument Chief Justice De Lancey spoke:

Gentlemen of the Jury, the great pains that Mr. Hamilton has taken to show how little regard juries are to pay to the opinions of the judges, and his insisting so much on the conduct of some judges in trials of this kind, is done, no doubt with design that you should take but very little notice of what I may say on this occasion. I shall therefore only observe to you, that, as the facts or words in the information are confessed, the only thing that can come in question before you is, whether the words, as set forth in the information, make a libel; and that is a matter of law, no doubt, and which you may leave to the Court. But I shall trouble you no further with anything more of my own; but read you the words of a learned and upright judge, in a case of the like nature [Lord Chief Justice Holt in the Tuchin case]. To say that corrupt officers are appointed to administer affairs is certainly a reflection on the government. If people should not be called to account for possessing the people with ill opinion of the government, no government can subsist; for it is necessary for all government that the people should have a good opinion of it; and nothing can be worse to any government than the endeavor to procure animosities. As to the management of it, this have been always looked upon as a crime, and no government can be safe without it be punished.

Delancy concluded by saying:

now you are to consider, whether these words I have read to you do not tend to begat an ill opinion of the administration of the government; to tell us that those that are not employed know nothing of the matter. Men are not adapted to offices, but offices to men, out of a particular regard to their interest, and not to their fitness for the places.

The jury withdrew and after a short absence returned. When asked for their verdict, the foreman, Thomas Hunt, said, "not guilty." As soon as the verdict was announced the people who had crowded the hall where the court was held and who were fully aware of the magnitude of the question at stake, and who strongly sympathized with Zenger, gave "three Huzzaz in the Hall." It was reported that the outburst was much to the chagrin of the judges, who had confidently anticipated a very different result. The crowd carried Hamilton from the courtroom on their shoulders and the next day New York gave him a key to the city in a golden box.

Zenger was released after having spent eight months in prison, and he and about forty New York citizens entertained Hamilton at the Black Horse Tavern for dinner. They wanted to express their thankfulness for his generosity and brilliant legal defense. When he departed from New York the next day he was saluted with the great guns of several ships in the harbor, "as a public testimony of the glorious Defense he made in the cause of Liberty in this Province."[6]

After Hamilton's return to Philadelphia the city rewarded him with the estate of Bush Hill which comprised the space from Vine Street to Coates Street, and from Twelfth Street to Nineteenth Street. It was carved out of the manor of Springettsbury and granted to Hamilton on the advice of James Logan. There Hamilton built a large and stately manor, where he lived until his death.

Most important was the national and international fame that Hamilton received from the Zenger case. Four editions of his speech were published in London in 1738 and one in Lancaster, Pennsylvania. His speech was also printed in Boston and Philadelphia, and continued to be reprinted as late as 1770 in New Jersey. "The trial of Zenger in 1735," said Gouverneur Morris "was the game of American Freedom, the morning star of that liberty which subsequently revolutionized America."

Hamilton's fame spread quickly to England, and the leading men of the English bar agreed that the subject of libel had never been so boldly treated in the courts of Westminster. The London correspondent of Franklin's *Pennsylvania Gazette* on 11 May, 1738 wrote:

> We have been lately amused with Zenger's trial which has become the common topic of conversation of all the Coffee Houses, both at the Court end of the Town and in the City. Our political writers of different factions, who never agreed on anything before, have mentioned the trial in their public writings with an air of Rapture and Triumph. A Goliath in learning and politics gave his opinion of Mr. Hamilton's argument in these terms: "It is not law, it is better than law, it ought to be law, and will always be law wherever justice prevails."

Basically, Hamilton had argued three propositions. One, that the jury have, in prosecutions for libels, the same right as in other criminal prosecutions, to determine the law as well as the facts under the direction of the court. Second, that as the alleged libel concerned public conduct of persons acting in public capacities, the publication was justifiable if the statements were true. The third, that whether they were true or false, the limits of fair discussion of subjects of general public interest had not been exceeded. Some scholars have suggested that the speech should be applauded more for the bold enunciation of principle than for the accumulation of learned citations and for its arguments from precedents. Hamilton did cite authorities with great skill, however, and dealt through them a strong attack on the royal prosecution and the court.

The impact on the autonomy of the jury in American law was great. Hamilton said:

> only claimed to liberate the jury from the authority of some disagreeable law and of an obnoxious court holding its appointment from the Crown. No lawyer can read that argument without perceiving, that, while, it was spirited and vigorous, though rather overbearing, harangue, which carried the jury away from the instruction of the Court, and from the established law of both the Colony and the Mother country, he argued elaborately what was not law anywhere, with the same confidence he did the better points of law.

In general, legal historians have judged the speech to be more than just a great forensic flight. Some have said it reflected his accuracy of scientific learning, and the result of his severe self-discipline as a lawyer. "His method of reference to authorities tests the depth of his research and the clearness of his judgement not less than the copiousness of his intellectual development. His learning must have been profound. But he made no parade of it." Furthermore, "it is obvious that he had educated himself in general public law, and was familiar enough with its principles to incorporate them with his argument without pausing to state them." His biographer further adds that "if short sighted men of his day thought him a demagogue, which I do not believe, those of greater forecast must have recognized the traits of a statesmanlike lawyer, whose works would produce their memorials to be appreciated in a future generation."

From a strictly legal standpoint it is probably true that the points that Hamilton argued were not "good law" at that time in America or England. Sir James Stephen called the speech "singularly able, bold and powerful, though full of doubtful, not to say bad, law." But exactly those points were to be embodied over fifty years later in Fox's Libel Act. Certainly a different result in the Zenger case would have delayed, for a while at least, the free political press in America. It may be argued that if the speech had never been made the framers of the constitution of several states might not have been prepared for the adoption of provisions like that of the seventh section of the Declaration of Rights in Pennsylvania. That provision stated that "the printing presses should be free to every person who undertakes to examine the proceedings of the Legislature, or any branch of Government; and no Law shall ever be made to restrain the right thereof."

After 1740 the Philadelphia bar began its rise to great eminence and during the period before the Revolution it attained unrivaled excellence. Andrew Hamilton was truly the father of the Philadelphia bar. He was the first to give great honor, admiration, and the highest of professionalism to the appellation "Philadelphia lawyer." After Hamilton that came to be the byword for a lawyer of exceptional prominence and ability.

2
Colonial Period: 1750s

Dr. Johnson once remarked that he did not care to speak ill of any
man behind his back, but he believed the gentleman was an attorney.
—Charles Lamb

In the 1750s, about twenty-five years after Andrew Hamilton's triumphant
return from New York, Philadelphia had grown greatly and was second only
to Boston in population. The city had become the "bread basket" of the colonies
because of the fertile land west and north of the city. The excellent soil plus
the German immigrants, who were considered to be the best farmers in the
world, resulted in high food productivity. Philadelphia became the main
supplier of foods from the colonies to the West Indies as well as to many ports
in southern Europe.

By the 1750s Philadelphia had become one of the major cities of the world.
In its seventy-year history it had developed far greater in a shorter period than
probably any city in history. Its was on the verge of becoming the largest and
most dominant city in America and second only to London in the British
Empire. Its wealth and upper class were firmly locked into British values, and
in most cases the education of men was as well. In no area of education was
that truer than in the learning of law.

The few outstanding lawyers in Philadelphia had been trained in London.
The four Inns of Court in London were and still are Middle Temple, Inner
Temple, Gray's Inn and Lincoln's Inn. They began their control over the
educational standards of English legal practitioners during the fourteenth
century when they started as voluntary guilds. Over time they gained great
prestige and recognition, and became the only means by which the Englishman
could practice as a barrister. By 1600, English lawyers were clearly professional
men by virtue of their education in law. They set their own standards and defined
who was to be admitted to the practice of law. Historically, the inns were never
connected to the universities, and therefore were not influenced by Roman
law or the general legal culture of Europe. The young men at the inns, if they
learned anything (and sometimes they did not), learned English law, English
pleading, and English legal experience. Their legal training was primarily
practical and not jurisprudential.

The earliest records go back to 1501, and they show that the four inns of court had already become well established as secular monasteries. During the years there were many great names associated with the Middle Temple including Lord Chancellors Clarendon and Hartwicke as well as Lord Chief Justices Coleridge and Reading and Sir William Blackstone. In literature there was Henry Fielding, William Cowpers, William Makepeace Thackery, and Charles Dickins. The patriots Sir Francis Drake, Sir Walter Raleigh, and Edmund Burke were there, and Oliver Goldsmith lived at the Middle Temple at the time of his death in 1774. The Middle Temple was the most important of the four inns in the training of Americans in law before the American Revolution.

The Inner Temple was recognized as a separate legal society by 1440 and out of that inn came Sir Thomas Littleton, the author of the great treatise on tenure, and Sir Edward Coke, the "father" of common law. It also produced Prime Minister George Grenville and writers Charles Lamb and James Boswell. Lincoln's Inn began in 1311, and among its great lawyers were Sir Thomas More and Richard Cromwell; its famous men included John Donne, Horace Walpole, William Penn, William Pitt, and Thomas Macaulay. Gray's Inn was as old as the Middle Temple, and it produced the two Bacons and Thomas Cromwell as well as Joseph Ball, uncle of George Washington.

To be called to the bar one must have been formally admitted to one of the Inns of Court, have established a residence, however nominal, and kept twelve terms, four to the year, and eaten dinner there at least six times a term. They were also expected to read law, participate in the debates, discussion, and moot courts; attend sessions of the Courts of Westminster; and become "imbued with the spirit of the Inn."[1]

At the middle of the eighteenth century there was only a limited legal literature so education was chiefly oral—by lecture, disputations, and debates. The legal education was very practical with a stress on the procedural and argumentative aspects of law. Moots and bolts were very important because it was strongly believed that argument fostered alert and original minds. Young men walking around the quadrangle were encouraged to put cases to one another, and those who were skilled became known as "out-case men." By the 1760s to be admitted to the bar one had to take an oath to the king's spiritual and temporal supremacy as well as an oath of obedience and allegiance to the Crown. That stopped several Americans in the 1760s, who refused to swear the allegiance, from being called to the bar in England.

The Middle Temple trained most of the Americans. All of the inns, by the middle of the eighteenth century, for various reasons, had undergone a decline. Law was not being pursued with the same intellectural and social class enthusiasm as it once had. (That may have been one reason for the willingness to accept wealthy colonists as students.) Before Blackstone the common law had been an undigested mass, without anything approaching scientific arrangement or organized treatment. That Blackstone, with such crude materials as were available at that time, could produce what he did, has long been regarded as one of the legal marvels of the ages. His first English edition was published in 1765, and the first American edition was published in Philadelphia in 1767. That book constituted almost all the knowledge of law available to American lawyers and judges.

About 60 American-born lawyers were educated at the Inns of Court before 1760, and about 115 between 1760 and the start of the American Revolution. Of the approximate 236 Americans who were born before 1815, nearly half were admitted to the inns between 1750 and 1775. Of that total Middle Temple had 146, Inner Temple, 43; Lincoln's Inn, 32; and Gray's Inn, 9. By States, South Carolina sent 74; Virginia, 49; Maryland, 33; Pennsylvania and New York each sent 23; and Massachusetts, 19. To go to the inns was very expensive, and only the sons of the wealthiest fathers could do so. To the English gentry many of the American young men were seen as having severe social handicaps, being from the colonies. Often the Americans felt they had to combat the view that they were simpleminded rustics. Many felt compelled to maintain their social appearances at great expense. In America, other than in New England, the common view was to attribute very high status to those young men who attended the inns.[2]

From the northeastern colonies only a few young men were sent to the inns. In part, that was because anti-common law values continued to discourage any professional training for the law. More important, however, was that Massachusetts had Harvard College, and New Englanders could see nothing to be gained by sending young men to England for either their general education or to study law. For the other colonies, especially in the South, where there were no large towns and few colleges, the wealthy had to send their sons to London, however.

Many Americans, although not always called to the English bar, returned home and became leaders in the development of the bar in America. Even though their education at the inns was often limited it still provided them with a distinct advantage over most of the lawyers trained in the colonies. Some of the Americans trained at the inns, along with young English lawyers who later became important, were strongly influenced by the tradition of the English bar. Those men had access to and were influenced by the beliefs in individual rights and liberty that at the time characterized English legal thought and that became the great American heritage taken from English common law. Many of the values that gave to the English bar an exclusive and aristocratic characteristic became even stronger in the colonies. Those values plus the absence of any American aristocracy based on hereditary privilege as well as no extremely wealthy upper class led to a dominance in social and political leadership by American lawyers. As a result the American bar became the most English of the American institutions.

At the inns many young Americans from the different colonies met one another and formed friendships as well as professional and political connections. Those contacts were very important because they helped overcome the traditional geographical isolation between the colonies. Those shared experiences also contributed to the American Revolution, especially among those trained in the inns, who were from the southern colonies and from Pennsylvania. Being trained in the tradition of English liberties and immemorial rights of the English, rather than just in legalistic technicalities, the English legal education contributed very significantly to the movement for American independence. In many instances those lawyers became the leaders and spokesmen of the American Revolution. For example, all three of the lawyers who came to the defense of John Peter Zenger—James Alexander, William Smith, and Andrew Hamilton had been educated at Gray's Inn.[3]

The Middle Temple could make some claim to being the cradle of the American Republic. For example, Ralph Lane, who became the first Governor of Virginia studied there. The plan for the incorporation of a Virginia chartered company had a leading part played by a Middle Templer, Sir John Popham. He had been treasurer of the inn from 1580 to 1587 and afterward the chief justice of the queen's bench. Among the original Virginia settlers from Middle Temple was George Percey who also became governor of Virginia. The close connection of the inn to the affairs of the Virginia Company continued up until the Revolution. Edmund Burke (himself a member) said in his speech on conciliation with the colonies: "In no country perhaps in the world is the law so general a study. . . . I have been told by an eminent bookseller that in no branch of his business, after tracts on popular devotion, were so many books as those on the law exported to the plantation. . . . I have heard they have sold nearly as many Blackstone's *Commentaries* in America as in England."[4]

A study of the fathers of seventy students recorded in the books of the Middle Temple before 1760 indicated that they came from America. In the years between 1681 and 1784 there were an estimated thirty-two Philadelphia lawyers trained at the Inns of Court, with twenty-three at the Middle Temple. Half of those young men were the oldest or only sons, and all but one of the rest were the second sons.[5] To send a son to the inn was for many wealthy American fathers the greatest reward and investment they could give and that usually went to their most valued son, the oldest. Distinguished Pennsylvania jurists trained in the inns between 1760 and 1783 were Pennsylvania Chief Justice Benjamin Chew, Thomas McKeon, Edward Shippen, Edward Tilghman, and Justice Jasper Yeakes. There were also the presidents of the Supreme Executive Council Joseph Reed and Peter Markoe. The number of Inns of Court trained lawyers was not large, but they were significant because of their great influence in the development of Pennsylvania law and the legal profession. Most of the early Philadelphia lawyers were not products of the inns but rather started as clerks in a Philadelphia lawyer's office. Because their mentors had often been trained at the inns, however, those apprentices were usually trained in the legal philosophies and values common to London. Given their relatively high level of legal training for the period in Philadelphia, they quickly became the core of the legal profession in Pennsylvania. All the lawyers of distinction in Pennsylvania had to practice in the city because that was where the most important courts held their sessions.

In early Philadelphia the pattern had been for the Quakers to avoid legal processes by raising laymen to the position of "common peacemakers." Although the early colonists might live without lawyers, they could not live without law. As the country became more populated and the commercial life became more complex, more and more men turned to the practice of law. Before the colonial period ended each had something approaching a legal profession, and each colony provided for its legal needs in its own way. The scarcity of professional structure along with the lack of licensing guilds in law encouraged an informal system of apprentice training. In America, except those trained in England, apprenticeship was the only way to enter the legal system.

In general what developed in the colonies was a kind of ranking, an informal grading of practitioners, by their education and experience. In some of the colonies only the better educated and most experienced were allowed to practice in the highest courts. In the South where large amounts of land were settled many of the large landowners by necessity had to learn some law.

In none of the colonies before the end of the colonial period were the courts run primarily by professionally trained lawyers. Another problem was that law books were scarce. Of about 150 volumes of law reports published in England before the Revolution, only about 30 were used in America. Where laymen were judges there was little incentive for advocates to be learned lawyers. In fact, technical legal knowledge could sometimes be a disadvantage. The lawyer was sometimes afraid that by showing his learning he would antagonize the judge by revealing the judge's ignorance.

The single greatest early influence on American law was Blackstone. He dramatically influenced the practice of law in the colonies by providing the means by which a literate person could grasp the outlines of traditional British common law. With nothing more than the four volumes of Blackstone a man could become an amateur lawyer. During the entire colonial period America probably did not produce a single lawyer who was deeply learned by strict English standards. America had many legal problems where legal precedent did not exist or was not available in America. The judges in America were often forced to draw from principles they barely understood or try to adapt English law that had limited relevance to their problems.

In essence a system of common law looks at what has been the legal action of the past to determine what ought to be done. For many Americans legal matters were more likely to be seen as tied to theology and philosophy rather than to practical considerations. The early American experience did not bring forth a learned specialist in law or anything else. Although there was a high level of legal competence among many men of affairs in America there typically was a vagueness between legal and other kinds of knowledge. Yet, with all these limits, the American Revolution came to be framed in legal language because that was the language used by literate men, and there was no other alternative.

In early Philadelphia there were only a few men with any legal background. In the first years of settlement David Lloyd, John Moore, Thomas Story, James Logan, and William Penn were the only men known to have been trained at the inns. Although Penn had spent one year at Lincoln's Inn he never actually practiced law and was in fact very antilawyer. In early Pennsylvania it was assumed that the members of the county courts would be men of prestige and respectability, but they were not likely to have been trained in the law. In addition to the lack of legally trained men, there was sometimes a lack of men of any community stature available to serve on the courts. Those men who served were paid very little, and frequently they felt they could not give up their living to serve in a judicial capacity.[6] As a result second rate men often became county judges.

James Logan was an early chief justice in Pennsylvania. Apart from William Penn himself, Logan was perhaps the best-known figure in the province. Logan served as head of the provincial council and also as the governor of the province during the years when Pennsylvania had no official governor. He was a scholarly man who could speak several languages. When he died in 1751 he left more than three thousand books to the Philadelphia library.

Despite the many attempts to suppress lawyers as a professional group there was by 1700 a small group of lawyers in Pennsylvania, mainly in Philadelphia. Experienced lawyers came to be seen as a necessity for the proper administration of justice if there was to be a stable law. Because of the Quaker hostility toward the litigious lawyer the Philadelphia bar was slow in developing. After 1740, however, the Philadelphia bar began its rise to great eminence, and during the decades before the Revolution it became the unrivaled leader in the colonies.

As to the early years of the lawyer in Philadelphia it has been observed that "they were distinguished more for their purity than for their learning, for their high standing in the community and their general capacity, more than their legal attainments." Although most law cases were simple in principle, readily understood, and easily disposed, there was still the tendency to view the legal profession with distrust and dislike. The law profession was seen as opposed to the views of peaceful good fellowship that Quakers believed to be an essential part of the true Christian character. In 1698 Gabriel Thomas said: "Of Lawyers and Physicians I shall say nothing, because this Country is very Peaceable and Healthy; long may it so continue and never have occasion for the Tongue of the one, or the Pen of the other, both equally destructive to men's Estates and Lives."[7]

During the eighteenth century part of the hostility toward the lawyer was because they were identified with wealth and power. Lawyers have often been viewed by many Americans as tools of the rich. Also, as law became more "rational" and "professional" the substantive nature of law became more confusing and remote to the merchants and businessmen. In general, lawyers came to be viewed as a necessary evil, because no modern society could do without them. As any society expands and becomes complex there will be problems for which lawyers have an expertise or at least a skill. Lawyers thrive despite the hostility because without laws a society cannot survive.

Among the colonists there was the often bitterly remembered heritage of English law and to a great extent the American opposition to lawyers had English origins. The Puritan Revolution, which had led many to move to the New World, was in general hostile to lawyers. The Puritans and Quakers believed they had suffered under the laws of England. In the colonies the legal profession was identified with the law officers of the Crown. There were also many persons who identified themselves as lawyers who were men of little or no professional competence.

In Philadelphia the rise of the lawyer came about with the significant reduction of Quaker influence in the active control of the city and the province. Philadelphia's first really important lawyer, Andrew Hamilton, was not a Quaker. His career points out the increased control of the city by other groups, especially the Anglicans. Increasingly, too, in entering law were the Scotch and Germans to whom controversy was the way of life. Those early colonials enjoyed a good fight. They were the exact opposite of the Quakers.

In Philadelphia the first significant legal family quickly become a major force in the social scene once Andrew Hamilton was firmly in place as the founder of the Philadelphia bar. His successor as attorney general and the leading lawyer of the city was Tench Francis who was related to everybody. Francis in turn was followed by Benjamin Chew and Chew's oldest son, Benjamin, Jr., who became the very model of Philadelphia's second generation. Although not a very good lawyer he did manage to strongly secure the Chew's top social position in the city, and he married an heiress as well as inherited several fortunes. It was said of Chew, Jr., that he devoted his life to doing nothing but doing it well.[8]

By the middle of the eighteenth century the complexity of commercial transactions, settlements of large estates and inheritances, and the searching and transfer of land titles had greatly increased. There were also maritime matters and admiralty law calling for the services and understanding of a new group of legal specialists. Added to that was the amassing of colonial statutes applicable to the new commercial society, and they also demanded new legal expertise. Lawyers were becoming increasingly indispensable. Those lawyers needed an extensive and costly education so they were drawn from the gentry.

The gentry could also see the importance of lawyers to their own personal fortunes and the economic future of their families. Therefore, they often wanted their sons to become lawyers, and the linking of the law to the gentry of Philadelphia became a very close connection.

The system of practicing law in America was much simpler than in England. In England at the top stood the barristers, the aristocracy of the legal profession. They came out of the Inns of Court and went into the High Courts, where they had a monopoly on that practice. Attorneys were not allowed to plead in court, and it was their function to set the machinery of the court into motion on behalf of their clients. Solicitors were the private legal agents, who were neither authorized to plead in the High Court nor set lawsuits in motion. They looked after routine legal matters for their clients. Barristers alone were "gentlemen" and therefore members of a true profession. None of those distinctions developed in America, however, and once admitted to the bar all lawyers had the same professional status and rights.

Colonial lawyers also played a major role in the founding and editing of important and influential literary magazines. The first magazine in America, *The American Magazine*, was published by Andrew Bradford in 1741 in Philadelphia. It was edited by John Webbe, a Philadelphia lawyer, who had previously made contributions to Benjamin Franklin's *Pennsylvania Gazette*. Many leading lawyers during the last half of the eighteen century frequently contributed to both the newspapers and the magazines. Many of their essays dealt with the significant political issues of the day, and their observations and arguments contributed greatly to the eventual American Revolution. As suggested, on the eve of the Revolution the legal profession, especially in the cities, were ranked at the top of the Colonial gentry. After a century of hostility and often bitter opposition they had significantly progressed in economic success, social standing, and profession prestige. "They had become professionally articulate and alert."[9]

Income from the practice of law varied considerably, depending on the prosperity of the colony, and on the ability and contacts of the lawyer. Well into the eighteen century incomes were extremely modest, and many lawyers had to enter other occupations to survive economically because of several factors. First, there was very little in liquid assets in the colonies to support a large and independent service profession. Second, person were allowed to plead their own cases, and men handled their own affairs so there was little demand for professional services. Furthermore, litigation was typically of a simple nature, and in some colonies fees were strictly regulated. The opportunity to acquire much wealth in the practice of law was not great. James Allen, a graduate of the College of Philadelphia in 1759 and a student at Middle Temple (he also studied with Edward Shippen in Philadelphia) estimated that he earned between £300 and £400 in 1773, his first year of practice.[10]

The emergence of the legal profession was also hampered by the lack of proper training facilities. There were no collegiate lectures on law before 1780 and no law schools before 1784. Also the study of law was seriously handicapped by the lack of authoritative law books. Most collections of law books in early Pennsylvania were privately owned and were mainly commentaries in book and pamphlet form on general concepts and rules of law. Although books supporting decisions of individual cases were relatively rare in both England and America there were a variety of commentary on general principles of law.

In talking about colonial lawyers Francis Rawle, wrote in 1772, about Benjamin Chew. "Perhaps no one exceeded him in an accurate knowledge of common law, or in the sound exposition of statutes. His solid judgement, tenacious memory, and persevering industry, rendered him a safe and steady guide." At the bar his language was pertinent and correct, but seldom characterized by effusion of eloquence. But at that time the sphere of the lawyer was somewhat limited. Before the Revolution the provincial courts discussed no great questions of international law. There were no arguments on the construction of treaties nor comparison of legislative powers with constitutional restrictions. Even admiralty cases had little interest. That was because everything of great and imposing importance was reserved for the mother country.[11]

Chroust has written that before the Revolution there were five general avenues to training in law. First, it could be done through one's own efforts and without supervision. The man picked up what he could of legal information and what he might find in available books, libraries, and reports. For example, Patrick Henry prepared himself for the bar by secluding himself for about six weeks to read *Coke on Littleton* and whatever Virginia statutes that he found available. That approach was not altogether successful and George Wythe, one of his "bar examiners refused to sign his license. John Randolph who passed him rather reluctantly 'perceived him to be a young man of genius . . . but very ignorant of the law.' "[12]

Second, the aspiring lawyer could acquire some legal knowledge and experience by serving as a scribe, copyist, assistant, or deputy in the clerk's office or in some court. He could supplement his scanty training by reading whatever legal materials were accessible. That was the common method among those without the time or money to enter the law office of a leading practitioner. This approach often limited the student from acquiring any familiarity with law as a science. As long as legal cases were settled in the old way, however, that class of lawyer could get along. It was said "they hated the subtleties of special pleading and they turned pale at a demurrer."[13]

Third, the student could enter as a clerk the law office of some outstanding or experienced lawyer, preferably one with a good law library. There he would learn the law by close personal association, observation, imitation, and sometimes the study of whatever law books were available. He would receive both direct and indirect instruction from his mentor. Much of his time would be spent copying pleadings and other legal documents as well as drafting briefs. He had to pay his mentor what at that time was a considerable sum of money. That kind of training often had some serious defects. The senior lawyer was often too busy or sometimes too haughty to pay much attention to the students who were often left completely to their own devices. The personal relationship between them was often reserved and could sometimes be very unpleasant.

James Wilson was probably the greatest Philadelphia lawyer of the Revolution era. About Wilson it was said that he hardly ever devoted any time to his student-clerks and that he was virtually useless as an instructor. "He would never engage with them in professional discussion; to a direct question, he gave the shortest possible answer, and a general request for information was always evaded."[14] The clerk in a law office quickly discovered that he had taken on a very difficult task. He was expected to "dig out the law by himself." For the most part he could expect little help from his preceptor when he found a new and strange legal phrase. Often he was totally confused by the obscure and frequently mysterious verbiage that was common to the law at the time.

Fourth, a student could go to England and become a member of one of the Inns of Court. That was, of course, provided he had the money. Once in London, aside from the instruction he received at the inn, he could also attend the courts of Westminster and come into contact with England's leading lawyers and judges. The fifth method was for a young man to attend one of the several colleges. In Philadelphia he could attend the college founded in 1756. Although none of the colleges taught any specialized course in the law during the Colonial period, the general education that was offered prepared young men for more profitable legal studies in a lawyer's office. During the later part of the eighteenth century some colonies insisted that only college graduates could be admitted to study or practice law. In other colonies, the college graduate might be granted certain privileges such as shorter periods of required legal study in the law office. As a result many of the more successful eighteenth-century lawyers were college educated.[15]

Meehan wrote that as Pennsylvania prospered and as trade and finance flourished the city of Philadelphia was drawing the best legal minds and forensic talents in the colonies. The two decades before the American Revolution saw the rise of a brilliant bar in Pennsylvania, and no colony, except South Carolina, had more lawyers trained at the Inns of Court. "Preeminent in their calling, of exceptional ability and broad culture, knowledgeable and skillful in the law, the distinguishing attorneys of Philadelphia were no less men of wealth, position and power in Pennsylvania. By the time of the Revolution the term 'Philadelphia lawyer' was current and the era of the 'special pleaders' begun."[16] In the early days the number of lawyers in Philadelphia were limited. From 1735 to 1770 there were on the average only about three lawyers admitted to the Philadelphia bar each year.

By the 1750s the legal community of Philadelphia was well established. It was closely linked to the upper class and to the political power structure of the city. Lawyers were already a significant force in helping to bring about the Revolution, and they would go on to be of the greatest importance to the new American government. The highly important position of the Philadelphia lawyer, with some short-term variations in prestige, would continue during the next two centuries.

John Dickinson, 1732–1808. Courtesy of the Historical Society of Pennsylvania.

Profile 2: John Dickinson (1732–1808)

John Dickinson was born on 8 November 1732 on a plantation on the eastern shore of Maryland. The plantation had been first settled in 1659 by his Quaker ancestor, Walter Dickinson. He was educated by a private tutor and when sixteen years of age was considered mature enough to study law. Dickinson entered the office of John Moland who was, following the death of Andrew Hamilton, probably the most distinguished member of the Philadelphia bar. Moland had been trained at the Middle Temple in London and was commissioned as the king's attorney to Pennsylvania. At that time there were only a few respected lawyers in Philadelphia and Secretary Peters had written back to England saying that all of them "except Francis and Moland are persons of no knowledge, and I had almost said, no principle."[1]

After three years in the office of Moland, Dickinson went to London and in 1753 entered the Middle Temple; the effects of that English training greatly influenced the views later important to Dickinson. Training at the Inns of Court influenced many of the attitudes of American lawyers regarding the controversial questions between England and the rights of the colonies. The views of the leading Philadelphia lawyers were very much influenced by their training in England. By contrast, in New England many lawyers were opposed to Britain because few of them had gone to England to be trained at the Inns of Court. Rather, almost all had received their education at Harvard and entered the law offices of Boston lawyers for their legal training. It was argued that "the resistance of the Central Colonies led by those trained at the Inns was at the beginning a constitutional resistance within the lines of the English common law. Whereas the others who were their opponents reflected a revolutionary resistance based on the ideals of the rights of man."[2]

In 1757 Dickinson returned to Philadelphia and began to practice law, but there is little known about his early legal efforts. One of his biographers wrote that after his return to Philadelphia "it was plain that he was not forced to wait long for clients." That writer goes on to say "unfortunately none of his forensic arguments have come down to us. But later it was said that he possessed considerable fluency, with a sweetness of tone and agreeable modulation of voice, not well calculated, however, for a large audience. His law knowledge was respectable, although not remarkably extensive, for his attention was directed to historical and political studies."[3] While he had been in London Dickinson had developed a great interest and love for books and that took him into areas not directly bearing on the law. He was very well read and a highly educated man for his time. Once the Revolution started it does not appear that Dickinson practiced much law.

In later years Thomas Jefferson suggested that Dickinson as a lawyer was more ingenious than sound of judgment, and still more timid than ingenious. He soon built one of the largest law practices in Pennsylvania, however. This was greatly facilitated because he belonged to the Philadelphia circle that included such old provincial families as the Pembertons, the Logans, and the Norrises. They were generally know as the Whig group. In that society Dickinson moved with easy grace, revealing himself as a sportsman, a poet, as well as a brilliant and popular conversationalist. Even in those early years he appears to have been wealthy, and when he retired in 1786 from public life his vast fortune had increased until he was one of the richest men in America.[4]

At the time of the Revolution, when taxation of the colonies was resisted on the grounds that constitutionally there could be no taxation without representation, the colonies had no real representation in England. Out of a total population of about 8 million there were only 160,000 electors. In England public morals had fallen to very low levels with seats in Parliament being bought and sold like commodities in the market. King George III was determined to reign both as king and minister. "Walpole and Newcastle had made bribery and borough-jobbing the base of their power. George III seized it, in his turn, as a base of the power he proposed to give to the crown. The Royal revenue was employed to buy seats and buy votes."[5]

This period followed the end of the French and Indian Wars that had been concluded by the Peace of Paris in 1763. At that time France lost her domination on the American continent. The cost of the war had been great, and the war debt in England was £140 million the colonies were expected to help pay. The Crown asserted that, in part, that debt had been brought about by protecting the colonies against the French and Indians, and therefore the colonies were justly bound to aid in paying the debt. That was the opinion of the king and his minister, George Grenville. That resulted in the passage of the Stamp Act, which contributed to the Revolution. The news of the passage of the Stamp Act caused universal excitement and alarm in the colonies and greatly accelerated the hostility toward England.

Dickinson made his political debut, not in defense of colonial rights but over the question of the Penn family's proprietorship. Franklin and Galloway had joined together to agitate for the overthrow of the privileged Penn family and to achieve a Crown-colony status for Pennsylvania. Dickinson opposed this and as a result was strongly criticized for his apparent conservatism. He believed that although the proprietary arrangement had faults at least the evils of proprietary government were known evils. Those he preferred to the alternative that he believed would be a much closer attachment to the British crown that might bring about many unpredictable evils.

In 1765 he opposed English legislature that would have made Pennsylvania a Crown colony. The colonists, Dickinson stressed, were Englishmen, with the privilege of taxing themselves. Consequently the mother country had no legal or constitutional right to levy stamp duties on American colonies. He further argued that Englishmen had the legal right to self-government wherever they might go, and the only bond between the American colony and the mother country was that of family affection. He made it clear that total separation was to be considered if Parliament continued to ignore the rights of colonists. He saw himself, however, as a proud member of the world's greatest empire and said: "Every drop of blood in my heart is British."[6] He believed that the most fundamental of historical privileges was the right to be taxed only by one's representation. That view was not shared by Parliament.

The evidence suggests that Dickinson was better fitted by education and personal values for the discussion of larger questions that engaged the attention of statesmen than he was for the more limited inquiries that were called fourth in the practicing lawyer. Following the passage of the Stamp Act Dickinson published his *Farmer's Letters* and that series of letters were printed in the *Pennsylvania Chronicle*. The letters, fourteen in all, were read by men of all social classes and political opinions throughout the colonies. From their appearance, up to the Declaration of Independence, they were of major influence on the destiny of the country.[7]

The effect of the *Farmer's Letters* was to crystallize opposition and provide the discontented with a rallying point around a common solution. Even those who were more radical felt it expedient to try the farmer's way before pushing forward on their own with more revolutionary approaches. Ben Franklin so highly approved of the *Letters* that he had an edition of them published in London for which he wrote a preface. The *Letters* were also quickly translated and published in France.

The tone of the letters was not hostile but rather conciliatory. Although Dickinson maintained that taxation was an invasion of the rights of the colonies, he pulled back from asserting what the consequences of the persistent refusal by England to change their oppressive measures should be. Instead, his solution was based on the development of a spirit of conciliation on both sides. He repeatedly impressed on his English readers the folly of their policy, by showing them the great value of the American colonies to them. He strongly argued that the trade and wealth of the English merchants were bound up in the adoption of a liberal policy toward America.

English history had long been one of popular reaction of constitutional authority against those kings and ministers who tried to govern as despots. It had been the power of the purse that allowed the House of Commons to resist royal encroachment on people's rights. Dickinson believed that the colonial assemblies should do the same. He repeated his calls for vigilance and recalled examples of the difficulty of restoring a former freedom once "any ancient law or custom" was broken. He was firmly committed to the birthright of Englishmen and completely agreed with John Adams that the desires of American patriots were not new, but that they wished only to keep their old privileges.

During the following years Dickinson's determination and patriotism continued to be very strong. He increasingly doubted there would be any return to political honesty on the part of the monther country, and the continued British oppression led him to feel that he might have placed too much reliance on the temper of the English people. Dickinson began to see increasing differences between the English liberties that he so highly valued and the actual practice of English politics. As a member of the First Continental Congress in the fall of 1774 he wrote a petition to George III appealing for "peace, liberty and safety." It was described "as penned with extraordinary force and animation, in many parts rising to a very high strain of eloquence."[8]

During the next eighteen months, as New England became more adamant and aggressive, Dickinson was viewed with less admiration. The Coercive Act remained, and in April and June of 1775 came the bloody fighting at Lexington, Concord, and Breed's Hill; there was no longer much hope for reconciliation or any kind of harmony. Nevertheless, Dickinson drafted the Olive Branch Petition early in July 1775 that asked for an end to further bloodshed and urged royal action toward reconciliation. Dickinson knew the king would refuse because the petition offered no concessions, but it did provide an air of injured innocence for the continental congress that sponsored it.

Although Dickinson is remembered as the "Penman of the Revolution" he is equally well remembered for his refusal to sign the Declaration of Independence and that cost him his popularity. Before that time, wrote one historian, "none but the illiterate or the remote frontiersman could have been ignorant" of the arguments of the Pennsylvania farmer, but afterward he was attacked by the radicals and even by the more temperate, for timidity and vacillation. Dickinson was too careful, too refining in thought to see an issue in black and white. He pleaded for a "mild and steady wisdom" in affairs of government. He wrote "We cannot act with too much caution in our disputes. Anger produces anger; and differences, that might be accommodated by kind and respectful behavior may, by imprudence, be enlarged to an incurable rage."[9]

During the summer of 1777 Dickinson served as a private soldier in the militia of Delaware and fought at the battle of Brandywine. After that battle he was appointed brigadier general of the militia of Delaware. Dickinson was one of the only two men in the Congress to actually take up arms in the Revolution. In January 1779 he was sent by Delaware as a delegate to Congress. In the autumn of that year he resigned and returned to his farm, and three years later in 1782 he moved back to Philadelphia. He was elected that same year a member of the Council for the County of Philadelphia.

He played a very active role in the federal convention that assembled in Philadelphia in May 1787. Powell writes that John Dickinson was one of the most prominent men in American political life when he arrived in Philadelphia to take a major part in the revision of the Articles of Confederation. His arrival was a matter of considerable interest to the delegates. "Tall . . . slender as a reed, pale as ashes, with white hair, carefully groomed in an out-of-date style, excessively modest, shy even, he was frail in health, which made him look older than his fifty-five years. Although he was not a good speaker, he was sincere, and what he said on the floor of the Convention was heard with respectful attention."[10] Possibly his greatest distinction at the constitutional convention was his strong support for the equality and sovereignty of the states. It was on his motion that the convention determined that the Senate should be composed of members, two from each states, chosen by their respective legislatures.

By 1787 Dickinson found that his temperate views toward governmental matters was more readily accepted than it had been in 1776. The independence of his political thinking appears to have regained for him the respect of many citizens he had lost in the radical victory a decade earlier. Also his record as president of Pennsylvania and the great patriotism he had shown by taking up arms in defense of a cause with which he did not entirely sympathize had made a powerful impression on his fellow Americans.

Dickinson's career was one of the most distinguished of the Revolution era. He was the author of most of the state papers of the continental congresses other than the Declaration of Independence and one of the several who framed the Articles of Confederation. He led a brigade in the Revolution and was again active in Congress in 1779. He was chosen president of "the Delaware State" in 1781, and a year later president of Pennsylvania. That officer at that time was the "first gentlemen of the land."[11]

Opinions of historians have varied in attributing the honor of the responsibility for the Constitution to certain of the statesmen concerned with its framing. It appears without question that the most important roles in the Convention of 1787 were filled by James Madison and James Wilson. Their work came from a theory of political organization that had emerged during thirty years of conflict. Their solution to the question of the relationship of state to empire was what came from American protests following each oppressive measure beginning with the Stamp Act of 1765. Each of those protests had come from the pen of John Dickinson. "In the years following 1765 no American had the influence in political thought which Dickinson attained, through his many signed writings and his activities as the leader of the dominant party in the Continental Congresses."[12]

John Dickinson died 4 February 1808, at the end of Thomas Jefferson's second term. Congress adopted resolutions lamenting his death as a national loss. Jefferson wrote: "A more estimable man or true patriot cannot have left

us. Among the first of the advocates for the rights of this country when assailed
by Great Britain, he continued to the last the orthodox advocate of the true
principles of our new government, and his name will be consecrated in history
as one of the great worthies of the Revolution."[13]

Dickinson was also a strong believer in education, and he sought to promote
that cause; Dickinson College, in Pennsylvania, was named after him. He was
also opposed to slavery and sought to bring about its abolition in Delaware.
One description of Dickinson is as follows:

> He was tall and sparse, his hair as white as snow, his face uniting with the severe
> simplicity of his sex, a neatness and elegance particularly in keeping with it; his manners
> a beautiful emanation of the great Christian principle of love, with that gentleness
> and affection which, whatever may be the cause, the Friends, or at least individuals
> among them, exhibit more than others, combining the politeness of a man of the
> world familiar with society in its most polished forms with the conventional canons
> of behavior. Truly he lives in my memory as the realization of my beau-ideal of a
> gentleman.[14]

John Dickinson was a great legal figure during the Revolutionary War period
and his outstanding achievements were as a statesmen rather than at the bar
or bench. That was a time when lawyers were crucial in bringing about the
change in government and in constructing the new one. As with Andrew
Hamilton and James Wilson he was not a native Philadelphia, but he was
strongly attached to the city.

Dickinson, along with James Wilson, were the two major Philadelphia figures
of the Revolutionary War era. Dickinson as a lawyer trained in the Middle
Temple succeeded as a lawyer in Philadelphia and amassed a great fortune.
As a Philadelphia lawyer, however, he is best remembered as a political theorist
and statesman. During the next 175 years few Philadelphia lawyers would
become successful statesmen or politicians.

3
Revolutionary War Era: 1770–1788

God works wonders now and then; Behold a lawyer, an honest man.
— Ben Franklin

In 1776, at the outbreak of the Revolution, Philadelphia was still a young city. It was less than one hundred years old and yet was the second largest city, next only to London, in the British Empire. The city continued to have something of a rural atmosphere as blackberries were still picked at the corner of Sixth and Chestnut Streets and wild strawberries along Spruce Street between Seventh and Eighth Streets. Every morning a horn was sounded on Dock Street, which ran along the Delaware River, to tell the owners of cows to turn them over to the cow man who drove them to the edge of town to pasture for the day. There were still a number of ponds around the edge of town where the frogs croaked in the summer and the citizens could ice skate in the winter.

In 1776, Philadelphia extended from the Delaware River to about Seventh Street and from Vine to Lombard Streets. That was a city area of less then one square mile. Living within that area, however, was a population of about 35,000 with almost seven thousand buildings. In 1774, 880 ships sailed into the river harbor of Philadelphia, and it was the busiest port on the American continent. The city was exporting the most cereals, cereal products, and lumber of all the colonies. By the 1770s it had become the leading manufacturing center, and because of its extensive trade the city developed a thriving industry in the production of barrels, hogsheads, and containers for the shipment of various foods.

By the time of the Revolution there was a strong belief that a man could improve his social position. Although most men never moved beyond the social level into which they were born, enough did to provide some models for the optimistic beliefs of others. It was certainly possible for a young man to achieve economic independence. For example, he might begin as a journeyman wage earner and realistically aspire to become a master worker. Among the wealthy their greatest advantage came from the economic resources of their families. For example, at least half of the wealthy merchants of Philadelphia had fathers who had been wealthy. Of the richest men in Philadelphia in 1765 more than half were merchants with one in five being professional men, and most of those were lawyers. Many of those men had as a major source of their wealth the ownership of property or rich returns from their business investments. Possibly one in seven of the wealthiest were self-made men, but they had not started out in the poorest families. In most instances those men had been sons of fathers in the urban middle class who had followed some trade and that provided them with a strong initial boost up the social ladder.

One basic belief shared by those of English origin was in the rule of law, and when in the late eighteenth century the colonists spoke of the "liberties of freeborn Englishmen" that clearly meant the rule of law. For the colonists to resist the government of King George III they had to prove to their own satisfaction that he had broken the law. The colonists did not see themselves as arguing to gain a new freedom but rather to affirm the freedom they believed they already had. The colonies were more advanced in self-government than was the mother country, and they also felt fewer pressures from many old customs. For example, the colonists had no tithes to support an established church, and the trades and the professions were relatively open and not castes. There were no guilds, corporations, or exclusive professional associations that rigidly stratified society. Overall there was an openness in the social structure of the colonies that did not exist in England.

The Sugar Act was the first law passed by Parliament with the explicit purpose of raising money in the colonies. The British government took the position that the colonists had to help pay the great expenses that had resulted from the French and Indian Wars. The Stamp Act, which was one section of the Sugar Act, required stamps on "every skin or piece of vellum or parchment, or sheet or piece of paper" issuing from any court. That included courts exercising "ecclesiastical jurisdiction within the said colonies." At the time there were no ecclesiastical courts, but a great fear had grown starting in the early 1760s that the Church of England might gain the authority to set up such courts under the bishop in America. The Church had been arguing for ecclesiastical jurisdiction over all of America. Although the Sugar Act struck mainly at the merchants, the Stamp Act hit every literate and influential person in the colonies because it affected lawyers, printers, editors, tavern owners, and even the dissenting clergy.

At the same time as the Stamp Act the British Parliament passed a new Quartering Act. That Act provided that if barracks were insufficient for housing the British troops being sent over public inns and even private barns might be used. As a result of that act mobs were organized, and they attacked the houses of the Stamp Act defenders intimidating the king's officials. In June 1763, the Townshend Acts were passed to raise money by placing new import duties on glass, lead, paints, paper, and tea. The crowning insult to the colonist was the provision that the salaries of the king's new appointees were to be paid out of the fines and judgments levied against violators convicted in the admiralty courts.

The court system in America obviously possessed many of the characteristics of the English court system from which it was given birth. The principle feature was a two-tier judicial system, with lesser courts set up on a territorial basis throughout the colonies. There was a central higher court to hear appeals from the lower courts. By the end of the Revolutionary War period the American system had evolved its principal legal structure. Laws were enacted by elected legislatures, administered by elected executives, and enforced by an elaborate system of courts. The legal framework was established by written constitution, and the means for making laws or amending them had been settled.

The Pennsylvania Constitution of 1776 called for a rotation of office. In England, office tended to depend on the Crown, but that system was firmly rejected by the states and later the Constitution. According to the Pennsylvania Court of 1776 "offices of profit" were not to be established because such offices led office holders to a state of "dependence and servility unbecoming freeman and created faction, contention, corruption and disorder" in the public. The Pennsylvania court also initially rejected the notion of politics as a career. Rather, political involvement was seen as a duty, a form of public service, opened to the concerned citizen.

The colonial government and the royal-controlled judiciary was often viewed as representing foreign domination, whereas the Assemblies were usually seen as the voice of local colonists. The Pennsylvania Court of 1776 gave "supreme legislative power" to a single House of Representatives, and there was no upper house or governor's veto to check its power. With time, however, there came to be a disillusionment with legislative supremacy and the objection was directed at the governor. As a result judicial power continued to increase at the cost of legislative power.

At the time of the Revolution the body of American law that existed had some qualities different from the English law from which it had derived. The foundation of American law had, of course, been the English common law and foremost among the rights the colonists had taken was the right to be tried by common law. An important factor of growth in America before the Revolution was the increasingly strong reaction in favor of the common law. In 1774, the Declaration of Rights of the First Continental Congress asserted "that the respective colonies are entitled to the common law of England.[1]

Each of the new colonies, in many ways, underwent their own evolution before they became states, and in their new directions they encountered new problems. First, they had to fight the war and resolve the domestic disruption and that called for a major effort in law making. In Pennsylvania, a state constitutional convention in 1776 declared a general amnesty and established a new form of state government where the old officials were replaced by new ones who were loyal to the Revolution. It was decided that the ordinary business of government was to continue whenever possible, but most of their efforts had to be directed to the war. After the British occupation of Philadelphia the state government created a Council of Safety that was given vast and summary powers. The council was to promote and provide for the preservation of the commonwealth, and it had the power to seize goods, "for the army and for the inhabitants, punish traitors, and regulate the prices of such articles they may think necessary."[2]

The general view of lawyers during the Revolution had seen negative and hostile attitudes directed at most members of the Philadelphia bar. Most of the leading lawyers were against the revolution. With about one-fourth of the former legal community being Loyalists that contributed greatly to the resentment toward lawyers. There were even some proposals to, in various ways, restrain, suppress, and even abolish the legal profession.

Certainly there was arrogance to be found in the legal profession. For example, in New York many prominent lawyers and judges were conspicuous and often offensive in their aristocratic bearing. Alexander Hamilton's description of the people as "the great beast" or Gouverneur Morris's view that "there never was and never will be a civilized society without an aristocracy" antagonized many patriots. The aristocratic frame of mind was not lost on the common man, and those views were responsible for much of the distrust toward the profession of law. During Shay's Rebellion in 1786 people demanded that the lower courts and all lawyers be eliminated.[3]

In Pennsylvania several statutes were passed to repress not only the legal profession but also the common law of England including the system of courts at the time. The opposition wanted lay referees instead of trained lawyers and trials without intervention by legal council. The situation became so severe in Pennsylvania that Charles Jared Ingersoll informed his friends that all the eminent lawyers of Philadelphia had their eyes on other cities where they might move. He added that his father, Jared Ingersoll, a barrister of the Middle Temple and one of Philadelphia's most distinguished lawyers of the time, when the city boasted the finest legal talent in the country, planned to move to New York.[4]

One major legal problem was the structure of the courts and their judges. In the common law system judges make at least some of the law, and American statesmen recognized that the values of judges and where they came from was of great importance. Therefore, how they were to be chosen and how they were to function on the court was a major political issue for the revolutionary war generation. The new American bench that emerged was far from homogeneous. The judges varied in their qualifications, and in the new American judicial system the range extended from local justices of the peace to the United States Supreme Court justices. Judges did not have to be politicians, although that was often necessary to win appointment. There was a clear trend toward professionalism, and laymen rapidly disappeared from serving on the higher courts.

The history of the legal profession reveals that at the time of the Revolution at least some of the colonies had a very able bar. There were differences between the colonies as to the acceptance or rejection of the common law of England and the organization of the courts as well as their quality. There were also differences in control over admission to the practice of law, and, at least indirectly, over the training and qualification to practice law. In general where lawyers controlled their profession there was a strong sense of solidarity and that solidarity brought about improvements in the quality of the bar.

There were professional problems, and they often differed between the various colonies. For example, in both Massachusetts and Pennsylvania, when compared with other colonies, religious opposition had held down the growth of the legal profession. By contrast, the problem in New York and Virginia had been that the dominant upper classes hindered the development of the legal profession. Yet, as mentioned, some of the colonies during the last decades before the Revolution were fortunate to have a substantial number of lawyers who had been trained at the Inns of Court. There were other colonies like Georgia, North Carolina, and to some extent New Hampshire that until the Revolution continued their fairly primitive "pioneer spirit" and did not develop a professional bar. In general important changes had started in the 1750s, and many of the colonies were positively influenced by the application of improved educational methods that were initially brought about by those lawyers trained at the Inns of Court.[5]

Lewis wrote that the opportunities for legal education in colonial Pennsylvania were very scanty. Furthermore, he wrote, there was a complete absence of variety in the methods of instruction. In fact, no courses of lectures were delivered upon legal topics, and no opportunity was afforded to young men to test their abilities before entering active practice. The belief became among some that an institution in the nature of a Law Academy was greatly needed. "The readings and mootings of the London Inns of Court seemed naturally the fittest model upon which to frame such an institution, and it was upon such a basis that in 1784 the first legal debating club was formed." It was composed entirely of law students. But it dissolved in a year or two when its members were admitted to the bar.[6]

With independence and the lose of many Loyalist lawyers there was an increasing need for new ones. Over the Revolutionary war era about nine new lawyers were admitted to the Philadelphia bar each year. Fortune, prestige and often political appointment were the goals of the successful city lawyer. In Philadelphia in 1770 Joseph Galloway earned over £2,000 a year and there were others who became as affluent through their law practices. Bridenbaugh writes that the phrase "Philadelphia lawyer" had not yet been coined, but many ordinary people looked with suspicion upon the lawyer with his green bag full of technicalities.[7]

No colleges gave law lectures, and no colleges were devoted to legal training in America until nearly the end of the eighteenth century. Before the Revolution, those who wanted to be lawyers and could not afford to go to London usually entered an apprenticeship at home. That could be expensive, and typically the higher the legal and social status of the lawyer-preceptor, the greater was his fee. At the time of the Revolution there was no uniform standard of admission to the bar, but some of the colonies had fairly strict standards. For example, New York demanded seven years of preparation for the right to practice as an attorney before the Supreme Court. Generally, more was demanded for admission to the bar in the city than in the rural areas.

Entrance to the bar in America was never an occupation determined directly by family lineage or by government-granted monopoly. The closest to a lawyer status based on inheritance or monopoly was in Virginia and Massachusetts, particularly in the generation before the Revolution. In Virginia the roots of possible social distinction lay in the practice of well-to-do planters sending their sons to the Inns of Court. In Massachusetts it was the roots of a self-perpetuating, more or less closed class of lawyers. That system was grounded in the admission of lawyers to practice in higher courts only after a preliminary period of admission to practice in the inferior courts. Those admissions were under the strict control of a strong local Bar Association. After the Revolution with the reaction against things English and the end of young men trained at the inns, however, there was a loosening of many restrictions.[8]

By the time of the Revolution a career in law had become the best professional means of social advancement. The American belief was not that everyone succeeds, but that everyone has the right to try. Even though some mobility could occur by becoming a lawyer, however, that did not mean the bar was no longer stratified. The stratification was increasingly controlled through admission to the bar. In 1778 the first State Board of Bar Examiners was set up in New Hampshire. From colonial days statutes had set down at least the general forms of requirements for admission to the bar. Before 1870, however, examinations were typically oral and were usually administered in a very casual manner.

There were a few colonial lawyers with an interest in teaching, and they moved away from the usual apprenticeship program and began to practice law less and spend more time with their clerks; the first law schools grew out of those specialized law offices. The earliest was in Litchfield, Connecticut, founded by Judge Tapping Reeve in 1784 and was very successful, attracting men from all over the country. The subjects studied were municipal law, master and servant, contracts, baron and femme, parent and child, executers and administrators, and fraudulent conveyances. Also taught were forms of action and pleading, commercial law, criminal law, and real property. The study of common law was taken back to the origins of the royal courts established in England after the Norman conquest. Reeves taught the law by lectures, but his lectures were not published. He knew to have published his lectures would have meant students would have had no reason to pay tuition and to attend his classes. His lecture plan was modeled on Blackstone's *Commentaries*, but the Litchfield lectures directed more attention to commercial law and less to criminal law. There were daily lectures lasting about an hour and a half, and the full course lasted fourteen months. The students were required to write their notes up carefully and do collateral readings. Every Saturday there was a strict examination on the week's work. By the 1820's the school began to feel competition, and it closed in 1833. More than one thousand students graduated during the fifty years, however.[9]

Law books were scarce in America, and as John Adams wrote legal education in America "suffered very much from lack of books." The first volume of American law reports was not published until 1790. For many lawyers and judges there continued to be little concern or value attached to legal training. That was reflected in the remarks of Judge Livermore. In his court he dismissed a reference to an earlier contrary decision of his own by observing that "every tub must stand on its own bottom," and it was his duty "to do justice between the parties not by any quirk if the law came out of Coke or Blackstone— books that I never read and never will—but by common sense as between man and man." Colonial America had produced no great legal systems or encyclopedia. What it did produce was a varied, dispersed, and miscellaneous results from hundreds of laymen, semilawyers, pseudolawyers, and a few men of solid legal training. There were many who believed that Blackstone had violated the spirit of the common law by putting it into a system. Blackstone, however, was to American law what Noah Webster's blue-back *Speller* was to American literacy.[10]

In Philadelphia in 1776, numerous legal commentaries, mostly by English authors, including Swinburne, *Wills*, Wood's *Institute*, Hawkin's, *Pleas of the Crown*, Tremaine's, *Pleas of the Crown*, Coke Littleton, *Jacob's Law Dictionary*, and Bacon and Seldon on government, were advertised for sale through local book sellers. Published books on decisions made by American courts did not exist until 1790, when Alexander Dallas's *Reports of Cases Ruled and Adjudicated in the Courts of Pennsylvania* appeared.

The most influential legal reference books to appear during the period was Blackstone's *Commentaries on the Law of England*. About one thousand copies of the English edition were sold in America. In 1771 a special American edition of fourteen hundred copies, subscribed for in advance, was printed in Philadelphia. For lay judges and pioneer lawyers alike, Blackstone was an authoritative reference to principles of the common law.[11]

The few available books were sometimes overvalued because they were all the aspiring lawyer had. Because he had so few books, those that he had were frequently thoroughly mastered. The early lawyer was in some ways served by not having many law books because the law he learned was practical rather than philosophical. Any system of common law examines what has been done to determine what ought to be done. It respects social change and looks to social functioning rather than legislative action. The development of law at this time was important not only for professional reasons but for political ones. The law was the substance of the Revolution, and the new federal, state, and local governments. As mentioned the American Constitution was framed in legal language because that was the language spoken by the literate community.[12]

It appears that at the time of the Revolution about forty-eight legal treatises had been printed in the colonies, but none was a treatise written for the use of the professional lawyer. They were primarily for the use of laymen and attempted to help them in daily business and community encounters. Law libraries continued to be scarce and small. When they could be found they were mostly limited to certain books on English law with sometimes a collection of local statutes.

Income from the practice of law varied greatly before the Revolution. How much one could earn depended on the prosperity of the community, and in that regard Philadelphia was economically rewarding for many of its lawyers. During the last decades before the Revolution incomes of £1,500 to £2,000 were not very common in the city. On the eve of the Revolution, William Smith, Jr., listed his income from the practice of law as between £2,000 and £3,000.

James Allen wrote in his diary on 30 October, 1773:

> I often reflect how happy it was for me when I took to the practice of law. Added to the uneasiness that it gave my father & all my friends to find after having served a regular clerkship & been three years at the Temple, I should continue an idle man I say added to this consideration I have now made myself easy to my circumstances. I compute my business this year 1773 will be between £3 & £400, which added to my estate will but little short of £1,000 per annum. For these last two or three years, which is the time that I resumed the practice of Law, I have read pretty diligently and have overcome the difficulty of speaking in publick. In short both the study & practice are becoming agreeable to me.[13]

For several Philadelphia lawyers, as with James Allen, what they earned from their practice was only part of their income. Because many were from wealthy families their law income was only a part of their yearly income. At the time of the Revolution in Philadelphia the most successful lawyers were almost all a part of the upper class. The family money had provided them with superior educations, opened the door to the most successful legal practices, given them the most profitable clients as well as financial support of their family resources. Clearly they earned more because of the great advantage brought about by having money and high social status with which to begin life.

As suggested in the aftermath of the Revolution, lawyers were often viewed with great suspicion and hostility. One reason was that money had became scarce at a time when the extension of credit was greatly needed to bring about the healthy development of a new economy. Shay's Rebellion was directed against taxes and the collection of debts as well as the unpopular courts. A few years later lawyers came under attack in the Whiskey Insurrection in 1794 in western Pennsylvania.

The laws of strict foreclosure and imprisonment for debt created many hardship cases. No property was exempt from seizure other than the clothes on the debtor's back. The sheriff could take the bed on which the debtor slept, the last potato in his cellar, and the only pig or cow in his barn. Because of so little hard currency the property at the execution sale brought only a fraction of what it was worth. Those who were owed were usually unremitting in asserting their legal rights, and if the proceeds of the sale did not bring the amount of the legal action and costs the debtor was sometimes put in jail. He was kept there as long as the creditor could pay his board, or until the debt was paid, or friends came to his aid. The lawyers were often singled out as the villains because the chief law business at that time was the collection of debts, foreclosure, insolvencies, and recovery of property.[14]

Lawyers were also involved in the detailed drafting of deeds, titles, and other legal documents. The recording of those instruments, contract negotiation, and formalities attending the payment of taxes led to many unpleasant dealings with embittered tenants. Certainly some of the lawyers who acted as land agents indulged in sharp practices that if not dishonest were close to it. It seemed that whenever the common man came into contact with the law or the court his experience was an unhappy one. The common opinion was that the law was nothing more than tricks and technicalities, run by unscrupulous men who built legal careers on the disasters of others. It was said that "lawyers are plants that will grow in any soil that is cultivated by the hands of others; and once they have taken root they will extinguish every other vegetable that grows around them." Lawyers often were seen as what the clergy had been in previous generations—parasites.[13]

After the Revolution some saw the lawyer as having been antirevolutionary. The lawyer sometimes appeared to stand in the way of the development of a truly free republic because he insisted on holding to the forms and ceremonies of law from before the Revolution. Often even the lawyer's dress set him apart from his fellow citizens. In Philadelphia several lawyers continued to appear at the bar with powdered hair and dressed in formal black attire. Those styles were carried over from the British and often were seen as inappropriate to the new nation. The lawyers were the only distinguishable social group that appeared to defy the new popular values. Their dress and behavior from the past often drew attention to them, and they became the only lightning rods visible to the general population.

It was often assumed that every new legal innovation or idea, however minor, had some sinister purpose or intent. Increasingly the charge against the lawyer was that an inevitable conflict of interest must occur when the same men who made the laws also applied them and profited from them. Many lawyers were profiting from the distress of others at a time when very few were profiting in any fashion. Among the most unhappy were the middle class who were anxious to protect their property rights against the new nation's threats they saw directed at them.

For the legal profession the revolutionary war era was one of very high prestige and social importance for the lawyer as statesman. That was followed by anger and hostility toward the lawyer as practitioner. The lawyer-statesman and the general population had a common enemy, the British government, and in his leadership role he helped bring about the Revolution. The values that went into making the Revolution, as well as the accepted behavior, were different from those that were needed to form the new government. That was illustrated by the fate of the leaders. Washington and Jefferson were great heroes at the time of the Revolution and for a while afterward. Once they entered the political realm, however, they became subject to increasingly hostile attacks based on conflicting political values.

The average citizen is not likely to encounter the law as a happy event, and the adversary system is based on someone being a winner and someone a loser. After the Revolution the function of the lawyer was no longer to create revolution but to construct the highly complex legal structure needed for the new nation. The lawyer had to apply the law, and the law took precedent over any compassionate needs that he might personally feel. The years after the Revolution, and up through the Jacksonian era, were an extended period of generally low status for the American lawyer.

Profile 3: James Wilson (1742–1798)

James Wilson arrived from Scotland at the age of twenty-three with a letter of introduction to the College of Philadelphia. He had been educated at St. Andrews in Scotland and had no problem in getting an appointment as a tutor. He quickly decided, however, he did not like tutoring. He also discovered that the most important and successful young men in Philadelphia were lawyers. He could see that those lawyers were going to be men of increasing importance in the city as they followed in the steps of the older generation of lawyers who were leaders in the power structure of the city. Several of those men had outstanding legal reputations. One was Benjamin Chew, a proprietary lawyer and the king's attorney, who was also powerful in Philadelphia politics. The older lawyer who impressed Wilson the most, however, was John Dickinson. He was seen as one of the most outstanding of all lawyers in the colonies.

Wilson studied law with Dickinson. He learned law by filling his notebooks with pleadings, forms, terms of contract, replevins, and torts; those notebooks came to reflect his values about law. For example, heading the first page was a citation from Cicero: "The house of the Lawyer is the oracle of the whole City." In 1767, after less than a year's apprenticeship with Dickinson, Wilson and his teacher decided he had completed his study and was ready to practice law. Because of the large number of young lawyers in Philadelphia at the time Wilson started his practice in Reading, the county seat of Berks County, located about fifty miles northwest of Philadelphia.

Wilson's law practice grew very rapidly. In the August 1768 term of the court of common pleas in Reading, he appeared in fourteen cases and came to be quickly recognized as an exceptional young lawyer. In January 1775, Wilson was chosen as a member of the provincial convention in Philadelphia. The main purpose of that convention was to approve the work of the continental congress. All conventions had at least one major oration and at that one the honor was given to Wilson. He addressed the delegates on "The Justice of the Colonial Cause and the Tyrannies of Great Britain," which gained him great recognition. When the second continental congress began to assemble in May 1775. Wilson's friends in the Pennsylvania assembly took advantage of Benjamin Franklin's return from England to add Wilson and Thomas Willing, as well as Franklin, to the Pennsylvania delegation.

Wilson became one of the most prominent figures in Congress because there was great respect for his outstanding legal abilities. Throughout the winter

James Wilson, 1742–1798. Courtesy of the Historical Society of Pennsylvania.

of 1776, John Adams and John Dickinson were battling for Wilson's political soul, and Adams was the winner. When Congress met, Morris and Dickinson, though present, did not officially take their seats; Wilson, Franklin, and Morton carried the state of Pennsylvania for independence. Even though Wilson was a continental statesman he was also very involved in Pennsylvania politics. Even with his many congressional duties he also led the fight in Pennsylvania against the radicals from the western part of the state.

In the winter of 1777, when General Howe's British army occupied Philadelphia, Wilson returned to his home in Carlisle, Pennsylvania. His leaving Congress was a turning point in his career. While in Congress he had made many friends of wealthy and influential men in the nation. With the ascendancy of the radicals, however, it seemed unlikely that political office would be available to Wilson. His interests changed, and he turned increasingly toward business ventures and land speculation. His two principle interests, business and politics, did draw him back to Philadelphia in June 1778, however.

James Wilson came to be a familiar figure on the streets of Philadelphia. He was a tall, thick-muscled man, inclined to put on weight. He had a ruddy complexion, wore a neat white wig, and used thick lens glasses. There was a stiffness in his manner; with strangers he was usually ill at ease, and his shyness led to an aloofness that his enemies saw as arrogance. He usually found himself more socially at ease with women than with men. To women he was courtly and attentive, and he once wrote that he valued the conversation of an intelligent and gracious woman more than that of a philosopher. He also had a reputation for somewhat eccentric behavior. Socially prominent people gossiped about his occasional lapses of social etiquette, which was probably a result of his rather humble origins in Scotland. Wilson clearly had not been born of the gentry and never made any attempt to suggest otherwise.

Few of Wilson's letters or records of his private talks, were preserved. The quality of his intellect was clear and sharp, however. He was a systematic and coherent thinker, who had read widely, and had completely mastered and digested what he had read. He embodied his observations and ideas in general principles and was prepared to apply them steadily and consistently. He also had the courage of his logic and was not afraid to maintain views that sometimes startled his peers.[1]

After the end of the Revolution several societies were reactivated or formed in Philadelphia, but the outstanding learned society of the day was the American Philosophical Society. Beginning in 1769 and having as members the most distinguished men in the country, the society elected Wilson a member in 1786. That was a reflection of the respect and eminence given to him as a political and economic theorist. As his biographer wrote "the life of James Wilson was in its essence a life of the mind, and although he was deeply involved in the events of his time, his greatest adventures were intellectual and his principal achievements those of an extraordinary mind."[2]

William Rawle said of Wilson that the views he took were luminous and conspicuous. His knowledge and information always appeared adequate to whatever the complexity of the subject, "and justly administered to the particular aspect in which it was presented." When he spoke his voice was powerful, though not melodious, and his cadences judicious though somewhat artificially regulated. In the courtroom his discourse was of reasonable length, and he did not affect conciseness nor minuteness. He would strike at the most important features of the case. "It must, however, be confessed, that Mr. Wilson on the bench, was not equal to Mr. Wilson at the bar, nor did his law lectures entirely meet the expectations that had been formed."[3]

Wilson did not have the easy and outgoing manner common to the successful politician. With all but his friends and relatives, he was emotionally inept, cold, and unresponsive. He had none of Robert Morris's genial heartiness, none of Thomas Jefferson's charm, nor John Adams's pungent wit. It was clearly among ideas and not among men that Wilson was most at home. His political writings, his law lectures, his speeches, all gave evidence of his insatiable reading of history, philosophy, and political theory. So formidable was Wilson's reputation for erudition that when William Findley, in the Pennsylvania Ratifying Committee, bested him on an obscure point about the constitution of Iceland, Wilson's enemies gloated over the triumph for weeks.

While lawyer, political theorist, politician, financier, businessman, and land speculator, Wilson was probably best known to his fellow Philadelphians as an orator. At the 4th of July celebration in 1788, which also honored the new constitution, Wilson was chosen to give the oration of the day. That was the highest speaking honor the new country could bestow. With his great imagery and flights in oration he was highly acclaimed. He was also described as being so physically imposing he was able to sweep his listeners along on the powerful tide of his rhetoric.

In the upper social circles of Philadelphia the Wilsons had no reputation for elegant parties. They were considered to be gracious hosts, however. After the Marquis de Chastellux had been invited to their home for dinner he said he found the fare "excellent" and was pleased by the "plain and easy politeness" of his host. The circle of Wilson's friends were close and congenial, and they were chosen for intellectual respect rather than social standing. Bushrod Washington, George Washington's adopted son, was taken into the Wilson family during his law apprenticeship with James Wilson, and he wrote of his affection and gratitude for the many kindnesses that the Wilsons extended to him.

The constitutional convention was the time of greatest achievement in Wilson's life. His work constituted a major contribution to the future peace and stability of the United States. No one man was probably more responsible for the final result of the Constitution than was Wilson. As one of the ablest political theorists at the convention, Wilson espoused more of those principles, which have become prominent features of American democracy than did any other delegate. Wilson, even more than his fellow Federalists, had a clear vision of the role of the chief executive as the national leader. Wilson saw the president as representative of all the people against, or above, the interests of any particular groups or of the individual states.

During the convention Wilson showed a practicality in that he often had to deal with other views, sooth alarms, or even "make a deal" with the selfish interests of opponents. The convention of 1787 found him reasonable and willing to accept compromises with good humor. "It would seem however that the immense influence which he exerted in that wonderfully able body was due less to any talent for persuasion enabling him to win over its members than to his argumentive power, to the clearness with which he saw and the force with which he expounded and applied the broad doctrines of political and legal science he had already thought out." He was as committed a Federalist as Hamilton, and he was more democratic in sentiment, with a greater disposition to trust the people, and apparently a more sanguine hope that in the hands of the people all things would work out right.[4]

In March 1789, the trustees of the College of Philadelphia received a petition from a group of law students asking that they be allowed to hold meetings in one of the rooms of the college, and the request was granted. The next year a plan was presented by a trustee's committee headed by Wilson for instituting a law course. Wilson drew up a plan that would cover constitutional law, international law, common law, civil law, and maritime law. The plan was approved, and Wilson was elected to give a series of law lectures at the college.

The lectures began soon after Congress first convened in Philadelphia. The first and introductory lecture occurred in the hall of the main college building on 15 December 1779. The day was described as raw and cloudy with a sharp wind, but the hall was packed well before the starting time. The gallery was filled with friends and admirers of Wilson. The floor was reserved for "Congress and Other Bodies." The president and the vice-president, members of Congress, the officers of the new government, the state senate and house, and local political dignitaries filled the main floor. When Wilson rose to address that audience, composed of the leading figures of the new nation, that moment was the symbolic peak of his great public career. His biographer writes: "Respected by both his friends and his oppenents, loved by few, locked within the confines of his blazing ambition and his awkward stiffness of manner—a stiffness perhaps compounded more of painful shyness than of pride—Wilson must have found the occasion a sweet balm to his restless spirit."[5]

His address was not a discussion of any random principles of law, but rather to lay what he saw as the cornerstone of a peculiarly American system of law and to cut the umbilical cord that bonded the infant "science" of American law from the common law of its English mother. Wilson argued that law should be studied and taught as a historical science. He said that "the study of law should, in some measure, and in some degree, be the study of every free citizen, of every free man." He asserted that all educated men should have familiarity with "principles and the elements of the law." He insisted that because the principles on which the Constitution of the United States are formed are different from those of England, so must the American law and education be different from that of England.

Wilson worked hard in preparing his future lectures, but only about half of them were ever delivered. The project seems to have been too ambitious to have been carried out in only a part of a single academic year. For various reasons it was not continued beyond the middle of the second term. Wilson's law lectures were a landmark in American jurisprudence, however. As a practical lawyer, Wilson was one of the outstanding legal figures of his day and as a theorist he had no serious rival. Wilson, one of the great political figures of his day, spelled out in detail his view of the nature of law, a view so broad that it encompassed philosophy, psychology, and political theory.[6]

There was never any question but that James Wilson would have a place on the first United States Supreme Court. When he was appointed by President Washington be was bitterly disappointed because he believed he should have been the first chief justice. Bryce writes that "it will always be a cause for regret that death at the age of fifty-six, when he had sat for nine years only, should have deprived the young Republic of those elucidations of the meaning of the Constitution which no one, not even Jay or Marshall, could have delivered with more authority of with more complete mastery of the principles of law and government.[7]

James Wilson, along with his brother-in-law, Mark Bird, had a mania for land speculation that was common to the time. They were not successful, however, and were both financially ruined. Wilson, although still a Supreme Court justice, had to escape from Philadelphia. He went first to New Jersey to escape debtor's prison and then fled to North Carolina where he died.

Wilson's life tragically ended away from Philadelphia, and there were no testimonials, eulogies, or funeral orations for Wilson. Always an anathema to his enemies, he had become a political liability to his friends. He was buried obscurely beside the waters of Abermarle Sound in South Carolina, far from the scenes of his greatest triumphs. "His forgotten bones, moldering in the little graveyard beneath the cypress trees, symbolized the eclipse of his fame." The very conditions of his death, as a fugitive from the law because of fraudulent business dealings, and hiding in a shabby Carolina Inn, made him an uncongenial subject for the biographers of the nineteenth cenutry.

Bryce writes that in that generation there were two men of great intellectual power for whom it took a long time for them to gain historical recognition. Both those men were Scottish immigrants. It was not until a hundred years had passed that one of those men, Alexander Hamilton, began to receive the honor because of his extraordinary gifts, "an honour which the extinction of the party he led and the emergence of new questions had for a time withheld from him."[9] Around the start of the twentieth century there was a revival of public interest in James Wilson, and in 1906 his mortal remains were removed from their resting place in North Carolina and reinterred in Philadelphia with great and solemn respect.[10]

Francis Rawle wrote about James Wilson and said that the views toward Wilson were that he was luminous and comprehensive. "His knowledge and information always appeared adequate to the highest subject, and justly administered to the particular aspect in which it was presented. His discourse was generally of a reasonable length, he did not affect conciseness nor minuteness, he struck at the great features of the case, and neither wearied his hearers by a verbose prolongation, nor disappointed them by an abrupt conclusion." Rawles went on to say, however, that "Mr. Wilson on the bench, was not equal to Mr. Wilson at the bar, nor did his law lectures entirely meet the expectation that had been formed."[11]

James Wilson was the greatest of the Philadelphia lawyers during the revolutionary war era. Although many saw him as ambitious, cantankerous, and greedy, he was the first to formulate in American law the concept that sovereignty resides not in the rulers but with the ruled, and not in the state but with the people. He must be judged by what he achieved in his brilliant career, and not by the unfortunate and tragic end. He was one of the greatest of all American political theorists and a major architect of the Constitution. He was a great lawyer as measured by his legal knowledge, his great skills as an orator, and his successes in the courtroom. He also was a justice on the first United States Supreme Court, and the first and inspirational force for legal education in Philadelphia. In the pantheon of the truly great Philadelphia lawyers, James Wilson followed in time the tradition of Andrew Hamilton and John Dickinson.

4

Philadelphia— Nation's Capital: 1788–1800

> Whenever a man has cast a longing eye on offices, a rottenness begins
> in his conduct.
>
> —Thomas Jefferson

Philadelphia during the decade of the 1790s was both the political and social center of the United States. The decade began with the death of Philadelphia's greatest man, Benjamin Franklin. In 1790, Franklin died at the age of eighty-four and twenty thousand people, nearly half the city's population, lined the streets for the funeral procession as it moved from the State House to the Christ Church burying ground. Between Franklin's death and ten years later when John and Abigail Adams moved into the new White House in Washington, Philadelphia was the center for almost everything in the new country. During that period the city gained great international recognition as it hosted not only American dignitaries, but also the great and famous from all over the world.

Wolf writes that the post-Revolutionary War period was a bitter sweet one for Philadelphia. There was the excitement of being the seat of government and the site of the Constitutional Convention. But that was leavened by political turmoil and terrible yellow fever epidemics. Prosperous growth alternated with inflationary depression and peace was followed by undeclared naval welfare. "Yet, by the end of the century, the city was well established as a center of culture, finance, and mercantile trade."[1]

Philadelphia took great pride in being the nation's capital, and it was a great disappointment when they lost it. There were many reasons why Philadelphia might have been chosen as the capital. The city had great tradition, and most of the achievements of the new government—the Declaration of Independence, and the framing of the Constitution—had occurred there. Geographically it was at the heartland of the eastern seaboard, and culturally it was viewed as equal to all but the greatest cities of Europe. It was also the city best known to Americans, and its societies, taverns, theaters, museums, and public entertainment met the needs of every taste.

The opposition argued, however, that the Congress should locate in a place of "less expense, less avocation and less influences than are to be expected in a commercial and opulent City."[2] Of even greater importance, however, was the growing desire by Congress to have a city of its own. They wanted a federal city that would be controlled by the national government, and in the end that undercut Philadelphia's hopes for being the federal capital.

The Revolution did not level the social classes, and the new American leaders had no intention of eliminating the upper class (of which many of them were a part) or in destroying social class lines and distinctions. The belief common to the new democracy was that a gentleman was made not just by birth and wealth, but also through his personal ability and effort. Such leaders as John Adams and Thomas Jefferson clearly believed that all men were not equal. They believed some men were better than others by virtue of health, strength, and intellectual ability. What was most important was not just wealth, but also lineage, education, attitudes, and dress. Of course it was wealth that made those other values possible. Above all the most highly regarded man was the gentleman.

In Philadelphia many fortunes were expanded through land investments as well as new fortunes that were made. The land activities opened up an important new source of legal work for lawyers as well as providing for some lawyers the opportunity to expand their own fortunes through land investment. The Revolution also gave lawyers greater access to power, and some entered social circles that a few years before had been closed to them. Prominent among the Philadelphia postwar lawyers were Joseph Reed, William Bradford, Charles and Edward Biddle, William Lewis, William Rawle, and James Wilson. Some of those men had consolidated their social positions through prudent marriage choices. For example, James Wilson's marriage to Rachel Bird allied him with a part of the provincial or rural society that maintained close ties with the colonial ruling class in Philadelphia. The Bird family had connections that reached into some of the oldest and most powerful families in Philadelphia—the Willings, Rosses, Franceses, and Binghams.

By the 1790s there were a number of Jews in America, and their success and influence was far out of proportion to their relatively small number. Most of them were Sephardic Jews who were descendants of Jews exiled from Spain in 1492, and they had first arrived in New Amsterdam in 1654. At the time of the Revolution there were Jews in all thirteen colonies. Newport had several important families and became the center of Jewish life in the northern colonies. Up until 1800, only a few native-born sons of established Jewish families went into professional careers. Maser and Sampson Levy had been admitted to the Philadelphia bar before the end of the Revolution. The first professionally trained Jew to become a lawyer in Philadelphia was Zaligman Phillips who graduated from the University of Pennsylvania and was admitted to the bar in 1799. After that it was several years before more than a handful of Jews entered law in Philadelphia.[3]

The new Constitution and the new democratic government provided nothing new for women. Abigail Adams expressed some concerns about the effect of government and laws on women. She wrote to her husband, John, that in "the new Code of Laws which I suppose it will be necessary for you I desire you would remember the Ladies, and be more generous and favorable to them than your ancestors. Do not put such unlimited power in the hands of the Husbands. Remember that all Men would be tyrants if they could. If particular care and attention is not paid to the Ladies, we are determined to foment a rebellion and will not hold ourselves bound by any law in which we have no voice or Representation."[4] But, of course, they were bound, and it was well through the nineteenth century before married women could vote, serve on a jury, get a professional education, hold elective office, enter into a contract, obtain custody of their own children, or control their own money, even when they had earned it.

The move from being a colony under the authority of British law to becoming a new nation meant many dramatic changes in the development and application of laws. The old laws from England had to be continued, adapted, or discarded. The legal transition was made easier because so many of the country's leaders had been trained in law. When the new government came into existence the relationship between intellectuals and political power was not a problem. That was because many of the leaders of the Revolution were the intellectuals, and often those intellectuals were trained in law. Control over the fate of the new country was mainly in the hands of an upper class elite and that elite was one in which men of intellect spoke with great authority. It was still a time of unspecialized knowledge, and the role of the intellectual as expert was not yet very important. Law was rapidly coming to be the first true profession, however, because it was a more specialized and technical field of knowledge than was either medicine or religion. Lawyers were emerging as the first elite and best-trained profession in America.

During the revolutionary period only a few men were educated, and being educated usually gave those men a great advantage in being placed in positions of leadership. The political leaders and the learned gentlemen were essentially the same men. The Revolution produced many of the great men of knowledge who were also the political leaders including John Adams, John Dickinson, Benjamin Franklin, Alexander Hamilton, Thomas Jefferson, James Madison, George Mason, James Wilson and George Wythe. Most of those men were educated in law.

It is generally true that the men who make revolutions are not the leaders who can over the long term successfully bring about the development of the new government. In America there had been men of character and great courage who were leaders of the Revolution and with great skill had helped to organize the new government. By 1796, however, the early leaders had become divided in their political values and beliefs. Often the divisions were a result of the strong conflicts brought about by the French Revolution. The leaders of the American Revolution lost much of their earlier solidarity, and although most of them shared a common membership in the ruling upper class the world of politics had set one against the other. Even George Washington, who had enjoyed great admiration and often veneration, was subjected to abuse and slander.

The United States, being a new country, had to develop its methods and means to operate the new form of government. In the 1790s in America there was a powerful feeling of breaking away and leaving the old behind. There was a new feeling of being distinct from the rest of the world, especially from England. Americans began to see their new country in its new relationship to the rest of the world, which contributed to a strong commitment and belief toward the future. The new American citizens quickly came to believe that they could control their own destiny and that their new society would be better than any other in the world.

Many of the leaders were greatly concerned and believed the new nation was faced with the choice of either a stronger union or anarchy. Congress was meeting in New York in 1786 when it sent out a call for each state to send delegates to a constitutional convention with the purpose of strengthening the federal government. The convention met in Philadelphia in May 1787. The seven elected delegates from Pennsylvania were James Wilson, Robert Morris, Gouverneur Morris, Thomas Mifflin, George Clymer, Jared Ingersoll and Thomas Fitzsimmons, later Ben Franklin was added.

The fifty-five men who came to Philadelphia to write the Constitution represented leadership by men from an established upper class. Two of them, Washington and Franklin, were also men of international fame. There were about a dozen who were national leaders, and the rest were more or less established local leaders. Those men were also highly experienced with America's political development. Three had attended the Stamp Act Congress, seven the First Continental Congress, eight had signed the Declaration of Independence, thirty had served in the revolutionary army, forty-three had served in Congress under the Articles of Confederation, and all except two or three had held public office. Most of the men were very wealthy and highly educated. Forty of the men held government securities or were bankers or money lenders, and fifteen were slave owners. Although only about a dozen were practicing lawyers, most had been trained in the law.

Not only were most of those men trained in law, but ten of them had served as state judges. They believed that law was reason codified as experience, and their legal realism allowed them to draw on the best features of the existing state constitutions and to combine them with some truly original contributions. Their contributions were most notable in the establishment of the federal system, a strong executive, and an independent federal judicial power. By setting up a government with distinct executive and judicial branches, completely separate from the legislative, the framers were able to make sure that each of the three great powers essential to government could be effectively implemented.

The American Revolution was not only the end of a political revolution, but it was also a revolution of lawyers. American law had developed in a kind of legal limbo, which caused the legal renaissance to blossom and to draw from the riches of the English law. Having created and defended the new government of the United States, the American lawyers had largely fulfilled their creative role. "And Kent, Story and Marshall, the leaders to come in the consolidation, would represent the twilight of the Gods."[5]

After the French Revolution there were several American liberals who were attracted to the concept of French civil law and saw the Napoleonic code as a symbol and model of clarity and order. That view had only a limited influence on the direction taken by American law, however, because only a few lawyers had any knowledge of French law. English legal authorities dominated in America and the English common law was strongly defended. For most Americans the common law was held to be the birthright of free men that had been perverted by the British under George III. It was still a vital reality for America, however. Those lawyers who strongly believed in common law were among the heroes of the Revolution and were the ones who drafted most of the state and the federal constitutions. The French legal system was never really a serious alternative to common law in America.

Much of the mechanism for the application of law in the United States was new. A novel development of the post-Revolution era was the establishment of the federal bar. The United States Supreme Court opened in New York on 2 February 1790, and three days later three lawyers were admitted to practice before it. Of the first nineteen attorneys admitted to the bars of the Supreme Court, two were senators, and nine were representatives attending the first congress that was in session in New York City. In 1791 the Supreme Court moved to Philadelphia, and there it sat until 1801. Most lawyers who were admitted to practice before it during that decade were members of the Philadelphia bar. Included were such great Philadelphia lawyers as Jared Ingersoll, William Bradford, William Lewis, Edward Tilghman, Alexander J. Dallas, and William Rawle.

Some of the reasons for the high reputation of the Philadelphia bar from before the Revolution no longer existed. There had been important changes in the city's membership at the bar. As mentioned, many lawyers, including some of the most eminent, had been Tories and had left the country, whereas others had grown older and retired. Also, the reputation of lawyers underwent change, and suspicions were often directed at lawyers because they were seen as instruments of the detested English. There was for a brief period a possibility that some states might eliminate the common law as the foundation of American law. In fact, several states, including Pennsylvania, passed laws prohibiting the citation of English doctrines to be handed down in court after independence. There was, as there often had been over the years, the belief by some Americans that laws and lawyers were obstacles in the way of securing true justice. Most Americans recognized, however, there was no way to ensure justice without laws and lawyers. It was clear that the political and economic nature required for the conquest of the continent had to have a legal system. Law was needed for the country to cope with the great growth in population, commerce, and wealth.

There was one group concerned with the common law because they saw it as often archaic, inflexible, and irrelevant. That group, whose needs it did not seem to suit, comprised many merchants and businessmen. Those men were often against the law of the lawyer because they believed that nobody wanted the common law except the lawyers. In the increasingly complex society, however, it was unrealistic to believe that lawyer's law could be overthrown and replaced by natural justice, whatever that might mean. Law had to meet the needs of the consumers and that was what increasingly happened in the nineteenth century.[6]

The distrust of law and lawyers was often strong in the rural areas and that reflected a general distrust of the city. For example, a rural delegate to the convention in Massachusetts to decide on that state's ratification of the federal Constitution in 1788 expressed his opposition. "These lawyers, and men of learning, and moneyed men, that talk so finely, and gloss over matters so smoothly, to make us poor illiterate people swallow down the pill, expect to get into Congress themselves, they expect to be the managers of this Constitution and get all the power and money into their own hands, and then they will swallow up all of us little folks, like the great Leviathan, Mr. President; yes, just as the whale swallowed up Jonah. This is what I am afraid of."[7]

Yet, with all the negative attitudes, in a short period of time the lawyer became tolerated if not always admired. Some lawyers who had been Tories were able to return if they had not been too conspicuous in their opposition during the Revolution. Initially, as suggested, many of the old political differences were not too important, and in the early 1790s national and political leaders mixed freely and openly. The gradual growth of political parties did not at first greatly influence the cordial nature of social and intellectual exchange. The Philadelphia politicians were mostly lawyers, and they were mostly conservative. Those conservatives, sometimes including Tories from the past, became successful in Philadelphia. Among the leading Philadelphia lawyers and judges of the 1790s were some lawyers who had during the Revolution remained neutral, for example, Benjamin Chew, William Tilghman, and John Ross.

Even such a professed Tory as Edward Shippen was able to become very successful in Philadelphia law. He was probably the first successful Philadelphian to come from an old upper class family. His behavior during the American Revolution was a reflection of the aristocratic and Royalist influence on him while he had been in London at the Middle Temple. When he was called to the bar in London he took an oath to the king, and he lived up to that oath. With all his aristocratic bearing, however, that did not stop him from being forgiven and greatly rewarded in the legal world of Philadelphia following the Revolution. At the conclusion of the war the need for skilled lawyers was great, and many of those who had remained loyal to the Crown were forgiven. In part, the shortage of experienced lawyers in Philadelphia had occurred because some with stronger commitments than those of Shippen had returned to England. With the new government there was also greater demands for trained lawyers. Although Shippen had been a Loyalist he had remained in Philadelphia, and his legal skills and social importance made him acceptable. Shippen was one of the first upper class Philadelphia lawyers to help direct the growth of the new American legal system. He was also among the first of the old upper class lawyers to have a strong involvement with the judiciary. That was an interest that would disappear for most old family upper class lawyers early in the nineteenth century.[8]

Some of the more troublesome legal cases were those of treason and confiscation following the war. They were only a part of the variety of cases and questions to come before the lawyers and jurists after the Revolution, however. Those legal views became in ever-widening circles the basis for decisions in Pennsylvania. For example, all bills creating corporations were referred to the judges of the commonwealth supreme court, and they were dealing with questions pertaining to granting of monopolies and relating to taxes and tariffs. The court was consulted on the wording of new and the interpretation of old laws. The state sought the court's opinion on the knotty and delicate legal and political questions relative to the disposition of Pennsylvania property. The lawyers in the state were active in the civic and social as well as on the legal front. The lawyers led the movement for penal reform, and for the reform of marriage and divorce laws.[9]

Edward Tilghman was one of Philadelpia's great lawyers of the period. He had studied law at the Middle Temple and was admitted to the Philadelphia bar in 1774. Horace Binney said about Tilghman that he seemed to possess an instinct, which seized the true result before he had taken time to prove it. "With him it was intuitive and he could untie the knots of a contingent remander or executory devise as familiarly as he could his garden." Tilghman had a strong aversion to both authorship and to public office, and he declined the chief justiceship of Pennsylvania. He represented the new tradition of the gentleman lawyer of Philadelphia with little or no interest in politics or the bench. Tilghman's interest was to devote his life to the practice of law, and his reference group was the legal profession.[10]

Another change among Philadelphia lawyers was in their training for the bar. After the outbreak of the American Revolution few Americans were trained at the Inns of Court. Although the overall number of Philadelphia lawyers who had been trained at the inns had not been great, they had been significantly overrepresented among the outstanding lawyers and judges of the city. They were often the ones who were training lawyers in their law offices, in their own images. By 1790 all lawyers were being trained through the practical work of an apprenticeship in a law office. The new lawyers were being trained to organize business, form partnerships, and handle credit instruments and the many details of real property, land titles, and transfers. Increasingly many of those lawyers became involved in constitutional law.

The old lawyers who were training the new generation were strongly committed to the common law. Through their training the new lawyers were turning to the common law, but in many respects it was a new common law that was based much more on American precedent. The basic question for the world of law was what part of the English law would remain. Because of the heritage England remained the source of all law that was not new or completely American. The habits of a lifetime in the uses of common law were not thrown over, and much of the new and indigenous American law was weak and derivative. One severe limitation was no general pattern of publishing American legal decisions and records. American case reports were not common until a generation or more after independence. To common law lawyers a shortage of cases was crippling, and to fill the gap English materials were used and English judges quoted as authorities.[11]

Even with the distrust commonly directed toward law and lawyers during the early days of the Republic, the practice of law provided more opportunities than did any other profession. It continued to be the most promising and attractive profession open to the young men of ambition and talent, and that was specifically true in Philadelphia. There was plenty of work for able lawyers because the many social and economic disturbances caused by the war had greatly increased litigation. At the same time the effects of the Revolution had been to reduce the number of available lawyers considerably.

In Pennsylvania, after independence, citizens were becoming increasingly involved in legal actions. That led to a dramatic increase in the demand for lawyers and judges. The urgent need for legal services effectively reduced the resistance to lawyers. Many of the city's lawyers had more clients than they could take care of, and there were opportunities for the younger lawyer to make his name. The profession lost many well known and established lawyers as Chew, Allen, Waln, Shippen, Dickinson, and Gallaway. The new lawyers turned to the task of proving they were the equal of their celebrated predecessors, and they matched the challenge. The highest and ablest of the new generation were William Lewis, James Wilson, George Ross, Jared Ingersoll, Francis Hopkinson, William Bradford, Jr., Stephen du Ponceau, Edward Tilghman, Alexander J. Dallas, and William Rawle. Those men won fortunes and reputations through cases that were strongly contested.[12]

Pennsylvania, by rule of the state supreme court in 1788, required either four years of clerkship and one year of practice in the court of common pleas, or three years of study and two years of practice as well as an examination by two approved lawyers for admission to the bar. Requirements were not nearly as demanding in most other parts of the country. That was especially true along the frontier where there was often barely any admission standards. For example, in Kentucky, one candidate who was not able to answer one question correctly during his oral examination was still admitted to the bar. The reason stated officially by the court, which acted as the examining board, was that "no one would hire him anyhow."

In 1790, Alexander Dallas published a volume entitled, *Reports of Cases Rules & Adjudged in the Courts of Pennsylvania, Before and Since the Revolution*. Sitting judges in Pennsylvania helped Dallas by providing him with notes on their current cases. Dallas wrote of a patriotic aim in that he hoped his reports would "tend to show the pure and uniform system of jurisprudence that prevails in Pennsylvania." In a second volume, Dallas added cases from the United States Supreme Court, which was then sitting at Philadelphia. In that volume, "quietly and unobtrusively began that magnificent series of reports, extending in an unbroken line down to the present, that chronicles the work of the world's most powerful court."[13]

In the one hundred years between the publication in 1687 of William Penn's extracts from Lord Coke and the issuance of the American edition of Gilbert's *Evidence* in 1788, not a single book that could be called a treatise intended for the use of professional lawyers was published in America. The first American legal treatises published after 1788 owed their origin largely to the general demand for "native" legal texts to be used by a variety of legal practitioners. The first legal texts after 1788 dealt with pleading, real property, maritime law, or maritime insurance. Most early American texts were clearly intended to be used by laymen—they were largely manuals for petty officials, justices of the peace, town officers, and the like. Those texts were of little value to the legal profession.

The first professor of law was appointed to the College of William and Mary in 1779. In Philadelphia in September 1787 there was a petition from a "Junior Law Society" for the use of one of the rooms. The petition was presented to the trustees of the college of Philadelphia. Again in March 1789 a petition for the use of one of the rooms was presented by what has been recorded as a number "of young gentlemen students in law." They were asking to have some formal legal education associated with the college. That helped bring about the appointment of James Wilson in 1790 to the position of professor of law. At that time Wilson was an associate justice on the new Supreme Court sitting in Philadelphia. Wilson, although eccentric and difficult, was probably Philadelphia's greatest lawyer during the revolutionary war decades.

Wilson, as professor of law was to be paid by his students up to the limit of ten guineas. At that time that was a considerable sum and must have excluded most young members of the Junior Law Society. The course conceived by Wilson was not so much for the young law students as for "gentlemen of all professions, and especially legislators, magistrates and other lawyers." Wilson's first lecture was delivered before President Washington and his cabinet, the governor of Pennsylvania, and members of Congress. His first lecture did not receive general approval because it was too political. Wilson delivered severe criticisms of Blackstone, and his extreme Federalist views concerning the power of the national government were not well received by lawyers or the general public. He discontinued the planned series of lectures because of a lack of interest by students. Not for another twenty-five years would the University of Pennsylvania appoint another professor of law.[14]

The chief method of preparing for law continued to be through the apprenticeship system. The apprentice would, it was hoped, acquire knowledge and certain skills by close association with and the observation and imitation of an expert lawyer at work. The student entered the law office and "read" law. He was taught by form and precedent rather than by principle. He often copied precedents without knowing either their application or the rules on which they were grounded. He received little formal instruction and legal theory, and principles were rarely discussed. The focus of American law for the student was practice rather than theory.

From 1776 to 1800, 211 lawyers were admitted to the bar in Philadelphia, an average of about 9 each year. Law continued to be practiced in the old court house in Philadelphia, and most of the lawyers had offices nearby with a number located in a small alley called Chancery Lane. That was the period of great transition in Philadelphia law. The 1780s and 1790s were bringing to the bar the great lawyers that would flourish down through the first half of the nineteenth century. The beginning lawyer at that time in Philadelphia started with the rich heritage of being in the city as the new federal government emerged. Those were the golden years in Philadelphia of unrivaled national leadership. In Philadelphia history, the 1790s were the time of the city's greatest significance and grandeur. It was also a time of transition—transition from the lawyer-statesman to the lawyer-practitioner.

William Lewis, 1751–1819. Courtesy of the Historical Society of Pennsylvania.

Profile 4: William Lewis (1751–1819)

Lewis was born on a farm near Edgemont, Chester (now Delaware) County, Pennsylvania. He attended a country school near his home and later entered a Society of Friends seminary at Willistown, Pennsylvania. He grew up wanting to be a lawyer, and his father to prepare him best enrolled him at the Friend's Public School of Philadelphia where he would receive instruction in Latin. His early formal education was probably not very good, but because of his very high intelligence he managed, on his own, to acquire a good English education. In 1770 he began to study law under Nicholas Wain of Philadelphia who was an eminent Quaker and a highly respected lawyer. On his own Lewis mastered enough Latin and French to read the *Entries* and *Reports*. He was admitted to the bar in November 1773 and again in 1776, after the adoption of the state constitution.

One of his contemporaries described him as a person of great intelligence in law and politics as well as in any other areas that were of interest to him. His early interests were in all aspects of law that were important at that time— common, constitutional, international, commercial, and maritime. Lewis from the beginning of his career believed that good pleading prevented confusion and was therefore the best way to practice law.

As was true of most members of the Philadelphia bar at that time Lewis was a Federalist and strongly anti-Jeffersonian. He was a close friend and was frequently consulted by General Alexander Hamilton, secretary of treasury. Lewis was one of the three major lawyers that in 1860 Horace Binney wrote about in his book, *The Leaders of the Old Bar of Philadelphia*. Binney said of Lewis that "he was fertile in the suggestion of doubts and quick in the solution of them, and had an admirable ability to discern, the strong and weak points of assault and defense." Furthermore, he was learned in the law, clear and logical in argument, and was recognized to be one of the leading lawyers of his generation. Binney also wrote that "he sometimes procrastinated in preparing his cases, and made use of many ingenious devices for gaining time." He had the "annoying habit of studying his case while it was in progress and introducing new points when he had the closing argument that led the court to make a general rule prohibiting new points by concluding counsel."[1] Binney wrote that it was generally agreed that no man of his day knew the doctrine of common law any better.

Lewis came to the bar of Philadelphia just before the adoption of the

Constitution of 1776. The first state supreme court, held under Chief Justice McKean, met in July and August 1777. The court, however, was forced to flee from the city because of the entry and occupation by the British military. Lewis's name first appeared in a case dealing with high treason in 1778, an area in which he became the leading expert. During the Revolution, and for years afterward, William Lewis participated in almost all the major legal cases and especially in those of high treason.

Lewis achieved an important victory at the bar in 1788 when the attempt was made to take away from the state supreme court one of its oldest and most necessary powers. As counsel, Lewis had asserted and maintained the right of the court to punish Colonel Oswald by fine and imprisonment, without trial by jury, for contempt of court, in the columns of a newspaper. He also defeated in the legislature a very active effort to impeach Chief Justice McKean and several other Judges for having exercised that power. Binney wrote that "for the most penetrating and corrupting of contempt, such as requires immediate redress, to take an obstruction out of the very path in which a court of justice is moving at the times, is a contempt *out of Court*, on the face of a widely diffused newspaper."[2]

The only judicial system in the new nation to deal with the laws of treason was in Philadelphia, and it was there that Lewis achieved his high stature as a lawyer. He continued to hold his high legal position with not much competition until the end of the eighteenth century. In the treason cases he was almost always on the side of the defendant and usually won his cases. Binney writes that his deep learning and facility in the law of treason and other high crimes was remarkable. "He had studied the law of treason with passion; and had mastered all of its details, the law of its process, evidence, and trial, as well as of the offense itself." Binney went on to say, "I cannot forget the vehemence, amounting to rage, with which in rebuke of some harsh general reprobation of a prisoner upon trial, he arraigned, as an example to be forever adjured, the Attorney General Coke, for his brutal language to Sir Walter Raleigh and the trial of the Bye and Main. 'Thou Viper! I chose thee, thou traitor. Thou are thyself a spider of hell. Go to, I will lay thee on they back, for the confidentest traitor that ever came to the Bar.' "[3]

Lewis's defense of those charged with being traitors was generally unpopular and sometimes dangerous. In those years immediately after the Revolution the common American view toward their fellow colonists who had supported the British was often very hostile because of the long and bloody war that had just ended. Lewis was a strong believer in the Declaration of Independence, but he was not severely proscribed by that adherence. He believed that professional assistance must be given to those who were hounded by the "public interest." Lewis was a republican, and even with his defense of "traitors," he was still a close friend of George Washington.

The years from 1783 to 1801 were the period of Lewis's greatest intellectual and legal powers. The country was only beginning to develop laws that would meet the new demands, and the demand for lawyers of high judicial skill and experience was great. It was in that atmosphere that Lewis emerged as one of the great legal leaders. He dealt with questions of prizes and the jurisdiction of the admiralty as well as questions concerning the rights of ambassadors and the privileges of consuls. He was also involved in the new legal questions on the constitutional powers of the federal courts and the powers of Congress. The most important question was dealing with the basic conflict between the authority of the state and those of the new federal powers.

In the summer of 1791 Lewis was appointed judge of the Federal District Court for the Eastern District of Pennsylvania. He only served for one year and chose to return to his very lucrative private practice in Philadelphia. He was elected a member of the Pennsylvania legislature in 1787 and again in 1789, when he was also chosen a member of the state constitutional convention.

Lewis was totally committed to maintaining what he saw as the just and proper authority of the court, the jury, and the rights of the bar. In criminal cases, whatever powers or prerogatives had been given by Magna Charta, the Constitution, or the law for the defense of personal liberty and reputation, Lewis strongly supported and defended. "He kindled at nothing sooner than an invasion of any of these great securities, on any side, to the prejudice of either Court or Jury, or of the independence of the bar, or of the full exercise of defence against criminal accusation."[4]

The public image of the great lawyer at that time rested only in part on the logic and development of his legal arguments. Far more important in the eyes of the public was his appearance, his manner, and especially his oratorical style and flair. When Lewis appeared in court he rarely stood still and instead often performed as a showman. When he was not trying or arguing a case he was quizzing or joking with everyone in the courtroom. But when he was engaged in his argument he was totally dedicated to his cause.

It was said of William Lewis that not only was he one of the distinguished members of early Philadelphia bar who gave it its high status in learning and ability, but he was also a leader in developing the ethics of the bar. It was further said that he would accept no fee that came to him with any taint of dishonor in the earning of it. If he found that a client had resorted to any disreputable proceeding in the interest of his case, he had no wish to be associated with him any further. On one occasion he was employed by a businessman of good reputation to represent him in defending a business transaction involving a large sum of money. The case went into court, and there Lewis presented it with his usual vigor and acuteness. As the case developed Lewis became convinced that his client had not told him everything and that he was furthermore guilty of fraud. He declined to have anything to do with the case and was about to withdraw from court. "Will you not speak for me?" asked the defendant. "No, Sir," said Lewis, "What then," inquired the client, "have

I paid you for?'' ''You have paid me,'' replied an angry Lewis, ''that you might have justice done; and justice will now be done without any further interference.''[5]

Lewis was about six feet tall, very thin, and stooped. He had a long nose on which rested his spectacles. He continued to wear knee britches all of his life, long after they were out of style. He also stayed with hair powder and a cue, and his suit was always black. He wore that outfit to make a statement about his intense dislike for all things French. That included pantaloons, which in his day were just coming into fashion. When he talked it was with a self-confident sweep of his head and in a deep baritone voice that would demand the attention of everyone. His typical style was to address the court with one hand between his waistcoat and shirt. He would open his address with no movement other than his head; then, with a quick movement, and sometimes with a little jerk of his body, he would bring both his hands to the side of his body and begin the action. It was said that his voice never failed him, and it was deep, sonorous and clear. ''His pronouncement was without the least affectation and always conformed to the highest standards of correct English. He was animated to the end without break or pause, except to lift his spectacles and look at his notes.'' Binney further writes that Lewis had at the tip of his tongue all the gibes and scorn that prosecutors spit into the faces of the accused in the oppressive spirit of that time.[6]

According to Binney he had two rather interesting habits. It was not common at that time to find many suggestions of indelicacies of speech or any suggestion of sexual innuendo. Therefore, any such suggestion was of interest because it was so rare. Binney wrote that Lewis was known to make ''indelicate allusion'' at the side bar. In his personal life Lewis appears to have been less than circumspect in his romantic and sexual references in front of his younger colleagues. Binney clearly did not approve of that behavior on the part of one of his heroes of the early bar. Even more upsetting to Binney, however, was that Lewis had a ''half-libertine life between his two marriages.'' Unfortunately for posterity Binney does not tell us what that meant in those days. Lewis's second sin was that he smoked constantly, and according to Binney ''he smoked at the fireplace in Court. He smoked in the Court Library. He smoked in the street. He smoked in bed; and he would have smoked in church if he had ever gone thee.''[7]

William Lewis took part, along with a few other distinguished lawyers of his time, in the formation of the Bar Association of Philadelphia. According to one newspaper account there were in Lewis's day, as there were later, ''not a few members of the bar belonging to the class commonly described as shysters.'' It was necessary to have those men put on their good behavior by subjecting them to punishment or weeding them out of the bar. At that time, as long afterward, nearly all the lawyers had their offices and usually lived, too, within five or ten minutes walk of Independence Square, and so it was not difficult for them to mingle together in frequent contact. It was thus that the *Bar Association* came into existence very early in the last century (Nineteenth), with probably a close acquaintanceship between one another on the part of most members. No lawyer could then perform a crooked act without a general knowledge of it passing quickly from mouth to mouth who saw him regularly in his comings and goings. "It was this intimacy and scrutiny which went far indeed to enable the strong and clean men of the profession to keep it true to the spirit of the ethics of William Lewis."[8]

In his book, Horace Binney observed that in the days at the end of the Revolution there were from Maryland to Massachusetts some persons at the bar who in the view of persons within several hundred miles loomed very large and overshadowed all other lawyers in the same state. Theophilus Parsons at Boston, Luther Martin at Baltimore, and William Lewis at Philadelphia were such overshadowing names. Although Lewis was the senior of the Philadelphia bar, and was in fact a very able as well as eminent lawyer, "his reputation was from accidental circumstances, more transcendent abroad than at home. It was very great at home; but there was at least one at his side who, in some respects, stood out in a clearer light before the members of his own Bar, and one or two others who were near to them."[9]

It is clear that in the years following the revolutionary war William Lewis stands out as one of the most distinguished practitioners of the law not only in Philadelphia but also in the new nation. Lewis, who lived for about the same period, may be contrasted with John Dickinson who was famous for his politics and statesmanship. Lewis was one of the very first models that would come to dominate the Philadelphia bar. His great interest and abilities were in the practice of law, and he had little interest in politics or the bench. William Lewis appears to have combined great legal ability and intelligence with the oratorical flair necessary at that time to be an outstanding practitioner of law.

5
New Nation: 1800–1830

Ignorance of the law excuses no one—but a judge, a lawyer or a member of the bar.

—Anonymous

When President Adams, and the rest of the federal government moved from Philadelphia to the new national capital in Washington, D. C., in 1800 that marked the end of Philadelphia's golden decade. Within a few years Philadelphia was replaced by New York as America's largest city. During those first few decades of the nineteenth century, however, Philadelphia continued to create its own identity as a major American city. The new image was being built more on the accomplishments of Philadelphians, and less on the great names and historical achievements of the Revolution. Philadelphians centrality in the cultural life of the nation remained long after the capital moved to Washington. The luster of the American Philosophical Society with Rittenhouse and Jefferson as successive presidents reached far beyond the shores of the ocean.

During the early 1800s Philadelphia continued to be the intellectual center of the nation, and among its leaders were such great lawyers as James Wilson, Alexander Dallas, and William Rawle. There were important differences between the intellectual leaders of Philadelphia as compared with Boston. Philadelphia produced a privileged upper class with little concern for the glory of the state or the nation. To the Philadelphians it was their city that was important. By contrast, the upper class of Boston was more into reading and writing than was the upper class of Philadelphia. In general, intellectualism was less valued in Philadelphia than in Boston.[2]

Philadelphia, however, did produce the nation's first successful literary magazine, the *Port Folio*, first published in 1801. Many Philadelphia gentlemen lawyers were contributors, among them were Nicholas Biddle, Charles Jared Ingersoll, Thomas Sergeant, Thomas I. Wharton, Horace Binney, Richard Rush, Joseph Hopkinson, and Thomas Cadwalader. They were gentlemen first, lawyers second, and literati on the side. The *Port Folio* was an excellent journal in its day, and its existence in Philadelphia showed what the city might have done had more in its educated classes been inclined to write and take

88

the lead in intellectual matters. They did not, however, and the *Port Folio* passed into history following Joseph Dennie's death.[3]

The first generations of the nineteenth century, led by the rising influence of the legal profession, developed the legal institutions of America that have been carried down to the present. The defining of the powers of the Constitution under Chief Justice John Marshall provided the legal foundation for the new nation. Constitutional law revealed the creative process that could be seen very clearly in the area of private law—for example, in such areas as property and contracts.

During those early years many aspects of national life were organized on a local basis. The state legislatures and courts laid the groundwork for industry and democracy by adapting English doctrines to meet the changing conditions in the new society. As the law grew so did the role of the lawyer. The written constitutions on both the federal and state levels placed lawyers in the center of questions on accountable power. Justice Story in 1829 described the common law as a collection of principles that constitute the basis of the administration of justice in England. That definition fed the fire of the Jeffersonian argument that an independent democracy should have nothing to do with English common law. They argued that the common law was not a construction of systematic reason. Instead, it was a haphazard accumulation of precedents, quirks, and obscure decisions. As Story insisted, however, when it came to trial by jury on habeas corpus, America had to resort to the common law for interpretation of those terms. Story, Kent, and others argued that the courts, without the aid of a statute, can call in the common law to support their verdicts. They further argued that the courts really had little choice because there was nothing if not common law.[4]

Even among those who were the most committed to the common law, however, there was a recognition that it could not be brought in its entirety to America because there was much that had little relationship to American society. There were also some who argued that Americans should trust their own judgment rather than to take over the English methods. For example, du Ponceau argued that because America had an explicit Constitution, the common law, for all its majesty, was a system of jurisprudence and nothing more. He argued that common law was not the source of power, but rather the means or instrument through which power was exercised.[5]

Kent believed that the evolutionary character of the common law made it especially appropriate to America, because it could develop along with a rapidly changing society. Possibly the slowness of lawyers in perfecting that justification was a sign of the inability to recognize the immense economic and subsequently legal reorientation brought about by the War of 1812. There was the new importance of admiralty law; the beginning of manufacturing; and the sudden need of policies for patents, the development of turnpikes and canals, and soon railroads. There was also the difficulty in shifting from a philosophy of law that was primarily contractual to one that was conscious of history.[6]

It was contended that pleading was not a model to follow blindly from the English common law. Pleading was often seen as an elaborate contest made by the lawyer where the techniques of winning a case frequently had little to do with substantive worth. In theory, pleading was suppose to distill, out of fact and fancy, one narrow issue on which the trial could focus. Those in America who had the skills had no desire to abandon the system. The country was not run by lawyers, however, and for many merchants, bankers, and land owners the "science of pleading" appeared nothing more than a lawyer's plot to manipulate justice and thereby frustrate the rights of the ordinary citizen.

The European system of law of evidence was simple as it allowed almost anything to be introduced and left it to the judge to separate good evidence from bad. American law distrusted the judge, however, and gave the jury full fact-finding powers and, in criminal cases, the final word on innocence or guilt. The law distrusted the jury as much as the judge and so the rules of evidence developed as a kind of offsetting force. The jury was allowed to hear only that part allowed by the law of evidence. The judge's options were also limited because if he allowed improper testimony, he ran the risk of having the case reversed on appeal. The rules of evidence came to bind and control both the jury and the judge. Later when the function of the jury changed to that of an impartial panel of listeners, the law of evidence underwent great growth.[7]

In 1800 a young man wanting to study law started by reading Blackstone, Coke and Littleton, and that frequently resulted in great bewilderment. During the next two decades, however, the learning situation changed greatly. By 1821 there were more than 150 volumes of *Reports*, and there was some concern that the new danger was of being overwhelmed by legal materials. The work of American lawyers quickly expanded because by 1815 there were common law, chancery, admiralty, criminal, registry, and orphans courts. Of great importance was that those practices were open to all American lawyers because there was no specialized profession as in England.

The influence of the *Reports* was great. They allowed the states to amass their own common law, as independent of the common law of England as well as other states, if they so chose. The *Reports* also allowed the states to borrow from one another.

The best courtroom oratory was also being published, and a body of practical legal literature rapidly emerged. Almost all of the literature was very practical as systematic legal theory was largely ignored not only by most writers but by the bar as well.

The founding fathers beliefs as to the natural rights of men led them to make a division between personal rights and property rights. The history of American law, from the beginning, has been to move from an emphasis on property rights to personal rights. The framers had carefully provided express constitutional guarantees for life and liberty as well as property. The direction of laws moved from giving each man his due to the expansion of individual self-assertion. American law became expansive rather than defensive in nature and stressed change rather than stability. If in the new society men were to be measured by their accomplishments, and not by their social status, the country had to encourage and support individual accomplishment. Natural rights increasingly came to be seen as the rights of individuals to enter a contract. It was those rights that the law had to maintain.

The radicals generally objected to the common law because it was British and therefore aristocratic and un-American. They also saw it as an instrument to protect creditors at the cost of debtors and property rights rather than human rights. Those radicals argued for laws based on natural rights. Most trained lawyers and most conservatives, however, had little use for enacted laws. Rather, they valued the common law for its organic nature, its time-tested precepts, and its provisions for personal rights and the sanctity of property rights. Story and Kent added to and organized through their court decisions the means for a greater acceptability of the common law. That was done by identifying it with the generally accepted law of nature. Those jurists supplemented the common law with comparative law, and translated many social and political ideas and practices of America into legal concepts that were in harmony with the English common law tradition. What made the new law acceptable to the conservatives was that it allowed for the expansion of commerce and the creation of new industries.[8]

In Philadelphia, as in other cities, the view of the law was one of respect among those of influence and power. Of course, the law generally worked to their advantage. That respectful view, however, was not held by most of those who lived in small towns and along the frontiers. Among those citizens there was a deep hostility to the legal profession, and many viewed the law as an insult to their native intelligence. They often saw judges as agents of social control over them. David Crockett, boasted in 1831 that his judgments were never repealed by the higher courts "as I give my decisions on the principles of common justice and honesty between man and man, and rely on natural born sense, and not on law learning to guide me." He proudly affirmed, while the nation applauded, "I had never read a page in a law book in all my life." Many believed that the complexity of law was a gigantic conspiracy of the learned against the helpless integrity of the common man. Almost as soon as the lawyers of the new republic began to mobilize the forces of the mind against the emotions of the heart they found hostility in the American mentality.[9]

In Pennsylvania lawyers were gaining greater political influence, and there was an expansion of new counties and county seats as well as courts. Many Pennsylvanians continued their traditional view that "the mystery of the law was a gigantic conspiracy . . . against their helpless integrity," and they kept intact their habitual distrust and resentment for the men of law. "A cause of bitterness," said Brackinridge, "was their wealth and connexion."[10]

From the beginning of the nation there have been severe and often hostile attacks on both the federal and state courts. Soon after Jefferson's election the Federalist judiciary system was seen as a thorn in the side of the Republican administration, and the Jeffersonians who controlled Congress launched an attack at the Supreme Court. Their strategy was to impeach one justice at a time, starting with Justice Chase. On 1 March, 1805 Chase was voted not guilty on five counts by a majority of the Senate and guilty, but not by a two-thirds majority, on three other counts. The plan was that if that impeachment had been successful the next step would have been to try to impeach Chief Justice Marshall.

In Pennsylvania in 1805, Chief Justice Edward Shippen and Associate Justices Thomas Smith and Joseph Yeates were impeached for an "arbitrary and unconstitutional act," namely for having fined and jailed Thomas Passmore for "constructive contempt." The argument against them was that punishment for contempt was a form of barbarism sanctioned by the English common law wholly unsuited to America and therefore illegal. In Pennsylvania dependence on English law could cause impeachment of a state judge. The trial of the three judges became the focus for renewed attacks on lawyers, the courts, and the common law in general. When the leading lawyers in Philadelphia, Jared Ingersoll, Alexander J. Dallas, and Peter du Ponceau refused to serve the state legislature as attorneys for the prosecution, the attacks became even more vehement. The three judges were acquitted only because the prosecution failed by three votes to obtain a two-thirds majority. Because their case was won by a legal appeal to the principle of common law of England, however, that brought about a renewed attack on the common law. In 1810, a statute was passed in Pennsylvania, and not repealed until 1830, forbidding the citation of any English decision handed down after 4 July 1776.[11]

During those years lawyers grew very uneasy under the attacks in Pennsylvania. "All the eminent lawyers," wrote Charles J. Ingersoll, "have their eyes on one city or another to remove to in case of extremes." Peter du Ponceau recalled in later years that "the bar was subjected to bitter attacks and constant invective . . . of lawyers." He recalled some advocated "nothing less . . . than their entire destruction." Although the attacks on lawyers and the judiciary subsided after 1810 lawyers continued to be sensitive to the suspicion in which they felt they were viewed. A Philadelphia writer of the 1820s described the popular view: "lawyers were slippery, rascally characters who accumulated a mass of knowledge, purposely complicated to render it unintelligible to the layman, and thus plied their mysterious trade at great personal profit. . . . If you seal one up in a quart bottle," said the common man of the lawyer, "he will get out through the pores of the cork and the wax."[12]

The openly political role of the judges was reduced, and with time most states turned to the elective process. That ended the impeachments, and the judges wrapped themselves in professional decorum. A part of the judge's job continued to be to make and interpret policy, but policy was separated from overt partisan politics. The view was that justice would be blind and wear a poker face. That image of the proper behavior for judges had enough truth and force to influence the role playing of judges, "and to hang some peace and consensus to issues of tenure, selection, behavior and removal of judges."[13]

The more erudite lawyers in America were calling on citizens to recognize the "scientific arrangement and harmony of principles." Horace Binney said that such scientific works as Newton's and Franklin's were of the character where the researcher pervades the whole. By contrast, however, the law is a "practical" wisdom that must from day to day retain the same shape. "A speculative, inventive judge is a paradox." Binney said "a good judge, like Tilghman, did not exhibit the magnificent variety of the ocean, at one moment serene and the next tempestuous." But, "instead," wrote Binney, "it is like the current of the river that safely bears upon its bosom the riches of the land." However, "if a river is to maintain an unvarying surface it may have to be restrained by dikes and other devices of flood control.[14]

Binney believed that although the War of 1812 brought destruction to American commerce, it also brought prosperity to the American bar. It was for that reason that after 1815 beside the old distrust of law there was also the suspicion of the courts. Those who practiced the legal "science" were aware that they were seen as a body of men who had reached their eminence and success only by subordinating their avarice and ambitions to the rules of their methods. In Philadelphia, where the bar had reason to compliment itself on its professional distinction the antilegal sentiment was especially strong. Still, however, the legal profession in Philadelphia prospered, both in wealth and prestige. That was primarily because those who were most vehement against lawyers had little wealth or power. Those who had the money and the power needed the lawyer.[15]

In general what happened to American law during the early nineteenth century was it underwent great changes to meet the increased need of all kinds of consumers. People came increasingly to see law as a utilitarian tool, a way to protect property and the established order. Beyond that there was also the desire to further the interests of the middle class mass, foster growth, and release and harness the vast inherent energy of the new nation. At one time any change in the law was looked on as a rare event and to be treated almost apologetically. In the nineteenth century, however, America made laws wholesale, and basically it was legislative law. Law was made by elected representatives rather than by judges.[16]

The development of equity courts in America was a basic part of the growth of law in the new society. Equity is law administered according to fairness in contrast to the strictly formulated rules of common law. Equity is based on a system of rules and principles that originated in England as an alternative to some of the harsher and more inflexible rules of the common law. Blackstone said very little about equity other than to make it appear unattractive. What he did say was "the liberty of considering cases on an equitable light should not be indulged very far, lest therefore we destroy all law." Blackstone further said that although common law without equity might appear hard and disagreeable, the public good would be less well served by equity without law. "Pure equity," warned Blackstone, "would make every judge a legislator and introduce the infinite confusion."[17]

The argument of equity vs. common law cut across political party lines. Many citizens saw equity as simply one more legalistic scheme to put limits on their liberties. Popular distrust first emerged because it did away with juries, and that became the central issue for argument. The concern was that an equity witness under oath was to be interrogated by a judge. The fear was in the distrust of the judge. Without the control of the jury, many believed the judge would give his opinions based on his own subjective biases.

The legal argument for equity was that it not only filled in the open areas of the law, but that it was also a distinct science. It was argued that equity courts could adapt to the varieties of circumstances that might arise and adjust to them the peculiar rights of all the involved parties. Story in 1820 said that in states where the concept of equity prevailed there was a tendency to make it a sort of arbitration law, or to decide cases on their particular circumstances, with no reference to any general principles. "But nothing could be further from this ideal of equity and nothing more harmful to the profession and the nation." In Philadelphia both Binney and du Ponceau in their eulogies of Tilghman asserted that his concept of equity had been as scientific as his law. For Tilghman equity never meant "as some have affected to understand the word, the fluctuating emotions of a judge." Rather, "those eternal principles of right and wrong, a science reduced to a regular system so rational that its superiority was admitted even by practitioners."[18]

As suggested, throughout the equity debate the use of juries was the basic issue. Although lawyers tried to persuade a complaining public that equity had its precedents, they did not effectively conceal their eagerness to broaden the range of cases to be tied in equity so fewer citizens would be meddling in trials. To reassure those who were worried, it was argued that there was no intention of eliminating juries where they played a legitimate part, like in criminal cases. The attacks on the Chancery reflected a continued apprehension that educated lawyers were planning to eliminate the juries of the uneducated. During most of the nineteenth century both opinion leaders and social policy were strongly supportive of business productivity and growth. Most government intervention and government regulation, carried on from 1800 to 1830, was by the states and not the federal government. There was increasing pressure toward large-scale internal improvement, and it was generally the states that brought about change. For example, the Pennsylvania Railroad was quite literally the railroad of the state of Pennsylvania. In the early years of the century the states were involved in the building of turnpikes, plank roads, ferries, and bridges. In the first half of the nineteenth century franchise was a key legal concept. The franchise was a grant to the private sector that came out of the inexhaustible reservoir of state power. Pennsylvania owned two-thirds of the capital in the Bank of Pennsylvania that was chartered in 1793. Later the states were less likely to own outright shares of banks, and their influence was more through enacted programs of regulation.[19]

Another important development in American law that would have great implications later in the century was regarding corporations. For centuries in England the right to operate business in a corporate manner was a special favor granted by the Crown to only a few favorites. At the time of Blackstone, corporate charters could only be obtained by an act of Parliament. The kinds of business and ends the corporation was to serve were narrowly defined. The American colonies took that procedure and decided the right to license corporations was to be among the sovereign powers belonging to each state. Those state powers were initially not often used. Before 1800 there were only 213 corporations in the country, and only eight of those were for purposes of manufacturing. The rest were bank, turnpike, and canal companies.

Before 1818 the value of a corporate charter was limited by the power of the legislative body that had issued the charter. It could be revoked or amended in whatever way a new legislature might be politically inclined. That changed with the *Dartmouth College case* in which the Supreme Court ruled that a corporate charter was a contract between a state and the proprietor of the corporation. Therefore, a corporate charter, once passed by the state, became to all intents and purposes embedded not merely in law but also in the Constitution. According to Article 1, Section 10, of the Constitution, a state was forbidden to pass any "Law Impairing the Obligation of Contracts." The corporation was an artificial person; however, did it have state citizenship? Justice Marshall very firmly said no. "That invisible, intangible, and artificial being, that mere legal entity, a corporate aggregate, is certainly not a citizen." In 1844, however, the Supreme Court changed the rules of the game and announced in the *Letson* case that for jurisdictional purposes a corporation would be treated as a citizen of the state in which it was chartered.[20]

Blackstone had tailored his great work to the needs of eighteenth-century England at a time when the gentry ruled as justices of the peace, and the House of Commons was their club. It was because Blackstone had addressed himself to legal intelligence rather than technicalities, however, that his work became so important in America. "Blackstone," said Parsons in 1852, "speaks of law as a scholar and a gentleman would wish to speak of all things." Story wrote "that only a familiarity with Greek and Latin can furnish such a polish as to impart that subtle elegance and grace which color the thoughts with almost transparent hues."[21]

The image of the lawyer came to have many contradictions in society.

Although the leaders of the bench were presenting a chaste and elegant liberality, in the state courts and in the United States Supreme Court, counsels were presenting exhibitions of forensic melodrama that rivaled the most dramatic performances of the theater. Those exhibitions were widely reported and attended by large crowds squeezing into the narrow chambers, "always on featured days, and including members of the fairer sex." On many occasions "the performer played shamelessly to the galleries and were hailed, like actor Edwin Forrest as geniuses." It was said of William Rawle of Philadelphia, "he argues with a pleasant voice and has great neatness, and even elegance."[22]

In the early nineteenth century there were many rich lawyers in Philadelphia, and the wealthiest were from the old families. In general those men owed their fortunes more to inheritance than to what they earned from the practice of law. Many of Philadelphia's leading lawyers, however, also gained or added to their fortunes from nonlegal family business activities. That was true of William Rawle, Thomas Wharton, and Thomas Cadwalader. Other Philadelphia lawyers from very wealthy families were Charles Ingersoll, Thomas McKeon Pettit, Richard Rush, George M. Dallas, Benjamin Chew, Jr., and Joseph Hopkinson. Several wealthy Philadelphia lawyers continued to follow the successful formula of adding to their family fortunes by marrying well. There were also several wealthy men who never practiced law and were only nominally lawyers. That was true of George H. Baker, Richard Vaux, and Thomas I. Wharton. Thomas Wharton and Charles Ingersoll were in real estate, and Nicholas Biddle, James Dundas, William Meridith, and Joseph P. Norris were in banking.

The Philadelphia bar was outstanding in the quality of its members as jurists and as civic and political leaders. "Joseph Hopkinson, Federalist congressman and Federal judge; Alexander J. Dallas, compiler of the laws of Pennsylvania, Madison' secretary of the treasury and secretary of war; William Tilghman, chief justice of the Supreme Court of Pennsylvania; and Richard Rush, attorney-general of the United States from 1814 to 1817, were among the luminaries." And beginning their long and distinguished careers were John Sergeant, Charles Jared Ingersoll and Horace Binney.[23]

Around 1820, most lawyers earned less than $1,000 a year with only a few earning as high as $15,000. One of the most financially successful was Alexander James Dallas who by 1801 was earning $10,000 and doubled that income by 1814. Lawyers increasingly had to seek new business, and they often found it necessary to advertise themselves. At that time there were no prohibitions against self-advertising, and they often put notices in newspapers. In those days of limited means of communication, however, word of mouth was the best way to get clients, and success was often based on their reputations in the courtroom. The flamboyance, tricks, and courtroom antics of those nineteenth-century lawyers was often more a matter of personal flair than any great legal knowledge or skill. Courtroom behavior was needed to create reputations because any lawyer who did not impress the public and gain a reputation found it difficult to survive. The entertainment of the courtroom action continued to be one of few shows in town, and citizens filled the courts and were familiar with the styles and reputations of various lawyers. The profession was also becoming increasingly competitive as it expanded. In Philadelphia, more than six hundred lawyers were admitted to the bar between 1800 and 1831, an average of about twenty per year.

As mentioned there had been from the beginning a small number of Jews who settled in Philadelphia. One of the early families was founded by Sampson Levy, and his son Moses practiced law, having graduated from the Academy of Philadelphia in 1772. The Levys were apostate Jews, and no professing Jew became a lawyer in Philadelphia until Zaligman Phillips, who graduated from the University of Pennsylvania and was admitted to the bar in 1799. Beginning in 1810, other second-generation American Jews, Joseph Simon Cohen, Benjamin Gratz and Elijah Gratz Etting entered the legal profession. According to Wolf and Whiteman, however, it was to be a good many years before there was more than a handful of Jewish lawyers in the city. "There was not the positive desire on the part of Jewish parents to see their children enter a field which they considered distinguished and above their own station. Consequently only a few Jews drifted into medicine and law."[24]

In 1811, a semipolitical society with Federalist leanings, The Washington Association of Philadelphia, was founded. Its members were many of the young lawyers of the city, who hoped that political connections would become valuable assets in their legal careers. Among those young lawyers were Benjamin Gratz and Henry Solomon. Solomon became secretary of the group two years after it was founded, and a few months later his brother-in-law, Zaligman Phillips, sponsored Solomon's admission to the Philadelphia bar. There does not appear to have been much anti-Semitism, and some of the Jewish lawyers were sponsored for admission to the bar by lawyers from old gentile families. For example, in 1816 Joseph R. Ingersoll sponsored Gratz Etting, and in 1819 William Meridith moved the admission of Moses Nathans. In 1825, Jonas Attamond Phillips received his masters degree from the University of Pennsylvania, and the following year he was admitted to the Philadelphia bar. He joined Phillips in what was the outstanding Jewish firm of the city for a generation.[25]

A mixture of admiration and hostility continued to confront the lawyer. Many saw lawyers as following the "most respectable and most lucrative" profession, and having great influence over citizens. The legal profession met criticism by asserting they were essential, politically capable, learned, upright, and were well paid because they deserved to be. There were some citizens who even though they felt lawyers were as liberal, honest, and respectable as any class of men also felt that the business of law was a public evil. The attacks on lawyers continued to be common throughout those early years of the nineteenth century. High fees were a universal grievance and were seen as enabling the lawyer to live in luxury. The growing wealth of some lawyers was obvious, and the feeling that they represented the rich rather than the poor led to their being accused of aristocratic leanings. Certainly in Philadelphia that was a legitimate charge against the most successful lawyers.

Horace Binney wrote that Philadelphia, at the beginning of the nineteenth century, was indifferent to its really great legal talents. "That she has been hitherto and perhaps immemorially indifferent or insensible to the abilities of her sons, who have gained their first consideration elsewhere." Philadelphia "has not taken, and never had taken, satisfaction in habitually honoring her distinguished men as *her* men, as men of her family." Binney said Philadelphia was more indifferent to her sons than to strangers, and he believed that may have come out of the Quaker heritage, with the values of moderation and personal modesty. Binney wrote that "while there is something like a general temperament in the life and manner of the city, there is no city whose significant population is less homogeneous." He believed that it was just to the individual and profitable to the city to give its most able men in every profession such prominence and decoration, "as will bring a due share of consideration from the country at large. It helps the community, it helps the individual." Binney further believed that full public recognition was not given to Tilghman, Lewis, Ingersoll, Rawle, and Dallas who occupied the front seats of the bar of Philadelphia at the end of the eighteenth and into the nineteenth century.[26]

In the early 1800s the education of lawyers was in the hands of practicing members of the profession. Recruits read law in the offices of an established practitioner on a diet of Blackstone, Coke, Grotius, Pufendorf, as well as available reported state cases. Their legal training typically was of little intellectual depth, and the emphasis was one of memory rather than comprehension. There was sometimes a lawyer supervising a half-dozen students by directing their reading, instructing them in the preparation of forms and documents, and watching over them in the daily routine of office work. The apprentices had weekly question-and-answer periods, went with their superiors to court, ate at their tables, and sometimes married their daughters. Those common experiences led to a high degree of closeness in the legal community of Philadelphia.[27]

Among the many customs imported from England, relative to members of the legal profession, was the practice of carrying their briefs and papers to court in what were termed "lawyers bags." The profession continued generally, until after the Civil war, to carry green cloth bags. And to say that a man intended to carry a green bag, was the same as saying that he meant to adopt the law as a profession.[27]

For some the apprenticeship was very limited, and they had to learn law with little directed study. They worked in law offices and drew up legal forms. They listened at court and once in a while heard a lecture on legal subjects. In 1817, attempts were made in Philadelphia to have along with the apprenticeship system a more systematic legal instruction. The University of Pennsylvania established a series of law lectures in hopes of building a law program, but apparently a lack of interest ended it after the first year. Four years later Peter du Ponceau, a leading Philadelphia lawyer, organized the Law Academy to supplement the work of the law offices. The academy continued for more than a century, but it developed more as a professional, social, and debating society then as a setting for legal education.

The aspiring lawyer was made familiar with judicial procedures by attending the county courts rather than by reading legal treatises and reports. There they learned the procedures of law, the functions of various court officials, the possibilities of challenging potential jurymen, the rules of evidence, the nuances of handling witnesses, and the legal erudition sometimes presented to a jury. There was little time or interest in abstract jurisprudence or with the traditional concerns of the educated man who had studied law. With legal business expanding rapidly that included the legal specializations related to business and maritime matters.

During this time nearly all practitioners of law had their offices and usually lived within a few minutes walk of Independence Square. It was not difficult for them to mingle in frequent and familiar contact. It was in that way that the Philadelphia Bar Association came into existence early in the nineteenth century and there was probably a close acquaintanceship between the members. "No lawyer could than perform a crooked act without a general knowledge of it passing quickly from mouth to mouth among those who saw him regularly in his comings and goings and who constituted the membership of the Bar Association."

In 1802, seventy-one members of the bar of Philadelphia associated themselves and were incorporated as The Law Library Company of the City of Philadelphia. The law library is the oldest in the United States. In the first three years the library accumulated 391 volumes. Those were texts, commentaries, and decisions of use to the lawyer learning his craft. Those books were written chiefly by British authors. There was nothing of consequence from the pens of Americans.[28]

There were only a few legal periodicals, and they usually had a short lifespan. Before 1830, twelve periodicals were founded. The *American Law Journal & Miscellaneous Repository* was one that was published in Philadelphia in 1808, but it died in less than a decade. Most of that journal was devoted to case reports and digests of statutes. Some secondary writing on various legal subjects was included. Those kinds of periodicals competed with the published *Reports*, which reprinted key decisions and other primary sources of law.

Of major importance during the days of the colonists and after the Revolution for the practice of law was the availability of a law library. In Philadelphia in 1802 there was the establishment of the Law Library Company. The articles of association were signed by seventy-two lawyers including all the prominent members of the bar of that day. Those included William Lewis, Edward Tilghman, and Jared Ingersoll, the leaders of the bar after the Revolution. Also involved in the library were the younger leaders such as Horace Binney and John Sergeant.[29]

From the Law Library of Philadelphia came the Philadelphia Bar Association, which is considered to be the oldest continuous bar association in the United States. In 1784, and again in 1798, some law students and younger practitioners in Philadelphia had formed unofficial societies to conduct moots and generally promote better legal education. They did not survive, but they did give impetus to the founding of the Law Academy of Philadelphia in 1821. Its purpose was to supplement the practical training received in law offices with lectures and moots. Sometime before 1821 a "professional society" had been established, later known as The Associated Members of the Bar of Philadelphia Practicing in the Supreme Court of Pennsylvania. They established a *Committee of Censors* to watch over the practice of law and report instances of unprofessional conduct for appropriate disciplinary action. One of the stated purposes was "generally to aim at maintaining the purity of professional practice." By the 1830s, however, there was clearly a deprofessionalization of the bar because of the anti-intellectual Jacksonian values.

At the time of the Revolution there had been no uniform modes of admission to the bar, but by the 1830s admission by local bars had become popular. What that meant was that the lawyer who could get himself admitted, even in the most slipshod local court, was a fully licensed member of the bar of that state and could practice before any court. Requirements for admission to the bar were far from uniform, and only a few states were very strict. For example, in New Hampshire, between 1805 and 1833, the federated county bars required five years of preparation for admission to the lower courts. New Hampshire was unusual, however. In 1800, only fourteen of the nineteen states or organized territories had a definite period of preparation for the bar. By 1830, only eleven of thirty jurisdictions had done so.[30]

The Associated Members of the Bar of Philadelphia, an organization founded in 1823, was formed because of the efforts of the most distinguished lawyers of old upper class Philadelphia. In the first organization the chancellor was William Rawle, who was from not only one of Philadelphia's most distinguished social families, but was and would be along with the Biddles and the Ingersolls one of Philadelphia's most distinguished legal families. The vice-chancellor was Horace Binney. The members of the Committee of Censors were Peter S. du Ponceau, Samson Levy, Charles Chauncy, John Sergeant, Joseph R. Ingersoll, Thomas Kitters, and John M. Scott. All of those gentlemen were upper class Philadelphians.

The first three decades of the nineteenth century saw the American legal system emerge, and saw the role of the lawyer move from distrust and suspicion to greater acceptability and respectability. In the next few decades, under the influence of Jacksonian democracy, the lawyer would once again come under attack as elitist and antidemocratic, however. In Philadelphia, during the early decades of the nineteenth century, law was highly regarded and dominated by upper class gentlemen. Those men were the leaders of the city who were interested in the practice of law and generally had little interest in playing an active role in politics. For only a few was there any interest in the bench. The Philadelphia values about the lawyer were well established—the Philadelphia lawyer practiced law.

Jared Ingersoll, 1749–1822. Courtesy of the Historical Society of Pennsylvania.

Profile 5: Jared Ingersoll (1749–1822)

His father was also named Jared Ingersoll, and his mother Hannah Whiting was from an old Philadelphia family. After the passage of the Stamp Act of March 1765 the senior Jared Ingersoll was asked to serve as agent for the distribution of the stamps in Connecticut. When the senior Ingersoll returned from England he was met with a hostile reaction toward him as an agent for the Stamp Act. After a very harsh and unhappy confrontation with the citizens Ingersoll resigned his position as agent. Soon after he moved to Philadelphia where he had been asked to organize the vice-admiralty court. The elder Ingersoll continued to be loyal to the British constitution and to the Crown, as did many other colonists at that time. During the ten years between the repeal of the Stamp Act and the Declaration of Independence, he could be described as more of an observer than an actor. Although he remained loyal to the Crown he was not aggressive about it.

The younger Jared Ingersoll was born in New Haven, Connecticut, and graduated in 1766 from Yale College. That was soon after his father had moved to Philadelphia. Ingersoll followed his father to Philadelphia where he studied law. Because of the bitter political controversies leading up to the Revolution his father sent him to England to study law at the Middle Temple. After spending two years in England and then traveling on the continent Ingersoll returned in 1778 to Philadelphia and was admitted to the Philadelphia bar in 1779. Soon after starting practice he married Elizabeth Pettit, who not surprisingly was from an old Philadelphia family. Although the senior Ingersoll was a Loyalist, the younger Ingersoll after his return from England rejected his father's Loyalist views.

Joseph Reed was president of the newly created Supreme Executive Council of Pennsylvania, and he asked Ingersoll to look after the interests of Reed's clients in Philadelphia. With that highly enviable start he very quickly became one of the most distinguished and successful lawyers in the city. That was a mark of considerable achievement because of the very high caliber of men at the Philadelphia bar at that time. Ingersoll became an attorney for the wealthy merchant Stephen Girard and also represented Senator William Blount, against whom impeachment proceedings were brought in 1797.

Ingersoll was admitted in 1791 to the bar of the United States Supreme Court. During the next year he was counsel for Georgia in the case of *Chisholm v. Georgia*, the first of several cases argued by him that involved various phases of federal relations. In 1796 in opposition to Alexander Hamilton he was an attorney in the first case involving the question of the constitutionality of an act of Congress. He was also counsel in several early cases connected with foreign relations as they were affected by constitutional law and under the jurisdiction of the new federal courts.[1]

Horace Binney writes that Mr. Ingersoll's success at the bar, like that of every other lawyer of eminence, was, and must have been, his own work. He also had some very favorable ties, however. He was friendly, and through his marriage, tied with President Reed during the three years of his presidency and until his death in 1785. He was also an executor of Reed's will. Binney writes, however, that Mr. Ingersoll wanted no other patron than his own talents, learning, integrity, and industry; "and if he had wanted any of these, no patron could have raised him to the great elevation which he attained at the Bar."[2]

Ingersoll held several public offices. In 1780 he was elected a member of the Continental Congress, and in 1785 he took an active part in the agitation for the revision or supplementing of the Articles of Confederation. He was also a delegate to the Federal Constitutional Convention of 1787 but took little part in its deliberations. William Pierce said of him: "Mr. Ingersoll speaks well, and comprehends his subject fully. There is a modesty in his character that keeps him back."[3] In local politics he was a member of the Philadelphia Common Council in 1789, and from 1798 to 1801 he was City Solicitor. From 1790 to 1799 and again from 1811 to 1817 he served as Attorney General of Pennsylvania.

For a short time during 1800 to 1801 he was U.S. district attorney for Pennsylvania, and in 1811 he was nominated by Pennsylvania Federalists for the vice-presidency. In politics he was at first inclined toward democratic views, but the events of 1801 appeared to have been considered by him "the great subversion"; thereafter, whenever he took part in politics it was as a Federalist. His main interest, however, was always the law and not politics.[4]

Horace Binney in his book *Leaders of the Old Philadelphia Bar*, published in 1866, wrote about the three men whom he considered the Philadelphia legal leaders in the transition from being a colony into a new republic, and Jared Ingersoll was one of these men. The other two were William Lewis and Edward Tilghman. Binney knew all three of those men when he was a young lawyer, and he had in fact read law with Jared Ingersoll.

Binney describes Jared Ingersoll as a Philadelphia gentleman:

He was tall, spare of flesh, fair complexion and light colored hair. There was a measure, and the observance of breeding in all that he said and did. He was full of attention when you talked to him and uniformly regardful of good manners. There was little playfulness, no jocularity, not the slightest attempt at repartee. He wore a full suit of black, or of light brown or drab in the warm season, with knee breeches and shoes, and long after others had abandoned the practice, hair powder and a cue. He was free of everything like assumption or presumption. He gave every member of the

Bar his due in civility and respect and to those whom his intercourse was intimate, he was both gracious and cordial. He was not generally familiar or communicative. He was a religious man, in open and full communion with the Presbyterian Church. His intimate friends were few and select.[5]

Ingersoll had considerable learning in the law as well as general information and a familiarity with literature. Binney in describing his work mannerisms said: "He would sit for a moment at his table and write, and then would rise and pace the floor, not infrequently stopping and holding out a hand, or nodding or shaking his head, and then return to his table, and write again, and so repeat the process. When he was making a presentation before the bar he did not resort to his brief with any frequency but was always clear, full, and precise. While he could not always write off hand an impregnable plea or opinion, he could criticize it on his legs with the greatest acuteness and strength. His cold opinions had not, by any means, the persuasion of force of his oral arguments. He was most complete and ready, at all times, in commercial law, in which from his great practice, he was most frequently called to think and to speak."[6]

Binney went on to say that

when he rose before a jury no lawyer could be better prepared with a knowledge of the facts and of the law that bore upon them and he choose his point of assault, and his field of defense, with the tact and decision that belonged to a first rate commander. If he was still doubtful of his victory, and the adversary made a mistake he fastened on to it with the grasp of death. His position was that if he could satisfy the jury that his antagonist was decidedly wrong on anything, they would not always distinguish whether it was in the main thing or not. His oratory was of a very high order. He was clear, concise and logically connected, rarely or never raising to the highest flights. Before the jury he seized with dexterity and effect upon every honest prejudice that could enlist the feelings of the panel. He never stumbled upon an awkward phrase nor was he voluble or rapid.[7]

Jared Ingersoll represented one of the last in the early tradition of the Philadelphia bar. After him no longer would the leaders of the Philadelphia bar be trained at the Inns of Court. He also represented a time when the gentleman lawyer had some involvement in politics and did his duty by serving some time on the bench. To a great extent that was due to a much smaller world of lawyers as well as that politics and the judiciary were seen as a natural part of the noblesse oblige of the leaders of the bar. In the new nation, however, as the number of lawyers dramatically changed and more important as the practice of law became more complex, there were far more options and rewards. Involvement as a politician or on the bench was becoming increasingly less attractive to the Philadelphia gentleman lawyer. Jared Ingersoll was also a member of what would be during the years one of the city's most distinguished legal families.

6
Jacksonian Era: 1830–1850

To fit up a village with tackle for tillage
  Jack Carter he took to the saw
To pluck and to pillage the same little village
  Tim Gordon he took to the law

A school chant in 1840s

Philadelphia was surpassed by New York as an ocean port city, and it became less a coastal city and more an inland one. As a result the city's concern with land transportation became much greater. In 1830 there started what was probably Philadelphia's most famous manufacturing business, the building of locomotives. Matthias W. Baldwin was born in New Jersey in 1795. He was a jeweler, silversmith, inventor, and stationary engineer who had been building stationary engines in a little shop in Philadelphia. Baldwin built "Old Ironsides," the ancestor of all American locomotives. Within thirty years his shop had expanded into the huge Baldwin Locomotive Works, which for years covered many blocks along North Broad street.

In Philadelphia, even before the end of the eighteenth century, Thomas Willing and William Bingham had become millionaires. By the 1830s the Philadelphia families with the greatest wealth were Baches, Copes, Cadwaladers, McKeons, Walns, Shippens, Biddles, Whartons, Wetherills, and Willings. Those were old families of wealth whose fortunes were built on earlier money. In 1840 it was said that Philadelphia had eleven millionaires, and another 350 citizens worth $100,000 or more. The richest Philadelphian at that time was Stephen Girard who was worth at least $6 million at the time of his death in 1831. Of the wealthiest citizens of Philadelphia, 77 percent were merchants, 11 percent were lawyers and doctors, 6 percent manufacturers, and only 1 percent mechanics. Almost all the initial wealth had come from land and business enterprises.[1]

Philadelphia during the age of Jackson underwent great economic change with the emergence of industrial wealth and power. Philadelphia continued to have its own cultural values, however, with the upper class patterns of life changing very little. It was in that world that the best-known, the most successful, and most powerful of Philadelphia lawyers played a major role. The earlier pattern continued, and very few of those men were ever active as politicians or statesmen. Instead, they were typically gentlemen who practiced law.

The United States continued to remain deeply indebted to England for the basic thrust of its law. The influential treatises of the Americans Kent, Story, and Greenleaf were adaptations of the English common law to the new American environment. Like American lawyers those authors started with the common law heritage and applied to it a mixture of reason, ideology, and empirical observation to elaborate new principles. Although they weighed precedent carefully, they were free from a doctrinaire acceptance of prior law that would make the legal systems too rigid.

Natural law was also tied to another unique American characteristic, the primacy of judicial review. Judicial opinion was based on the doctrine of natural law, and the tendency was to interpret natural law as a guarantee of the right to satisfy man's natural acquisitive instincts. The structure of law was designed for accommodation and compromise rather than radical change; wherever the social structure needs were questioned, a need existed for legal specialists. At his best, the pre-Civil War lawyer exhibited subtle balances in temperament, a respect for authority, and a willingness to revive a respect for the English common law, but only as suitable to America. The conscientious lawyer rarely questioned the aspirations of the middle class coming into greater power because he was often a part of that group. There were not many of the profession interested in championing the underprivileged. It was a legal order that emerged in America that successfully assimilated change.[2]

Along with a strong resistance to common law there was also a reluctance to systematize the law. It seemed strange to many, however, that in a democracy with a deep distrust of common law there were objections to making the law rationally coherent. William Rawle in Philadelphia picked up in 1824 where James Wilson had left off thirty years before and called for a reduction of "the uncertain coruscations of Pennsylvania equity, to the safe and steady light of chancery." In arguing against codification lawyers reiterated the same arguments that had been used or were still being used to win American consent of the common law. One argument was that codification was a ruse of the pettyfogger, and under the charge of confusion in the law was marked "a superficial knowledge of law" because it was merely a knowledge of practical law. Codification was a knowledge sufficient to confuse the student with perplexities and doubts, but that did not extend to a comprehension of the great principles and illustrative analogues by which such difficulties were removed. The Spanish Inquisition had been a very simple, energetic court. Was this what the codifiers wanted? It was also argued that in elegance and refinement the French did have the advantages, "but in what is really valuable, they are always behind . . . . They have the ruffle but we have the shirt."[3]

One legal procedure from the Jacksonian era is the jury system. The jury system was the epitome of the egalitarian belief that nothing was beyond the capabilities of the common man when he used his native intelligence. The intent of the jury system was to bring forth the common experience of men to bear on the problems of guilt and innocence. That belief had a great effect on the practice of law because different views and appeals of the law could be effectively used to influence a jury than could be used to influence the bench. The result was the greater stress placed on rhetoric rather than legal substance to convince a jury.

Distinct specialization in the practice of law did not become significant until near the end of the nineteenth century. Early in the nineteenth century, however, different methods of commerce and business developed that brought about the growth of various types of law practices. Commercial instruments, security documents, and collections had become familiar to the Philadelphia lawyer by 1825. The city had became the center for the insurance of goods and capital invested in commerce, and the war years had resulted in several complex insurance battles. For example, Horace Binney began his career as the eventual leader of the Philadelphia bar with his successful handling of a major insurance lawsuit. Lawyers were also finding increasing work in bringing order to financial affairs and in handling the problems of insolvent debtors.

The nineteenth century in American law came to be the century of the contract. The new society was in a hurry, and the contract was the legal instrument that helped them to move fast. Before the Industrial Revolution the common law of contracts had been narrow in scope and technical in application. Those early laws had put individual conscience and judgment first. The assumption was that if men were willing to act, legal consequences must be attached to their free expressions of will, and everyone must abide by the consequences of their free choice. The law was to impose liability if a man failed to do something he had agreed to do. The law of the corporation came to be one of America's most indigenous legal products, however. Of course, the corporation had arrived on the American scene before the Jacksonian era. The first important American development was the legal recognition of the business corporation as a legitimate instrument by which to achieve economic ends. American judges came to look with approval on the corporation as a method of doing business. By allowing corporations to operate nationwide, the courts provided great stimulus to economic expansion.

Corporations were no longer seen as quasi-public institutions, with their primary purpose to benefit the public interest. For the courts to have blocked the further creation of charters would have been to endorse the executive privileges and elitism that were being challenged by the Jacksonians. Increasingly the view was that charter privileges should be available to anyone who sought them. It was the Jacksonians, in the name of antimonopoly, who laid the foundation for the corporate monopolies that would dominate the post—Civil War industrial era.[4]

In Pennsylvania there were 2,333 special charters granted for business corporations between 1790 and 1860, and of that total about 1,500 were for transportation companies, with fewer than 200 in manufacturing. Until the middle of the nineteenth century, however, the corporation was not the dominant form of business organization in America. Most commercial enterprises were partnerships that consisted of two or three partners who were often related through blood or marriage. The partnership was used by all kinds of business, ranging from the small country storekeeper to the great merchant bankers. As the economy continued to expand rapidly, the new entrepreneurs increasingly made use of the corporation. In no field was that truer than in the development of transportation.

Eternal life was not the rule for the early corporations, and limited liability, now considered one of the main objects of incorporation, was not universal in the nineteenth century. Between 1800 and 1850, however, the basic nature of the corporation did change. No longer was the business corporation a unique, ad hoc creation that vested exclusive control over a public asset or natural resource in one group of favorites or investors. Instead it became a general method for organizing a business that was legally open to all with very few important restrictions as to entry, duration, and its management.

State partnership in corporate enterprises seemed natural in the early nineteenth century. First, many corporations were chartered to do work that traditionally was a function of the state, such as road building, banking, and the digging of canals. Second, each franchise was a privilege and favor, and the state had a right to charge a price and that price could include strict controls and sometimes even profit sharing. Third, state participation was seen as a good way to help an enterprise because it was a way of supporting important enterprises that would in turn enrich the economy. Fourth, public participation enhanced public control because if the state owned stock and its men sat on the board, they could make sure the company acted in the public interest. Lastly, state investments could bring money into the treasury. When the dreams of the enterprise were realized then big dividends would flow into public coffers. Pennsylvania not only owned stock in the banks, but, after 1806, the commonwealth invested in turnpikes, bridge companies, canal companies, and finally in railroads.[5]

Pennsylvania experimented with mixed public and private enterprises. At one stage in the state's marriage with railroads, in the 1830s, Pennsylvania furnished the locomotives, whereas private companies supplied the other railroad cars. The participation by the state was only a passing phase that occurred during periods of crashes, panics, and depressions. Furthermore, state investments were often lost and that contributed to a disillusionment with the idea of state participation. In 1844, a referendum in Pennsylvania approved the sale of the Main Line Railroad to private interests, and the Pennsylvania Railroad bought the line for cash and railroad bonds. In exchange the state gave the railroad all tracks and equipment of the line, and exempted it from "the payment of taxes upon tonnage or freight carried over said railroad."[6]

The great success of the corporation as a form of business association had its problems, and the corporation was a source of great controversy during the first half of the nineteenth century. In part that was because most corporations were transportation monopolies, banks, and insurance companies. The acquisition of capital was often seen as the "few" against the "many." When compared with farm and industrial enterprises those corporations were not producing any product. As a result they were often viewed as parasitic, and as having great power but no soul. One common fear was that corporations would bring together the worse ambitions among many groups of men. That fear existed because the economic power of the corporation was not controlled by the neutrality of any one person, or by any of the traditional family or moral considerations. The opposition to corporations never gained the strength or consensus to stop their emergence, however.

No issue more persistent in the period from 1815 to 1850 than public control over corporations. *Dartmouth College v. Woodward* (1819) decided that no legislature could change the terms of any chapter that a previous legislature had granted because to do so would be to "impair the charter." That decision brought forth a great howl of protest because many felt it a great blow to popular sovereignty, and believed it took away from the people and their elected representatives a "large part of the control over social and economic affairs." The purpose of the decision had been to secure property interests, however, and to protect ownership and management rights from shifting with the winds of public opinion.[7]

The corporation in the language of law is an artificial person. It has a legal entity, which, like a person, can sue and be sued, own property, and transact business. Unlike natural persons, however, the corporation can survive the death of any particular member(s). The birth of the corporation begins with a charter, and it ends when the charter expires. A perpetual charter became common for the twentieth century corporation. In the early nineteenth century the legislature had granted charters by statute, one at a time. Almost all the early colonial corporations were churches, charities, or cities or boroughs. For example, New York City was a chartered corporation.

During the first three decades of the nineteenth century there was a shift from the appointment to judicial offices to one of election. Nash observed that the primary attention of reformers was directed at political issues, especially toward the extension of the electorate's power at the expense of the executive. Strong antilawyer feeling continued, however, and the nineteenth century saw a continuation of the sentiment against lawyers as being aristocratic and of giving to themselves special rights and privileges. In Pennsylvania, in 1837, a constitutional convention had as one of its major proposals the aim to circumvent strongly the powers and influence of the legal profession. At that time amendments were made to make elective various legal offices such as prothonotaries, justices of the peace, court clerks, recorders of deeds, and registers of wills. Those amendments were drafted, debated, and passed. Another article abolished lifetime judicial appointments, prescribing instead tenures of fifteen, ten, and five years.[8] In 1850, an amendment to the Pennsylvania constitution mandated the election of judicial officers, which remains the manner of judicial selection today.

The lawyer delegates to the constitutional convention had not been completely opposed to the demands of the reformers, and that lack of unanimity reflected the lack of solidarity in the legal profession. Charles Brown, a lawyer-delegate from Philadelphia, was a leader in the fight to abolish lifetime judicial appointments. He was supported by Thomas Earle and Joseph Doran, also lawyers from Philadelphia. Other attorneys from Philadelphia such as Jared Ingersoll, John Sergeant, Charles Chauncy, and William Meridith were also strongly opposed. John Sergeant pleaded at the convention that he would yield anything rather "than go home with the slightest apprehension that any human being should be tried for his life, his liberty, his property, or his reputation, by popular clamor or the popular will."[9] The main opposition, however, came from the old Philadelphia family lawyers who were the most distinguished lawyers in the city. Those men had a strong distrust of egalitarian virtue and what that would mean for the way courts would be run.

The popular cause prevailed, however, and the first half century of the 1800s saw a steady attempt to undercut and dilute the power and autonomy of the legal profession. As the popular cause kept winning, the old Philadelphia lawyers continued to fight a losing battle. "What can elected courts give of security of honor," wrote Horace Binney in 1859, "if the wheels of the instrument receive a twist or bias through party fear or favor, or are so ignorantly and presumably governed, as to let them cut into each other, until they work falsely or uncertainly?"[10]

The attacks on lawyers traditionally had been related to the rises and falls in the business cycle. For example, in Massachusetts, during Shay's Rebellion, there were uprisings against the courts as well as lawyers. Often there were strong feelings that lawyers were overly zealous in their oppression of debtors. Many layman believed that law was nothing more than tricks and technicalities, used by unprincipled men who built their profitable legal careers on the misfortunes of others. At various points in American history the lawyer has been labeled a Tory, parasite, usurer, land speculator, corrupter of the legislation, note shaver, panderer to corporations, tool of the trusts, shyster, ambulance chaser, and loan shark. Some of the bad feeling was the result of the lawyer often being a hired hand to the rich and the powerful who had the money to hire them. Also, lawyers in American were upwardly mobile and often reached for any available opportunities.

The American lawyer has not always been viewed as a learned man, but has often been seen as a man of action and cunning. The role of the American lawyer was shaped by concrete events and circumstances. The Revolution had been an attack on the British government as it was represented by specific men. Those men had been the local agents of a tyrant British king, and many of those who represented him had been lawyers. Later with the rise of Jeffersonian and Jacksonian democracy, the dominant political party opposed the idea of government by experts. That value implied that either some limits be placed on the power of the bar or that the bar be open to all. Under the pressure of American practical politics no legal elite profession like that of the English developed.

Against the protests of beginners who felt that all they needed to know were American statutes, Thomas Sergeant of Philadelphia argued that those treatises were indispensable. "Maybe they were not always finished, nor need they always serve as authorities," he said in 1838, "but connecting scattered principles and cases, they shed light upon the law without which no science can easily be taught or understood."[11]

The training of lawyers in Philadelphia remained fairly high at least for those who were accepted and could afford to enter the office of one of the top lawyers in the city. George Wharton Pepper described the training of students in the law office of his Grandfather Wharton before the Civil War. Pepper said that the process of preparing students for admission to the bar made them at the time members of the preceptor's household. "After the semi-weekly quiz, which lasted from 7 to 9 in the evening, my Grandfather would lead his 10 or 12 students upstairs to the drawing room where my grandmother and her six daughters were waiting to receive them. Somebody would play the piano, while the others danced. Cake and wine were served and at half past ten the students went home. Whatever may have been the educational shortcomings of this process it at least had a civilizing influence on the students."[12]

The work of the lawyer tended to focus on procedure as his concern was with proper forms and safeguards, and in general to keep his clients out of trouble. The resourcefulness of the lawyer was mainly in the legal methods necessary to accomplish the limited objectives set for him. That made the American lawyer an able technician in dealing with the scope and growth of corporate power. Foreign observers such as Burke, Tocqueville, and Bryce all noted how legal minded Americans were. They typically saw American law as strongly individualistic, and usually explained it as an expression of Puritanism and the frontier spirit.

The attack on the legal profession by the Jacksonians was simple. They believed that any white male could practice law and "every man his own lawyer" became their slogan. The state constitution of Indiana probably went the furthest in 1851 when it said: "Every person of good moral character, being a voter, shall be entitled to admission to practice law in all courts of justice." Those values continued to lower the standing of the legal profession, and that in turn made for greater incompetency. One consequence was an ever-increasing complaining about the growing incompetency. When the rugged frontier lawyer, who was often incompetent, lost to the eastern lawyer it was rationalized that he an honest man of the soil had been done in by the sharp city slicker.

The regulations of the time often allowed anyone to practice law, medicine, or any other occupation without being officially licensed by the state. This was a result of the hostility toward the guild system of England. Many felt the need to raise the prestige and credibility of their profession, however, and so the more learned and successful practitioners tried to establish voluntary associations. Those professional groups were viewed with suspicion by the general public, however, who saw them as the special enclaves of men of privilege. There also existed the egalitarian belief that all occupations were of equal merit, and the farmer or small businessman was just as good as any of the more learned occupations. There were many large and aggressively vocal elements in society hostile to any form of special privilege, whether they were medical associations, chartered banks, or bar associations.

A common belief was that lawyers had deliberately made the administration of law complex to preserve their monopoly. Popular opinion was that to speak of an occupation as a profession and set standards of admission to it was un-American. Many of the complaints about lawyers heard today are the same as they were in the past. Some of these included the great expense of legal proceedings, the uncertainty of the law, and interminable delays. Typically, contact with the legal system occurs when there are problems, and in the public mind lawyers have always been associated with pain and trouble. Quite simply, lawyers are not often sought out on happy occasions.

The great lawyers of the early nineteenth century, when not filling the halls of Congress or their state legislature with resounding assertions on the political issues of the day, were often seen as in the courts as gladiators who defended the rights of the oppressed against the owners of property. That legend of the early courtroom lawyer was a romantic exaggeration, and their practice was much more related to property rights than to those of personal rights. In the *Dartmouth College* case in 1819 and in *Gibbons v. Ogden* in 1824, Daniel Webster was dealing with questions not very different from the modern corporate lawyer. "Or William H. Seward, known for his defense of an insane Negro murderer in which he braved a local mob, and for his argument in the *Ohio Fugitive Slave* case, the foundation of his modest fortune was his handling of the readjustment of the affairs of the Holland Land Company in western New York of the Panic of 1837, and from the late 1840's through the 1870's the major income of his Auburn firm and of the next generation of partners came from patent cases."[13]

The practice of law was often more technique than substance. Horace Binney, midway through his long and brilliant career, candidly declared that the practice of law added nothing to the lawyer's intellect. "The lawyer," he said, "is concerned to win, but win or lose, he forgets the case as soon as he is paid."

Binney said the physician learns new facts and increases his knowledge from every patient, but the lawyer's facts are unproductive of all benefits, except to the fortunate client. Binney asserted that "all of this justifies the sneer which is commonly directed at 'mere lawyer.'"[14]

In America, and in no place more so than Philadelphia, was the law generally the best path to wealth, distinction, and political influence. Among the older Philadelphians many felt a deep responsibility toward the society in which they earned their fame and wealth, and many of them strongly believed in a tradition of public service. Horace Binney was the classic example of the early Philadelphia lawyer's social commitment. Binney was a towering figure among Philadelphia lawyers for more than half a century, and he was involved throughout his life in community service. For Binney public service was not active politics, but the discreet behind-the-scenes activities of civil committees and panels. By early in the nineteenth century politics was increasingly being left to the less successful and less gentlemanly lawyer.

For many of the leading Philadelphia lawyers their courtroom style was one of impassioned legal discourse, and they would present their arguments in a grand and flamboyant fashion. It was those lawyers in Philadelphia and in the other cities who laid the foundations for American jurisprudence and government, however. Their main spokesmen presented law as not simply a trade, but as a social agency for shaping rules and adjudicating disputes, as a philosophy of government in the broadest sense. "The lawyer was cast not in the role of scrivener or a pedantic dealer in words, but that of a man grappling with the problems of men. Lawyers became the cement of the young society."[15]

In Philadelphia the law continued to be where the best-educated gentlemen were to be found. It was the commonest profession of the educated man, and an education was expensive. It was also difficult for the beginning lawyer to earn a living. To come from a wealthy family provided not only the economic means for education but also entrée into a successful law practice. A person of humble background might become a lawyer in Philadelphia, but it was difficult for him to break into the legal establishment. Also the upper-class distaste for politics meant that by the 1830s many more middle-class lawyers saw the bench and politics as their best means of success.

Although the bar was theoretically open to almost all men, there clearly were still many barriers. The limited mobility of the bar reflected the high degree of stratification. From 1800 to 1850 there were no large law firms in Philadelphia, but there were a few rich lawyers and many poor ones. The rich lawyers were those who represented wealthy clients, whereas the poor were those who tried to make a living by handling petty claims in the lower courts.

Getting started in the practice of law was very difficult. For example, David Paul Brown, started with every advantage but in his first year did not have one client. What was worse, not a single visitor came into his office as even the beggars kept away from young lawyers. In fact, his first visitor was a fellow lawyer who told of a similar experience that had lasted for several years.

What made getting started so difficult was that the system dictated that any worthwhile case which might stray into the hands of a novice had to be turned over to his preceptor. Brown wrote "There is no important case in which a young man has any chance of distinguishing himself; and in an unimportant cause no one can distinguish himself."[16]

The city of Philadelphia produced a bifurcated legal system, mainly based on differences in social class origins. The city's position as the nation's center of commerce and banking up until the 1830s encouraged a large legal group. Nash wrote that in Philadelphia law was in the air and nowhere in the country could be found such an outstanding body of men expert in commercial, criminal, and maritime law. A British traveler of wealth and education remarked in 1833: "I have never met a body of men more distinguished by acuteness and extensive professional information than the members of the Philadelphia bar." As Nash also observed at that time, however, the resistance to the egalitarian ideology was abnormally high in Philadelphia. "Almost every European observer saw a tight-knit upper-class clique entrenched in Philadelphia to a degree unparalleled in other American cities."[17]

Nash believed that the breakdown of the bonds of common origin and outlook probably began shortly after the beginning of the nineteenth century. The egalitarian cries against lawyers and demands for wider access to the profession began to loosen the hold of the upper class on the bench and the bar in the first decades of the century. By 1825 a lawyer of lower-class origin, Edward King, had been raised to president-judge of the Philadelphia Court of Common Pleas. That was much to the distaste of the older members of the bar who lamented that "precedents had been violated in thus elevating a man whose birth and position were not up to the old-time judicial standards."[18]

The behavior of judges in the courts was also changing. For example, judges had been in the habit of giving oral instruction to the jury and would also often instruct the jury about the law in a nontechnical and natural language. That practice died out, however, as the instructions became technically written documents, drafted by the lawyers with each side drawing up their statements of law. The judge picked out those that were in his judgment, legally "correct," and gave instructions that were often technical, legalistic, and incomprehensible to juries.

During that period one of the most influential teachers and judges in the city was George Sharswood. He devoted his entire life to law and saw in it the ultimate perfection of the reasoning mind. He emphasized the necessity for a dignified and respectable attitude toward the court, and insisted that excitability and irritability must be suppressed. He believed that when noting exceptions to the opinions of the court the manner must be polite and never contemptuous or insulting. He warned against attempts to exert improper influence on the courts. "Nothing is more certain than that the practitioner will find in the long run, the good impression of his professional brethren of more importance than that of what is commonly called the public."[19]

Sidney George Fisher wrote in his diary on 12 March, 1848. "He (George Sharswood) is now President Judge of the District Court, an excellent appointment as he is a good lawyer, has a mind and character well suited for judicial duties and is a worthy and honorable man. He is rather dull in conversation, however,—heavy prodding sense and very heavy and absurd nonsense."[20]

In Philadelphia there was some concern that fewer men were being recruited into law who possessed college educations. The foreign born and non-Protestants, however, still found the legal profession nearly unattainable. What did occur was an infusion of middle class young men who somewhat broadened the social class range. The aristocratic legal profession was, at least in numbers, slowly giving way to a somewhat more socially heterogeneous bar. There was an increasing erosion of respect for the bench and bar. The agitation of the egalitarian view was making the judiciary more and more influenced by politics. An increasing number of legal positions that had been held through professional merit were becoming political offices. That had been brought about by the political attack on the lawyers as elitists who were dangerous to democratic values. There was a viewpoint that American democracy had no place for aristocratic lawyers, and that Philadelphia would be better off to revert to William Penn's old system of arbitration before disinterested citizen referees. There were others would have been content to see the law deprofessionalized.[21]

In the years from 1826 to 1855, more than 850 lawyers were admitted to practice law in Philadelphia. In McElroy's *Philadelphia Directory for 1842* there were 220 lawyers listed. In using the *Social Register*, published near the end of the nineteenth century as a measurement of old upper class families, it is estimated that at least 40 percent of the lawyers in 1842 came from upper class families or went on themselves to found upper class families. The pattern of old families providing lawyers is reflected in the 1842 listings that included three Biddles, two Binneys, two Chauncys, two Hares, two Ingersolls, three Lewises, two Norrises, three Rushes, three Sergeants, two Whartons, and two Whites. There was one lawyer from the families of Armstrong, Bayard, Bisphan, Brewster, Brown, Cadwalader, Cope, Dallas, Duane, Fisher, Hopkins, Hopkinson, McCall, Mifflin, Morris, Price, Reed, Sharswood, Tilghman, and Wheeler.

The lawyers of Philadelphia continued to have their offices along a lawyer's row in the city. That was where most of the higher-status lawyers had their offices and sometimes their residences as well. The offices were in houses from Samson to Walnut Streets and on Walnut, between sixth and seventh Streets.

By 1830, in that era, were found the offices and homes of the most prominent members of the bench and bar. Most of the houses had been built in early colonial times as residences in the neighborhood of the old court house on Independence Square. It was along Walnut Street that the older and more aristocratic, "as their humbler brothers of the profession called them made their homes and had their offices. They derisively termed the houses along Sampson and Walnut, to which the younger attorneys had their offices, as 'Poverty Row.' "[22]

In many respects, even though increasingly influenced by egalitarian values, the practice of law was becoming more complex. By 1829 there were more than 150 volumes of reports and decisions published; the different states were appointing official reporters. Story, Greenleaf, and Bishop, among others, had written texts. Legal periodicals, although not always successful, were launched to help find and analyze the law and discuss issues. *The Pennsylvania Law Journal* in 1842 disavowed all theorizing and offered to their readers a "medium of communication concerning legal matters of fact useful and interesting to gentlemen of the bar." The bulk of every issue was devoted to the bare reporting of recent court decisions, in advance of their appearance in official volumes of reports. There was a heavy emphasis on law as it is rather than law as it ought to be.

The more complex social conditions were making increasingly necessary the specialization of law—for example, corporation, criminal, and admiralty law. There were also new patterns of thought emerging regarding training in law. One was a belief in a rigorous training along with the duty of the young lawyer to apply himself to systematic study of "the amiable and admirable secrets of law." The second related theme was the condemnation of the narrow training of the typical lawyer. That was a sensitive point among those who wanted lawyers to be liberal and cultivated men. They wanted the preparation for the lawyer to, besides his legal education, require a comprehension of literature, the rules of rhetoric, and other fields of knowledge. Of course, that education was considered superfluous and aristocratic to the Jacksonians.

There was also an increasing disagreement about the lawyer entering politics. Some believed it was not consistent with the dignity of the profession that men would enter law as a stepping stone toward a political office. Often, the lawyer who became a politician was viewed by his former colleagues as something of a renegade. The appearance of a code of ethics was another sign of the lawyer attempting to become professional. Many of the older members of the bar were trying to upgrade their profession and to force the lawyer to perform his traditional functions—in Chief Judge Shaw's words, "in a manner most honorable to himself and useful to his age and country."[23]

Beginning in 1827 the *Law Association of Philadelphia* not only controlled the profession in the city, but was the locus of the prestige and power of the old Philadelphian lawyer. From 1827 to 1900 there were twelve chancellors and thirteen vice-chancellors, and every one came from or was a founder of an upper class family. The names of those early chancellors were a roll call of the great old Philadelphia upper class lawyers. Rawle, du Ponceau, Sergeant, Binney, Ingersoll, Meridith, McCall, Biddle, McMurtie, Townsend, Bisphan, and Dickson. Also the Law Association officers of treasurer, secretary, censors, and even librarians were overwhelmingly upper class Philadelphians.

In 1832 the *Law Academy* petitioned the Board of Trustees of the University of Pennsylvania for the establishment of a law department. The impetus appears to have come from the law students who were restless about the limits of their training in the law office. They wanted to follow the example of New England and establish a systematic and less inbred program of legal education to be run under the auspices of the university. There was strong opposition from the legal establishment, however. It may have been that the very success of the Philadelphia bar was what delayed the development of formal legal education at the University of Pennsylvania. The leading members of the bar also had a stake in perpetuating an apprenticeship system that allowed them to choose their young clerks and maintain control over the bar's membership. Those apprentices, or law clerks, paid fees to their patrons, did routine work around the office, and accompanied their patrons to court. Their legal education depended, however, on the whims of their sponsors rather than on any formal curriculum. The opposition in 1832 came from the city's foremost lawyers including Chew, Binney, Hopkinson, Cadwalader, Sergeant, Ingersoll, Rawles, and the Biddles. As a result of the active opposition from the legal profession the university took no action on the proposals of the Law Academy, and for almost two decades nothing was done.

In 1849, law students once again appealed to the University of Pennsylvania for a legal education, and at that time the profession did not offer much resistance. The movement was led by George Sharswood in 1850. He was a well-known city lawyer but not of the old upper class. In 1850 the new law department enrolled its first students and two years later awarded the degree of bachelor of laws for the first time. To gain admission one did not have to have had a college education. In the first ten classes only 21 of 116 students had more than a high school education. That was a smaller percentage of college graduates than was generally reaching the bar because the better-educated and the wealthier were still training in the law offices. The law department fees were low enough to open the doors to all but the very poor. Initially, the Law School was a means of social mobility for the poorer student.

There was a strong desire among the reformers to gain access to positions of power, influence, and wealth where they might reduce the requirements for admission to the bar. They were especially upset by the long periods of required study that they saw as working against ambitious young men of limited means. Response to those "undemocratic" qualifications was widespread. In 1800, fourteen of nineteen states required between three and seven years of preparation for bar candidates. By 1840, however, the definite periods of legal instruction were required in only eleven of thirty jurisdictions. The low point was reached in 1860 when only nine of thirty-nine states made such requirements, and four states required only proof of good moral character and attainment of twenty-one years of age for admission to the bar.[24]

In the 1840s, a few states eliminated all requirements for admission to the bar except good moral character. One was Maine (1843); another was New Hampshire (1842). Yet those rules cannot be taken too literally because laymen did not practice law, even in Maine and New Hampshire in the 1840s. The values of Jacksonian democracy was a major cause as to the bar letting down on admission standards. Other social forces were also in operation, however. Government control of occupational standards was generally very weak and diffuse. There were many jurisdictions, and no one of them could really define standards for itself; the weakness of one was the weakness of all. It was a society where many people, not just the noble or lucky few, needed some rudiments of law, some forms or form books, some know-how about the mysterious ways of courts and governments. It was a society that needed a large and open-ended profession, and some loose standards were probably inevitable. The market for legal services was sometimes an efficient control because it pruned away the dead wood, and it rewarded the adaptive and the cunning. Jacksonian democracy did not make every man his own lawyer, but it did encourage a scrambling bar of shrewd entrepreneurs.[25]

The Jacksonian era was one of low status and often severe harassment of the bar. In many respects, however, Philadelphia was able to minimize those attacks because the old gentlemanly lawyers controlled the bar. Furthermore, with the withdrawal of old Philadelphia family lawyers from politics they were often "above" the fray. Many of those old lawyers went quietly about their business with great success. It appears likely that the lawyers of Philadelphia were less susceptible to the extremes of anti-intellectualism and antilawyer feeling during the period than were lawyers in any other city in America.

Sidney George Fisher, 1809–1871. Courtesy of the Historical Society of Pennsylvania.

Profile 6: Sidney George Fisher (1809–1871)

This profile is different from the others presented in this book. Although Fisher was a lawyer he was far from successful. Fisher began keeping a diary in 1839 that continued intermittently until his death thirty-two years later. It is his diary that gives him importance. The selections that follow reflect some of Fisher's impressions of law over those years in Philadelphia. Fisher was clearly a social snob who was constantly worried about money. He wrote, "My birth, fortune and education gave me a place in society, but want of means prevent me from playing the part which I could, would and ought to do." He graduated from Dickinson College in 1827, studied farming for a time and became a member of the Philadelphia bar. He had little regard for the legal profession and practiced only to try to supplement his inherited income. Not only was he a failure as a lawyer but because of his absentee direction of his farm that too became a financial disaster. He did attain some distinction as a writer on constitutional and political questions during the Civil War era.

Fisher's diary is a rich historical source on Philadelphia for more than three decades including the Civil War period. He was a man who came from an old and distinguished Philadelphia family and was a part of the upper social circles of the city. In his diary he often comes across as bitter because of what he saw as his restrictive economic resources and because of his sense of superiority to almost every other person in the city. Fisher lived in a world he felt never gave him his due nor sufficient financial means to live at a level he felt he deserved.[1]

22 DECEMBER, 1836

Mused over my wasted powers and do-nothing life. Yet what am I to do; I do not so much want the will as the opportunity and sufficient motive. Make money? I dislike my profession, its associations and labors. I consider them calculated to narrow the mind, degrade the feelings and blunt the moral susceptibilities. Time can be more pleasantly employed in reading and society, and tho not rich I have enough for comfort and independence, and can slowly but surely increase my property by other means more suited to my taste. Luckily fortune small as it is and my social position command respect from the mass. I must look for my enjoyments to domestic happiness, the intercourse and good opinion of my friends, and to such occupations as are suited to my tastes and intellectual bias.

15 JANUARY, 1837

At 9 went to Harrisons. This is one of the few houses left in the city, where one does not meet these vulgar, nouveau riche people, who are now crowding into society, and are seen at all the parties. The good, respectable, old-family society for which Philadelphia was once so celebrated is fast disappearing, and persons of low origin and vulgar habits, manners and feelings are introduced, because they are rich, who a few years ago were never heard of. If they were agreeable, cultivated, intelligent or beautiful there would be some compensation for the innovation, but they are all commonplace and uninteresting, many of them vulgar, stupid and ugly.

2 OCTOBER, 1838

I have been regularly in Court in the morning and have read law every day. I have four cases, which I hope will be the sources of other business. Have been received and treated courteously and kindly by some of the older members of the profession. Although I have had no practice I am not without reputation, and am as well known as any man my age in town. This is a great advantage, as it gives me at once a respectable position, and I do not feel much doubt about acquitting myself creditably in such practice as I may be able to get.

1 JANUARY, 1839

I shall make an effort to gain enough practice to prevent the mortification of having failed in an attempt, and to add to my income. But I hate it, utterly and perfectly, and a slave to it I cannot and will not be. I will believe that a different and higher destiny awaits me than that of even a successful lawyer at such a bar as this. If other schemes fail, literature, farming, and the solitary independence of Mount Harmon would be far better and more congenial to my tastes.''

29 DECEMBER, 1839

Went to court, as usual was disgusted. I think, although I have some business I am further than ever from becoming a lawyer. I cannot conquer my utter hatred for the profession and all its labors, habits and associations and would rather live on a farm.

7 JANUARY, 1890

John Cadwalader [later his father-in-law]—he always shows a friendly disposition to me, and, though his manners are somewhat repulsive, I like him. He has been very successful at the bar and makes $10,000 a year, but is working himself to death. He advised me to stick to the bar and said he considered, and always had, that my success was certain if I made the proper exertion. I am minded to follow his counsel. My income is not sufficient to support me as I wish to live. As a man grows older, his sources of expense increase. As a bachelor, to be easy, I want $4,000 a year. At the utmost my income is only $2,500. To make the other $1,500 or more would occupy but part of my time, leaving me still more leisure.

5 OCTOBER, 1840

Went to Court to hear William M. Meridith's argument in the d'Hauteville case. His speech was powerful and eloquent. Many clear thoughts, correct and strong feeling, sarcasm, indignant declamation and rebuke, humorous and touching pathos, all expressed in language plain but fluent, nervous, and perspicacious and with a manner and voice, never o'er stepping the modesty of nature, but according always with the varying sentiments of his case. He is beyond question the first man of the bar, with a wide gap, as regards natural talent, between him and the rest.

3 OCTOBER, 1841

The routine of each day is nearly the same. In the morning from 9 to 2 business, if I have any to do, sitting at Court, reading. From 2 till 5 riding, which at this season is a great enjoyment. At 5 dinner. I have adopted this hour for dining whether I ride or not. I find it far preferable to the usual hour here, 3 o'clock, which breaks in on the best part of the day. I have thus a long morning for business, study and exercise, and come to the table with a good appetite. After dinner till 7 or 8, a book, an easy chair, and cigars, and then society or study until 1 or 2.

17 JANUARY, 1842

My income is $2300 independent of my practice and what I can make by occasional operations with money. If I can make it in all $3,000, it will do for a bachelor until he is 40 very well. After that a man needs more. This (what he has) is, a small fortune, but it procures the substantial comforts and some of the luxuries of life. It gives me food, clothes and fire without working for them and it gives me independence. My pittance gives me a comfortable home, servants, a good table, wine, a horse, books, "country quarters," a plentiful wardrobe, the ability to exercise hospitality in a small way—and as the greatest of all pleasures freedom, leisure, the sense of independence, the control of my own actions. Add another $1,000 to it and I would be rich. Add a little more and I might venture upon a wife.

17 DECEMBER, 1843

Have been busy with the green bag business, as we call it. It brought me to court several times and I have the satisfaction to think I conducted it respectably, was successful, and shall get some money for it. I find that the 3 or 4 cases I have give me a good deal of occupation and that the excitement is rather agreeable than otherwise. I find also that I transact it with ease and confidence in myself. I made the other day before the Court the longest professional speech I have yet made, without even notes, and I found I was without the least embarrassment and capable of expressing my ideas clearly and fluently. I have always felt I possessed enough of the faculty of public speaking to make me successful in those duties of the profession where its exercise is required. But I am deficient in legal knowledge and in habits of business.

JUNE (DATE TORN OUT) 1844

Mr. [George Mifflin] Dallas is a gentleman by birth and education, amiable in private life, very bland and courteous in manner, too much so indeed, or rather too indiscriminately so, to give one an impression of sincerity and truth, a reckless partizan [sic] totally devoid of principle and capable of upholding or relinquishing any opinion whenever his own or his party's interest requires it. His talents are very moderate, his acquirements scanty, he had an inferior position at the bar, no one would give a dollar for his opinion and his practice is for the most part in jury cases unless when political influences introduce him into an important case.

2 MARCH, 1845

This is my birthday, am now 36. Well, so be it . . . . I am resigned to the idea of a single life, but if I can marry prudently and according to my wishes, may be tempted to take the plunge. One thing is certain. I must not think of marrying a poor woman. With my temperament and habits, dependence on business for a support would make life wretched.

21 MARCH, 1849

Horace Binney is a man I cannot like. He is too hard and cold and impervious. He has a clear, accurate, highly trained intellect, powerful sharp, and adroit in its sphere, but the sphere is narrow, he wants imagination and he wants heart, and these are the chief elements of greatness. He has no sympathy with others, there is nothing genial about him. He does not so much receive graciously as demand haughtily deference and homage. His appearance is strikingly handsome and commanding and though 70 he is admirably preserved. Though very rich (he is worth at least half a million) he still does a large business as counsel, though he never appears in court. Though not loved he is more than respected and Philadelphians are very proud of him and boast a good deal about him abroad. It is said that Philadelphia is celebrated for three things—the Fairmount Waterworks, the Wonderly Butter and Mr. Binney.

25 FEBRUARY, 1849

I have been made junior counsel to the Reading road, which will give me more work to do than ever I had. It will give me also $500 a year, with the chance of increasing business. Henry's [Cadwalader] influence got it for me, of course. Am glad of it, for I want the money and don't object to the work.

27 MAY, 1851

Married Elizabeth Ingersoll, the object of long attachment. Our prospects are not very bright. We are neither young nor rich, but neither old nor absolutely poor. I have an object and purpose in my life. At the same time I am not without care and anxiety, and have no longer the feeling of independence and freedom which I have so long enjoyed. Mr. Ingersoll had settled $1,000 a year on his daughter. My own income will be at least $2,000. We can live with comfort on $3,000. To attend to business, to read law, to have intercourse with vulgar, ignorant businessmen seems such a sacrifice of life and waste of time when there are the rich fields of nature and literature and art, filled with sources of pure and noble delight open to me. But it is necessary to make the effort. Live on S. 7th, we have 3 good servants. Small as house is we manage to give nice little dinner occasionally.

31 DECEMBER, 1851

Business does not increase. I have none of any consequence except the Reading road, and my connection with this is for various reasons so disagreeable that I would gladly resign, but I cannot afford to lose $500 a year. I fear I am not likely to succeed. I cannot even desire success, tho it is so important for me to make money. To attend to business, to read law, to have intercourse with vulgar ignorant businessmen seems such a sacrifice of life and waste of time when there are rich fields of nature and literature and art filled with sources of pure and noble delight open before me. But it is necessary to make the effort.

IN FEBY. OF 1853

I went to Washington. I was counsel in a case for the Reading Railroad that was argued in the Supreme Court, My experience was not agreeable. For the first time in my life I became embarrassed and lost presence of mind in speaking. I did not exactly breakdown, but I felt that I made decided failure. I had gone to court every morning for a week, prepared, and each day the case was not reached. The day before it was reached, I took a violent cold, which had a depressing effect. It was a very solemn tribunal, new to me, and I was nervously anxious not to fail.—to crown all, in consequence of something that was said on the other side I was so unwise as to change the order of the argument I had prepared, just as I rose, and became entangled in it. I felt much mortified.

JANUARY 1855

I could bear it no longer and resigned, and my only regret is that I did not do it sooner. That I ever accepted the place at all. My connection with this company [Reading Railroad] and all that it revealed to me have completed and confirmed my aversion and disgust at all business and businessmen. They live in a very base and inferior world,—The only way to have property is to inherit it, and the universal feeling of world that makes this the basis of the position of a gentleman is founded in truth and knowledge. Tho but having a small income I have been willing to sacrifice my inclination to some extent, to add a little to my means, desiring to do only a little business for this purpose, reserving the larger part of my time and thoughts for better and higher things. This has been a great mistake in life. To gain a little success at the bar requires entire devotion to it, which would obtain a great success.

15 FEBRUARY, 1867

The movements in favor of female suffrage seems to be gaining strength. The idea is so absurd and so repugnant to all the feelings universally received of the true position of women, that it would seem impossible for a scheme so extravagant to be seriously discussed. But we live in a time when nothing is impossible except virtue, wisdom and moderation.

15 SEPTEMBER, 1869

The learning necessary for practice is a dry mass of details of no interest and the practice itself has become little better than a mere trade under the degrading influence of democracy. It by no means follows that a successful lawyer is a gentleman, that he is a man of honor, or that he has received a liberal education; and indeed those who are now most successful at making money, the great object of all, are notoriously deficient in these qualities, which were once regarded as prerequisites. The bar and the bench, too, have fallen very far below the dignified and respectable position it held when I knew it thirty years ago. I saw and knew the last of the old set who gave so much influence and reputation—Rawle, Binney, Sergeant, Chauncey, the two Ingersolls, Scott, etc.—all of them gentlemen by culture, birth and manners, all of them distinguished for learning and ability, Binney and Sergeant pre-eminent for eloquence and power, all of them, too, with scarcely an exception, worthy of all confidence and respect for integrity, professional honor, and moral worth. The courtroom in those days, every morning when the bar was assembled, was like a drawing room, filled with elegantly dressed gentlemen of courtly and refined manners. Many a times have I gone to hear Binney or Sergeant speak and to enjoy the conversation of these men, for they were very gracious and kind to young members of the profession; and I always remember their courtesy to me with pleasure, whether, when I met them in Court, or enjoyed, as I constantly did, the hospitality of their homes. All of this is now changed—culture, elegance, refinement, courtesy, eloquence, wit, scholarship have vanished.

Fisher died 25 July 1871 at the age of sixty-three. He led a comfortable and privileged life, but he was far from happy with his lot. His high expectations for himself, based on what he believed to be his right by virtue of birth, never materialized. At best his practice of law was to add to his income, but he rarely achieved any personal satisfaction from it as a profession. In fact, there were many times when he hated being a lawyer. Fisher's wife died less than a year after his death. They had one son, Sidney, who was educated at St. Paul's School, Trinity College, and Harvard Law School. Like his father, however, he was not strongly committed to the practice of law and interrupted his legal practice to write several books on American history.

7

Civil War Era: 1850–1870

If there were no bad people there would be no good lawyers.
—Dickens

The United States at the beginning of the Civil War had passed through the early stages of the industrial revolution and the development of factories had led to a decline of domestic and craft shop manufacturing. The demand for skilled arisans decreased, and the ranks of the unskilled worker were being filled with new immigrants. The great economic success of industrialization was also creating a new capitalistic aristocracy in America. The opening of the Erie Canal in 1825 had ended the dominance of Philadelphia as the leading American city. That distinction clearly belonged to New York.

In contrast to its commercial decline, however, Philadelphia's importance as a manufacturing center was only slightly behind that of New York and far greater than any other American city. For example, Philadelphia's manufacturing production in 1860 was almost as great as the combined efforts of all eleven of the Confederate states. Industrial production in Philadelphia continued to be mainly in small establishments, although the Baldwin Locomotive works sometimes employed as many as a one thousand workers. Few other factories had as many as five hundred employees, however. Manufacturing was bringing into the city many immigrants, and by 1860 about 30 percent of the population was foreign born. About half of the immigrants were from Ireland, more than a quarter from Germany, and the rest from England and Scotland.

During the Civil War Pennsylvania raised one-sixth of the total Union armies. Officers and men served in every major campaign, but it was at Gettysburg that Pennsylvania made its greatest contribution. One-third of the Union troops there were from Pennsylvania as well as its commander, General George Gordon Meade. In severe fighting and outnumbered and outflanked, the Union force nevertheless turned back several Confederate attacks. The Union forces continued to hold their lines until 3 July when they won the crucial battle of Cemetery Hill. It was that battle that turned the tide of the war and led to the northern victory.

On 13 December, 1860 a citizens meeting was called in Independence Square. Nearly everybody who was in the city attended the meeting. The bar was out

127

in full force. Mayor Henry, Joseph R. Ingersoll, Theodore Cuyler, and Judge George W. Woodward gave stirring pro-South speeches flavored with many concessions. Afterwards conciliatory messages were sent to the southern states.

Philadelphia was a principal concentration point for New England troops and its depots and refreshment stands were filled with Union regiments on their way to the battle front. But there were a variety of strong feelings in the city. There was also apathy and bitterness that interfered with the patriotic efforts of the soldiers and most of the civilians. Southerners and their sympathizers continued to be an important part of the city's population. Many of the most prominent families in the city were torn apart by conflicting beliefs between their members.[1]

Some of the young lawyers of Philadelphia played a small part in the battle at Gettysburg. Battery A, First Pennsylvania Artillery, had been organized in 1844 by the Philadelphia bar to help control the riots of that year, and in 1862 it was reactivated. One of the new recruits was Private John G. Johnson who would go on to become possibly the greatest of all Philadelphia lawyers. The total experience of each of those lawyers in the army was only a few weeks, but it was a professional bonding experience that had a positive influence for many in their future social and legal relationships. One of the lawyer members of Battery A, besides Johnson, was James T. Mitchell, later a U.S. circuit judge. Robert L. Willson, William B. Hanna, and Clement D. Penrose also became judges. Others serving were George W. Biddle, Charles Chauncy, Albert A. Outenbridge, and Thomas Hart, Jr. Another young lawyer was Charles E. Morgan who became the founder of Morgan Lewis & Bockius, the largest law firm in Philadelphia and one of the largest in the United States today. A part of that firm's success was due to Johnson, who at his death left a significant share of his practice to the Morgan firm. That first tie between those two lawyers went back to their shared experience during the Civil War.

The Civil War was the severest constitutional crisis in American history. The end of the Civil War proved not that American government was stable and permanent, but that crisis and change could be accommodated within the language of the Supreme Court. The major legal novelties following the war were the Thirteenth, Fourteenth, and Fifteenth Amendments. The Thirteenth Amendment abolished slavery. The Fifteenth Amendment guaranteed the right to vote to all citizens, regardless of "race, color or previous condition of servitude." The Fourteenth Amendment said that all persons, born or naturalized in the United States were "Citizens of the United States and of the States wherein they reside." No state could abridge their privileges or immunities. In addition, no state could deprive any person of "life, liberty, or property, without due process of law" nor could any state deny "to any person within its jurisdiction the equal protection of the law."[2]

Equity had been the underlying concept of the American legal system since it was proclaimed as a "self-evident truth" in the Declaration of Independence.

Before the Civil War the great debate in public law dealt with the nation-state problem. The turning point in American public law, however, was 1868. The Fourteenth Amendment had been originally intended to protect the freed slaves after the Civil War from any coercive action by the southern states. In practice, however, the Fourteenth Amendment did far more than transform the relationship between the state and the citizen. It influenced and nurtured the basic economic instrument by which the United States economically expanded during the nineteenth century—the corporate charter.

By the 1850s the duration, alteration, and repeal of corporate charters had become controversial political issues. The problem of reaching a balance between encouraging business initiative and preventing abuses had become a problem for the legal profession. Being immune from individual liability for the debts of the enterprise, which in today's world is considered the chief advantage of the corporation, was strongly opposed. The idea of corporate privilege was attack as being contrary to the natural law doctrine of the Revolution. Small business argued it was unjust to expect them to compete with incorporated firms who had the advantage of limited liability. The economic pressures were powerful, however, and as the factory system developed the increasing competition forced a change in attitudes. As shop owners and merchants began to invest their wealth in domestic manufacturing their opposition to the corporate form and limited liability decreased. The economic fears that industry would not be attracted to a particular state overcame its anticorporate arguments. After 1830, the individual states began to adopt general incorporation acts as necessary to their own economic survival.

The concern that growing enterprises might be strangled by costs underlie *Murray v. South Carolina Railroad Company*. The court held that a worker, injured through no fault of his own but through the negligence of a fellow servant, could not sue the common employer. That was made into law by the Shaw opinion, *Farewell v. Boston & Worchester Railroad* in 1843. Through the 1840s the declarations and decisions of the courts asserted two major principles. First, the private right of an individual must yield to the *eminent domain* of government whenever the public good requires it. Second, to equalize the burden, and avoid all hardship, the owner of the property so taken is to receive a compensation, which shall be full and just.[3]

The greatest legal achievement of the pre–Civil War period had been to build on the Constitution a legal system that could meet the needs of the new nation and the new industrial era. Although the original starting points were based on English origins, the new principles were adapted to the special needs of American society. The result was a molding and reshaping of the emerging common law usually brought about through the judicial process. Judges were constantly reviewing and reshaping the common law, and the law came increasingly to emphasize free individual action and decisions. For example, the burden was placed on injured persons to show why the law should shift the loss onto the one who caused the injury. As a result liability became a corollary of fault and that was being attached with little discrimination to all acts causing injury.

The American law of damages was based on the need to encourage men to take risks in the interests of productivity. The belief was that the law should not add more risks to those economic risks already inherent in business situations. Basically, the laws said that every adult male must take responsibility for himself and should not expect to be saved from himself through any legal paternalism. The fellow-servant rule was an expression of the powerful individualism of nineteenth-century law. The individual was seen as free to pursue his occupational choice, but he also assumed the risks of his chosen profession. That included any harm that might befall him as a result of negligence by his fellow workers.

As suggested in previous chapters the legal reputations of Philadelphia gentleman lawyers were made mainly in the practice of law. Over the years, only a few members of such distinguished old families of the Hopkinson, Hare, Cadwalader, Sergeant, and Biddle families served on the bench, and the Ingersoll family, one of the most distinguished legal families in Philadelphia, never had a family member serve on the bench. President John Adams had offered Jared Ingersoll a position in the federal judiciary, but he was not interested.

John Cadwalader, the most distinguished of his clan, did serve on the United States District Court from 1858 to 1879. The Sargeants were another of the foremost Philadelphia legal families. Jonathan Dickinson Sergeant had played a prominent part in the Stamp Act controversy and his two sons, John and Thomas, were leading members of the city's bar. John Sergeant was a close associate of Horace Binney, a member of Joseph Dennie's circle at the *Port Folio* and served several terms in Congress. Like several of other distinguished Philadelphia lawyers Sergeant's status can be measured by the offices he turned down. Those included a seat on the United States Supreme Court, a cabinet post under Harrison and the embassy of England under Tyler. The waspish Sidney Fisher wrote of Sergeant at his funeral in 1856: "He led a dreadful life, drank to horrible excess, died of delirium tremens. For many years he had lived with a mistress, openly, as if she were his wife. He was, however, a manly good hearted fellow, a gentleman in his manners and of considerable talent. His mistress was in the church, a handsome woman."[4]

By 1860 the general temper of Americans had come a long way from their deep distrust of law and lawyers as well as the ethics of advocacy that were common at the beginning of the nineteenth century. For example, by 1860 what was being published were typically guidebooks to courtroom techniques or the demonstration that such techniques constituted a manifestation of evangelical piety. William Rawle voiced the distaste that was becoming the common refrain of lawyers. "The heart of the philanthropic patriot sinks," he said, "at the sight of the dark and portentous cloud which hangs over this sublime and magnificent landscape—a cloud compacted of riots, lynchings, and licence." Rawle went on to say that "if the law cannot vindicate itself against this self-destroying principle then life and liberty will be of uncertain tenure, and the slave who bends under the yoke of Russian tyranny is safer, happier and more free, then he who can boast the proud name of American citizen."[5]

Miller wrote that midway through the rise of the legal profession the clear threat was that its progress might be checked, or even destroyed, unless it could decide for itself "where its own dedication, its own highest obligations, lay." Throughout the constitutional debates of the 1840s and 1850s and down to the fatal actions of 1861, "that was the issue that drove them, that haunted them, that led many to reminiscent falsifications of their careers. The inability of the best minds to understand what they had to deal with, their often pathetic efforts to preserve their reputation for consistency, amounted to both the glory and the tragedy of the era."[6]

One Philadelphia lawyer, writing in 1856, offered the following observation about his profession:

> The lawyer is not only bound not to delay his clients cause for lucre or malice, but not to delay his clients the cause of his adversary. Always mingle as much kindness as possible, with the permanence of duty. A lawyer has the right to take all advantages, his learning and talents afford him, in order to sustain a good cause or defeat a corrupt one. Flippancy, frivolousness, exhibited by the youthful toward the aged barrister, is a marked vulgarity and low breeding. Let a lawyer dress as he pleases, provided he always dresses as a gentleman.[7]

Brown contended that of the nearly five hundred lawyers in Philadelphia not five were tainted with the vice of intemperance; however, he said back in 1810 of the one hundred lawyers appearing in court about five would appear under the influences. "The time use to be when drinkers excited sympathy, but not anymore." He went on to advise that an exception should be noted to the bench in an agreeable and respectful manner. As to rules for the beginning lawyer he believed that firmness and fidelity were perfectly reconcilable with courtesy and kindness. "By all means, in all circumstances, maintain your composure; if you lose that you lose all. Never retire to bed without having arranged all your business for the next day. Keep your table always clear of surplus documents and papers."[8]

Brown went on to say that orderliness varied among different members of the bar. "Mr. Lewis's office was an Augean stable; Mr. Rawle's was much better, but nothing to boast of; Mr. Ingraham's was one where you could find everything and nothing. On the contrary, Mr. J. R. Ingersoll's, Binney's, Sergeant's and Channey's were models of cleanliness, neatness, and system." Brown's further advoice was "keep your appointments as faithfully as possible.

Want of punctuality is the vice of the indolent. For the new students civility and politeness could also be part of their learning."[9]

It was still the age of forensics. The tempo was leisurely, entertainment was limited, and an education was something to be proud of. The lawyer was a celebrity. He came into court in formal dress and in every variation of the tailor's art. His performance was as important to his position as was his legal ability. The audience and the jurors expected to be entertained. "They wanted an excellent speech, garnished with classical allusions beyond their scope and delivered with great emotion."[10]

One of the more picturesque figures at the bar during the Civil War era in Philadelphia was Benjamin Harris Brewster. It was said that he tried to distract from his scarred face by his dress that was more appropriate to the earlier colonial style. Especially noticeable were the frills and ruffles that he had attached to his shirt. In one of his confrontations in court his adversary commented on Brewster's scarred appearance. Brewster used that in his closing speech to the jury by saying:

> May it please the court and the gentleman of the jury. I know that I am often referred to in a kindly fashion, but, in my absence, as "Burnt-Face Brewster." But it remained for my learned opponent to endeavor to scarify my soul by reference to my scarified face. Reluctantly I must ask you to bear with me while I recall my boyhood. When, to rescue a little sister from a fire which was burning her little dress I was myself in great danger. Suffice it to say that is visible and I will carry it to my grave, a scarred and mutilated countenance, which when I had completed my rescue was as black [turning to and facing his antagonist] as my learned opponent's heart.[11]

The story was questionable but it did win him the verdict.

George W. Woodward, in his book, *Law and Lawyers* (1859), had some observations about the lawyers of his time. He wrote that outside the profession, law was regarded almost universally, with terror rather than affection.

> For some it was seen as a grim tyrant delighting in the tortures it inflicts. Others may think of it much as they do of a juggler who excites expectation only to disappoint them, and appeals to our senses only to confound them. Whilst everybody looks upon us as a monster of unwieldy proportions and of uncertain steps sometimes wheeling capriciously in his tracts, and sometimes staggering to and for like a drunken man *we* know that the law is personified by the grave and reverent image of Justice holding aloft the equal scales. The best bloods of the world, tried as by fire, have crossed and co-mingled to make the American lawyer.

The Philadelphia lawyer, Woodward went on to say,

> is called to a more diversified practice than those of his brethren who stand in Westminster Hall, or in the Common Law courts elsewhere. He unites in himself the several functions of Counsellor, Attorney, and Barrister, besides adding very frequently the duties of Conveyancer. The Courts under which he practices retain

the common law principles of pleading and evidence, and yet administer much equity under common law forms, besides sitting, as they now do frequently, as mere courts of equity."[12]

Woodward further wrote that "the lawyer must be adaptive, as ready for the severe logic of special pleading as well as for the didactics of the bar. He must, above all, be thoroughly versed in legal science. The Philadelphia student in the office of the practitioner, if he belongs to the Law Academy and attends the lectures at the University has excellent opportunities for learning the common law." But he "must also be a diligent student of history. There is no professional fame or fortune without the aid of good character and living in the midst of preeminent temptation, the lawyer shall be preeminently honest. Nothing will betray the well trained lawyer into manners unbecoming a gentleman." Furthermore, "a lawyer will not assert a legal proposition which he has not good reason to think true, any more than he would assert before the judge, not to corrupt or mislead, but to enlighten and guide his judgments."[13]

The American bar was beginning to take a more aggressive stand about the practicing of law. The *Law Reporter* in 1846 wrote that lawyers "insist upon the wrong with the same pertinacity, earnestness and personal feeling, that they do upon the right." The *Law Reporter* went on to say that "while lawyers may select causes and refuse retainers, the sober truth is that the more mercenary our profession is, the more it will deserve respect." In 1859, the *U.S. Monthly Law Magazine* asked what was disgraceful in bringing before the judicial mind all that can fairly be urged on either side of a doubtful question? George Sharswood told his students in Philadelphia that no profession, including the sacred ministry, more demanded "a high-toned morality, be he alone with those apologists protested that their morality is entirely compatible with arguing any and every case." He said the advocate is not a moral censor, and it does not matter as to his private conviction. "The Judge is there to adjudicate the law, and the jury to determine the facts. His sphere in the proceedings consists in endeavoring, if possible, by all means, to obtain a favorable decision from both. There is nothing immoral in this."[14]

At the time of the Civil War the advocate was still regarded as the most honorable and respected of all professionals, and law was still a goal for many intellectual and ambitious young men. Eloquence was one of the principal attributes that distinguished the advocate, and the intent of the orator was to vindicate eloquently the morality of right and justice. It was believed that the study of metaphysics and logic, history and literature, language and poetry were basic to the development of the orator. Law and the lawyer, however, were slowly beginning to move away from the traditional role. In part, the change was due to the decreasing need for the orator as more and more the questions of law did not reach the courtroom. This pattern, developed increasingly up the present, is to make less and less the percentage of legal work that ever reachs the court.

In 1851 judgeships in Pennsylvania became elective rather than appointive. That had a dramatic impact on those who filled judicial positions, which has continued to the present. In the 1850s running for a judgeship was a career option for the lawyer. It was firmly based in politics and called for no evidence of any particular legal ability. During the years that meant that the state courts produced judges who were very often not successful lawyers. The question increasingly became why would a successful lawyer want to become a judge because for him a judgeship would mean a lower income and lower professional status.

The judges, with all their incompetency, were often seen as arrogant. One observer, in the 1850s, said that the average newly elected judge, fresh from daily and hourly close identification with his brethren at the bar, immediately became infested with the "Grand Llama of Tibet contagion." He wrote that it was too much the custom to refer to "great and exulted" judge and indulge in such ascription of "compliments and object praise as are only employed by inferiors in their communications to superiors."[15] Sometimes if the lawyer was not properly subservient he was in danger of proceedings against him for contempt of court.[15]

The decision in 1851 that made state judgeships at all levels elective was strongly opposed by the Philadelphia legal establishment. The opposition was strong because the elective method was seen as taking away the independence of the judiciary and making them subject to politics. Philadelphia leaders of the bar such as Ingersoll, Sergeant, Rawle, and especially Horace Binney took the lead in what became a losing battle. Binney believed that the integrity of the bench depended on an independent judiciary. He wrote:

> A good Bar cannot exist long in connection with a favor seeking Bench,—a Bench on the lookout for favors from the people or from anyone. Such a Bench is not an independent body, whatever some of the judges may be personally. The Bench therefore as now constituted is raised sufficiently above the Bar, to command it by the power of its political constitution. The Bar is constitutionally the higher body of the two, the more permanent, the more independent, and, popularly, being with the most power, the more controlling body, though only for its personal and several ends. The subordinate becomes the paramount, the private and personal will control the public; not by reason, not by virtue, not always openly, but by influence.[16]

The political parties were finding it difficult to get "gentlemen" to run for office, but there were some exceptions. Charles Jared Ingersoll was a Democratic congressman from 1840 to 1849, and his brother Joseph Reed Ingersoll went to Washington as a Republican in 1846. The most colorful was Richard Vaux, an aristocrat who dressed in the latest fashions. He was elected Mayor in 1856. But the most outstanding Democrat was George Mifflin Dallas, vice-President of the United States from 1845 to 1849, the highest public office attained by any Philadelphian.

During the Civil War era law firms with partnerships or associates were not common. Wister wrote that he could remember only three, C. G. Fallon, Clay and Horace C. Jones, and Charles J. and Craig Biddle. He further noted that all the law offices were in a front room, which was a reception and student's room and an inner or back room for the lawyer. There would be book cases and paper cases or boxes in both rooms. "There were no large offices, with sundry rooms and library accessible to all of them, such as now exist [in 1900]." [18]

Clement Penrose, in his reminiscences, said that in 1847 when he came to the bar, and for a considerable time afterward there were few lawyers whose offices were not in their residences. In later years, when the trend was growing to have the office away from the place of residence Henry J. Williams said he did not see how it was possible for a lawyer in active practice to do that. "When I was practicing I went to my office as soon as I had finished breakfast, and saw clients until it was time to run over to the court. At 3, I came home to dinner, going at 4 to an audit; then coming home, at 7 we had tea, after which I spent the evening in my office." Williams also had some comments on what was needed for success. He said, "Mrs. Williams and I concluded that desserts were unwholesome and we never ate them. Men must exercise who overeat." He referred to a well-known lawyer who had died still a young man because he was too fond of good living. "I met him one day with a basket on his arm. He opened it to show me the fine lobsters. That is just the kind of man to die young." [19]

Wister wrote that with the common neighborhood of lawyer's offices and their homes they could often call on each other for business and social reasons. Wister said that "sometimes the back offices were used by female members of the family, and when a stranger entered they might be seen flitting away to avoid recognition or observation." Wister relates that "once a gentleman called at Mr. McCall's and found a student sitting in the back office with his feet on the window sill. When he heard someone enter whom he took for a fellow student, he neither rose nor looked up to see who it was. The gentleman, in a very sharp voice cried out: 'Say to Mr. McCall that Mr. Joseph R. Ingersoll called, and it was the first time he had called here without having Mr. McCall or some gentleman get up to receive him.' " [20] Furth wrote that unquestionably, the most unique interior in the way of an old-fashioned office was that of Colonial Charles J. Biddle. That office was located on Sansom Street just above Walnut Street. "Colonel Biddle had some odd and explicable notion about the upper stratum of air in a room; for his private desk was placed on the top of the large office table. His accustomed seat at this desk was reached by a series of steps extending from the floor to the table top. No doubt, many others, with myself, were astonished when first confronting this apparition in green spectacles inspecting the visitor from his elevated 'coign of vantage.' ''[21]

The *Legal Intelligencer* was first published in Philadelphia in 1855. The advertisements that were carried give some indication of items that were of interest to lawyers. For example, offered for sale were such products as Venetian blinds. One could hire house, sign, and ornamental painters. For the office there were blank books and stationery as well as fireproof safes. For one's personal life were canes of every description, fancy goods, fine pocket cutlery, vintage wines and liquors, French brandies, and Holland gins. For those nearing the end of their practice of law there were undertakers and burial plots ready to take over.

One of the law offices of the period that left records of income and expenditures was that of John C. Bullitt and Frederick Furthorn. In 1849 they received seventy-six fees totaling $1,577.94. Only one of the fees was for more than $100. In 1850, there were 581 items resulting in an income of $5,476.36. There was still only one fee for more than $100. In 1851 the total income was $6,277.19, including three fees of $100 and one of $275. In 1866 they listed the following office expenses: brushes, brooms, and buckets, $8.21; spittoon, $0.15; lock for outside toilet, $2.50; parchment, $2.25, green bags, $3.00; post office box rent, $2.00; and a wash basin, $0.37. The office boy was paid $1.00 a week.[22]

The courtrooms of the city were described as drab, unornamented, and sometimes unfurnished. The ceilings were often in need of repair, and it was reported that on at least two occasions judges narrowly missed death when loose plaster fell. The rooms were heated by crude stoves, and the judges held court in their street clothes, including great coats, in the cold weather. In their later years, however, the old timers would often forget the discomfort and recall only the mutual courtesy and the high standards of conduct they recalled as governing the relations of attorney.

The 1850s were well before the invention of the typewriter. At that time the introduction of the steel pen and blotter was considered a questionable substitute for the traditional quill and sand. One lawyer reminisced that

> despite its drab setting, the bar of the 50's held an unchallenged glory in the tradition of those who had gone before and in the work of the men who were active. It was still the age of forensics. The tempo was leisurely, entertainment limited, and education something to brag about. The successful lawyer was a celebrity and he came into court in formal dress or in every variation of the tailor's art. His performance was as important to his position as was his ability to work justice. The audiences and the jurors expected a thrill and they desired a first rate speech, garnished with classical allusion beyond their scope and delivered with an extravagance of emotion beyond their ability.[23]

In the decades of the 1850s most of the men who were leaders of the

Philadelphia bar had family roots back to before the Revolution. George Dallas, William Meridith, William Lewis, Edward Tilghman, Charles Chauncey, Jared Ingersoll, John Sergeant, Horace Binney, Francis E. Brewster, John Cadwalader, Eli Kirk Price, and Thomas Earle were the older members with roots to the past. Peter McCall, Richard C. McMurtie, Moses Dropsie, George Wrundel, J. Alexander Simpson, and David Sellers were gaining recognition; they, too, were mostly of Old Philadelphia stock.

One reason for the increasing interest in the study of law during the Civil War was its intellectual appeal. Several early American lawyers found in the study of law a liberation from the severe theological restrictions of their youth. There was a "romance" in law, said L. J. Bigelow, "but the principal effect on the practitioner is a loss of faith in humanity. In the legal perspective, much more than evangelical, this hard working, pushing society appeared headed for catastrophe and lawyers saw themselves the only guardians. As a result lawyers rose so rapidly to social and financial eminence to the tune of keening despair over the future of the nation."[24]

In 1850, George Sharswood took over the direction of the newly established law department at the University of Pennsylvania. In time the law school broke down the control by the elite barristers over legal training and replaced the long apprenticeship period with a two-year law study course. In 1856 the Supreme Court of Pennsylvania accepted a degree from the law department as evidence of qualification of the applicant for admission to practice. That resulted in some democratization of the Philadelphia bar. In 1799, 72 percent of all the Philadelphia lawyers came from high-income, upper class families; however, by 1860, it was about 35 percent. None of the lawyers in 1800 had come from families of clerks, shopkeepers, or non-English immigrants; however, by 1860, more than one-fourth of all practicing lawyers did. That was because the law school provided greater opportunities for the poorer students than did the elite private law office.[25]

Most new lawyers continued to be trained in law offices. For example, George M. Wharton, a graduate of the University of Pennsylvania, was admitted to the bar in 1827. Henry E. Busch writes that he entered Wharton's office as a student in 1855 and stayed with him as an assistant until Wharton's death in 1870. During those years twenty-five men entered Wharton's office and were directed in their course of reading in law. Wharton did not hold regular examinations, but had an occasionl quiz and frequently held evening meetings when he would talk on some subject of interest to him at the time. He usually drafted his own pleadings, paperbooks, and documents and would require his students to make copies of them for filing or serving on opposing counsel.

Neatness and order were characteristic of Mr. Wharton and his surroundings. There was no confused pile of papers on his table. The papers in each case were carefully folded, endorsed, tied in bundles and made so they would be accessible at any time.

Mr. Wharton possessed an agreeable manner, a good temper and unblemished personal character. Occasional interruption whilst addressing the court or jury never seemed to ruffle his temper or confuse his thoughts. His industry was untiring, he worked without ceasing, the business of his clients was ever on his mind. He seldom, if ever, took a real vacation. He might go to the seashore but would return for visits to his office.[26]

Samuel Dickson wrote:

that when the office was in the dwelling house and the evenings devoted to study and work, it was easy for the preceptor to direct the reading of his students, to test their progress with frequent examinations and to start them on the drafting of documents, pleadings and opinions which made the vocabulary of the law familiar and its technicalities intelligible. But even more valuable were the intimacies which grew out of such relationships, and students lived in an attitude of admiring and affectionate regard for the teacher and exemplar, to whom he looked up—as his learned master in the law. The force and the value of these influences upon the discipline of the bar cannot be exaggerated. After three years in his office the certificate from a gentleman that the applicant for admission was of good moral character meant something, and the friendship between men of different ages as well as between fellow students and contemporaries, gave homogeneity and unity to the bar.

Dickson also wrote that until 1874 "the old District Court was a sort of lawyer's exchange, where all met once a week for friendly and social as well as professional reasons."[27]

Coxe, in writing about the earlier Philadelphia bar also comments on the closeness that came out of the office learning experience. He said "the personal intimacy existing between preceptor and student made it possible for the fame of the lawyer with numerous office students to endure." Coxe felt "the tradition and historical impact of the old offices were of importance to the beginning lawyer. He described the office of Mr. Barclay in the Athenaeum Building on Sixth Street. "The dust of ages, apparently sacred in Mr. Barclay's eyes, for never would he permit its disturbance, covered the myriad pamphlets and the old documents in red tapes, the text books of an earlier era, crazy tables and chairs, carpet that once had a pattern—here with a foxy wig, a rusty suit and silk had still rustier, but a dignified and cultivated gentleman in any garb, however poor or plain."[28]

John C. Bullitt had his office in 1858 at 32 South Third Street. He and his family occupied the upper floors until prosperity and the increasing size of his family led him to acquire the adjoining house, between which he cut doors. In his office Bullitt was described as an autocrat and regarded all of his employees as his personal chattels. At the time of the opening of the new Law School the principal address was made by Mr. Justice Harlan of the United States Supreme Court. While he was in Philadelphia Harlan stayed with Bullitt and made his office his headquarters. Walter Harris was assigned to take care of him, take dictation, do copy work, and do anything else Harlan wanted him to do. "Some years later," Harris wrote, "I was in Mr. Bullitt's office one day taking dictation. When he finished he sat back in his chair and said, 'Harris, did I ever tell you of something that happened while Judge Harlan was here?' I told him he had not, and he said, 'Well when Harlan was leaving he said, "Bullitt, I like that young man who has been doing my work and I would like to take him to Washington with ." I told him he could not have you' Thus," said Harris, "I was disposed of with nothing to say on the matter."[29]

The old successful lawyers of Philadelphia continued to oppose the formation of a law school at the University of Pennsylvania because they wanted to retain control of the training and entrance to the Philadelphia bar. There was some revolt from a few law students who were "restive in the confines of the law offices and eager for a 'less inbred program of legal studies.'" In 1832, when the Philadelphia Bar Association petitioned for an appointment of a professor of law, they compared the University of Pennsylvania unfavorably with Harvard, Yale, and the University of Virginia, which had facilities for the study of law.[30]

In April 1850, George Sharswood, a judge of the Philadelphia District Court, was elected professor of law at the University of Pennsylvania, and he originated a series of law courses. Sharswood began by giving courses more practical than had any of his predecessors. He devoted the first course to the institution of the law of Pennsylvania. There were two classes for beginners, each meeting twice a week, using Blackstone and Kent as textbooks, with formal lectures, informal recitations, and occasional moot courts. Before the second year was over the usefulness and popularity of the system was so great that on 4 May 1852 a complete law faculty was established. It consisted of three professors to cover the institution of law, practices, pleading and evidence, and the law of real estate.

With time Sharwood's new law department broke the control of the city's elite barristers over legal training and replaced the long apprenticeship period with a two-year university course. That had little significance in opening up the chances to enter law, however. The two years at the university plus the law school was something a very few young men could afford. The degree of bachelor of laws was first given at the commencement of 1852 and was granted to thirty men, some of whom were already members of the bar. Soon the degree was given only to students who had attended and passed examinations in the lectures of all three professors for the two years.

Many of the older lawyers and the courts were not very happy about the new law school. The district court, court of common pleas and the state supreme court gave only a slight and grudging recognition to the value of the law school degrees in their regulations for admission to practice. The Law School never had many students, with the average number of graduates from the beginning until 1881 being only fifteen. The size of the Law School work did not require a large faculty, and those who taught continued their law practices after being elected to a professorship. Those men were largely chosen because of their eminence in practice. The University of Pennsylvania law department remained small and local for the rest of the nineteenth century.

In the 1850s there prevailed among the older lawyers the view that the Philadelphia bar was rapidly deteriorating in learning, eloquence, and character. That was undoubtedly due in part to a nostalgia for earlier days distorted through recollection. The old guard's generally low opinion of the young lawyers was that they were uneducated and that was the reason for the general low regard for lawyers. "It permeates all classes, tingeing even educated and liberal minds with prejudice. It has crept into the literature. Be it tragedy, or farce, if a lawyer be introduced, he is the villain or dupe of the piece." The writer said, however, "if the profession of medicine and divinity were subjected to the same trial, how would they endure the test? Let every prescription of the physician and every homily of the clergyman be subjected to rigorous cross-examination, and an acute analysis, by a disciple of some hostile school, while a competent umpire summed up the controversy, and twelve impartial men pronounced their verdict on it and how much quackery and heresy would be laid bare to vulgar eyes?"[31]

Another famous Philadelphia lawyer of the period, F. Carroll Brewster, wrote in 1861 about the rights and duties of the lawyer. He told the beginning lawyer that with their admission to the bar they also had conferred on them privileges and certain duties. The privilege to uphold the law, "it is also your privilege to represent another's cause. Your profession protects all and the fruits of all alike. You are the guardian of the law. He went on to say "you must deny yourself all the temptations which lure you from your office; you must be neither sportsmen of the turf or water; your office must be your theater, concert room, race ground, your home, your everything. Save your church." And he said "if you are not equal to this you are equal to nothing, certainly not equal to success." And above all if you want to succeed you must "cultivate the faculty of being able to sit upon your office chair and stay there. Allow no itching for political distinction to lure you away from your business. If you have spare time, employ it to study. The habit of self preparation is the great secret of success. Trusting to chance leaves the council without a chance. Place yourself in the camp of your adversary."[32]

Of all the professions, up to the time of the Civil War, the lawyer was recognized as the social and intellectual aristocrat of the land. In Philadelphia the ties between the lawyers from old family backgrounds were especially strong. That resulted in several positive factors that could operate on behalf of the favored individual. For example, John I. C. Hare's father was a wealthy man, and Hare was able to study law and become successful as a teacher, writer, and judge. His career was helped along, not only by an old and wealthy family background, but also because he had studied in the office of William M. Meridith and married Horace Binney's daughter. The ability to achieve success often depended less on innate abilities and more on the inheritance of wealth and social standing. By the end of the Civil War era, however, there was some change in the overwhelming dominance of the upper class control of the Philadelphia bar.

Nash did a study of lawyers admitted to the Philadelphia bar from 1800 to 1805 and from 1860 to 1861. He found a striking uniformity of both ethnic background and nativity during both periods. In the two groups only about 6 percent of the lawyers were foreign born, and all of them were British born. Also about 80 percent of the men in both groups had fathers who were American born. For the most part the lawyers were third generation or longer, and overwhelmingly of English and Scotch-Irish extraction. Although the evidence was fragmentary there did not appear to be any clear religious differences between the two groups. Main groupings were Presbyterians and Episcopalians with a few Catholics, Jews, and Methodists. The relative absence of Quakers, especially in the early group, when they were numerically and socially important in Philadelphia, was because they avoided the legal profession.[33]

The two groups did have significant differences in education. Even though college training in the early period was rare, 69 percent of the 1800 to 1805 lawyers were college graduates. By contrast, despite the growth of collegiate education after 1800, the 1860 to 1861 lawyers had only 48 percent college graduates. That was due to a broadening range of economic and social backgrounds from which lawyers were drawn. Nash found that in the early group, lawyers came predominantly from families of wealth, status, and social importance. For those lawyers for whom family background could be determined, 72 percent of them were of upper class derivation. Seven of the forty-three were sons of landowners of considerable wealth, which allowed them to live at leisure on large tracts of land, often acquired by their colonial ancestors. The fathers, with their wealth and status, guided their sons into law. Eleven of the lawyers were from families of mercantile interests. The fathers were numbered among the most illustrious personages of their community. Included in that group were Richard Bache, husband of Ben Franklin's only daughter; Bache later became postmaster general of the United States. Charles Biddle, great uncle of Nicholas Biddle and William Coxe, father of Tench Coxe, were also in that group. Fifteen other lawyers were sons of professional men—lawyers, doctors, doctors, and clergy. Of those fathers, most were scions of prominent, well-to-do families. The rest of the lawyers came from middle or lower class backgrounds.

By 1860 the preponderance of upper class representatives reaching the bar was yielding some ground to an upward surge of the middle class. The drop was from 72 percent in 1800 to 44 percent in 1860. The drop was almost completely the result of the success of the middle class in raising their sons to the profession. About 12 percent, coming out of the lower class, did not change during the sixty years. Many of the old-timers at the bar were upset by the change. One said in 1856, "if the present course be pursued the past glory of Pennsylvania Jurisprudence shall never return."[34]

Nash argued that there was no longer a legal fraternity in Philadelphia in 1860 to 1861 characterized by the unity that earlier bound lawyers together as "a band of confiding brothers." Although the percentage of the bar from the upper class was reduced, however, they still maintained great power and influence in Philadelphia legal circles. Many of the middle class lawyers of 1860 would in time themselves become upper class primarily because they were of the "right" ethnic and religious background. All they needed was wealth and prestige, and several did become very successful. George Sharswood was an example. Many of the middle class lawyers went into the judiciary and politics, areas that generally did not interest the upper class. In legal participation in important cases, the ones of greatest fame, and in the areas of greatest profit, however, those upper class lawyers controlled far more than their 42 percent share in the Philadelphia lawyer market in 1860.

Also important was the organization of greatest legal prestige, the Law Association of Philadelphia. It was organized by upper class lawyers, and they continued to dominate it. In 1855, of approximately 400 lawyers in Philadelphia, 173 belonged to the Law Association. Of that group, at least 70 (40 percent) were from or were themselves of upper class families. That was almost exactly the same percentage of lawyers that Nash found in the upper class. The Law Association had been founded in 1827 and from that date until 1902 there were twelve chancellors and thirteen vice-chancellors (often the same men). Every one of those men were of the Philadelphia upper class. That was also overwhelmingly the case for those lawyers filling the offices of treasurer, secretary, censors, and librarians. The first six chancellors running through 1873 were William Rawle, Peter S. du Ponceau, John Sergeant, Horace Binney, Jospeh R. Ingersoll, and William M. Meridith. Those men were among the greatest of Philadelphia lawyers in the nineteenth century. The Law Association also owned the law library. The cost of membership was $100 for a lifetime membership, and a regular membership was $30 for the first year and $19 each year thereafter. Only those who were fairly wealthy could afford those fees. The library was exclusively for the use of its members, and therefore those who could not afford to belong had no other comparable law library in the city to use. That put them at a severe disadvantage in their practice of law.

At the time of the Civil War there were no women in the practice of law in Philadelphia or anywhere else in the United States. Some of the prejudices against women as potential lawyers is shown in an article published in the *Legal Intelligencer* of Philadelphia in 1855. The article says, in an attempt at humor, that if women were admitted to the bar new rules would have to be made. The following are the writer's twelve new rules:

1. No lady lawyer is ever to kiss the Judge for an arrest of judgement.
2. No lady lawyer is ever to say "My Dears" to the Jury.
3. No cradles allowed in Court, and Attorney's clerks or nurses must stay outside the railing.

4. No consultations with milliners allowed while in session.
5. No argument of Counsel in an ordinary assault and battery case, is to last longer than four hours, and in the case of promise of divorce, not over three weeks to each of the Counsels.
6. Paregoric, Godfrey's Cordial bottles, will not be allowed to be lying around loose in the Court room.
7. Pap spoons are not to be included in the stationary usually furnished to counsels.
8. Apostrophes to infants, such as "Mommy's itty darlin" or "eety tweety cherub ah," and others, will be considered irrelevant and highly improper.
9. "Ride a cock-horse," "Buy a baby bunting," and other melodies are strictly forbidden.
10. The comparison and mutual admiration of babies, will be deemed highly exceptionable, and will be treated as such.
11. The Sheriff, if a man of family, will have the supervision of the Attorney's desk. If he is single, it will be the clerk's duty, and in the case the latter should be too good looking, they will be consigned to the care of the ugliest tipstaff attached to the Court.
12. The penalty for the infraction of the above rules, shall be striking the names of the offending party from the Roll of the Court, and obliging her to attend to her household duties, which latter, is a punishment as severe as any humane Court can allow itself to inflict.[35]

The preceding rules, as well as the rest of the article, not only reflect the contempt for the idea that women might be lawyers but a general contempt for the roles of women. The male view was that by the very nature of being women they were unsuited for the practice of law. Yet, at that time the profession of medicine was opening up for a few women. In Philadelphia, The Women's Medical College of Pennsylvania was the first organized school for the medical education of women and it opened in 1850. Eight women graduated in the class of 1852. Up until that time women had never been trained in the same way as men for the profession of medicine. One of those first women, Hannah E. Longshore, was the first woman to go into practice in Philadelphia. Crowds gathered outside her office to ridicule her and druggists refused to fill her prescriptions. Most male physicians would have nothing to do with her. She did persevere, however, and practiced medicine in the city for forty years.

The Civil War era did begin to see some changes in the Philadelphia lawyer. Although the old upper class continued to dominate there were more opportunities for others. The opportunities were often in the judiciary and in politics, which the old elite continued to reject as unworthy of themselves. Also, with the emergence of the corporate business world, there were significant changes in the practice of law.

Horace Binney, 1780–1875. Courtesy of the Historical Society of Pennsylvania.

Profile 7: Horace Binney (1780–1875)

During the years there have been many great Philadelphia lawyers. Above all the rest, however, tower two giants: Horace Binney and John Graver Johnson. Both men lived exceptionally long lives, and their legal careers overlapped. As a result, between them, they were of major influence on the Philadelphia bar for about one hundred years. Both men were totally committed to the view that the practice of law was the ultimate and true role for one trained in law. Neither man ever had any interest in political positions nor any interest in serving on the bench. Both Binney and Johnson, on at least two occasions, turned down appointments to the United States Supreme Court (see Profile 8: John Graver Johnson).

Horace Binney's father came from Boston to Philadelphia to study medicine and later served with George Washington at Valley Forge. Binney's mother was the daughter of a successful Philadelphia lumber merchant. His father died when he was seven years old, and four years later his mother married Dr. Marshall Spring of Massachusetts and the family moved there. Following a brief period of private tutoring Binney entered Harvard College in 1793, at the age of thirteen, and graduated in 1797 with high honors. Binney first planned on studying medicine but was discouraged from doing so by his stepfather. He returned to Philadelphia where he planned on entering a mercantile office but found no vacancies. Instead he entered the office of Jared Ingersoll to study law.

Ingersoll was one of the two or three most eminent lawyers in Philadelphia at that time, and Binney throughout his life expressed his gratefulness for his chance to have studied law with him. Later in writing about his legal study he said, "this, which may be called the old way, is a methodical study of the general system of law, and of its grounds and reasons, beginning with the fundamental law of estates and tenures and pursuing the derivative branches in logical succession, and the collateral subjects in due order, by which the student acquire a knowledge of principle that rule in all departments of the science, and learn to feel, as much as to know, what is in harmony with the system and what is not—the profession knows this by its fruits to be the most efficient way of making a great lawyer."[1]

As Binney pursued his legal studies he maintained his interest in the broader cultural learning that had been a major part of his experience at Harvard. The beginning of the nineteenth century was still a time when being a lawyer was also to typically be a liberally educated man. Binney continued his extensive reading of both the classics and of general literature. He wrote that he strenuously resisted the social temptations that assailed a young man in a large city, "especially if he can play pretty well on a flute and sing an agreeable song, which I could."[2]

After two years of study, in 1800, he was admitted to the Philadelphia bar. he was twenty years old; however, as he later observed, no attention was paid to the qualification of age, or for that matter anything else. Binney started to practice law at the beginning of the new nation and at a time when the eminent men in American law were strongly concentrated in Philadelphia. In 1800 most of the outstanding lawyers had made their reputations as statesmen and politicians. With the end of the Revolution, and with the move of the federal capital to Washington, D.C., in 1800, the practice of law came to take on new importance. In the decade Philadelphia had been the federal capital several Philadelphia lawyers had made great names for themselves. Along with Jared Ingersoll, there were William Lewis, Edward Tilghman, William Rawle, William Tilghman, and Alexander James Dallas. It was commonly believed that those old leaders of the Philadelphia bar would have graced Westminster Hall in its greatest days. Those were men with a variety of accomplishments and power, and they handled almost all the important legal work in the city. For many of the young men starting in law the future did not look very optimistic because of the dominance by the older generation of lawyers.

Horace Binney, having studied with Ingersoll, gave him some entree into associations with the leaders of the old Philadelphia bar. Nevertheless, Binney had to bide his time, and during the first five years of practice he had only a few clients. He wrote in his memoirs that if he had been compelled to season his porridge with the salt earned by his first years he would have found it quite tasteless. In later years he also wrote that the time was not lost because he would attend the courts and watch the trials. He would also hang around the courts ready for any legal work that might turn up. "If attentive one can learn as much in court as they can in their offices during the same hours, and it will be more use to them as regards the art of managing causes." Those early days of the new country were a time when the insurance business was rapidly developing in Philadelphia, and it was in that legal area that Binney got his start.[3]

Although it took a few years to get started it was not long before Binney was very highly regarded in the Philadelphia legal world. In 1806, when he was only twenty-six years old he was chosen a trustee of the University of Pennsylvania, and by 1812 his income had increased sufficiently to allow him to build a house on Fourth Street just west of Walnut Street. He had built a one-story office adjoining the house, which he occupied the rest of his life.

Horace Binney was a Federalist and believed that a strong, stable, and orderly government was an absolute essential for the preservation of liberty. He believed that the worst enemy of liberty was the unreasoning popular prejudice that was emerging in the politics of parties. Binney held that fidelity, obedience, and submission to the Constitution and to the laws of each state were required of all citizens. For him allegiance was to the nation alone, and his views of Jeffersonian and later Jacksonian political beliefs was never anything but total abhorrence. Horace Binney remained a staunch Federalist all of his life, and after the party was gone he never had any other party affiliation. His judicial hero was John Marshall, who Binney believed applied Hamiltonian principles on the bench as chief justice of the United States Supreme Court from 1801 to 1835.

In 1816 Binney was persuaded to become involved in Philadelphia politics and was a member of the Philadelphia Select Council from 1816 to 1819. On several occasions he declined to be a candidate for Congress, but he once said that, like his preceptor, Jared Ingersoll, "he had at no time in his life a warm predilection for politics." He did have a strong sense of duty as a citizen, however, and he felt that serving on the council met that obligation.

His legal practice continued to grow, and he argued many cases, although none stirred any great interest in the world at large. As one of the counsels of the Bank of the United States, he wrote many opinions on points of commercial law. He also served as an officer in various institutions for philanthropic education and other public interests. He did not in those early years feel that his life was in any way especially eventful, and he held few illusions about the importance of a lawyer's life. He wrote:

if a lawyer confines himself to his profession and refuses public life, though it best for his family, and therefore for his own happiness, it makes sad work for his biographer. You might as well undertake to write the biography of a mill-horse. It is at best a succession of concentric circles, widening perhaps a little from year to year, but never, when most enlarged, getting away from the original centre. He always has before him the same things, the same places, the same men, and, the same end. It is surprising to what extent he has the same clients. His work is always the same in kind and he pursues the same method of doing it. One trial is very much like another and one speech of a lawyer very like all the rest of his speeches. Every question in the longest life of the bar comes within the range of one or two inquiries. Does the thing in controversy belong to A or B, or has C done something to D which he ought not to have done? And after a lawyer has for 30 years employed himself in such inquiries he may write his life in a single sentence. He spent his time investigating facts, which when known did not make him any wiser, or in investigating principles which were of little use but to enable him to investigate and apply the facts. This constitutes the greatest drawback from the profession of law, not merely that the life of the lawyer has great sameness, but that the investigation which cost him the most time and labor do not in the slightest increase his stock of useful knowledge. The facts are forgotten as soon as the verdict is given, and well for the lawyer that they can be forgotten. The biography of lawyers, however eminent, *qua* lawyers, is nothing."[4]

Despite his disparaging comments on the impact of the lawyer there was no calling Binney viewed as higher than that of the law.

Maritime insurance litigation was becoming increasingly important in Philadelphia because of the maritime measures adopted by Great Britain and France against each other's trade during the Napoleonic War. Those measures seriously affected United States commerce and were constantly raising new questions about insurance law. The first important retainer Binney received was in *Gibson v. Philadelphia Insurance Company* in 1808. That involved the correct mode of adjusting a particular average under a clause in a respondentia bond. He demonstrated such ability that he soon had all the insurance business he could handle. In 1808 appeared the first volume of Binney's, *Reports of Cases: Adjudged in the Supreme Court of Pennsylvania*, which he did at the suggestion of Chief Justice Tilghman. That work ultimately reached six volumes and covered all important cases up until September 1814. Those reports were considered very valuable and their accuracy was never challenged. In January 1808 Binney was elected a director of the First United States Bank. His first case in the United States Supreme Court, which he won, was *United States Bank v. DeVeaux*, respecting the rights of a corporation composed of citizens from one state to sue a citizen of another state in the federal courts.

By the 1820s Binney was clearly established as one of the leaders of the Philadelphia bar, and his reputation reached throughout the country. In 1823 he argued the case of *Lyle v. Richards*, one of the two great cases on which his reputation as a lawyer was based. That case involved an intricate discussion of the application of the common law to real property in the state, and his contention was upheld in the court. In 1827 the bar of Philadelphia nearly unanimously recommended his appointment to become chief justice of Pennsylvania, and in 1829 President Andrew Jackson was urged to appoint him to the United States Supreme Court. Both movements were unsuccessful, and he had not been consulted on either occasion. He had no interest in taking a seat on the bench, and he again declined in 1830 an offer for a position on the Supreme Court of Pennsylvania.

By 1830 the strain of long hours of work had began to affect Binney's health. He also felt strongly that the changes brought about after Chief Justice Tilghman's death had seriously affected the comfort and dignity of the practice of law. As a result of those changes he planned to withdraw gradually from the business of the court. He was also very concerned with the federal government because of his strong Federalist principles. Andrew Jackson was to him the incarnation of all that was horrible about Jeffersonian democracy. He was also offended by Jackson's boorishness and social crudeness, and believed that Jackson's veto of the bill to renew the Second Bank's charter was both stupid and reckless.

Even though he wanted to reduce his legal participation, powerful influences were directed at him, and he was persuaded to become a candidate for Congress on the anti-Jackson ticket in 1832. He consented on the understanding that he would not be required to support a protective tariff, that a vote for him should only be considered a vote against Jackson, and that if elected he would not be bound to any party. Binney was elected, and when Congress began in December 1833 he found little attractive about Washington. To Binney it was still a primitive new city of twenty thousand. The journey from Philadelphia was usually by steamboat through the Delaware and Chesapeake Canal to Baltimore and then overland by stage coach. It took most of two days, and in the winter involved considerable exposure and discomfort. Binney found the boarding houses of Washington a poor substitute for his home. His work strain also brought on serious inflammation of the eyes that bothered him all the time he was in Washington.

In the House he was an outstanding figure, but he could do nothing in the face of the Jacksonian majority. Binney felt he could accomplish little in the Congress with its strong currents of political prejudice and partisanship. As a debater he was outstanding, and his speeches were almost always at a very high level. He detested the environment, both physically and politically, and refused to be renominated, however. He said that the experience was a mistake and from that time on he emphatically rejected any suggestion that he return to public office. Binney once said that for him public life would be a perfectly useless martyrdom. He was not a modest man and made it clear he would be wasting his vast talents in the arena of politics.

In 1837 when Binney retired from all court work he was the unquestioned leader of the Philadelphia bar. Even though his career in Congress had been short it had not hurt him in the eyes of Philadelphians. From that time on no other man in the city commanded greater respect or had more influence if he chose to use it than Binney. After his retirement from court work he confined himself to giving opinions, particularly regarding land titles.

Although Binney never had any personal interest in serving on the judiciary, he did have very strong concerns about the courts. He was strongly opposed to the amendment proposed in the Pennsylvania Constitutional Convention of 1837–38, making the tenure of judges for a term of years only, instead of during good behavior. He published an eloquent address to the people appealing to them to vote against it, but the amendment was passed.

As suggested in 1827 when his name was put up for the state chief justice, he played no part in the attempt. He later wrote, "In the time of General Washington and of his immediate successor Mr. Adams, I think it would have been thought less strange for a man to solicit a judgeship than for a lady to solicit a gentleman in marriage." As Burt observed, "Binney declined, as any good Philadelphian should, an appointment to the United States Supreme Court and then, in 1869, after the death of Taney, the Chief Justiceship of the Supreme Court."[5] Binney came to be the model for the Philadelphia lawyer—one who practices law, and later in life, if your peers so value you, gives advice, serves on boards, writes and eulogizes your less durable cohorts. Given the fact that Horace Binney lived until the age of ninety-five, he had the chance to deliver many eulogies. That was the settled and unadventursome life of Binney until he was called forth to argue and win his greatest case and to gain immortality in the annals of American law.

Girard Case

Stephen Girard had been born in Bordeaux, France, in 1750. He became a cabin boy at the age of fourteen and a merchant captain at the age of twenty-three. He settled in Philadelphia in 1777 and entered trade, and was possibly the greatest of all early American financial success stories. In 1812, when the federal government refused to recharter the United States Bank, Girard bought its building and started his own bank, and he also continued his business as a merchant. He died on 6 December 1831, a childless widower, with the largest fortune any man had, until that time, ever amassed in America. In his will he left to his relatives more than $200,000, and several bequests for charitable purposes and public improvements. He left the bulk of his property, worth at that time the unheard of amount of $7 million, to the city of Philadelphia, however. It went to the city in trust to establish and maintain a college for poor white male orphans, between the ages of six and eighteen.

To Girard's way of thinking there was an unfortunate multiplicity of religious sects in America, and he desired "to keep the tender minds of the orphans free from the excitement which clashing doctrines and sectarian controversy are so apt to produce." He provided that the young scholars should be taught "the purest principles of morality," but that "no ecclesiastic, missionary, or minister of any sect whatsoever should ever set foot, even as a visitor, within the college grounds which are to be surrounded by a high stone wall."[6]

Girard's relatives were less than grateful for what they had been left, and they filed a bill in the United States Circuit Court to have the trust declared void. Their grounds were that the city could not be a trustee and that the object of charity was too vague and indefinite to be executed. Later they also attacked the exclusion of ecclesiastics, urging that the college would become a means of propagating infidelity. The case was first argued in the United States Supreme Court in 1843, where three of the justices were absent (among them Story, the recognized authority on equity). A reargument was set for the next term to occur before the full Supreme Court.

The complainants retained Daniel Webster, whose fame at that time was the highest of any member of the American bar. Webster was also a member of the United States Senate. The city of Philadelphia turned to Horace Binney, although he had not been before a court in seven years. During those years he had repeatedly refused to attend court and would deliver no arguments. Great pressure was put on him, however, and his great pride and loyalty to the city finally moved him to take on the case. The early argument had been made by another great Philadelphia lawyer, John Sergeant, who had built his case mainly on Pennsylvania decisions. Binney thought it was necessary to investigate the principles of charitable trusts, however, and the second argument before the court was not simply to be a repetition of the first. Binney had made his acceptance conditional on Sergeant remaining with him on the case, however.

Binney set for himself the very difficult, but at that time still possible, task of studying the legal history of charitable trusts as they had never before been systematically studied in America and probably not even in England. He found that charitable trusts for uncertain beneficiaries had been well known to common law and repeatedly upheld. At the time of Binney's appearance before the Supreme Court, Chief Justice Taney was too ill to sit, and so the case was heard before seven justices with Justice Story presiding.

Binney arrived in Washington in late January with the case to begin on 2 February. The cold weather was very hard on Binney, and he wrote to his son on 27 January, "My cold continues and is to wear off with a cough. I want my voice as much as Old Jenkins said he did when he expected to speak at his hanging." On 5 January, when Binney made his opening statement, he showed that Girard had been quite liberal to his relatives and that, in consequence of the residuary clauses of the will, they could gain nothing by a judgment adverse to the trust. "The only effect of it, beyond their own destruction, is to give [the property] to the City, for her appropriate municipal uses, and to defeat, without the slightest benefit to themselves, the noble charity that their kinsman has instituted for the poor."[7]

The complainants had contended that the law could not uphold a trust in favor of indefinite, unknown persons. Binney undertook to show that the most perfect charitable gift was that where the beneficiaries were least known to the benefactor. He proceeded to establish the validity, demonstrated by references to group after group of unassailable authorities, the successive proposition that the trust was good by the common law of England, which was the common law of Pennsylvania. His accomplishment was to place the Girard trust on absolutely solid legal grounds.

Daniel Webster rose to speak—and did so for the next three days. Most of his oratory was about how the will was an attack on the clergy of America, and he contended over and over that the trust was designed to foster atheistic education among young boys. It was later revealed that Justice Story saw Webster's speeches as being an address to the prejudices of the clergy. Story at the time wrote to his wife, "Even the space behind the Judges, close to their chairs, presented a dense mass of listeners. He [Webster] will conclude on Monday. The curious part of the case is that the discussion has assumed a semi-theological character. I was not a little amused with the manner in which on each side the language of the Scriptures and the doctrines of Christianity were brought in to point the arguments and to find the court engaged in hearing homilies of the faith and expositions of Christianity with almost the formality of lectures from the pulpit."[8]

Webster united his piety with patriotism and confidently expected that a profession guided by Kent and Story would support that Christianity being the fundamental part of common law, and therefore the basis of the American system, would decree that such a contrivance of "French atheism" must not be tolerated in a free republic. Webster did not disappoint those who came to hear him soar into heavenly exultation. He brushed aside Girard's notion of rational benevolence and propounded the thesis that Christianity was basic to common law and thus the fundamental law of Pennsylvania. He asserted that because religion is to be taught only by the clergy, by excluding them, Girard manifestly intended to ridicule them and so send those hapless youth into the world with only deism or atheism as their guide, "equal in defiance of heaven, and in the scorn of law." Webster went on to state that the common law had never sanctioned such a scheme, and the law of Pennsylvania, of which Christianity is a part, must disown and reject it. He said "Girard's project could not be considered charity, either in the Christian sense or in the sense of jurisprudence."

As Webster worked himself up to his ultimate paroxysm of eloquence he wept—and the ladies wept, as did some of the judges. All the founders of America—Puritans, Quakers, and Presbyterians—he thundered, had brought with them the principle of Christianity inherent in the law of the land.

> And where there is any religious sentiment amongst men at all, this sentiment incorporates itself with the law. *Everything declares it*. The massive cathedral of the Catholics; the Episcopalian Church with its lofty spire pointing heavenward; the plain temple of the Quakers; the log church of the hardy pioneer of the wilderness. The mementoes and memorials around and about us, the consecrated graveyards, their tombstones and epitaphs, their silent vaults, their moldering contents; all attest it. The dead prove it as well as the living. The generation that are gone before speak to it and pronounce it from the tomb. We feel it. All, all, proclaim that Christianity, general, tolerant Christianity. Christianity independent of sects and parties, that Christianity to which the sword and the argot are unknown, general, tolerant Christianity is the law of the land."[9]

While Webster, the audience, and some of the judges wept, Horace Binney did not. Binney had asked Sergeant to argue the equity parts of Girard's benevolence. When Binney stood he said the matter before the court was and had to be altogether a matter of law, because the court considers and decides no questions but questions of the law. Binney asserted that the justices had no warrant to ask whether Girard's directions were expedient or disrespectful of the clergy. With his total commitment to legal clarity Binney destroyed Webster's specious piety. Some argued that Binney went on to strike a blow from which the Protestant apparatus never recovered. He quietly and without theatrics said:

> I have no pleasure in a public investigation of even points of law, that requires me to speak on the subject of religion. I desire, therefore, if possible, to raise myself

above those dangers, by treating this question as I have a right to treat it, as a question of law, to be submitted by the court under the responsibility of my professional character and not under the guarantee of my religious opinions. I do not mean to make any profession of them, or to speak of them. I will not suffer my conscience or my conscientious belief to be even named by me. My remarks will be directed to the judicial conscience of the court and if I satisfy that, I can easily satisfy myself that the rest belongs to a different forum.

Binney's argument presented a nineteenth-century concept of legalism demanding that the particular case be examined on its merits. "After eloquence has done its best and worst," Binney said, "counsel must ask whether pains have been taken to discover Girard's design, or only to fulminate ignorantly against what Webster supposes it to have been. The simple and clear question," Binney said, "is whether any of Webster's elocution has for a single minute fairly interpreted the will of Stephen Girard."[10]

Story's decision (in which his fellow justices concurred without altering a word) was an overwhelming defeat for Webster. Story upheld the will and refused to even consider Webster's argument by dealing only with the legal question. For that Story was attacked in the churches. He said that the court had no right to interfere with the state unless it demonstrated contrary to the federal Constitution. He went on to say that Girard had not been malevolent. As long as society agreed that benevolence was, as it must be, the supreme manifestation of Christian culture, there was no reason to accuse his school of atheism. By thus identifying Girard's use of the term "benevolence" with a residual Christian spirit, Story emerged as the champion of secularism which need not be accused of infidelity "in a country composed of such a variety of religious sects as our country." Benevolence allowed Binney to plead that the wealth of the nation could be used for something other than the promotion of the Kingdom of God. "What Binney wrought, whether or not it was his intention, was a fatal dislodgement of Webster's thesis, appropriated from Blackstone, that Christianity in any theological definition must be deemed a part and parcel of American law."[11] The reasoning of Binney took a long time to be understood by either the legal profession or the public.

One dramatic consequence of the famous case was the extent to which the loser lost and the winner won. Webster, who was at the time a U.S. senator, had believed that the case would be a stepping stone to the presidential nomination the following June. The defeat at the hands of Binney, however, was probably the reason he lost that nomination to Henry Clay. For Horace Binney his argument was remarkable for its erudition, scholarship, and power. There are legal scholars who consider it to have been the most brilliant argument ever addressed to the Supreme Court. It came to be universally recognized that the establishment of charitable trusts in general was based on an unassailable legal basic in the United States because of Binney's work. That was Binney's last appearance in court and his greatest triumph.

Binney returned to Philadelphia and for several years he devoted himself to an office practice, investigating and giving opinions on legal questions. That work continued to increase as the years went by. In the spring of 1850 some very severe work brought a recurrence of a serious inflammation of the eyes. He saw that problem, plus his being seventy years of age, as a warning to give up his professional efforts, and thereafter he refused any work except occasionally for a friend. He was not ready to fade into a life of retirement, however. As far as his eyes would permit, and they did get better, he kept himself fully occupied. He was free to read and write what he chose, but rarely did he appear at public meetings. In 1852, John Sergeant died, the last of Binney's fellow law students and his close friend. At that time Binney succeeded Sergeant as chancellor of the Law Association of Philadelphia, of which both men had been among the founders. After two years he declined reelection because of his age.

In 1858 Fisher wrote about Binney in his diary:

> He has a trained, exercised, clear and powerful understanding, a strong energetic character, a combination which forms what he eminently is, a man of affairs, successful in action and business and bringing to both the influence of honorable but not generous or liberal sentiments. He wants imagination and reason, has no vivid perception of beauty or the higher order of truth, prefers the practical and finite to the intellectual and infinite, statesmanship and law to philosophy or poetry. He is a great lawyer, and, except in a democracy, would have been a great statesman. He has not only amassed a great fortune, but was for many years at the head of the bar and consulted on every affair of importance in the city. He is in fact an institution in Philadelphia: an oracle, universally respected.

Fisher went on to write that Binney was "a product of ideas and manners different from those of the present—Binney is respected and admired, but not loved. He is not genial, but hard and cold, exact and severe. He rarely unbends. He seems always conscious of his position. He is, however, courteous and kind in ordinary intercourse. He has always been gracious to me, at times particularly so, recognizing with ready praise and appreciation anything I did worthy of either."[12]

Coming into the 1860s Binney was very concerned with the deepening split between the states. The move toward the breaking of the Union was, in his eyes, the greatest crime against liberty and civilization. Writing in 1860 he said that generally democracy had nothing to do with liberty. "That from the time the Democratic party attained power its aspiration had been for power. It was not power in the government, nor in the law, nor wholly in the party, but it was power in the individuals who formed the party. "The power to partake of the party strength and to seize on it for personal profits and advantages" Binney went on to say, "for sixty years I have seen this accursed love of power, debauching the mature and the young—in the overthrow of judicial tenure, in stripping the judges of the power to appoint their own clerks, in bringing every office down to the individual vote and claim of every man, in lifting up to every man of every sort to clutch at every office or position that will increase his own power, and to culminate and revile everyone not of his party as an enemy of liberty."[13]

Binney also wrote in 1860 that

the democracy of the South is better disposed to good government in general than the democracy of the North; but they are incurably vitiated upon the subject of slavery, and bent on making it a Federal institution. The South has promoted constantly the enfeeblement of the Federal government by interpretation, by internal policy, by arrogance of the States. She had introduced a standard of political morality which gentlemen cannot live by, Both the policy of the South and the bearing of their public men are intolerable to me. I think their bearing must be so to every man in the North who wears a clean shirt preferably to a dirty one. And their institution will keep it so.[14]

With the outbreak of the Civil War Binney supported the Lincoln administration, though he did not approve of all of their actions. The war, however, gave occasion for the first of his series of habeas corpus pamphlets, *The Privileges of the Writ of Habeas Corpus under the Constitution* (1862). In that work he upheld the legality of the president's action in suspending the writ. Two subsequent pamphlets elaborated his argument, and the three together composed what came to be held as a very valuable constitutional treatise.[15]

Horace Binney died 14 August 1875 at the age of ninety-five. His great position in the legal establishment of Philadelphia was undoubtedly due in part to his long life. Binney was a man who in his own lifetime tied the Revolution together with Reconstruction. He had seen and known George Washington, Alexander Hamilton, and the Adamses as well as Abraham Lincoln and Ulysses S. Grant. He had strived to perpetuate the Federalist party in the days of Madison and had fought against the rise of Jacksonian politics. He had defeated Daniel Webster in legal argument and toward the end of his life brought his still highly acute mind to the aid of Lincoln and Grant. Both those men came to Philadelphia to visit him, and pay him the respect due one of his age and great reputation.

His opponents could and did criticize him. They never impugned his motives, his sincerity, or his courage, however. He once wrote, "I may say to my children that I never knowingly committed an injustice toward a client, or the opposite party. I never prosecuted a cause that I thought a dishonest one. I at all times disdained to practice any stratagems, tricks, or artifice for the purpose of gaining an advantage over my adversary." Those might sound like the remarks of self-aggrandizement, but they were also the observations stated even more emphatically by Binney's opponents as well as his friends. Horace Binney might have had as an epithet, "He was the consummate gentleman lawyer of his time."[15]

Although Binney did not come from an old Philadelphia family, his background was highly respectable, and he founded a Philadelphia upper class family. He was for many years unquestionably Philadelphia's leading citizen who was honored and beloved by the city. Burt writes that there is always in Philadelphia at least one Grand Old Man who was the opitome of Old Philadelphia—a man of professional prominence, devotion to the city, extensive participation, impeccable reputation, personal charm, physical handsomeness, family connections, and money. "That was Horace Binney. he was also in Philadelphia's highest tradition not a politician and avoided at all costs publicity and notoriety. Probably no Philadelphian has ever embodied all those traits any better than Horace Binney."[16]

8
Corporate Era: 1870–1890

What do I care about the law? Hain't I got the power?
Commodore Vanderbilt

In the 1870s Philadelphia had 125,000 buildings, three hundred miles of paved streets, 86,000 gas lights, and 339 businesses turning out $335 million worth of goods each year. There were rolling mills, stove works, soap factories, distilleries, brick yards, flour mills, and textile and carpet factories. There were also locomotive works, a wide range of smaller workshops, as well as stores and warehouses. In 1870, the city's population of 675,000 was spread five miles along the Delaware River and had moved west across the Schuylkill River into West Philadelphia.

Not all of the legal questions and the practices of Philadelphia lawyers were overly serious or profound. One example was the legal battle about the church bells of St. Marks, on Locust Street near Rittenhouse Square, which was finished in 1851; however, it was not until the 1870s that the belfry was fitted with the bells made in England. Once the bells were in place they began to ring at 6:45 A.M. on Sunday and three times thereafter for a half an hour at a time. Close at hand lived the best of old Philadelphia society, and they were very unhappy with the loud bells. One account asserted "the bells are loud and harsh, and are rung by a person or persons unskilled in such matters." "My baby," complained a mother, "starts up out of his sleep at the sound of the bells, and it is impossible to put him to sleep again." Because everybody who was anybody lived in the neighborhood something had to be done. The rector refused to stop ringing the bells, however, so the residents did the obvious—they sued. They hired William Henry Rawle, a member of one of the great old upper class families of law in the city. The church countered by hiring George Washington Biddle, of an equally famous old upper class legal family.

Newspaper accounts of the trial reported that forensic eloquence had never known a better day. Rawle compared the bells, as a nuisance, to abattoirs and pig sties, citing ancient precedence. He also impugned the character of Mr. Biddle, but all in fun because they were close friends. He quoted Shakespeare, "Me thought I heard a voice cry sleep no more, Macbeth doth murder sleep." Rawle went on to intimate that the Reverend Dr. Hoffman, "a high-handed priest," was the Macbeth of Locust Street. As for the witnesses, Rawle refused to contrast "the affidavits of Harrison and Cadwalader and Norris" with those of "Michael Fitzgerald, Catherine Harkins, Adeline Blizzard and Patrick Maloney, many of whom cannot read or write and whose signatures had been collected by the Church as those who said they like to hear the bells ring early in the morning."

Biddle, when it came his turn, quoted Cowper, "How soft the music of those village bells," and he made the most of Rawle's class conscious remarks about the witnesses. "Blizzard perhaps is not a highly aristocratic name," he admitted, "but such people who, after all, have to stay in town all year, have their rights and should not have their little pleasures disturbed. Let the rich plaintiffs move on. Let them cross the Schuylkill and go West. Let them follow Horace Greeley's advice," he said, "and cease this petty wrangling, which will do more harm to their delicate systems than any amount of bell-ringing." Despite the appeal to Democracy and the Little People, the court judged that the bells were a nuisance, quite apart from the social station involved. The rich people happened to live right opposite the church, the poor people in sheltered back alleys. The court granted an injunction restraining the defendants from ringing their bells, and the injunction still stands.[1]

In 1870, one in every four Philadelphians was foreign born. In general immigrants, although poor, were quick to adjust their material expectations to American standards. A British consul in 1880 observed that English textile workers in Philadelphia were living very comfortably for workingmen. Back in Staffordshire, he said, "a potter was content to wear a flannel shirt and a handkerchief around his neck from one week's end to another," but soon after he arrived in America he bought "a white shirt and white collar and a nice necktie and a pair of patent leather shoes." A mill owner in Paterson, New Jersey, complained that English immigrants "can make at least half as much again here as in England, but they do not live in the same penurious manner. They come here to enjoy rich food, and want meat three times a day, whereas in England they would be satisfied with cheese and porridge."[2]

The disinterest for political office continued to be the hallmark of the old upper class Philadelphia lawyer. The Senate of the United States has sometimes been called the most distinguished club in America, but during the entire first century of the Philadelphia Club's history (1834–1934) no club member ever sat in the U.S. Senate or inhabited the governor's mansion in Harrisburg. When Senator Logan refused to stand for reelection in 1807, he became the last senator to be elected from Pennsylvania until Boies Penrose went to Washington in 1897. "In fact, Logan, George Mifflin Dallas (appointed in 1831–33), Penrose, and George Wharton Pepper (appointed in 1922 on the death of Penrose and defeated for reelection) were the only members of the First Family sample to represent the state in the Senate."[3]

Between 1850 and 1900 American law continued to undergo dramatic changes. The Far West was settled, and the United States became a major industrial power with transportation and communication vastly improved. The social order became more complex with the development of new social organizations centered around the many new economic interests. There emerged powerful labor unions, industrial combines, farmer's organizations, and occupational associations. Those interest groups vied for power and in doing so strongly influenced and shaped American law. People were coming together in groups, not simply for mutual help, but often in defining an enemy and to make common cause against the outsider. Organization came to be a law of life, not simply because life was so complicated but even more because life appeared to be a constant competitive struggle. For example, it was often believed that life was a game: If the railroads won, farmers lost; if labor won, employers lost. Competition was the economic theme, and it was increasingly between large organizations.[4]

The complex new world of machines led to a rapid increase in personal injury suits and those suits were of major legal importance as well as a new source of income for lawyers. With the great expansion of commerce also came a wide variety of contracts, both maritime and domestic. The increase in the value of land meant greater complexity in title searches. All of those changes raised new questions that often involved intricate points of law. After the Civil War what was needed was a legal system that would provide uniformity, equality, and certainty. The major source of social change was economic and that affected every aspect of life including the legal order. The new methods of manufacturing replaced individual artisans and new combinations of power and resources demanded the vast amassing of capital needed to carry out the new activities. The old values of liberty, liability, contract, and property based on individual concepts were giving way to new interpretations based more on the concept of social independence. "Where the law of the first half of the nineteenth century was developed in the direction of strengthening and preserving individual rights, the law of the second half was developed in the direction of creating, reorganizing, and regulating the great combinations that were emerging."[5]

Any concept of business is dependent on laws to govern the many complex relationships. Each of the parties have a vested interest that has to be resolved in a way acceptable to all concerned. Increasingly that became the function and responsibility of the legal system. Business law, like any law, had to be enforced, or it would be meaningless. As late as Blackstone the word "contract" was a rarity in English (and thus American law). When it became necessary in the eighteenth and nineteenth centuries to develop a complex body of business law and fit it with appropriate government action, neither the British nor American legal professions had much legal precedent on which to build.

Friedman writes that in hindsight the development of administrative law seemed mostly to have been a contribution of the twentieth century with the creation of the Interstate Commerce Commission (ICC), in 1887, seen as the genesis. The ICC was the first great independent regulatory commission by the federal government. In a wider sense, however, there had been a great deal of administrative law in the later decades of the nineteenth century—for example, the federal post office. The ultimate tests of the effectiveness of law and government were pragmatic because American society was making more and more demands on and through government. Control came to be the key concept; in a society of mass markets, mass production, and giant enterprises, the individual became relatively insignificant. To the general public it seemed the only workable means of control was through the law, and the solution was for the agencies of control to become increasingly administrative. That is, more and larger agencies of civil servants were charged with a continuous, steady job of monitoring some segment of business or of life. That was because the traditional agencies of government could not regulate big business nor were the courts very effective as regulators.[6]

There were two publicly expressed reasons given for the general corporation laws. The first reason was to protect the public from the special privileges that corporations had devised for themselves when each could draw up its own act of incorporation with the support of a friendly state legislature. The second was to encourage commerce and industry. There was great economic risk in an industrial society, and the corporation had obvious advantages in reducing the risk. Division of ownership could be offered through stock to small investors who knew they would not be personally liable for the debts of the company. Although the stockholders could share any windfall profits, they were protected by "limited liability" and so were protected from unanticipated losses. "The high priest of the new metaphysics of property were the lawyers. Lawyers came to preside over the mysteries of corporation law. No layman could imagine all the new ways of building, combining, and controlling corporate wealth which lawyer's might concoct. They made the subtleties of Duns Scotus and Aquinas look like child's play. Property became a new realm of the occult."[7]

The advantages of the corporation were very clear. When a man did business by himself or in partnership he could go bankrupt, have his home, land, and any other property seized if he guessed wrong in his ventures. Each partner would be fully liable, personally, for all losses. If the business was done as a corporation, however, the worse that could happen would be the loss of the money already invested. If the corporation went under it was the creditors or other victims, but not the proprietors, who would be responsible for the financial losses.

By 1870 corporations held a commanding position in the American economy. By the 1880s the religious and political reformers were shouting against trusts and antitrusts. In 1890 the Sherman Antitrust Act was passed, but there continued to be strong controversy. Change occurred, but it was around particular kinds of corporations—those of banks, railroads, and insurance companies. For the most part corporation law developed through private practices with court legislation playing only a minor role. The pattern was for courts to turn practice into law as they encountered it through litigation, and the general trend was to allow corporations to do largely what they wanted.

One intent of the Sherman Antitrust Act had been to create a doctrine of greater honesty toward stockholders and creditors, but the act only did so in so far as honesty did not interfere with the efficiency of business. Management and directors were allowed to run their business so long as the courts believed their business decisions were made in good faith. In the ordinary course of business, stockholders had little legal recourse if the business decisions turned out wrong. That was justified as a calculated risk the individual investor took against the great potential profit. Those developments meant that corporations hired lawyers in large numbers and therefore contributed greatly to the rise of many law firms.

After the Civil War the belief increased that law was a subject that should be taught in the universities, and the major impetus came out of the Midwest through the establishment of the land grant colleges. In 1868 the University of Iowa established a law school, as had a private institution, Washington University in St. Louis, a year before. The pattern of the early law schools was to have lectures given by professors with their students taking extensive notes. There was little or no class discussion involving students.

There continued to be strong resistance among many lawyers to law schools taking over the legal training. In Philadelphia the resistance came mainly from the old establishment lawyers. One commonly stated objection was that what law schools taught would have little application in the real world of the practicing lawyer. Probably the main concern was that the law school would take away from the old guard control of who could practice. Once the law school did became important, however, it was taken over and controlled by the old Philadelphia bar. The old guard ran it, did the teaching, and continued to control who was admitted to the bar.

John Marshall Gest wrote about the legal education he experienced at the University of Pennsylvania in about 1880. He described legal education as a method or system of reading, instruction and observation that was designed to fit a student to practice at the bar. First, it meant method. The course of education must be systematic. Second, it required reading because the law was found only in books. Third, the student should have instruction by preceptor and law professor to guide him. Four, the student must observe the routine of legal procedures and methods of practice of courts and lawyers. Last, the object of legal education was to fit the student for the actual practice of the profession.[8]

In 1879 in Philadelphia the rules for admission to the bar required that an applicant must, before registering with the prothonotary as a student at law, be in the office of a practicing attorney. The candidate had to undergo an examination covering the branches of what were considered a good English education. If he held a diploma from the University of Pennsylvania, however, that was accepted in place of the examination. The student was then required to serve a regular clerkship in a law office, under the direction of his preceptor for three years and then, having attained the age of 21, pass an oral examination. That was given by the Board of Examiners, appointed by the judges of court of common pleas and the orphans court. The examination might be dispensed with in the case of a graduate of the University of Pennsylvania Law School, provided the candidate had been duly registered and served a clerkship in the office of his preceptor.

As those changes occurred in the education of the Philadelphia lawyer many of the older lawyers were not happy with them. For example, Robert Coxe, in writing about the 1860s and 1870s in Philadelphia, described the cheerful Sundays and bright summer holidays in Fairmount Park "when and where was wont to congregate a coterie of lawyers. The recollection of these incomparably enjoyable episodes compels the thought that the picturesque and genuinely social side of our professional life is no longer a distinguishing feature of it." He wrote "that was no longer a feature of professional life and conditions had changed, mostly because of legal education. It is open to question," he wrote in 1906, "whether the Law School turns out as good lawyers as were the best types of those who served their undivided apprenticeship in the old fashioned and sufficiently equipped and conducted law office. In truth there is nothing like the association of youth; and no attachments can take firm root in the lecture room or the moot court like those developed in the intimacy of the front office."[9]

Coxe went on to write that "daily there was an affectionate intercourse between what was, really, a preceptor, and what were, really, pupils. One substantial evidence of this is found in the unquestionable fact that the lawyers of today are, in the main, of a monotonous pattern. Of course, their work is well enough done, but in court and out of court the individuality has departed and the picturesqueness of the social side of life has left it." Coxe further asserted that "one fact proves the law office was more successful than the law school as an agent for maintaining a standard of conduct—the several individuals who have of late years been disbarred for unpardonable violations of professional ethics, were, without exception, the exclusive products of law school. An unprincipled or dishonest youth is speedily discovered and unmasked in the law office."[10]

Women in Law

Women were able to obtain university and professional training in the Midwest and West before they could in other parts of the country. It was estimated that by the 1870s more than eleven thousand women were enrolled in about 580 institutions of higher education, with most of them earning degrees in education. Women in the late 1800s were severely restricted by a system that clearly defined what and where they could be educated. The eastern cities, when compared with the Midwest, had more rigidly enforced views as to appropriate behavior for women. Basically, education was seen as acceptable for women as long as it was a pastime and not a preparation for a professional career. Under no circumstances should it ever interfere with her roles of wife and mother.

Women found it much more difficult to become lawyers than doctors, although both professions were extremely difficult to enter. In 1885, there were in Philadelphia approximately thirteen hundred lawyers of which only one, Caroline Kilgore, was a woman. For the same year there were about fourteen hundred physicians in the city, and fifty of them were women.[11] The difference may have been because the legal profession was more institutionalized and generally had control over licensing powers earlier than did the medical profession. Arabella Mansfield was probably the first woman in modern times to be allowed to join the bar when she was admitted in Iowa in 1869. The first woman law student in the United States was Lemma Barkaloo, a Brooklyn woman who had to go to St. Louis to get her legal education. The first woman to receive a law degree was Ada Kepley in 1870 from Union College of Law in Illinois (later Northwestern University).

The federal courts were even slower than some of the states to admit women. In 1869 Myra Bradwell was denied admission to the Illinois bar. The United States Supreme Court upheld that exclusion with Justice Joseph Bradley giving his notorious opinion that "the natural and proper timidity and delicacy which belong to the female sex evidently unfits many of the occupation of civil life. The paramount destiny and mission of women are to fulfill noble and benign offices of wife and mother. This is the law of the creator. And the rules of civil society must be adapted to the general contributions of things, and cannot be based on exceptional cases."[12] Although schools like the University of Michigan and Boston University admitted women in 1870 the elite law schools of the East continued for years to reject them.

There were a variety of sexist explanations given by the law schools for their refusal to admit women. Given were such reasons as coeducational classes creating a serious diversion of the attention of the male student or because women "had not the mentality to study law." Another assertion was that "only a woman of dubious virtue would want to know about cases of rape, adultery, and prostitution." Still another rationalization was that women could not be successful at the bar because they were too kind. An example of the typically pompous explanations was "the law of nature destines and qualifies the female sex for the bearing and nurturing of children and for the custody of the homes of the world and their maintenance in love and honor. And all life long callings of women, inconsistent with these radical and sacred duties of their sex, as in the profession of law, are departures from the order of nature; and once voluntary, treason against it."[13]

Belva Ann Lockwood graduated from the Law School of the National

University in Washington, D.C., and was admitted to practice in the district courts in 1873. In 1879, by an act of Congress, women lawyers were permitted to argue cases before the United States Supreme Court, and Lockwood was the first to do so. By 1882 there were five-sixty women attorneys in the United States, of whom thirty-one had graduated from law schools.

The famous trial lawyer Clarence Darrow once said to a group of women lawyers in Chicago: "You cannot be shining lights at the bar because you are too kind. You can never be corporation lawyers because you are not cold-blooded. You have not a high grade of intellect. You can never expect to get the fees men get. I doubt if you can make a living." In New York State, women were not permitted to practice law until 1886. The *New York Law Journal* printed an editorial opposing the idea and suggested that women would play with the law in much the way they play with fashion; one year contracts would be short; the next year, they said, women would make them stylishly long.[14]

The first woman Philadelphia lawyer was Caroline Burnham Kilgore. She had been orphaned at the age of eleven and managed to support and educate herself entirely on her own earnings, first as a domestic worker and later as a teacher. She was also the first woman to receive the M.D. degree in New York State. Kilgore moved to Philadelphia in 1871 and applied for admission as a student at the University of Pennsylvania Law School and was turned down. She then studied privately and in 1873 applied to the Philadelphia Board of Examiners for admission to the bar. The board refused to examine her on the ground that there was no precedent for the examination of a woman for admission to the Pennsylvania bar. She next applied to the state supreme court, but, although the chief justice complimented her on her argument, he also denied her appeal. In 1881 the state legislature passed a bill allowing women to be admitted to the legal profession, and she then applied again for admission to University of Pennsylvania Law School and was accepted. In 1883 she received her degree of bachelor of laws.[15]

Kilgore's battles were not over. She was admitted to orphan's court in 1883, but when she applied to Common Pleas No. 2, Judge Hare refused her admission on the ground that the eligibility of women was a matter for the legislature. Her application to Common Pleas No. 3 was denied for the same reason, plus the additional ground that she was a married woman. Finally, Common Pleas No. 4, in an elaborate opinion, admitted her to practice, which she did for the rest of her life in Philadelphia. Initially she was in practice with her husband but after his death took over his clients. In a newspaper story in 1908 Kilgore, in referring to her early days, said "those were the days when lawyers were students of the law, when cases were tried carefully and when one went into the courts with the implicit faith that justice would be obtained. And those were the days when men were so narrow-minded that it was 16 years after I started the study of law before I was admitted to practice in the courts of Philadelphia."

In 1886, Kilgore was named a master of chancery in Philadelphia. She was a very strong supporter of the suffragist movement and gave powerful speeches on the rights of women before the Pennsylvania legislation. After completion of her term as master of chancery one writer said, "Mrs. Kilgore has won the respect and the confidence of the bar and the courts and the character of the business intrusted to her proves that she has gained the confidence of the public." It appears that Kilgore never tired of new challenges. In 1909, the year of her death, she was actively involved in a new pursuit—hot air ballooning.[16]

Once the first women achieved the right to study and practice law many believed there would be a great surge by women to enter law. Some argued that would be good because it would humanize the law as a result women's alleged "finer natures." Others saw the possible increase as bad, however, because they believed women were inferior by virtue of their gender and would distract from the high esteem of the Philadelphia bar. Whatever the beliefs, however, the number of women who actually sought a career in law were very few for many years. In Philadelphia it was not until 1900, seventeen years after Kilgore's admission to the bar, that another woman lawyer appeared.

In New York it was not until 1886 that the first woman, Kate Stoneman, was admitted to the bar. Unlike Philadelphia, however, there were several women entering the bar by the end of the century. The demand for legal educational opportunities in New York City for women grew dramatically. That was because of a combination of increased technology and cheap immigrant labor that freed many middle and upper class women from many of the household duties that had occupied their time. Some of them turned to education, and they wanted something more than the busy work with which many women were forced to be satisfied.[17] The New York bar, although far from open toward women, was better than Philadelphia. The upper class dominance of the Philadelphia bar continued well into the twentieth century, and they made it practically impossible for women to enter the bar.

Black Lawyers

It was during the Reconstruction period that many American colleges and universities were establishing law schools. With the establishment of law schools that allowed for qualifying to practice law careers opened up for the first time for blacks to enter law. Howard University and several other Southern colleges founded law schools during that period. Charlotte E. Ray was the first woman graduate of Howard Law School in 1872. Between 1871 and 1876, 62 students received the L.L.B. degree from Howard, and from 1881 to 1903 there were 319 graduates.[18]

Segal writes that blacks who dreamed of becoming lawyers believed that Philadelphia, home of the Quakers who had been supportive of them during their slavery years, would be a likely place to enter the practice of law. They found that it would be many years before that dream would be realized, however. Blacks were systematically barred from any practice of law in the city. The best information suggests that Philadelphia had its first black lawyer after the Civil War. One study, a careful listing of occupations of blacks in Philadelphia compiled in 1859, had no evidence of any black lawyers. According to the *Directory of the Colored Members of the Philadelphia Bar* the first black lawyer appearing there was Theophilus J. Minton, admitted in 1887. Aaron Mossell, Jr., became a member of the Philadelphia bar in 1893, and five more blacks were admitted before 1900. DuBois noted in 1899 "There are at present 10 practicing Negro lawyers in the City [Philadelphia]. . . . Two of those are fairly successful practitioners. . . . Three others are with difficulty earning a living at criminal practice in police cases, and the rest are having little or no practice."[19]

After the Civil War, as specialization and greater social stratification of the bar occurred, the top lawyers and the new law firms were taking over the highly rewarding new fields of tort liability, patent law, and corporate reorganization. The prestige attached to the corporate lawyer put the big city lawyer at the top of the legal hierarchy. The period also saw the continued shift from advocacy to counseling as the frock-coated courtroom orator was being replaced by the "office man." The new corporate-styled leader of the bar was policy oriented, and his managerial role directed him to look at the major issues that threatened his client's welfare. The principle of loyalty to one's client was becoming paramount rather than any ethic of public interest.

There was a lack of professionalism of the bar during the "era of decadence," which lasted until about 1870. Pound said that "there came to be, not a bar, but so many hundred or so many thousand lawyers, each lawyer unto himself, accountable only to God and his conscience—if any." The formation of the Association of the Bar of the City of New York in 1870 marked the end of the decline. The association was originally formed by a small group of leading New York lawyers, principally to combat the Tweed Ring's corruption of New York lawyers. That revitalization of the organized local bar led to the countrywide movement by the formation of the American Bar Association in 1878. In addition, many more local bar associations were organized. The development of legal education owed a great debt to the cooperative effort of the organized bar and law teachers.[20]

The American Bar Association began in 1878 at Saratoga Springs, New York, with 75 lawyers. Francis Rawle of Philadelphia attended and became the first treasurer, and for twenty-four years he was an influential member of the organization. The first period, from 1878 to 1892, was a time of professional development and the leaders were mostly the older lawyers from the Civil War era. In the early years the membership was fewer than 1,000, and the annual meetings were attended by only 75 to 150 lawyers. For the first years the association was mainly a social organization where the elderly gentlemen met on the porch after lunch and planned what the association was going to do during the next year.

The Law Association of Philadelphia was founded in 1827 and until 1900 was almost totally dominated by the old upper class lawyers of the city. Each of the first thirteen chancellors was either from an old upper class family or the founder of one. Those chancellors, the great lawyers of the nineteenth century in Philadelphia law, included William Rawle, John Sergeant, Horace Binney, Joseph Ingersoll, George W. Biddle, and Samuel Dickson. About the only great name missing was John G. Johnson, and that was because he had very little to do with the association. To most lawyers in the city, however, to become Chancellor of the Philadelphia bar was the highest professional honor a lawyer could ever achieve.

The Law Academy of Philadelphia was organized in 1821 and continued until 1882. It functioned as a social, and to some extent professional, association for the older lawyers in the City. Possibly its greatest value was for the younger, beginning lawyers. The Law Academy made some contributions to legal training when the law school was not meeting that need by providing its members with a library as well as moot court experiences. John Marshall Gest joined in 1879 and wrote that they met every Wednesday night in one of the court rooms of Common Pleas Court No. 2 where the young men presented arguments before a group of judges and distinguished lawyers. "The arguments were well attended and after adjournment some of us were apt, in walking home to stop for liquid refreshment in saloons that adorned Samson Street or stopped at Pinelli's for a half dozen of his incomparable fried oysters washed down with a mug of ale."[21] The Law Academy was also dominated by the lawyers of old Philadelphia families. There were only three Provosts over its almost fifty years, Peter Stephen du Ponceau, Thomas Sergeant, and George Sharswood, all of whom were or became upper class Philadelphians. Of thirty-one vice-provosts during those years thirty-three (74 percent) were upper class.[22]

Gest in writing about admission to the Philadelphia bar in 1880 said "it was delightfully informal. It was conducted orally by the Board of Examiners that were appointed by the Judges. There were ten of them, all practicing lawyers, who soon ascertained, when faced by the trembling candidate whether he knew anything. It lasted about one-half hour. My question was mainly on the second book of Blackstone and on the practice of replevin, foreign attachment and suits in promissory notes. When a candidate showed himself to be uncertain on one subject, the examiner tried him on something else, and sometimes he was grilled for hours."[23]

By 1880 the population of the United States was slightly more than 50 million with a little more than 64,000 lawyers in the country. That was a ratio of 1 lawyer per 770 population, a significant increase from 1870 when the ratio had been 1 to 945. In Philadelphia the ratio of lawyers was higher than nationally, with 1 lawyer per 614 of the population. Of those Philadelphia lawyers it has been estimated that probably less than one-third of them were self-supporting, and not more than 100 of them had incomes of more than $5,000 a year. There were a few, Bullitt, Dickson and Johnson, who earned $100,000 a year or more.

During this era there was a dramatic increase in the number of lawyers being admitted to the Philadelphia bar. During the Civil War period the average had been about 50 each year. But during this time span the average number of new lawyers each was about 90.

The increase in the number of lawyers meant a greater awareness and desire for professional control within the legal world. In 1880 the Law Association amended their charter in order to adapt greater power to existing requirements and to make them more efficient. The Association's objectives were: (1) general supervision of the conduct of members of the bar; (2) the improvement of the law and its administration; and, (3) keeping up the law library. At that time the law library had nearly 16,000 volumes, "the collection being especially strong in Reports and in Sessions Laws of the different United States."[24]

By 1880 the great stylistic orators were disappearing, although a few remained who could "cultivate the art of eloquent utterance before juries." John P. O'Neill was described as "a cultivated gentleman with a Trinity College, Dublin degree, delightfully fluent speaker, gifted with handsome winning presence, possessing an educated Irishman's thorough command of the very best English; and a fascinating delivery." Another was David Paul Brown. It was said that "his style of addressing juries was pompous and ponderous. There was more of the actor than the forensic orator in his performance. He had, with a really meager equipment, acquired a popular reputation as a great orator, and in his day, the prestige accompanying this preposterous estimate of him had, undoubtedly, great influence with juries. Such a theatrical poseur as Brown, with his dandified manners, his conspicuously displayed gold snuff-box, the elaborate costume with which he clothed his bejewelled person, and his stilted and deliberate utterance, might amuse present-day audiences and juries, but he would neither seriously entertain or control."[25]

The oratorical style of practicing law had become best suited to the small community with relatively simple legal questions. With the rise of big business and new and complex legal practices that rapidly cut into the monopoly held by the old oratorical style, however, there came to be new and different ways of getting, keeping, and serving clients. "Then, too, the sheer mass of business had an effect, as dockets became swollen there had to be an end to the leisurely pace of litigation."[26] Furthermore, after 1870, there was increasingly a more matter-of-fact attitude and a distaste for litigation because it was becoming too costly, and increasingly the successful lawyer kept his clients out of court.

From early in the nineteenth century there had been some partnerships among lawyers, but there were no law firms with large memberships until near the end of the century. The earlier partnerships were almost always a two-men affair where the division of labor was typically one "office" member and one "court" member. Those men frequently operated without a formal agreement of partnership. In 1872 there was only one law firm in New York City listed in Hubbell's *Law Directory* with as many as six partners.[27]

During much of the nineteenth century, law partnerships were considered unprofessional and even to locate a law office near the commercial centers was in frowned on in practice. Toward the end of the nineteenth century, however, the great increase of commercial business forced the need for law partnerships. In Philadelphia, as in other American cities, New York served as the model for the development of law partnerships. Efficiency and reduction of costs were seen as their great advantages. The great Philadelphia lawyer John G. Johnson never felt the need for partners, however. He, at various times, would take on a few capable lawyers who were glad to work for him as his assistants. His great brilliance and capacity made him a law firm in himself, and at his death his clients provided the major impetus for the growth of several Philadelphia law firms.

The new law firms that developed in Philadelphia seldom had more than three or four partners, and they took in no legal associates except for a few unpaid students who were preparing for their bar examinations. In the new corporate era, lawyers, who had previously rarely been called into business transactions until litigation occurred, were being called on to organize the new corporations and to supervise the increasing number of security issues. The most important corporate retainers went to those lawyers who had already achieved high professional success. It was in that new setting of corporate law that John G. Johnson made his fame and his millions. The practice of law was increasingly the drafting of legal documents to create, consolidate, and reorganize corporations and to affect public issues of securities. Corporate lawyers were also advising on a variety of questions of law and business that arose daily in the business operation of their clients.

In the 1880s in Philadelphia, title companies and trust companies were gaining a solid foothold, much to the distress of the bar. Traditionally it had been the bar that had acted as conveyancer, title searcher, and general depository; those tasks had provided an important source of income for many lawyers. The 1880s were still a time when estate funds were often placed in personal strong boxes and in accounts set up by the lawyer with the lawyer's honor and conscience as the only safeguards. Increased competition, cut-rate fees, and a continuing economic depression were undermining the financial success of the legal profession, however. "The old guard shook its head sadly and blamed it on the newfangled law schools as they asked what better could be expected of those machine-turned, store-clothed graduates?"[28]

The press was heavily into muckraking, and popular targets were the leaders of the bar—especially those who were making money from the big corporations.

Most strikingly, the one great exception was Johnson, to whom the press was uniformly friendly. Although he made great amounts of money, he was also known to help the poor by taking on their cases. Even though Johnson was highly admired, that was not always true of other top lawyers in the city. For example, John C. Bullitt was criticized for running a "law factory" with thirty young lawyers working for little or no pay. The bar was also in conflict in other ways. For example, when Judge Amos Briggs ran for reelection, two-thirds of the bar attacked him for his egotism, eccentricity, overbearing manner, and submission to those of influence. It was a time when fist fights between lawyers would break out in court.[29]

The corporation was providing their lawyers with legal work that was never ending because the very nature of the corporation as a legally created artificial entity made lawyers continuous participants in their activities. There were always new questions, new conflicts, and new procedures that called for legal expertise. As the corporations grew larger the lawyers were increasingly rewarded. Many of those lawyers earned their rewards because the hard-driving first generation of great capitalists put strong pressure on their lawyers to justify their corporate interests legally. "The lawyer who started out at the beginning of post-Civil War period as the intellectual architect of the newly expanded corporation found himself as the end of the period as also the interpreter and/or repulser of restrictions imposed by the federal government."[30]

There was also the emergence of the contingency fee. There were few other issues that cut so deeply into the social mores of the industrial age. That was because of clear social class and ethnic biases. Those who had industrial accidents and surviving members had to bear the full cost of the risk of being in dangerous work. Legal services were available to only those who could afford them. The contingent fee was a necessary financial means to attain legal services by personal injury victims who had no other resources. The negligence lawyer claimed a high percentage from his successful suits to compensate for his many losses. The costs to the legal system were high, however. There were enormous pressures to litigate with great expense and long delay, which worked to the employer's advantage.[31]

Lawyers were making public policy because that was the nature of the political process in America. Because public policy was being established by lawyers along legal lines lawyers alone were familiar with the vagaries and intricacies of the law. A great part of the modern esteem by which the legal profession is held comes from the careful work those early lawyers did in the foundation and development of big business empires. The corporation lawyer was in reality a businessman; he had something to sell—an intangible. "The intangible could be the advice or the outline of a unique course of action which the lawyer presents to bring about the results desired by his client. The lawyer inhabits literally, a paper world; when he looks at capitalism he sees an endless vista of contracts, in one form or another, prescribing duties, rights, obligations, promises."[32]

The corporation lawyer learned to work quietly and anonymously behind the scenes. He also learned, as a professional duty, to be even more close mouthed than the banker, because the whole basis of the lawyer-client relationship rested on the client's ability to confide freely to his lawyer. The names of many of the greatest of those lawyers were unknown to the general public. That was a far cry from the earlier lawyer well known because of his courtroom oratory where his publiic fame contributed to his reputation and his rewards. Law was continuing to change from the open and often powerful impact of the spoken word to the closeness of the technically written word of the legal craftsman, however.

The practice of law was also being influenced by technological change. By 1875, the typewriter that revolutionized general office procedures, including those of the lawyer, came on the market. An advertisement in the *Legal Intelligencer* in 1875 read: "This wonderful machine can be played by a child. In a short time you can write 50 to 100 words per minute. Will manifold from 3 to 20 copies at once. No repairs, inking, or oiling. Always ready for use. Saves printers bills. Over 100 law firms now using them. Price $125."

The new work of the lawyer was within specific limits because he geared his service to meet the needs of a particular client. Of course, from the largest corporation to the individual citizen, what was always wanted was a legal decision most favorable to the client. The competition among lawyers became intense because for a modest fee there were a variety of practitioners of varying skills also seeking clients. In Philadelphia there were still a relatively few lawyers with the proper social backgrounds who monopolized the most rewarding clients, and they were the lawyers who gained great power and wealth. For the rest the practice of law was often perilous, and there was a constant need for sharpness and aggressiveness if they were to survive. Many of them did not survive as lawyers. Although what was important in law was often very different from the past it was still men of the old upper class background who dominated the financially rewarding practice of law in the city.

There was sometimes hostile criticism directed at the new corporation lawyer. For example, in the eyes of some of his legal colleagues, David Rudley Field, a leading New York lawyer, was guilty of chicanery because he promoted the interests of such "criminals" as James Fisk and Jay Gould. As a result of those clients Field came close to being expelled from the Bar Association. There were certainly several corporate lawyers who if not breaking the law were certainly bending it. Some lawyers found fortune if not fame in devising legal formulas by which monopolists rode to power while escaping the penalty of the law. Those in commerce and business, absorbing as they did the lion's share of prestige, left some lawyers of taste and traditional ideas doubtful about the country of their birth.

History has not given corporation lawyers of the nineteenth century much respect or admiration. The usually anonymous office lawyer was without the glamour, real or imagined, of the old courtroom orator. Levy suggests it may be that in academic circles and among social critics there has been a "liberal" orientation that blinded those writers from being able to see any authentic inventiveness of creativeness among the early corporation lawyers "even though the intellectual and social creativity of these men within their own framework may be breath-taking."[33]

In 1885, in Philadelphia, of all lawyers listed in the *Social Register*, 73 percent of them lived in the city. Almost all the rest lived in the suburbs of Germantown, Chestnut Hill, or along the Main Line. Of those who lived in the city about one-third lived in the immediate Rittenhouse Square area, and nearly all the rest were between Market and Lombard and Third and Twenty-fourth Streets. There was only one *Social Register* lawyer who lived north of Market Street, where simply "nobody" lived.

With the ever-increasing number of lawyers in Philadelphia, a decreasing percentage of them were of the old upper class. In 1875 there were approximately eleven hunderd lawyers, and by 1885 about thirteen hundred lawyers listed in the *Philadelphia City Directory*. Of those lawyers, 22 percent in 1875 and 19 percent in 1885 were also listed in the *Social Register*. The Philadelphia Bar Association continued to be dominated by the upper class mainly because most other lawyers in the city did not belong. In 1875 there were 38 percent; in 1885 39 percent of all lawyers in the city belonged to the Bar Association. In 1875 42 percent and in 1885 37 percent of those who belonged were listed in the *Social Register*. As mentioned earlier, however, the leadership of the Bar Association was almost totally dominated by lawyers of the old upper class.

One of the chancellors of the bar during the period was George W. Biddle. Because of his social background and his natural ability he was seen as the logical successor to Judge Sharswood as the leader of the city's legal profession. It was written of Biddle that his manner equaled his position, and a certain austerity overlay warmth and humor. Furthermore, it was said "his citations were moss covered and whenever he could he drew from English law." Biddle had been helped when he started on the bench by Judge Allison. In one of Biddle's early cases he turned to his colleague, who was listening to the long argument with his usual patience. "Why, Judge, have you any doubt about this?" he asked. "Not the slightest," replied Judge Allison, "but you know if we are going to decide against him, we must hear him."[34]

Richard C. McMurtie, brother-in-law of George Biddle, was another chancellor of the Philadelphia bar. He was described as having for the law a feeling of loyalty like that of knight to the lady of his choice. Biddle took judicial decisions he believed to be unsound as a personal insult. He did not have the long-winded style of many advocates because he spoke briefly and to the point, often expressing himself with almost brutal frankness. To a judge who interrupted him to express dissent he said: "Your Honor, I am addressing myself exclusively to those members of the court who do not make up their minds until the conclusion of the argument." Once, when appearing before

President Benjamin Harrison to urge the appointment of Samuel Hollingsworth to a federal judgeship he forgot where Harrison had practiced law. "It is well known that nobody west of the Alleghenies knows any commercial law. 'There may be two opinions on that point,' observed the President, smiling. 'Possibly—, but only one of them is correct.'" Hollingsworth was not appointed.[35]

With the great social changes following the Civil War those who lived through that period often looked back with fond recollection to what they remembered, but those practices were no longer to be found. One older lawyer looking back from the early twentieth century wrote that the law had been more of a profession and less of a business in the past. Commercialism and materialism existed before, but were not pervasive and manifest. The same lawyer said, "I don't think the filthy lucre was quite as filthy then." The practice of law was much less complicated—especially the federal law. There was no income tax and no federal estate tax. There was no national bankrupt law, no Public Service Commission, no Interstate Commerce Commission, and no Fair Trade Commission. The lawyer went on to say, "the ordinary citizen came into contact with the Federal Government through the gentle medium of the postman, and as a general rule did not know what a Federal judge looked like. I knew a man in those days, we all loved him and called him Uncle Sam; he had a wonderful constitution, but he took no care of it, he went to quack doctors for fancied and trifling ills; he allowed it to become impaired, and so he aged prematurely."[36]

Other values of the period are reflected in an 1888 article written by Edward M. Paxson who offered some practical hints for new members of the bar. He said that the beginning lawyer should attract business by participating in social intercourse, making himself prominent in many ways, and doing good works. "And if his conversations in life are suitable to his high calling, he may make friends and in the end clients. But personal solicitation is unprofessional, and charlatanism is unbecoming a gentleman." Paxson went on to say "the moderate measure of success I met within my own career was in great part owing to the fact that whenever practicable I kept my clients out of law. Especially do not encourage them in frivolous litigation. Procrastination is not only the thief of time, but it is also the lion in the path of many a lawyer." Furthermore, he said, "there is no road to success to a lawyer who does not carefully prepare his cases. And most important Virtue will be rewarded. I have actual knowledge of the case of a member of the bar, who, when a comparatively young man, without any considerable financial responsibility, was made executor of a large estate for the reason that he did not drink wine. There are no drinking saloons, licensed or unlicensed, on the Road to Success."[37]

J. Hay Brown, another Philadelphia lawyer, also wrote about conditions he believed necessary to a lawyer's success. He said that the successful lawyer is one who is loyal to is profession and that no man can succeed who is not true to himself and frank with his conscience. Brown believed that of great importance was that the educated lawyer must also be an educated man. "The words of the law lecturers will fall with no profit on the ears of his hearers, unless they qualify themselves to hear what he says by tireless and unremitting study of the masters." As to dedication to the profession he said "the first exaction made upon the lawyer who seeks the highest end of professional exertion, is singleness of devotion to the law. She is indeed a jealous mistress, tolerant of the love of no other. There must be patience in wooing and waiting for the favor of the law. If the office is fit to receive them and its occupants to care for them, they will find their own way to it in time, never to leave it."[38]

Brown went on to write there were two allurements, like the mariner of the Grecian story, and that the young lawyer must seal his ears to their ravishing music. "One is political office. It will sweep away cool judgement and with, his general interest in his client and in himself. The second allurement deals largely with business and commercial interests. This can lead the lawyer to divide his time and talents between his professional labors and outside interests. There must be supreme devotion to the law itself."[36]

William H. Ashman, University of Pennsylvania professor of law, also wrote in 1889 about the dangers of distraction to the young lawyer. He said that the student of law must be a man of serious conviction. "There are too many men who watch the political and social barometer, as the sailor watches the sky; and who get between decks, at the first appearance of a cloud, or the first patter of rain." He said, however, "the student of the law must be a universal student. The student of the law must cultivate honor—or rather he needs to have it, for that quality must be indigenous. When I hear the vulgar practitioner flaunting his cheap law before the courts, or hurling his shattered English in the face of a helpless jury; when I see the peripatetic lecturer peddling his small wares to country lyceums, or listen to the political declaimer hurling his balderdash to a cheering mob; and when I read in respectable journals that these men are orators, I confess I am sick."[40]

For the beginning lawyers success at the bar often took a great deal of time and patience. David Paul Brown was a Philadelphia lawyer whose reputation as an advocate was mainly because he was ornate in his style and fond of pedagogical quotations, mainly from Shakespeare. Six months after he was admitted to the bar he met a man who had been admitted to the bar at the same time and asked him how he was getting along. The man said "as well as could be expected." Brown replied, "I can say that much at least, and more too; I can say that I have got along much better than I expected, and it is not saying much after all, for I have had but one client since I have been admitted, and I gave him such wretched advice that I wonder he did not return and kick me out of my own office."[41]

There was during this time period changes in the court system of Philadelphia.

"By the Constitution of 1873 it was provided that on and after the first Monday, January 1875, the then existing Court of Common Pleas and District Court, should be abolished, and all their powers and jurisdiction should be vested in four new courts of equal and co-ordinate jurisdiction, to be composed of three judges each and to be called the Courts of Common Pleas, No. 1, No. 2, No. 3 and No. 4."[42]

Each of the four courts had a president and three associate judges. There continued to be some influences by the old upper class in the courts. Of the 16 judges, six of them were from high status old Philadelphia families. There was always for some, but not many, in the upper class a willingness to serve on the bench.

In Philadelphia the common pleas courts were expanded to four by the Pennsylvania constitution of 1873. In the 1880s crowds were still sometimes drawn to the courts to hear the well-known lawyers of city perform. Some of the judges were also great crowd pleasers and with only four courts the judiciary was still small enough for some of the judges to stamp their individuality on the legal community. Judge Allison was seen as gentle and patient, whereas Judge Biddle was less indulgent but witty. In addition, it was said that Judge Cadwalader often lost himself in the depths of his scholarship and subtlety.[43]

Judge John Innes Clark Hare has been described as probably the most learned lawyer that ever administered justice in the courts of Philadelphia. His work on the *Law of Contracts* long endured and was regarded as a great contribution to philosophical commentary and interpretation. Hare had the custom of sometimes leaving his old district court room at sixth and Chestnut, crossing the street, taking a drink of whiskey at a neighboring bar, and returning to his judicial duties—without any attempt at concealment. When he was "in the saloon he was treated with the unqualified reverence and respect which both his position and his gentlemanly demeanor unconsciously expected; and gossip did not and could not venture a breath of unfavorable comment."[44]

The bench was often not highly regarded by the bar, however. Coxe wrote that in Philadelphia the average newly elected judge, fresh from daily and hourly close identification with his brethren at the bar, "too often becomes immediately infected with this grand Lama of Tibet contagion, and is, thenceforth, a permanent, chronic victim of its virulence." He went on to say there is "too much adulation of judges. The custom for the speakers at meetings to refer to the 'great and exulted' judge and abject praise as employed by inferiors should cease. This is forced upon the profession by the judges but a little more courage on the part of the lawyer would have prevented this judicial pretentiousness."[45]

The corporate era was one of great change for the American lawyer. The Philadelphia lawyer, as a part of that change, saw the further emergence of success for the lawyer resting outside the courtroom and the traditional role of the advocate to the privacy of the emerging law firm office. There his legal counsel was mainly directed at keeping his client away from any legal difficulties. In Philadelphia, while the legal profession was increasing in size and the upper class decreasing as a percentage of all lawyers, the status and wealth separating lawyers was continuing to increase. The old upper class lawyers were a smaller percentage of all lawyers, but they had gained dominant control over the new and complex practice of law coming out of the corporate world. That meant that the wealth and power being gained by some lawyers was far greater than any of them would have dreamed of in previous decades. Furthermore, with a few exceptions, that kind of law practice fit well the upper class values. It was private and done without the public exposure of the courtroom. The values of privacy were well suited both to the social and legal lives of the Philadelphia upper class lawyers.

Profile 8: John Graver Johnson (1841–1917)

John G. Johnson was born 21 April 1841 of ancestors who had been farmers and artisans. Johnson's father was a blacksmith and his mother a seamstress. His mother taught him to read and write at an early age, and he had access to a private library in Chestnut Hill (a suburb on the edge of Philadelphia) while he was a young boy. Central High School, built in 1838, was Philadelphia's only public high school, and it drew academically qualified boys from all over the city. Johnson was twelve years old when he started, about two and a half years younger than the average beginning student; by his second year he was academically the top student in the school. The boys who attended Central High School came from all social class levels throughout the city, and there was strong competition to gain admission. The teachers were as well qualified as the faculties of most colleges at that time.

Another student, at Central High School, two years behind Johnson was the great American painter Thomas Eakins (1844–1916). It is a further coincidence that Johnson in later years became a noted art expert and art collector, and he was a strong supporter of Eakins who had many problems with the social and art establishments of Philadelphia. In later years Johnson represented Eakins in several legal matters.

At the time of Johnson's graduation from Central High School the school was informed that the law office of Benjamin Rush wanted to hire the top student in the graduating class. The faculty's verdict was unanimous, and Johnson got the position. He started in Rush's office with the title of "scrivener." His job was to copy hundreds of legal papers, serve summons and subpoenas, run errands, and in general do whatever he was told. Along with his great intellectual abilities he also had good handwriting, a highly valued skill at that time. Johnson had to copy all papers, writs, affidavits, rules, and briefs three and four times. There was no mechanical means for making copies, and therefore each copy had to be tediously done by hand.

Johnson quickly decided he wanted to become a lawyer. At that time the best procedure was to be accepted and registered in a recognized law office. That was not easy because only a few offices were acceptable to the Bar Association, and they charged a high fee for the training. There were also strong social class barriers that restricted the chance to train in many of the city's law offices. The old upper class ties between families and between the leading members of the Philadelphia bar and bench were many and strong. Having

John Graver Johnson, 1841–1917. Courtesy of the Historical Society of Pennsylvania.

an acceptable family background was of the greatest importance in being accepted by a prestigious law office. The acceptance into a high-status law office was the most important hurdle to overcome if one wanted to become a successful lawyer. Once accepted, with a reasonable level of intelligence and a willingness to work fairly hard, one could in a few years begin a potentially successful and high-status career at the Philadelphia bar.

Johnson started in the office of William F. Judson. That was not one of the city's high-status law offices for training the beginning lawyer. Judson offered no special routine and no defined relationship as a preceptor to Johnson as a student. The two front rooms on the first floor were piled high with the old Rush dossiers as well as many other legal files, however, and they provided Johnson with an opportunity for learning. Most of his legal training came from his daily chores in the office and from his private studying after work. With his great intellect and commitment Johnson learned law on his own, and he knew that with Judson's sponsorship he would be able to attain admission to the bar.

About that time Johnson's father died, and he was left as the sole supporter of his mother and brothers. He worked long hours, often overtime doing special work for attorneys and conveyancers. He ran errands, collected rents, and searched titles. By 1862 he was being encouraged by Judson to move more actively toward admission to the Philadelphia bar. As one step toward that goal he was encouraged to seek the training available through the Law Academy. He also enrolled for law courses at the University of Pennsylvania. All that meant at that time, however, was that he paid his fees for the right to attend several lectures. Those lectures were given by three well-known Philadelphia lawyers, George Sharswood, Peter McCall, and E. Spencer Miller. The lectures combined some of the practical law experiences of each lecturer along with some academic observations. They were not complete lectures in so far as covering the body of law. Of greater importance in his legal education were Johnson's personal notebooks that he had filled with more comprehensive legal knowledge. In those notebooks he included cases and principles as well as his personal digests that covered various phases of legal practice. Johnson always believed his notebooks were of far greater value to him than what he acquired through the Law Academy lectures.

The methods of law study then in vogue contrasted sharply with the modern case system with the emphasis upon outside research and moot court training. Little progress had been made in codifying the law, but broad principles were of greater importance than isolated rulings. The books of recognized text writers laid the foundation of a legal education, and a few leading decisions of the English courts formed the pattern from which American case law was derived.

The academy in the 1860s could trace its history back to the first provost, Peter Stephen du Ponceau, who had served under General George Washington. Since 1855 George Sharswood had directed the work of the students. Sharswood was assisted by several leading lawyers who provided subjects for arguments and presided over the student debates. The moot courts were considered an essential complement to the legal theory taught in the law school. The minutes of the meetings in 1862–63 contain references to Johnson's participation in the moot court arguments. That was Johnson's only real association with the law group as he had no interest in holding even minor positions in the group. That was not due to reticence or shyness but rather because of the demanding problems of earning a living. Even with all the demands on his time and energy, on 7 February 1863 Johnson was admitted to the bar at twenty-one years of age.

The spring of 1863 was one of great anxiety in Philadelphia as the Confederate armies moved into Pennsylvania. The main body of the southern army had moved up the Chambersburg Pike and into the Allegheny foothills. The Confederates crossed the Susquehanna River on 16 June 1863 and in Philadelphia, Mayor Henry ordered businessmen to close their stores, factories, and workshops. The city dug trenches and put up earthworks in preparation for the Rebel armies reaching Philadelphia.

Battery A, First Pennsylvania Artillery, had been organized in 1844 by the Philadelphia bar to help control the riots of that year, and in 1862 it had been reactivated. One of the new members was Private John G. Johnson. Battery A left Philadelphia on 26 June, arrived in Harrisburg that night, and the next morning crossed the Susquehanna River where they dug trenches. The first fighting in the area began on 1 July, and a section of Battery A went with a regiment of infantry toward Carlisle, Pennsylvania. The lawyer-soldiers encountered some sniper fire, but because of their lack of training and being poorly equipped they were held in reserve and not sent into the lines.

When Johnson returned to Philadelphia he found plenty of work as a new member of the bar because many lawyers were still away in military service. Generally, the first years of practice meant the beginning lawyer rarely earned much more than bare subsistence. Traditionally if any worthwhile case fell into the hands of the novice he was expected to turn it over to his preceptor. Johnson's career from the start was very different and very exceptional, however. He had already achieved a reputation, far beyond any other young lawyer in the city so that along with the bigger cases coming to Judson's office he was also getting several referrals on his own. Johnson continued his participation at the Law Academy where Judge Sharswood brought students together once a week in his home to discuss moot questions of office and court practice. It was also possible for Johnson and other young lawyers to follow litigation occurring in the common pleas courts.

In estates work Johnson was doing the research as well as arguing cases in court. This soon brought Johnson up against some of the older members of the Philadelphia bar. Johnson's reputation was such that some established lawyers—for example, Biddle and Wharton—were beginning to consult with Johnson on estate matters. His fees were modest but what was more important to his future was the kind of client he was attracting. Johnson was getting established businessmen, real estate operators and speculators, builders, and the heads of some of the newly developing industries in the city. Johnson was rapidly broadening his reputation to the point where he clearly was *the* lawyer in business matters.

Shortly after the end of the Civil War, and before the age of thirty, Johnson added to his reputation and fortune by handling a difficult and complex sale of land that had been viewed as useless swampland in South Philadelphia. He first handled the sale from private ownership to the city and then the sale from the city to the federal government. The swamps became League Island, a major naval shipyard on the Delaware River. His client was the Pennsylvania Company, one of the most successful trust companies in the city. That highly profitable transaction was so well handled by Johnson that he became the permanent counsel of the company. Johnson, with the help of a few associates, was making more than $100,000 a year by the 1880s. That was in a city of about fifteen hundred lawyers where fewer than an hundred made more than $5,000 a year. That extraordinary income came from hard work and outstanding legal judgment rather than from very high legal fees. That was the method by which he amassed his great wealth throughout his career.[1]

After the Civil War Johnson remained mainly uninvolved with political activity going on in the city, and he had no interest in the upper class social world. His name was familiar to those in high financial circles both in and outside of Philadelphia, however. In 1870, Judson died, and Johnson at the age of twenty-eight took over the total practice. Johnson's life continued to be devoted completely to the practice of law. He handled the added responsibilities brought on by Judson's death by adding an hour in the morning and another at night to what was already a very long day. Johnson had clearly moved well out in front of his legal peers and was one of the legal stars of the city.

Because of his strong work values he often became irritated by the formality of the older lawyers. Their common procedure of seeking court delays was especially aggravating to him as he was busy and wanted to finish a case so he could move on to the next one. Johnson enjoyed the battle of the courtroom and was taken on as a senior by many older men who needed his great legal talents. His work routine was to spend the early morning at his office, five hours a day in forensic discussion and two or three hours each afternoon before examiners. He would then return to his office work, have a late dinner, and work in his office until midnight.

Increasingly the word among storekeepers, realtors, builders, and many middle-class men and women was: "You had better see Johnson," or "John G's the man for that." Literally, no case was too big or nothing too small for Johnson to handle. He would take minor cases that usually fell to beginning practitioners if they were of interest to him. Johnson kept his office in an old dwelling house on the south side of Walnut Street, below Eighth Street. There were a front and back parlor with wide double doors between the rooms that were always open. He sat at his desk in the middle of the back parlor, his chair tilted back, with his hands behind his head and gave each client his absolute and total attention as he listened. In the front office the wealthiest client waited his turn along with the poorest. On more than one occasion J. P. Morgan sat there waiting his turn. For Johnson, nothing else existed but the particular client and his problem at the time he was dealing with it.

Johnson was making legal history, through the substantial issues, the highly technical questions, and in the jury trials. There was a myth of Johnson's invincibility, but he lost many cases because if a case interested him he would take it. He was often approached by other lawyers who brought him cases that had no real chance of success. Unlike many trial lawyers, for Johnson it was the legal challenge and not a string of victories that mattered.

Of great importance to his developing legal career was his realization that very few lawyers had any substantive or procedural knowledge of corporation law. With little significant competition at this intellectual level, Johnson became the expert in American corporate law. The last three decades of the nineteenth century were a time when large businesses, in the form of corporations, were under the favorable climate of the new corporation laws, which were growing tremendously. Johnson was recognized as the outstanding corporation lawyer in the United States, and he came to play the leading role in most corporate cases that were argued before the United States Supreme Court.

Johnson's appointment as General Counsel of the Pennsylvania Company rapidly increased his number of new clients. What made Johnson's success so exceptional was that it began with his first year at the bar. It reached out year by year in widening circles as more and more clients wanted him. No case was too big, nothing too small for his personal attention in the office or the courtroom. Johnson rarely admitted defeat, and when a jury brought a verdict against him, he battled for a new trial with great force.[2]

Big business was developing many new products, methods of production, and means of transportation. All of those had to be clarified and given legal meaning through the courts, and it was there that Johnson was also the leader. He was the counsel when the city of Philadelphia tried to extend their transportation lines to new streets, and when railroads were reaching beyond the city and into the suburbs. Johnson had no commitment to any particular interest, however, but rather went where his legal curiosity took him. Furthermore, he did not restrict himself to one branch of the law but continued his general practice.

The years when Johnson first started to practice law were years when the public measurement of a lawyer was largely measured by the impact of his verbal skills in the courtroom. Johnson was a star courtroom performer at a time when forensic oratory and courtroom tactics were frequently still areas of great public admiration. Many of the lawyers of the 1870s and 1880s had a glamour usually associated with the great actors of the stage. What often impressed the public were the lawyer's swagger, his distinctive dress, and his grandiose speech. Those were not the courtroom characteristics of Johnson, however. His talents were simpler and generally free of affectation, and in the courtroom he could and often did vary his role. If he felt the occasion called for it he could roar like a lion, but his more common technique was to underact. His favorite technique was to talk to the jury as he might talk to a neighbor over the back fence.

Changes were occurring in courtroom style, and flamboyant oratory was beginning to lose some of its impact on the jury; increasingly success came more from the techniques commonly used by Johnson. That was to present the evidence to the jury rather than to try to persuade them through vocal histrionics. Johnson was earnest and simple, and his arguments were seen as models of briefness. Although his legal knowledge was great, he knew that little of past legal decisions was actually needed to make his case. A common comment was that few lawyers could say as much in fifteen minutes as could John G. Johnson.

Johnson varied his reactions to fit different situations, and with some clients he could be cold and distant. With women his manner was of deference and the chivalry common to the gentleman of his day. It was said that "when he spoke, paperbooks would lie unopened on the bench, for the Judges who heard him knew that the facts of the case would be correctly stated."[3] On cross-examination he could be formidable, and his style varied with the case and the witnesses. He would help some witnesses and coldly destroy others. Some he would cajole, and others he would ridicule; some he would confuse, and others he would terrify. In one case concerning a contested will he destroyed the composure of a self-satisfied and smug witness with the opening remark, "Now, Major, let me sharpen my teeth on you."[4]

Johnson, as a young man, was self-sufficient and discreet, and it does not appear that he had any close friends. He had no time for social relationships in his younger years ofter than in his practice of law. Johnson did not have any hobbies and no recreations at that time aside from occasionally going to a baseball game and once in a while playing poker. He spent little time sleeping, and did not drink or smoke. When he attended dinners at the Pennsylvania Company, where vintage wines and rare liqueurs were served, his standing order was for a large pitcher of lemonade to be sat at his place. His clothes were chosen with little interest and worn with indifference. When he was just past thirty years of age, he was still tall and thin, and was considered a handsome and imposing man. As he grew older, as did many men of his day, he grew quite heavy.

There were various opinions as to how phenomenal was Johnson's memory. The differences, however, were only about how truly fantastic his memory really was. He probably had almost total recall of anything he had ever read or written. One common story was that when he was a boy in high school he memorized all of Shakespeare's plays. He could at the mention of the name of a case in the *Pennsylvania Supreme Court Reports* turn to the volume and page where it was cited. He could also read a page at a time, as fast as he could turn the page, and completely absorb it. He had the ability to give his absolute attention as a listener. He would lean back in his chair with his hands crossed over his great belly and shut his eyes as if in a trance. He would listen to the client, brief the problem in his mind, and immediately know the best legal argument. John G. Johnson was unquestionably a genius and must have possessed one of the great minds in any profession in American history. Certainly, there was no question that that was the belief among his contemporaries.

By the mid-1870s Johnson was clearly the leader of the Philadelphia bar and one of the most highly regarded lawyers in America, a position he would hold for the next forty years. The meetings, dinners, and clubs of his profession he rarely attended; his success at the bar was a result of his great mental and physical powers rather than through the cultivation of others. Yet, with few exceptions others in the legal profession not only respected him but personally liked him. It was recognized that his lack of sociability was not because of snobbishness but rather because of his total commitment to his work.

Johnson first met his future wife, Ida Powell, as a client. Her first husband, Edward Morrell, had died in 1871 leaving her with three young children. She went to see Johnson for help about the small estate left to her by her husband. Mrs. Morrell came from an old upper class Philadelphia family. On her father's side her lineage was through the Hare, Powell, and Willing families of Philadelphia and on her mother's side through old New York families, the Van Courtlands, Schuylers, and Beekmans. It took some time for Johnson to settle her estate and only a few assets could be saved.

Mrs. Morrell, when she first came to see Johnson, had accepted widowhood for herself and her three children. Johnson from the beginning, even in pursuing his courtship, was patient and understanding about her problems as a widow. He greatly enjoyed her children, and began to visit her and bring gifts such as special French bonbons and candied fruits. They were married 15 July 1875 and moved into a big house at 426 S. Broad Street, across the street from the Academy of Music. Mrs. Johnson assumed the social position in Philadelphia based on her old family heritage. The new family household centered around Johnson's work habits, which changed very little after his marriage. He would leave by eight in the morning and return home for a late dinner. Johnson's private life changed dramatically and quite happily for him, however. Dinners at home became happy events and were completely free from any pressures from his work. He was totally committed to his children, and the word "stepchild" was never used in his family.

Even the closest of Johnson's associates and clients were rarely invited into his home. Although his wife had an active social life, he rarely participated. If he came home and his wife had a gathering in the drawing room he would go upstairs through the rear entrance. His wife's social background was the final touch needed to place him among the most upper class men of the city.[5] That, too, was of little importance to him because he had little interest in social elegance or conspicuous display.

One measure of Johnson's great esteem in the community, based on his professional achievements, rather than his marriage, was his becoming a member of the Philadelphia Club in the 1870s. The club is the oldest men's club in America. In Philadelphia it was and still is the very top of the pinnacle of high status men's social clubs. In Johnson's day a few highly successful men on occasion would be invited in as new members. Most of the new members each year were the younger members of impeccable old Philadelphia families. Johnson was not only highly successful, but his family background, although not of the upper class, was old and of "proper" lineage. Johnson was certainly not a club man, and his daily schedule was not geared to the club lounge. He would hurry in at noon, for a brief period, eat his dozen oysters on the half shell, and scan his newspapers. If his favorite corner table was occupied by someone not aware that it was his, he would stamp out to eat at a nearby oyster bar.

Francis Biddle, in his autobiography, tells the following story:

> Once after an argument in the District Court he [Johnson] walked 5 blocks back to his office, rolling along, with the pockets of his shabby gray Prince Albert bulging with briefs and papers, gradually becoming conscious of the little boys who stared at him at street corners and jeered as he went by. Reaching his office he discovered that he had taken the wrong hat — apparently his opponents, two sizes smaller than his immense derby. He burst out of the office, threw the offending headpiece on the floor, jumped on it 2 or 3 times, shouting his rage, and was kicking it about the floor when a mild and apologetic owner came to claim it. Johnson took one look at him, burst into prolonged shout of laughter. 'Too late!' he shouted, and plunged back into his office, with its long untidy table, and the 3 or 4 well used horse hair armchairs.[6]

Johnson took a leading part in many of the big legal cases both in Philadelphia and in the United States. His first really big case was in 1880 when he won the fight for Philadelphia's first buses. The passenger railroads had objected to the omnibuses on Market and Broad Streets, but Johnson won the Bus Company the right to license coaches, although the rights had already been given to the railroad to lay the tracks.

By the mid-1880s Johnson was being hailed in America as the legal wizard to whom nothing was impossible, and he was retained by the Sugar Trust. At that time, sugar refining was controlled by one of the largest corporations in America—the Trust. They were a loose combination of manufacturers, who had, to circumvent the Sherman Antitrust Act, consolidated themselves into a single company. The company was capitalized at $85 million and was paying huge dividends. The Trust had also created great public resentment by driving up the price of sugar. Furthermore, it was also a time when the denunciations of trusts and monopolies were very loud and strident. To many Americans it seemed clear that trust manipulation was the reason for most of the nation's economic problems.

The case started in the Circuit Court of the United States as a legal case in equity. Later there were indictments of the heads of the Sugar Trust in a criminal proceeding. Johnson had no hesitation in taking on their defense in both cases. He did not believe that the case could be fought and won by showing the economic basis for the mergers, and its benefits to manufacturers and consumers. Rather he felt the fight had to be made not in facts but in law. He hammered at what he saw as the one vulnerable point in the government's complaint by arguing that manufacturing was not interstate commerce. Johnson was able to convince the court that the proof required under the Sherman Antitrust Act, to protect trade and commerce against unlawful restraints and monopolies, could only be met by proof of a monopoly in interstate and international trade. He argued that to ignore the distinction between interstate commerce and manufacturing would bring about concurrent power over all industry within each state. The decision in the *Sugar Trust* case was a clear-cut and resounding victory for Johnson.[7]

His reputation was further enhanced by the results of the seven criminal prosecutions in the *Sugar Trust* case. That investigation was held before a committee of the United States Senate. Those men had been indicted by a grand jury for refusal to answer pertinent questions on matters deemed "vital to the dignity of the Senate." The seven men had not answered when asked if as officers of the American Sugar Refining Company they had made contributions to the political campaigns of several U.S. senators during 1894. Furthermore, they also refused to produce the books of the company. They had given money to both political parties so there was a strong bipartisan interest in squashing the case. Johnson was involved in planning their defense, but the cases were dismissed for political reasons. That ruling was met with a great outcry by the press. Yet, there was little resentment directed toward Johnson. In the criminal proceedings, even more than the civil, he was viewed as a hired advocate who had performed a highly skilled legal feat. That was always one of Johnson's greatest achievements. No matter how distasteful or disreputable his client, when Johnson represented him he was rarely negatively affected by the defendant's activities.

When his fee in the *Sugar Trust* case became known that contributed greatly to his legend. His total bill was $3,000, and all the other lawyers involved in the case went into severe shock and strongly protested his small fee. How could they present their far greater bills? Johnson refused to reconsider because he said that amount was exactly what his services had been worth. That was the Johnson pattern as he often charged fees that were a small percentage of what he could have claimed and that his clients would have been happy to pay. Although Johnson became a very wealthy man, he undoubtedly could have doubled or tripled his wealth if he had chosen to charge fees as great as others were getting in similar cases.[8]

The *Northern Securities* case centered around the effort to unite the Great Northern and Northern Pacific railroads through a holding company. Johnson had expressed his opinion that the formation of a holding company was not in violation of the Sherman Antitrust Act. The federal court had decided, however, that the ownership of two railroads by a single agency was in violation of the act. The case came before the Supreme Court of the United States in December 1903, and there was great national interest. At noon when the justices of the Supreme Court entered to be seated the courtroom was filled. Already seated were senators, representatives, judges, diplomats, and lawyers from every one of the states. At one table sat Attorney General Knox, described as "clean cut, smooth faced, and keenly alive to the responsibility of his first assignment." Seated alongside him were his assistants. Counsel for the Northern Securities was grouped at the other table, and there sat Johnson along with several other lawyers. It was Johnson who was the center of attention. The politicians, the legal establishment, the public, and the press were all there to see the great Johnson perform. A venerating newspaper account described Johnson "as a tall, finely built man, with a strong but kindly face. He stands out even among the strikingly forceful figures of the lawyers ranged beside him." The newspaper reported that Johnson opened the case in a plain, business-like manner. "He had not spoken five minutes before everybody who heard him was convinced he was no ordinary man. Void of affectation he held the attention of the court by his remarkable clearness and conciseness—plus the qualities of gentle warmth and a vein of humor which render it a delight to listen to him."[9]

Johnson's strategy was not to allow himself or the court to become lost in the maze of facts that led to the development of the two giant railroads. He believed that if that happened it would distract from the broad principles that he wanted to emphasize. Furthermore, there was little disagreement as to the facts. In general, Johnson argued that the formation of the Northern Securities Company was a defensive measure. He said it was for the purpose of guarding the stock of the two railroad companies against a raid similar to the one that had been made by the Harriman interests on the Union Pacific Railroad. Johnson placed his emphasis on the national and international implications of the case, and he pictured his client Hill as the creator of an empire that was linked with the flow of the nation's commodities to China and Japan. Johnson argued that the real competition was not between the Great Northern and the Northern Pacific, but rather between those two railroads and the Canadian Pacific and Pacific railroads that operated to the north of them. His argument insisted that there was international competition and that it had to be met by America. "If it was not," said Johnson, "the competition from England, Germany and other European nations would take away the vast rade with the Orient from America."[10]

According to one press account Johnson "sketched the project of raising a bankrupt corporation into life, and creating a great traffic, through the genius of a single mind grappling with a formidable railroad problem. Though apt at detail the great Philadelphia advocate lifted the case, as it were, into a higher region of thought and debate." The newspaper accounts also contrasted the much greater positive impact of Johnson when compared with Knox. "Mr. Johnson was cheery, good humored and optimistic while Mr. Knox was severe, and inclined to admonish and deplore."[11]

In his closing argument Johnson said: "You may strike down this corporation, and undoubtedly you will strike it down if you find that its existence is in violation of the law, even though in doing so you destroy a commerce of magnitude and almost beyond our powers of imagination for the future. But we respectfully submit that you ask the Attorney-General when he demands that you strike it down the presentation of some law to you that clearly and unmistakably pronounces as a crime that which he asks you to condemn." On 15 March 1904 the nine justices handed down a five to four decision for the government. That loss in no way hurt Johnson's great reputation, however, and he continued to be the dominant American figure in corporate law.

During the first fifteen years of the twentieth century practically no great case was argued before the United States Supreme Court in which John G. Johnson did not appear. He was at various times retained by the Amalgamated Copper Company, the Pennsylvania Railroad, New York Central Railroad, United States Steel, and American Distilleries among others. Altogether he was retained by between sixty to eighty banks and practically every great corporation in America. It came to be a proverb among financiers and lawyers that "JGJ's opinion was tantamount to a judicial decision." Yet, at no point in his career could Johnson be defined as a legal specialist. Although he was best known in the area of corporate law he also handled cases in patent law, admiralty, and criminal law. If he liked a case he took it and his predilection usually rested only on an interesting point of law. The number of reversals that he secured in the higher courts ran into the hundreds. To him the real function of law was to present one side in any controversy with the greatest possible legal proficiency. He was on all sides of a mooted question, acting more often as a part of the court than as a paid advocate. There are 350 bound volumes of Johnson's paper books, chiefly dealing with his appellate work. He argued 1,525 cases in the Supreme Court, Pennsylvania, 60 in the superior court of Pennsylvania, 16 in the United States District Court, 53 in the circuit court of the United States, 198 in the United States Circuit Court of Appeals, and 168 in the United States Supreme Court. There were so many cases in the Pennsylvania Supreme Court argued by Johnson that the clerk of the court made it a practice to lump them together as the "Johnson cases."[12]

In some sessions before the state he would appear to argue a half a dozen different cases. As each new counsel took his place at his table Johnson would stay at his table to argue one case after another. As each case was reached he would present his argument, and if the justice asked a question he would usually answer very briefly. After his presentation he would sit down, pick up the brief of the next case, and begin turning pages rapidly. He was studying the next case to be heard. His powers of concentration were such that he was also attuned to his opponent and if need be he would object, and then go back to studying the next case. When the judge noted the next case to be heard and it was Johnson's, he would be on his feet and ready to go. He would on some days run through a dozen cases.[13]

John G. Johnson never held a political office in his life. He always had an interest in politics and often represented city, state and county officials, however, and he knew all the politicians and political bosses of his days. He believed that the men of industry and finance were far more important than the political bureaucrats who often tried to control them. For Johnson it was clear that the future of America rested with big business. His ego needs were such that he was never tempted to run for public office. Getting elected had nothing to do with what mattered to him in his life as a lawyer. Johnson was a part of the long Philadelphia upper class tradition that saw involvement in politics not only as a waste of time but also as inappropriate.

Johnson not only had no personal interest in the judiciary but he did not care for public honors. He turned down offers of high appointments. He twice refused appointments as a justice of the United States Supreme Court. Once it was offered by President Garfield and on another occasion by President Cleveland. He also turned down the post of attorney general in the cabinet of President McKinley. After turning down one of the offers to the United States Supreme Court Johnson was reported as saying: "I would rather talk to the damn fools than listen to them."[14] Here, too, Johnson personified the ideal model of the Philadelphia lawyer—be an active member of the bar and practice law, not adjudicate it.

There was another very important role in Johnson's life, considered by many to be as significant and impressive as anything that he achieved in the practice of law. That was his role as art collector and art expert. Beginning in the mid-1880s, at the time of this marriage, he visited the major capitals of Europe where he spent his summers visiting the art galleries and museums of Europe. For several years before he began personally to collect art he very carefully studied painters, read widely about their methods and techniques, and studied art by visiting the galleries of Europe. When Johnson started, his interests in art were as carefully specialized as they had been in law when he initially dealt with estates and corporations.

The 1880s was a period when Americans were buying and transferring to the United States great amounts of European art. Some of the most wealthy American industrialists, including Vanderbilt, Morgan, Hill and Whitney, were buying huge amounts of art on the European market. Those men had their selections made for them by teams of professional art experts they hired. Many of those art collectors were into art primarily as an investment. Often their interests were in works of art that were rare, very costly, and often publicly the most sensational. Johnson was a very different collector, however. He had grown up, largely through the influence of his mother, with a love for design and color. In 1892 he published a small volume, *Sightseeing in Berlin and Holland among Pictures* and gave copies to friends, art lovers he had met, and private collectors. The book clearly established Johnson as an able art critic. In overall wealth Johnson could not compete in the European art markets with the great wealth of a Morgan or Vanderbilt in collecting art. Johnson's approach was to insist on quality rather than quantity, and he built his collection around the representative works of great artists rather than trying to buy their more famous and costlier works. Johnson became an outstanding art authority, and he was highly respected and often asked for advice by other collectors. His tastes became wide, but over time but he leaned toward the Italian Renaissance, the eighteenth-century French and nineteenth-century French and Dutch Schools, particularly the Flemish. Although there were many more valuable art collections in America there was no great art collector in America who could compare with Johnson in scholarship and expertise.

One writer, familiar with Johnson's collection, observed that in his art collection were Rubens, Rembrandt, and some of the Dutch genre painters, such as Jan Steen and Adriaen Brouwer, and they were among the best. Also among his English painters, the collection of John Constable's was considered outstanding, containing twenty-three works. His group of paintings by Carot was also considered notable. Among the more modern painters his taste leaned toward the French artists, particularly Rousseau, Degas, and Daubigny. In the later years of his life he served as a director of the Metropolitan Museum of Art in New York.

Johnson continued to live in his large house on Broad Street across from the Academy of Music. At home he would spend many hours on a Sunday afternoon looking at his paintings that were scattered around the house, many of them unframed. He would change the painting every now and then in the easel that stood before his great armchair in the living room. Francis Biddle wrote that he once heard Johnson say to his maid, Martha, "go upstairs to the third floor bathroom and bring us down the Botticelli picture that is leaning against the tub."[15]

During the years of collecting art Johnson organized his work schedule so that at the beginning of the summer he would leave his office to his assistants and sail for Europe. For the first week at sea Johnson would read a year's supply of detective stories. He would read each book as fast as he could turn the pages and as he finished would toss it overboard. He would then spend the rest of the trip studying the latest art catalogs and preparing himself as an art collector. His world as an art collector and critic was completely separate from his world of law. In his art collecting, as in his private life, Johnson indulged his sentimentality and the softer side of life. He could also on occasion show a hard side in art, however, because he had a trader's delight in outsmarting the other fellow.

The early twentieth century saw the rapid development of the large law firm in New York City, and to a lesser extent in Philadelphia and other American cities. Johnson's office was never large, however. In 1905 he joined the movement of the bar westward in Philadelphia to the new offices built around the new City Hall at Broad and Market Streets. He moved into the new Land Title Building, but his law suite was very plain when compared with those of other law firms in the building. The waiting room was not impressive, and the furnishings were simple. The chairs were hard oak with wooden seats, brought from his old office. No members of his family ever came to his office, and there were no art or paintings hanging there. Everywhere in the office were books, as he had one of the best private law libraries in the city at the time. He refused to be the nominal head of a large legal firm, and he was the last of the great general practitioners in the city. After his death his law business was so vast, however, that it provided a major impetus for the development of four or five large law firms in the city.

John Graver Johnson died 16 April 1917 at the age of seventy-six. He died a very wealthy man, and he left his proudest possession, his great art collection, to the city of Philadelphia. For tax purposes the collection was assessed at $4.4 million, but it was actually worth far more. He also left his home on Broad Street to house the art collection, along with $2 million for maintenance expense to the city. The value of the remainder of his estate was never made public. Johnson's art collection became a very important part of the Philadelphia Art Museum and significantly helped it become one of America's great art museums.

One observer wrote shortly after Johnson's death that "he had never filled judicial station, never discussed public questions and never wrote a legal thesis, because he would have thought it in evidence of vanity. What he did have in his life was the profound intellect and comprehensive attainment of the law. He was a lawyer who kept his conscience clear and loved his sacred calling. The lawyer whom every advocate and every judge in the land today feels was the greatest of all."[16]

When Lord Chief Baron Palles, a noted Irish jurist, visited America a few years before Johnson's death he told his Philadelphia host that the one man in America whom he was anxious to meet was John G. Johnson. "Of course, everybody knows," added the Baron, "that Mr. Johnson is the greatest lawyer in the English speaking world."[17] Once when Mr. Justice Brown of the United States Supreme Court was asked, "Would you kindly tell me who you regard as the greatest lawyer in the Country?" the Justice said, "Speaking among ourselves, we call Mr. Johnson the King of the American bar." Owen Wister, author and close friend of Theodore Roosevelt, who knew all the great men of the day rated Johnson above them all. George W. Norris, journalist, lawyer, and financier wrote, "John G. Johnson was the possessor of the greatest mind with which it has ever been my privilege to come into contact."[18]

There were many myths and legends about Johnson during his lifetime. One myth was of his courtroom invincibility, but he lost many cases. There was also the belief that he was a complete loner and never belonged to any group or participated in any social events. That was not completely true because he did belong to the Bar Association and the Philadelphia Club. In his later years he would on some occasions attend dinners to honor one of his colleagues of the Philadelphia bar. He disliked social events in his honor, however. In 1915 he agreed to accept the degree of LL.D. from the University of Pennsylvania. He fidgeted uneasily on the platform, and back in his office he discarded his academic robes and flung the mortar board cap across the room, vowing never again. His personal needs were met through his family and his art.

Johnson's resistance to publicity or honors are reflected in his total entry in *Who's Who*. "Johnson, John G. Corporation lawyer. Address, Land Title Bldg., Phila." The sincerity of his dislike of any social display for himself was reflected in the instructions he left for his death. At his funeral he wanted no pallbearers, and no representatives from the Philadelphia Club, or from the bar or the bench. Only four people attended his funeral: his brother and his wife, and his son and his wife. He left orders that nothing approaching a monument was to be erected, simply a plain low head and foot stone marked with his name, date of birth, and date of death.

John G. Johnson was both different as well as the epitome of the traditional upper class Philadelphia lawyer. He was different in that he did not come from an old upper class family and was not trained in the law office of one of the city's elite and high status lawyers. He both learned law and reached upper class standing on his own exceptionally powerful intellect and drive. He epitomized the traditional Philadelphia lawyer, however, through his total commitment to the belief that a lawyer practices law, and does not waste his knowledge and talent on being a politician nor by serving on the bench.

A final picture of John G. Johnson may be seen in a quote from George Wharton Pepper's autobiography. Senator Pepper was commonly recognized after the death of Johnson to be the leader of the Philadelphia bar. Pepper wrote, "He [Johnson] was the most prodigious man I have ever known. He had a big frame and radiated power. When he entered the courtroom he at once dominated the situation. The Judges treated him with the kind of deference more usually shown by the Bar to the Bench. He was a tireless worker and drove himself relentlessly, always carrying home after a long day an old fashioned cloth bag stuffed with papers to be worked on after dinner.'' Pepper went on to say,

prominent lawyers from New York and other cities were frequently seen in his anteroom, waiting their turn to enter his office. In court he usually selected one point on which to stake his case and drove it home as if he were hitting a spike with a sledge hammer. He always played fair and never distorted any authority. While Mr. McMurtie would rather lose a case than make bad law Mr. Johnson would take an impish delight in successfully making the worse appear the better reason. His record of cases won and lost throw no light on his capacity. Desperate cases were often brought to him as a last resort. But he fought them all with equal vigor.

Pepper goes on to write,

only once when I was new did he make me wince. On the technical question of equity pleading—the responsiveness of an answer—I had made an overelaborate argument, discussing dozens of cases in law school fashion, attempting to fit them into categories and to deduce an applicable principle. Mr. Johnson rose as if to reply; looked at me with withering scorn, turned to the Court, uttered not so much as a word, but gave a great grunt like a bull moose, gathered up his papers, walked out of the court— and won the case. I am sure that he regretted what he had done for he afterward went out of his way to be cordial.''[19]

9

Progressive Era: 1890–1910

About Harris Brewster, one of Philadelphia's great court orators:
It was too obvious that he found an intense satisfaction in hearing
himself talk, as, perhaps, why should he not?

—Anonymous

By the beginning of the twentieth century American cities were the dominant centers of the new industrial society. They were great urban sprawls, filled with industry and commerce, and a rapidly expanding labor force. The urban population of the United States doubled from 1880 to 1900. New York had a population of 3 million, Chicago of 1.5 million, and Philadelphia was the third largest city with a population of more than 1 million. Philadelphia still had some rural qualities, however. R. Sturgis Ingersoll wrote that in 1892 he could look out the front window of his house at 124 S. Nineteenth Street, and watch sheep and cattle driven west on Sansom Street to abattoirs in West Philadelphia.[1]

This was an era of increasing social concern and criticism. Lincoln Steffens, the best known of the muckrakers, wrote that "Philadelphia was indeed corrupt; but it is not without significance—with 47 percent of its population native born of native born parents, it is the most American of our great cities. Philadelphia has long enjoyed great and widely distributed prosperity. Philadelphia is sure that it has a real aristocracy, more so than any other place in the world. Philadelphia is simply the most corrupt and most contented." Steffens went on to say that Philadelphia was unique in that its machine had truly disfranchised its citizens. "The New Yorkers vote for Tammany Hall. The Philadelphians do not vote, they are disfranchised." Steffens cited the case of Rudolph Blankenberg who sent out before one election a registered letter to each voter on the rolls of a selected division. Sixty-three percent were returned marked "not at," "removed," or "deceased."[2]

By the 1890s business had come to be much more than simply an occupation, it was often a philosophy and a morality. The young man felt the necessity of finding the right business to enter. "In the ominous future of the boy— only industry and obedience and accuracy and neatness and a contempt for the pleasures of idleness could give him a leg up to success. There was no respect for college. College men did not stick to business, they thought too much. Those who were dreamers and were despised because their dreaming produced

194

nothing, dreamers were thinking of unprofitable things." Pennypacker further wrote in his autobiography that no one ever urged a young man to go into politics. "It was the broken man, or the weak incapable, who found it easier to be genial than to work, that became politicians. They took care of the necessary but inferior functions of civilization: crime prevention, the institutions, ash collecting, making roads,—the superior functions, business, law, social intercourse, getting rich were out of politics."[3]

This era was also the time of great immigration into Philadelphia. In America of the total population of 76 million in 1900, 10 million were foreign born and 26 million were of foreign-born parentage. Until the mid-1880s most immigrants had come from northwestern Europe. The new immigrants were largely peasants from Russia and Poland, parts of Austro-Hungarian empire, Italy, and the Balkan states. The immigrants were often blamed not only for lowering the wages of American labor, but also as being responsible for the conditions causing the diseases, vice, and crime associated with urban slums.

City Hall, begun in 1872, was to have been completed in ten years at a cost of $10,000,000, but it took much longer and cost much more. The tower was finished in 1887 and the statue of Penn raised in 1894. On a site about 475 feet square with a courtyard in the center, the massive structure when built was larger than any other single building in America. The legal community moved westward to be around the new courtrooms. The business community also moved and the new center of the city was around the city hall.[4]

The idea of the gentleman continued to be powerful in Philadelphia upper class. One pursued a career because it was his duty, and he did as well as he could, because that was the measurement of his worth. For the men of old Philadelphia families no occupations were more sacred than law and medicine. Those were followed by insurance and banking, with brokerage as a dubious modern adjunct. After these, running the family firm, no matter what its nature, was correct. Old Philadelphia families had from the beginning been legal families, medical families, then banking, iron, railroad, and coal families, and proud of it. Of approximately 2,200 Philadelphia men listed in the 1898 *Social Register*, 323 (15 percent) were lawyers, and 204 (9 percent) were medical doctors.

Some lawyers, in looking at the American legal system in 1900, saw an evolution that seemed similar to that of the biological world. It appeared to them that the law, like nature, must proceed on the natural selection principle. That society, both individually and collectively, could best attain its highest development by being left free from government control. The American Bar Association President James M. Woolworth said in 1897, "Under our system, the gates and avenues are open to all who will run the course. . . . There is no favor for any, but the best wins."[5]

American law continued to be based mainly on the traditional concepts of the liberty of the individual and the sacredness of private property. Laissez faire was the central value in all branches of the law including those governing relationships between private individuals. The general function of law was seen as providing the legal tools to create the framework within which economic growth could occur. There was little legal worry about such inequalities as existed between the bargaining powers of capital and labor. At the beginning of the twentieth century the right of property, like that of control, reigned supreme. The role of law relative to private property was primarily to make it secure from encroachments from others. The law dealt with property through the will of the owner, and his right to acquire and his use and disposal of property was strongly protected. Of course, the last quarter of the nineteenth century saw the phenomenal growth of the corporation.

The law of torts was not significant before 1900 because the common law had little to say about personal injuries brought about by carelessness. The modern law of torts came about as the machines of the Industrial Revolution had an unheard of capability to damage the human body. Historically, legal systems attempt to redress harm done by one person to another. The new machines added a frightful increase to the range of dangers to the individual, however. The great profits from the new machines also brought about increases in injury and death. That was different from human-to-human injuries because there were no ties of blood and love to prevent the suing of the machine and the owner. The economic expansion of the nineteenth century saw that as a great danger. The fear was that lawsuits and damages would undercut and subvert the growth of many marginal enterprises. That needed to be stopped because the machines were the basis for economic growth and national wealth for the greater good of the total society.

Most of the important early cases in tort law were connected with the railroads. More than any other industrial development the railroad was the key to industrial development. The railroads had already settled the wilderness, tied cities together, and linked the farms to the cities and to the seaports. They had also contributed greatly to the North's victory in the Civil War. The trains, however, were also sometimes out of control as they roared through the countryside, killing livestock, setting fire to houses and crops, smashing wagons at crossings, and mangling passengers as well as destroying freight. Sometimes boilers exploded, trains hurled off the tracks, and bridges collapsed. As a result railroad law and tort law developed together in America.

The concern in the law of torts was to decide on a line that divided those cases in which there was liability for harm done from those in which there was not. At the beginning of the twentieth century the line was fixed almost completely on the notion of blameworthiness. By 1900 the rule that liability was a corollary of fault had virtually been converted from a rule of common law to one of natural law. A law that considered the rule of no liability without fault a legal absolute placed the heaviest burden on the industrial worker. The cost of pain and mutilation related to production was borne by the worker rather than by his employer. Not only did the worker injured on the job have to prove negligence on the part of his employer, he also had to overcome the fellow servant rule and doctrine of assumption of risk. The combined requirement that the injured worker prove negligence, and that the injury was not due to a voluntarily assumed risk, made the worker's right to recover in industrial accident cases not common. The employee was a free man; he chose to work in an employment where he ran the risk of being injured. The employee must stand or fall by the consequence of his own conduct.[6]

Fault meant a breach of duty to the public, and it meant that the defendant had not done what a reasonable man should be expected to do. Absolute liability was rejected. To be more accurate, it was never considered because it might have strangled the economy. The aim of the judges was to limit damages to some moderate measure because their capital had to be spent for industrial development. The basic idea of contributory negligence was simple. If the plaintiff was negligent himself, ever so slightly, he could not recover from the defendant. The plaintiff had not only to prove that the railroad was negligent but also that he was faultless himself. If he was injured at a crossing, in relatively open country, with a clear view of the train, the court could take the case from the jury with clear conscience.[7]

By the beginning of the twentieth century the contract had also reached its great importance in law. A paper delivered at the 1900 American Bar Association proclaimed, "there is . . . complete freedom of contract; competition is now universal, and as merciless as nature and natural selection." The expansion of contract blossomed into a broadside freedom of contract that was considered the basic part of the liberty safeguarded by the due process clause. This resulted in an unprecedented accent on the anatomy of private decision makers. The law was devoted to providing legal tools, procedures, and compulsion to create the framework of reasonable expectations within which economic growth could occur. Freedom of contract was the chief article for those who wanted to minimize the function of the state. The right of contract was regarded not as a phase of freedom, but as the essence of liberty, posited as permanent and absolute. Impairment was not to be suffered, except within the most rigorous limits. "Contracts," said the Supreme Court in 1878, "mark the progress of communities in civilization and prosperity."[8]

The body of law had grown tremendously. Hundreds of volumes of reports were published each year. Every state published reports at least for its highest courts. As a matter of course, decisions and opinions were published in an endless stream. By the end of the nineteenth century there were very few high courts or federal judges any longer writing opinions of sweeping power and persuasion because they were rushed, and the dockets had become crowded. In the past the leisurely style of oral argument had been accompanied by a relaxed style of writing opinions. That was no longer true, however, Furthermore, the modern trend was for judges to be protectors of law rather than creators or builders.

Early in the twentieth century rights of property, like those of contract, reached their peak. The role of law vis-à-vis private property was largely to secure it from encroachment from others. The very word property meant the unrestricted right of possessing, enjoying, and disposing of a thing. A prominent text in 1889 said "Property is the realization of the free will of a person, the external sphere of his freedom." The law recognized and dealt with property exclusively through the will of the owner. "His right to acquire, use, and dispose of property was protected as never before, or since, in American law, for the all-inclusiveness of property rights was considered and essential aspect of the free society."[9]

"The lawyer", said Justice Brewer in 1895, "is evermore the leader in society" because from the beginning they have always been the rulers of the Nation. "How could it be otherwise?" as a speaker at the American Bar Association in 1892 observed "when the bar is and should be . . . that priestly tribe to whose hands are confided the support and defense of this Ark of Covenant of our father, the security of which against the profane touch of open and covert foes in the noblest function and the most patriotic purpose of our great profession."[10]

Government institutions were increasingly dominated by the legal profession, and especially significant was the creation of the new administrative process in the lawyer's image. For example, the first chairman of the Interstate Commerce Commission was Thomas M. Cooley, noted Michigan jurist and law professor. The greatest expansion of law in the twentieth century would be that of administrative law. That occurred as federal and state government assumed more power and responsibility through the creation of various types of boards, commissions, and bureaus.

From the beginning, when the Sherman Anti-Trust Act was passed in 1890, it was recognized by perceptive observers as a gesture, a ceremonial concession to the strong public demand for some kind of control over the trusts. Theodore Roosevelt's administration failed to prosecute many trusts, however, and failed to hold down the accelerating business consolidations that occurred during his administration. Roosevelt did not even believe in the trust-busting philosophy, and he was quite candid in saying so. "The man who advocates destroying the trusts," he said early in his presidency, "by measures which would paralyze the industries of the country is at least a quack and at worse an enemy of the Republic."[11]

The legal establishment was for the most part antilabor. For example, during the Pullman boycott, the usually liberal senior editor of the *American Law Review* applauded the railroads for having entered the struggle "with an unknown and appalling force, which threatened to revolutionize the very foundations of society and to reverse all the processes by which our splendid industrial society as been built." The *Railroad Age* observed, "It is probably safe to say that in no civilized country in this century, not actually in the throes of war or open insurrection, has society been so disorganized as it was during the first half of 1894; never was human life held so cheap; never did the constitutional authority appear so incompetent to inform respect for the law.''[12]

In Europe professional training in law was generally the result of university education, but that was not so in America. Instead of a requirement of special knowledge of history, literature, and language most of the new law schools were willing to admit anyone who would pay the required fees. Many law students worked in law offices and devoted their hours outside the classroom, not to library research but to earning a living. David Starr Jordan writing in 1895 said, ''From the streets any man can walk directly into the profession of law, disregarding even the formality of matriculation or graduation. In many of our States, it requires no more preparation to be admitted to the bar than to be admitted to the sawbuck.''[13]

The initial relationship between the law school and the university was very different from that it came to be in the twentieth century. The LL.B. was not a postgraduate degree because law schools did not require any college work for admission and many ''university'' law schools were very loosely connected to their parent institutions. By 1900, there were 102 law schools in the United States, and they were open for whatever business they could get.

In the early law schools faculty members were often locally known judges and lawyers, and full-time law professors were rare before the 1880s. Jordan wrote that in 1895 ''we find in most of our law schools lawyers who have turned incidentally to teaching. Usually the chair of law is occupied by broken down lawyers—old men who read old lectures to audiences inattentive or occupied with newspapers, or who conduct a lifeless quiz from lifeless text-books.''[14]

By the beginning of the twentieth century a body of professional teachers of law, outside the ranks of practicing lawyers, was beginning to emerge. They were developing as an independent force within the legal profession. As the full-time teaching lawyer replaced the part-timer, they developed an independent sense of professional consciousness that led to a broader conception of the law professor. Those men were increasingly concerned with new legal concepts and procedural reforms, deeper professional responsibility, and criticism of the courts. The law school teachers would increasingly take on the role of keepers of the professional conscience.

The modern University of Pennsylvania Law School was built by William Draper Lewis. He was a lecturer in the law department as well as in the Wharton School and was appointed the first full-time dean of the Law School in 1896. Lewis paid little attention to colleagues who said the teaching of law was a hobby rather than a profession. He took the position at the age of twenty-nine and agreed to give the position his full attention. Lewis was a Philadelphia Club level of the old Philadelphia upper class. He brought in a distinguished group of professors from outside Philadelphia. Under Lewis's leadership the Law School prospered and by 1914 awarded seventy-eight degrees.

Early in the twentieth century several nightime law schools emerged, and they usually had little in common with the university-related day law schools. The first, the Columbia College of Washington, D.C., was in operation in the late 1860s. It had been set up to reach employees in the government departments after they left work as three o'clock in the afternoon. The night schools were practical, and they had no interest in providing any intellectual legal training. Their emphasis on the local practice of law was to a far greater degree than in the full-time day law schools. With few exceptions, they lowered the level of legal education. The argument justifying them, however, was that they opened the door of legal training to the poor, the immigrant, and the working-class student. They became the breeding ground of the ethnic bar as they turned out Polish, Italian, Jewish, and Irish lawyers, many of whom went back to their ethnic neighborhoods to practice. Their graduates also contributed heavily to the lower court judges and local politics.

Temple University Law School in Philadelphia opened in the fall of 1895, and it offered an LL.B. after four years of school at night. When it started it was the only part-time law school in the United States that required four years instead of three. Temple University Law School was also the only law school that did not confer the degree until the student had actually been admitted to the state bar. It had its first commencement in 1901 and graduated sixteen, and the Law School was accredited in 1907.

For most of the nineteenth century there was no professional organization that could speak for the bar as a whole. Lawyers had for years formed associations, but they were mainly social; there was no general bar group until the last third of the nineteenth century. In 1870, a group in New York acquired a house in New York City, and during the first year about 450 lawyers joined, representing the "decent part" of the profession. Those first members were mainly well-to-do lawyers and predominantly of old American stock. The American Bar Association before 1900 was never much more than a gathering of dignified, well-to-do lawyers who enjoyed the comfort and elegance of their annual meetings at the resorts of Saratoga, New York.

Despite its restricted membership and agenda, the American Bar Association had a strong impact on the legal profession. It inaugurated a new era of professional activity that led to active bar associations in each state and many localities. There was a revival of the tradition of professional organization that had virtually disappeared from before the Civil War. The association on the local level spearheaded the movement to improve standards and instill pride in the legal profession.

The main significance of the American Bar Association was the way that it expressed, in concrete form, the ambitions of the "best men" of the bar for status and organization. Speeches and reports at the meetings usually voiced conventional sentiments about law reform, and ways and means to keep the profession decent, well liked, and well paid. The lowlifes of the bar—the ambulance chasers, the sleazy lawyers who hung around the criminal courts, the small-time debt collectors—were definitely not represented.

On 29 August 1906 at the St. Paul, Minnesota, meeting of the American Bar Association there was an address that had a great impact on reform in American law. The speaker was Roscoe Pound of Lincoln, Nebraska. He was in his mid-thirties and unknown outside his home state. His paper, "The Causes of Popular Dissatisfaction with the Administration of Justice" was dramatically different because it was not the usual eulogy to the "most refined system of justice yet devised by man." Rather, Pound said that dissatisfaction with the administration of justice was as old as law. He then jolted his audience by asserting that did not justify overlooking the fact "that there is more than the normal amount of dissatisfaction with the present-day administration of justice in America." As he read his bill of particulars his conservative audience sat in dismay. "Our system of courts is archaic. Our procedures behind the times. Our courts have seemed to obstruct public effort to get relief. They have been put in a false position of doing nothing and obstructing everything— their time is frittered away on mere points of legal etiquette. Putting courts into politics has almost destroyed the traditional respect for the Bench." That speech elicited hostile and virulent criticism, but it served as the catalyst for reform efforts.[15]

The Pennsylvania Bar Association in 1900 with a unanimous vote said that a State Board of Examiners should be created in Pennsylvania, and that a uniform standard of examination should be established for the registration and admission to the bar. On 1 January 1903 the state board was established. After 1910, all candidates had to either pass a preliminary examination, or present an academic degree from some college or university approved for that purpose by the state supreme court. Between 1903 and 1910, a total of 1861 applicants appeared for preliminary examination and of that group 45 percent failed on the first attempt. Ultimately 71 percent passed and were registered as law students. On the final examination for admission to the bar abour 73 percent passed on the first trial, with ultimately 92 percent passing.

The Philadelphia Bar Association was in many respects an organization for the upper class lawyer. In 1895, of about thirteen hundred lawyers in the city 20 percent of them were in the *Social Register*. Of all the lawyers in the city only about 40 percent belonged to the Bar Association. Of that group more than 50 percent of them were in the *Social Register*. Even more significant was that the leadership of the Philadelphia Bar Association continued to be dominated by upper class lawyers. There was also a Lawyer's Club incorporated in the city in 1892 "to encourage among its members social intercourse and a full discussion of matters affecting the standards of professional ethics—the maintenance of a club house and a library for the use of members." That club was apparently organized for those lawyers outside the upper-class establishment. Of the 570 members only 8 percent of them were in the *Social Register*, and the club appears to have disappeared in a few years.

By the end of the nineteenth century there were more lawyers in the United States than in any other country. The lawyer had come to be seen as absolutely indispensable to American society, and it was still relatively easy to become a lawyer and be allowed to practice. It was estimated in 1880 that there were about 60,000 lawyers in America, and by 1900 the figure had nearly doubled to about 114,000. In Philadelphia the number of lawyers went from about 1,300 in 1885 to about 1,900 in 1905, an increase of 45 percent.

William W. Porter wrote about the status of the legal profession in Philadelphia in 1907. He reminisced that there was a time when to be a lawyer was to be seen as well above the level of the layman and to be regarded with respect and consideration. "In this so-called era of reform the profession seems to be subject to attack. For many years past, with increasing emphasis, the profession has been charged with what is called 'commercialism.' " That appeared to mean that law had become more business and less professionally oriented. Porter went on to state that a mere glance into an active law office in his day furnished the foundation for his assertion. "It is no longer a modest room adorned with book cases where sits a learned semi-recluse writing to bestow his wisdom in the law and satisfied if compensation shall come as an honorarium." Instead, today there is "a large suite of offices resembling a place of business. Law books are often relegated to a separate library. Clerks, cashiers, messengers, bookkeepers, stenographers, typewriters and telephones are there. The chiefs of such offices are quite as much men of affairs as students of law."[16]

Another change in Philadelphia law practice was the disappearance of the old conveyancers. Although they were not always members of the bar, they had an intimate familiarity with the laws of real estate and of decedents. Their work was frequently a matter of inheritance, and the "good will" of an established conveyancing office was a very material and enviable asset. The conveyancer was commonly, too, the depository of clients' title papers, wills, and other documents. The relations between the parties was confidential and sacred. "It bred an exceptionally high type of man and the propensity of the corporate enterprise which supplanted them was due in a large measure to the honorable traditions which substantially embodied their legacy to their successors."[17]

Coxe also wrote that "all the elaborate and time-consuming labors incident to the taking out of searches in the various courts and scattered public places of record, the drafting and engrossing of deeds and mortgages and other instruments were speedily and forever done away with, under the new Title and Trust Companies." In the preparing of deeds and mortgages the introduction of the typewriter, "an innovation long resisted, practically and ever after the business was transferred to these corporations, caused the art of engrossing, to become completely a thing of the past as the writing of letters and legal documents by hand." Coxe wrote that earlier there had been resistance to the steel pen, when it was first employed, as being a "too unbusinesslike, unsentimental, and unpoetic substitute for the more romantic quill." [18]

Another writer observed that until the end of the first decade of the twentieth century there had not been many changes from thirty years earlier in the actual practice of law. He said that a successful law practice required a few substantial corporation clients to provide a comfortable cushion after paying expenses and with that would also go the fees of a general practice. Through that period lawyers were still generally advocates, and when they were not in court they were likely to be preparing for a trial or argument. There were also wills to be drawn, real estate to be bought and sold, and agreements to be prepared. By far the greater part of lawyers' time and energy, however, went into work that was already in or on its way to court. That work took the form of preparing preliminary opinions, pleadings, memorandums, and briefs. There was waiting in the courtroom for a case to be called for trial and eventually trying it; arguing a rule or motion either before or after trial; and finally arguing an appeal to a higher court. [19]

John Dos Passos wrote in 1907 that the age of forensic eloquence had passed, and the courts had rules that limited the length of time for courtroom presentations. As legal oratory was curtailed the use of "briefs" were greatly expanded. The brief became necessary to supply that which could not be spoken, or "to instruct an ignorant, too busy, or indolent judiciary." The lawyer's skill in jury trials came to be in the handling of witnesses, the capacity to twist and magnify facts, and the placing of all the circumstances in a dramatic light. "No modern lawyer is apparently satisfied with himself unless he can shout and use passionate and furious gestures. The Judge now gives an advocate hardly time to clear his throat. Of course, some tendency of lawyers to talk on infinitum. Hardly a lawyer ever believes he has said enough." [20]

Lawyers often said that the law had lost much of its distinctly professional character and had become a business. That may have been based on a somewhat exaggerated recollection of the law during an earlier era, however. Many older lawyers were convinced that their profession had declined in its intellectual standards as well as its moral and social position. Around 1900 the professional talents of courtroom advocacy and brief making were often referred to as "lost arts," as the occupation of the successful lawyer centered more and more on counseling clients and offering business advice.

The new law practices involved far greater sums of money than in the earlier days. In part that was because the legal problems were far more complex and required much more time and effort. It was also increasingly true that the line between a legal question and a business question was difficult to draw. The new practices were far more rewarding than the old because lawyers often realized far greater profits from clients' transactions. Counselors served as legal engineers, for questions involving larger sums of money; therefore, clients were ready to pay higher fees for legal services. "By the 1890's many of the former great advocates were not only devoting most of their time to the new corporate practice but had drawn around themselves other lawyers whose abilities lay rather in negotiation in the conference room and in drafting documents than in persuasion before the courts."[21]

There was in Philadelphia a great concern with the "ambulance chasing" lawyers. Porter wrote in 1907, "it is a disgraceful fact that among the first to call at the house when someone is injured is the agent of a rapacious attorney who wants to preempt the case." Porter went on to say that the crowding of the law profession along with the amounts paid in damages were responsible. The slightest accident was hunted up and reported by runners in the employment of lawyers of doubtful standing. In addition, there were many physicians in league with the lawyers. "Also—rumor has it that the defendants in damage cases do not always deal on the highest levels of honor. The eminent counsel to the great corporation which wish to keep on the shady side of law, and which retain lawyers at enormous salaries, to advise them, not what the law is, but how it may be violated with impunity."[22]

Coxe also wrote that negligence law had become a new means that allowed some younger lawyers to survive economically. He commented that "when I was a beginning lawyer accidents sometimes occurred in which persons were injured. But," he wrote, "there were no longer accidents. That was true because every injury a man received, even if the result of his own negligence, it was sought to hold someone liable." "The theory appears to be that for every injury which a man, especially a poor man, receives someone should make compensation. A corporation if possible and if not, some private person with a large estate. The person whose direct act caused the inury is seldom molested, the skillful practitioner flies his hawk at higher game. The advantage of this class of business is the young lawyer, if moderately frugal in his habits, can live upon one case per year, provided he gain it in the Common Pleas and not wrecked in the Superior Court."[23]

The question of the morality of Philadelphia lawyers was discussed in an article in the *Philadelphia Bulletin* in 1903. "Charlatans, tricksters, and fomenters of litigation are to be found on all sides, but only at long intervals does the public hear that any of them has been disbarred." The writer went on to say the "last occassion was when a lawyer named Maires was dropped from the rolls because he was a concocter of litigation who took cases for damages 'on spec' and received for himself the greater portion of the money obtained." For every lawyer, however, "that has been thus dealt with, it is certain that there are a dozen that ought to be among the pettifoggers of evil who solicit business, employ runners, cook up provocations to law suits, set up fictitious claims, exhort inordinate fees for damage, and cast all conscience to the winds in protecting the people who live on habitual fraud and vice."

The article pointed out that "in the fierce struggle for clients a poor and youthful man needs a moral fibre of the stoutest texture to enable him to live up to those principles in the face of the propsperous breed of blackguards and cozeners who treat them as obsolete or absurd." A few years before "the late Judge Arnold had remarked that about 3/5ths of the bar was strictly honest and faithful to their oath, that 1/5th were easy going or indifferent, and that the other 1/5th were shady and would deserve to be kicked out of the profession if any proof of their chicanery could be fastened to them." The point of this newspaper article was that the Board of Censors of the Philadelphia Bar Association must begin to take serious action against unethical and dishonest lawyers.[24]

The advice of George Sharswood in the 1850s for the young lawyer to wait for business to seek him out was of little reassurance to the new immigrant lawyers. Clearly the upper class monopolized the most lucrative business, and the rest of the lawyers had to scramble for a share of what was left. The lawyer without contacts either hustled, or he starved and often moved into areas looked down on by the successful members of the profession. For many, however, those "seedy" areas were about all that were available to them.

As mentioned, one important change in the practice of law was less involvement in litigation. In the past the ruggedly independent merchants would often, with their lawyers, go into the courts and do battle. The modern corporate client, however, expected his business to be handled so as to keep him out of the courts. The pattern increasingly was to avoid litigation. That change was reflected in the career of Morris Bockius who was the driving force behind the development of Morgan Lewis & Bockius, one of the oldest and largest firms in Philadelphia. Bockius was a lawyer with vast experience in business affairs but never appeared in any court at any time during his entire professional career.

As the system of codes became more and more dominant in law the need for the ancient pleading arts decreased. "The slow estrangement of the lawyer from his old and natural haunt, the court, was an outstanding fact of the practice in the second half of the century." Many lawyers at the beginning of the twentieth century still went to court, but not true of the new Wall Street lawyer. He often never spoke to a judge except socially, made more money, and had more prestige than any courtroom lawyer could ever attain. The change of function reflected changes in the law itself. Life and the economy were more complicated; "there was more, then, to be done, in the business world especially; and the lawyers proved able to do it."[25]

By 1900 lawyers as a group were more heterogeneous than they had been thirty years before. The large and successful firms were headed by the wealthier, more influential, and more conservative members of the profession. They were also the lawyers who were most dominant in the bar associations. In Philadelphia those lawyers were old family and for the most part wealthy.

The young men who would come to join them and eventually to take over the expanding firms came from the same social backgrounds. At the beginning of the twentieth century there was no opportunity for women, or members of minority groups. The firms were clearly anti-Semitic. Although they did take some young men in who were not quite of the upper class, they were ethnically "acceptable." Those lawyers entering the influential Philadelphia firm were Protestants and almost always the product of the University of Pennsylvania Law School.

Most lawyers in Philadelphia were in partnerships or sole practice, and their livelihood was modest at best and nonexistent at worst. As the situation of the sole practitioners deteriorated many of them drifted into ambulance chasing and taking on negligence work on contingency fees. Those poorer lawyers were viewed with little sympathy by the successful elite. "Much of the talk of the Bar Association about improving legal ethics represented the unsympathetic efforts of the richer lawyers to improve the reputation of the profession, at the expense of their weaker colleagues."[26]

The sole practitioner was being affected in other ways. Much of his traditional work was being taken away from him by real estate, trust and insurance companies, collection agencies, and banks, as they took on themselves larger and larger amounts of what had once been entirely legal business. A speaker at the meeting of the Baltimore Bar Association in 1911 estimated that 70 percent of the members of the profession were not making a suitable living.

In 1905, approximately nineteen hundred lawyers were listed in the *Philadelphia Business Directory*. There were fifty-five partnerships of two names, ten with three names, and one with four names. The size of some of the small firms was undoubtedly larger because they often did not list junior members. There were only a few firms in the city that had listed between six and ten lawyers.

Law partnerships were mainly a creation of the twentieth century. With the growth of industry, and especially with the bankruptcy of the streetcar companies at the turn of the century, clients' problems became to complicated for the individual lawyer to handle. Often the primary distinction in a partnership was between the office lawyer and the courtroom lawyer. That was a natural division of labor in those days of a still relatively simple law practice.

By the beginning of the twentieth century law offices had taken up the use of telephones and typewriters, and started to employ office workers skilled in the use of the new business machines. Also the salaried lawyer was becoming commoner. For example, Cravath in New York, in 1900 paid beginning lawyers $30 a month. Lawyers on the full-time payroll of large businesses were rare in 1850, but by 1900 they were beginning to be found. To be general counsel of a major railroad after the Civil War was to hold a position of great prestige and huge salary. Those in the positions were very high-status lawyers. There were also some railroad presidents who had started out as lawyers.

At the beginning of the twentieth century law offices were scattered over a wide area of the center of the city. The profession included nearly 2,000 lawyers and while all of those were not in practice those who were became too numerous to enable anyone of them to see much of the others in their ordinary pursuits. It was, therefore, much easier than it formerly had been for a member of the bar to save himself from professional condemnation when he was guilty of illicit, venal, or malodorous practice. In a 1903 newspaper article it was written that "charlatans, tricksters and fomenters of litigation are to be found on all sides."

In that same article it was said that the late Judge Arnold had remarked that about three-fifths of the bar were strictly honest and faithful to their oaths, that one-fifth was easy going or indifferent, and that the other fifth were shady and would deserve to be kicked out of the profession if any proof of their chicancery could be fastened on them.[27]

In Philadelphia the decades around the beginning of the twentieth century saw a move of the courts and the law offices. Almost from the beginning the courts and law offices had been located around the Independence Square in the fifth Street area. Slowly the move was westward to be close to the new City Hall at Broad and Market. That move from the old area was viewed by some as a real loss. Coxe saw it as the loss of professional individuality, and he nostalgically recalled that there was a personal distinction when the lawyer had a front office and especially when it was a part of his own home and fireside. "The removal of the professional center from the neighborhood of the old State House to the vicinity of City Hall had its very great stress in disturbing, not to say destroying, previous most pleasant conditions."[28]

An obituary in the *Philadelphia Bulletin* in 1912 provides a nostalgic description of the old law office area. The obituary was written at the death of William S. Price who had practiced law for seventy years. The article described him as the oldest of the few lawyers who had maintained offices under the same roof as their homes. Price, the article said, could never allow himself to leave the scene of his professional pursuits and his domestic pleasures. His house was described as "a quiet, genteel abode, on the North side of Walnut, below 7th Street. A little black tin sign, with the words which time had gently worn as if half-dimmed: W. S. Price, Attorney at Law." The article said he was not at all a great lawyer, but he was a sound and trustworthy one. Law firms, fancy offices, a corps of clerks, and a battery of typewriters were professional changes he could not altogether accept when he remembered how the greats of the Philadelphia bar received their clients in offices with a carpetless floor, a table with a green baize cover, a copy press, a few wooden chairs, a coal stove and scuttle, and, perhaps, a capacious spittoon.[29]

Most of the newspaper accounts reported the successes of the various outstanding members of the Philadelphia bar at time when they were being honored or at their death. Philadelphia had plenty of lawyers who were not seen as honorable, however. Around 1900 the newspapers, when they knew about them, reported scandals of all kinds and sold many newspapers. A sensational divorce, the antics of the more colorful lawyers like "Chippy" Patternson or "Foghorn" Fow, the elopement of lawyer Piggett with another man's wife, gave the readers lurid accounts of bar activities. There was a story of a rich young lawyer who was spending too much time at the race track, the disbarment of the former district attorney in Lancaster, or the spectacle of a local practitioner in the prisoner's dock on a minor charge.

On the more positive side there was an article in the *Philadelphia Bulletin* in 1903 about the Bar Association. In the article the writer related that William Lewis would accept no fee that came to him with any taint of dishonor. On one occasion he was employed by a businessman to represent him in defending an important transaction involving a considerable amount of money. As the evidence began to be developed Lewis suspected that all the facts had not been told him by his client and when his suspicions were confirmed he declined to have anything to do with the case. "Will you not speak for me?" asked the defendant. "No, Sir," said Lewis. "What then," inquired the client, "have I paid you for?" You have paid me," replied the now aroused lawyer "that you might have justice done; and justice will be done without any further interference."[30]

There were still very few women in law. By 1900, there were approximately one thousand women lawyers in the United States. The few women who graduated from law school found it impossible to attain good positions. In 1905 Alice Dillingham graduated first in her class at New York University Law School, but not one Wall Street law firm would consider hiring her because she was a woman. Eventually she found a $10-a-week job with the Legal Aid Society.[31] In Philadelphia, in addition to Caroline Kilgore who was admitted to the bar in 1883, there were only two other women in the 1900 *Philadelphia Business Directory*. They were Diana Hirschler and Ruby R. Vale. By contrast, in the same year, 120 women physicians were listed.

The egalitarian system that determined the selection of judges made sure that those individuals were not very talented. The American system was very different from that of the European one in which a student in law school decides whether he wishes to be an advocate or a judge. If he is to be a judge, he rises through the administrative process rather than through private practice. In his training he acquires at each stage skills and information that will help him to sit on the bench. In Great Britain the judges are drawn entirely from the limited ranks of barristers, and the appointments are made by the lord chancellor who is in a position to know about the candidate. (When Chancellor

Lyndhurst was asked what method he used in making judicial appointments, he replied, "I look about for a gentleman, and if he knows a little law so much the better.)

In American courts at the turn of the century statute law had in many instances come to replace common law. The judicial view came to be that statute laws were to be "construed strictly"—that is, the legislature was to be assumed not to have wished to change the common law unless it unquestionably said so. A classic example of that point was reached in the United States in 1902 when the Circuit Court of Appeals for the Eighth District ruled against a railway conductor who had lost a hand trying to couple together a locomotive and a railroad car that could not couple automatically. Under the common law, the conductor would have been held to have assumed the risk of losing his hand when he accepted the job. Congress, however, had passed a statute requiring railroads to equip their cars with automatic couplers, supposedly to put an end to such accidents. The court admitted the controlling force of the statute, then pointed out that both cars were in fact equipped with automatic couplers (though of different designs that would not lock them together automatically). One was a locomotive rather than a car, however. The court ruled that if Congress had wished to include locomotives in the law it would have said "locomotives." So the statute did not apply, and the railroad was not held liable.[32]

As the Philadelphia bar expanded there were many persons from various social backgrounds entering the law. They did not often reach positions of power in the city, however. Although the number of lawyers from the upper class remained about the same as thirty years before, their percentage of the total Philadelphia bar had decreased. They had constituted 22 percent of the Philadelphia bar in 1875, but in 1905 they were only 12 percent. They were also decreasing as a percentage of the Philadelphia Bar Association. In 1875 the upper class had made up 42 percent, whereas in 1905 it was 29 percent. They were still disproportionately represented in the leadership of the bar, however.

In 1900 of the adult males listed in the *Social Register*, 19 percent were lawyers, and 10 percent were physicians; there continued to be lawyers from some of the old Philadelphia legal families. For example, in the 1898 *Social Register*, there were twenty-five male Biddles listed, and six of them were lawyers and three physicians. Of five Cadwalader adult males listed three were lawyers and two physicians. Of twenty-two Norrises five were lawyers and three physicians, and of six Rawleses there were three lawyers.

Some evidence suggests that lawyers continued to be more often from older Philadelphia upper-class families than were physicians. In comparing membership of lawyers in the Philadelphia Club, the Rittenhouse Club, and the Union League 54 percent of the lawyers were listed in the 1898 *Social Register* but only 33 percent of the physicians. The lawyers were also more likely to belong to country clubs (although this was much less socially significant in 1895)—44 percent vs. 29 percent.

In 1898 the upper class lawyer was still well represented in the courts. Of the Pennsylvania Superior Court there were seven members of which two were in the *Social Register*. There were in the four common pleas courts and the orphans court, sixteen judges of whom eight were in the *Social Register*. These judges included such old Philadelphia legal families as Biddle, Hare, Pennypacker, Thayer, and Penrose.

The period around the turn of the century saw the continued importance of the corporation in the practice of the successful lawyer. The new evening law schools were providing education for many immigrants and their sons. Those men rarely went into the emerging law firms in the city but rather were increasingly to be found in politics and the judiciary. Those continued to be areas of the law of little interest to the old Philadelphia lawyers.

Profile 9: Samuel Whitaker Pennypacker (1843–1916)

This portrait is different in two respects from most of the others. First, Samuel Pennypacker was not of an old Philadelphia family; second, most of his career was served on the bench and in politics. He did come from an old Pennsylvania family, however, that had emigrated to America before 1700. The founder of the family in Pennsylvania, Hendrick Pannebecker came to Germantown in 1699 and moved to Skippack in 1702 where he practiced as an attorney. Samuel Pennypacker's father studied medicine at the University of Pennsylvania and settled in Phoenixville, about twenty-five miles from Philadelphia, where the son was born. As a young man growing up he worked in a country store, taught in a country school, and served for a few weeks in the Union army in 1863. He then studied law and was admitted to the Pennsylvania bar in 1866 at twenty-three years of age, and a year later he graduated from the University of Pennsylvania. He was elected to successive offices in the Philadelphia Law Academy. That reflected the high regard with which he was held among the other young lawyers in the city.

For several years his law practice was small because he had to develop his legal career as a lawyer slowly and patiently without Philadelphia family and social class connections. With time he did acquire some important clients, and in 1889, he was appointed judge in Philadelphia Common Pleas Court No. 2. That was followed by his election to a ten-year term, and he was later in 1899 reelected for another ten-year term. Pennypacker became President Judge of the court two years before his reelection. He has been described as "showing patient attention to counsel, ample learning, sound sense and promptitude in disposal of his cases which made his judicial services very satisfactory to the bar." On the bench he was described as not an innovator, and as one whose strong convictions and strong prejudices did not affect his legal decisions.[1] From 1885 to 1889 he also served on the Board of Public Education of Philadelphia.

In June 1902 he was nominated for governor of Pennsylvania and was immediately attacked for "Quayism." Matthew S. Quay was the political boss of the state, and he was also related to Pennypacker. The two men also shared common literary interests and were very close friends. Pennypacker ran an open campaign and was elected by an unprecedented large vote. His record

Samuel Whitaker Pennypacker, 1843–1916. Courtesy of the Historical Society of Pennsylvania.

as governor was characterized by an independence in appointments that were relatively free from political influence. His four-year administration did have conflict, however. From his judicial experience he had developed strong convictions that legislation was excessive, and that many statutes were absurd. He believed that there was far too much miltiplying of statutory crimes. By pressure, vetoes (63 in 1903 and 123 in 1905) and threats to veto, he cut by half the legislative output as well as improving its quality. He also held to other strong convictions. For example, he did not believe that corporations should be chartered with nominal capital as mere trial balloons or with capitalization too small to protect the public. Nor did he believe that water companies should be delegated powers of eminent domain. He also established a department of health and advanced conservation of forest land and historic sites in the state. He paid off the state debt and left a large balance in the treasury, without new taxation and despite the costs of a new state capital.[2]

The building of the state capitol did lead to one of the political turmoils that occurred while he was governor. Although the furnishings of the capitol involved corruption on a large scale, there was never any hint or belief that Pennypacker was corrupt. There were some who believed he should have detected the "jokers" in the contracts. His "libel bill" of 1903 and his supporting measure roused tremendous opposition. The statute authorized actions for damages against newspapers for publication of untruths as facts when there was negligent failure to discover their falsity. He required the newspapers to publish the names of their editors and publishers.[3]

Pennypacker had become interested in serious historical studies before 1872 and built a major collection of about ten thousand items on Pennsylvania history. He was the president of the Historical Society of Pennsylvania from 1900 to 1916, and he wrote several articles on local history and law. Pennypacker wrote *The Autobiography of a Pennsylvanian*,[4] published in 1918. One chapter in the book of particular interest was about the Philadelphia bar. He writes about his arrival in Philadelphia in 1865 to study law. Following are some of his comments about his experiences of becoming a lawyer in Philadelphia at the time of the Civil War.

Pennypacker arrived in Philadelphia to study law in the office of Peter McCall. McCall was of an old Philadelphia upper class family and had been the mayor of Philadelphia as well as Professor of law at the University of Pennsylvania. McCall held a position at the bar, "everywhere recognized as close to the top. Throughout the Civil War his wife, a southern woman, openly avowed her hope for the success of the southern cause, and he was frequently denounced as a Copperhead. He did for a time lose some clients and some of his students left him. But by the end of the War there was again respect for McCall."

Pennypacker wrote of his first morning going to McCall's law office. "I reached the offices, No. 224 South Fourth Street, in the early morning. They consisted of two large rooms on the ground floor. No one else had arrived.

Securing a book, I selected a large and comfortable chair, drew it to the front window and began my studies. Presently a tall young man with dark whiskers entered, and coming over to me said 'It is a custom in this office that the oldest student occupies that chair and I will thank you to give it to me.' I surrendered with due meekness and had received my first lesson in discipline."[5]

Students were expected to run errands and to respond when called on for any sort of manual assistance. Instead of mailing letters Mr. McCall would say in his blandest manner: " 'Mr. —. I wish that on your way home this evening you will be good enough to deliver these letters.' Once O'Brien [a fellow student] said by way of protest, 'Mr. McCall, is it the custom for students in a lawyer's office to carry letters?' 'I think it is, Mr. O'Brien,' was the answer, and therefore whenever a letter was deliverable at any unusual distance this particular student was pretty sure to get it."[6]

Among the students, Pennypacker was the only one who had not at that time graduated from college. At that time the method of training lawyers for the work of the profession was to have the student read on the subject in the office of a practicing attorney and under his direction, and to have his progress measured by occasional examination. "The reading was confined almost exclusively to dissertations upon the law and text-books and there was little or no reference to particular cases. A principle was affirmed and if a case was cited it was an elucidation of that principle. The judges were presumed to have known it and have decided accordingly. In Mr. McCall's we learned nothing of causes and I have many a time wondered what I should do if perchance in the future an actual case ever came to me."[7]

Pennypacker also provides a description of what his personal life was like when as a young man he arrived in the city from the country. He writes that through his first summer he boarded in the Pennsylvania Dutch Hotel on Third Street near Callowhill. The Hotel was patronized by clerks working for local merchants and farmers coming into the city. "I had a little room in the third story with one small window, a bed, a bowl and basin on a rough stand, two Windsor chairs, a strip of rag carpet along the bed and no other furniture except a jordan. In the dining room we sat on stools as a long table. There were not, however, stools enough for all the guests, and as a result there had to be two services. When the gong sounded the doors were thrown open, there was a rush for the stools in which men were jammed and clothes torn and when the stools were filled the doors were closed again. On Sundays, I went to Franklin Square and, sitting on a bench there, read Gibbon's Decline and Fall of the Roman Empire."[8]

Pennypacker was introduced to the Law Academy while a student, and in 1865 was elected its assistant secretary. Through two winters he attended law lectures at the University of Pennsylvania given by George Sharswood, P. Pemberton Morris, and E. Spencer Miller, paying each of them $60 for the two terms of the year. Miller had the reputation of being the least capable lawyer and the best lecturer. A nervous combative little man, he had a practice that was said to net him $30,000 a year and had made him rich. Sharswood had one of those kindly dispositions that made everybody fond of him. "He had no presence, no voice and a troubled utterance."[9]

When Pennypacker was admitted to the bar in May 1866, on the Board of Examiners were George W. Biddle and William Henry Rawle among others, and John Cadwalader, Jr., acted as secretary. "They made an entry in their minutes that I had passed the best examination which had come before them during their term, much to the delight of Mr. McCall and myself. Biddle, long regarded one of the leaders of the Bar, never forgot me and frequently recalled the impression of me then made." Pennypacker's grandfather had paid for his legal education. "This was extended through the two and a half years in the midst of the high prices of the war. The costs included $200 paid to his preceptor and $360 paid to University Professors, and including room and board, the total was $1,260."[10]

Because of his highly successful examination, Pennypacker was offered positions in three different offices—those of E. Spencer Miller, Daniel Dougherty, and Frederick Heyer, at a salary that ranged from $600 to $800 per year. Pennypacker decided he would rather start on his own, however, and he rented the front room at 705 Walnut Street from a lawyer George L. Crawford. "His clients passed through my office and I had the great pleasure of seeing them daily go by me in numbers." Pennypacker took part in the arguments of the Law Academy and was elected secretary in 1866. He wrote that a little clique of "cultivated men" conducted the affairs of the Law Academy. "There was the unbroken custom that he who filled the office of Prothonotary for one year should, if he so desired, be elected the President for the following year. At this time J. Vaughan Darling held the position of Prothonotary and supervised the serious labor of preparing all the cases to be argued during the winter's sessions." Pennypacker goes on to relate that in taking part in the management of the academy and during a speech he used the word "gentlemen." Darling, "in a supercilious way said 'Mr. Pennypacker will find his ideas and ours of what constitutes a gentleman are quite different.'" Pennypacker said that remark cost Darling the presidency. "The membership of the Academy had felt such things before, were ready for revolt, and only needed a leader. I organized a rebellion which proved to be a revolution. Our candidate won."[11]

Pennypacker writes that when he came to the bar, Horace Binney could occasionally be seen on the streets although long retired from practice. William M. Meridith could be heard at rare intervals in the courts, and Eli K. Price, in his canny way, was heaping up a fortune. There was also Theodore Cuyler, the counsel of the Pennsylvania Railroad, a suave and subtle man. He was perhaps best described in the epigram of Samuel Dickson, who said of him that "He had every quality of an advocate. He could persuade a jury to render a verdict contrary to the facts and the Supreme Court to render a decision contrary to the law."

Pennypacker also wrote about Philadelphia lawyers of his day. One, Daniel Daugherty, had the reputation of being an orator, but he was only an orator. Like so many other American orators, he was an Irishman. I once heard him make a powerful appeal to the jury, in an important case in which he was opposed by William W. Ker, who had only force and experience. When Ker arose he said quietly, "Gentlemen, you are to be congratulated. Those who generally hear Mr. Dougherty, listen for an hour at the Academy of Music and pay a dollar for the privilege. You have heard him for four hours for nothing." Ker won the case.[12]

Pennypacker wrote that the most eccentric character of the bar was a man named Lucas Hirst. "He had offices on Walnut Street above 6th, and ate his meals and kept a woman at the same place. Thin, with sandy complexion and red hair, he had a high, rasping voice. Other lawyers kept away from him as much as possible. Not only had he ability and readiness for the encounter, but papers had a way of disappearing and sometimes they did not remain at the end of the suit as they had been at the beginning." Another lawyer named Black was described by Justice Miller. "As a man he was simply abominable, but there was no one who appeared before the court to whom it was so agreeable to listen. In hearing him you felt that you did not care a damn whether he was talking about his case or about any other case, but there was a wealth of illustration, a knowledge of the Bible and of Shakespeare wrought into his arguments which made you feel that you would like him to go on forever."

Pennypacker wrote that during his first year of practice he received fees of $800, and his annual returns slowly increased. When he got married in 1870 he was earning about $2,000 a year. "At that time I moved my office to 209 S. 6th Street, where I had a room to myself. When I went out a tacked a card to the door. For years I carried my lunch to my office in my green bag and walked from my home at 2002 N. Marvine Street."[13]

Pennypacker was during the Victorian era one of the more distinguished cultural and civil leaders of his adopted city of Philadelphia. He was proud of his Pennsylvania Dutch heritage but also proud that he had become successful in Philadelphia. When he was elected president of the Historical Society of Pennsylvania in 1900, he wrote that "the event marked an innovation in the conduct of the Society. Up to my time the president had always been selected from among the families long identified with the life of the city and had always dwelt south of Market Street." He was a strong booster of his adopted city, especially in comparison to Boston. He wrote that Pennsylvania is an achievement above any other state because of "the law of nature" and the "scientifically proved" fact that "the crossing of allied stocks leads to the increase of vital activities."[14]

Pennypacker was one of the rare Philadelphia lawyers not only to practice law but also to be on the bench, serve in a high elected office, and also to be a scholar. Although he did not come from an old Philadelphia family, he founded one, and his descendants became a part of the Philadelphia gentry.

Common law
statutory law - ?

law made
by judge?
- unwritten?
precedent

lawyers
clergy - personal property

"The house of the
lawyer is the oracle
of the whole city."

James Wilson p.65
Chp. 3

GAD
MEN ARE SLOW!

10
World War I Decade: 1910–1920

He that has the worse case makes the most noise.

—Anonymous

When World War 1 ended in 1919 Philadelphia's population was 1,850,000. By 1910, there had been enough skilled workers, small businessmen, and white-collar workers who could afford the two- and three-story row houses, and as a result over a quarter of all Philadelphians owned their own homes. Between 1900 and 1920 the population of West Philadelphia more than doubled. Most of the new building before World War I had created "street car suburbs" within the city limits. The new patterns between the place of work and where one lived were complemented by new ways of shopping. The old market houses, curbside markets, and pushcarts were becoming rare. After 1900, mail-order sales, grocery chains, and downtown department stores had greatly changed the city's shopping habits.

Philadelphia continued to undergo dramatic changes in its population makeup. Pennsylvania attracted more immigrants than any other state except New York, and by 1920 the foreign-born population for Pennsylvania was 16 percent. The great Italian immigration to Philadelphia came after 1910 and extended into the 1920s. At the end of the 1920s the Italian and the Russian-Jewish populations each reached nearly 200,000. There was also a large population of both gentiles and Jews from other parts of eastern and central Europe. The second great stream of migration came from the American south, and Philadelphia had a black population of about 50,000 in the 1890s and by 1920 more than 100,000.

In the half century before World War II, the city's factories and mills dominated vast sectors of American manufacturing. The city led the nation in the production of such diverse products as locomotives, streetcars, saws, steel ships, textiles, rugs, hosiery, hats, leather and cigars. It held second place in the production of sugar, fertilizer, foundry castings, petroleum products, chemicals and drugs. The United States Census listed 264 manufactured articles produced in 1910 and Philadelphia produced 211 of them.[1]

The Philadelphia gentleman had been around for more than two hundred years, and in Philadelphia an inherited position was still clearly more rewarding than a self-made one. The old Philadelphian's education and training were not designed to make him get ahead. He was meant to turn out to be a credit to the family, a pillar of the establishment, and if he could not always be outstanding he could at least be a member in good standing. First of all was his education. One did not become a good Philadelphian simply by accident of birth. One also had to be groomed and trained. "After education comes Life—life can be Work, Good Works, Play and plain living. In Philadelphia the customary professional hierarchy of English upper classes as a pyramid topped by a career in Politics, the Army or Navy, and the Church had been inverted." Not for the Philadelphian was there the devotion of the Bostonian to the pulpit and its offshoots, professorships, and moral literature. Nor was there the southern respect for soldiers and statesmen. In Philadelphia the Church, the armed forces, and politics were not for the upper class. "For one thing, as a clergyman, soldier, politican, or teacher, one stands a good chance of being moved away from Philadelphia. A career away from Philadelphia is out of bounds, doesn't count. Instead the Old Philadelphian is supposed to confine himself to certain specific callings—law, medicine and banking.[2]

There was little of significance in legal development during the decade of World War I. Although the laws of the corporate world were coming under attack, they were still being interpreted by the courts in ways favorable to the corporation. The principle of immunity, itself a product of the recent legal developments, had become elevated into a right inherent in free government. It was held that government intervention could only be productive of ultimate harm. For example, on workmen's compensation one strong view saw that as a way of stifling enterprise, producing discontent, strife, idleness, and pauperism. The outlook for its enactment did not appear very good. By 1900 workmen's compensation was an idea whose time had come because the failure of the common law to provide for the injured worker had become intolerable. In 1917 and 1919 the Supreme Court finally held state workmen's compensation laws as legal, and the state courts speedily followed.[3]

In the first decades of the twentieth century intellectual life became even more specialized and professional. That was apparent in the rapid shift from the older apprenticeship systems of training doctors and lawyers to a dependence on the professional school. The professional training in medicine and law continued to suffer from lax standards even at the leading universities, however, and from the practice of diploma selling in chartered institutions. In those early years of the new century the growth and influence of university law schools paralleled the expansion and power of the corporation law firm. A law school hierarchy developed in which Harvard and other schools like Columbia and Yale were providing a professional elite of lawyers. The night and part-time law schools were preparing minority groups and poorer people for limited careers as sole practitioners, for politics and other areas of noncorporate law.

The first pronouncement of the American Bar Association regarding law school entrance requirements was made in 1897 when it called for completion of high school or its equivalent. In 1900 the association approved lengthening the course of night schools to four years and in 1912 merely required that the library be "available for the use of students and that it be adequate." In 1918 the association approved the action taken by many of the law schools in requiring two years of a college course as a condition of admission.[4]

By 1910 there were 124 law schools using the casebook method as their fundamental educational tool. The development of the Langdell era at Harvard and the emergence of the professional bar association, however, raised difficult questions regarding both the purposes of legal study and the future of the profession. For example, should legal education train practitioners, or should it make law into a responsive social institution? By emphasizing law as a science, by "detaching process from purpose," lawyers in the Langdell mold could avoid nagging questions of political and social importance—and at the same time claim that law was "an avenue of service, not a means for private gain." Similarly, the law profession could insist on the need to prepare lawyers for roles of service to the community and at the same time train them for employment in the large corporate law firm. "If young lawyers chose to enter private corporate practice, and few outstanding graduates from the best schools did not, it was in part because they had been so well prepared for their jobs in law school."[5]

Harvard Law School underwent change beginning in 1916 when Roscoe Pound was made dean, a position he held until 1936. He was a brilliant writer and teacher whose impact on the law and lawyers gained him the title of schoolmaster of the American bar. He brought into law and the teaching of law a social approach, and the range of his learning and his ability to call on it was awesome. "The number of things Pound knows," said Holmes, "drives me silly." A Harvard colleague declared that "Pound knows three times more about every subject we teach than the man who teaches it." His knowledge was legendary, but was used without pretension, and Pound assumed that his encyclopedic mind was not unusual. In his famous jurisprudence seminar he would discuss the books students should read, listing German, French, and Italian as well as English and American volumes. Finally he would refer to a work in Portuguese and then add, "For those of you who may not read Portuguese, there is an excellent summary in Italian."[6]

Francis Biddle was a student at Harvard Law School from 1909 to 1911 and describes in his autobiography some of his impressions. For the beginning student he said it was chaos because it was a strange world that spoke a foreign language. "It was concentrated and enormously stimulating and everything outside of work was immediately thrown aside. But the work was adventurous because it smacked of the world. The case system was at its height and hardly supplemented by an occasional textbook. The student was given a casebook on pleading, on contracts or first year property." Biddle said the classes were large and not divided into sections. When the student was called upon he was asked to state the facts, whether he agreed with the conclusion, and why. "Gradually the English common law grew in your mind like a slowly reaching tree of knowledge. It had governed the English speaking people across the world for 700 years. The customs of the merchants, the manners, the symbols and loyalties, the longings and the conflicts of the English, whose law and language were our law and language, were the stuff from which the common law was made. I felt it in my bones as understanding dawned and deepened, and law was no longer alien."[7]

Biddle described the teaching as Socratic and the study inductive. Students were not being prepared to ply a trade but rather were trained to practice a profession. The object of the examinations that came at the end of the course, and most ran through the year, was not to ascertain the student's knowledge but to probe his intelligence. New and unsolved problems could be picked up from actual life, and the different combinations of hypothetical facts were unlimited. Biddle said that by the last year he was bored as were many of his classmates by the long preparation that seemed to postpone coming to grips with reality.[8]

There were 102 degree-conferring law schools in the United States in 1900, 124 in 1910, and by 1920 there were 146. The sharpest division between the law schools was for those full-time and those part-time. In 1890 there were 51 day and 10 night law schools, but by 1920 the number had increased to 80 day schools and 62 night schools. The night law schools developed in the large cities, in part to fit the limited economic ability of the student but also to carry out a "practical" concept of legal education. Part-time students were at first usually men who were clerking in law offices, and the primary aim of the night law schools was to prepare the student to pass the bar. That was in part a combination of the old law office with some training in the law school.

George Wharton Pepper wrote that in his teaching days at the University of Pennsylvania the trend was clearly in the direction of law school training for the bar. He saw that trend as having two regrettable evils, however. One was the growing estrangement between the cloistered teacher and the lawyer in the arena. The second was the removal of the student from the civilizing influence of a responsible preceptor and the substitution of business for professional standards. "If the student is to develop a sense of trusteeship he must be exposed to the influence of a preceptor whom he respects and who himself has the right point of view." Pepper also believed that for teachers a considerable amount of past law practice ought to be required. "Under classroom conditions the teacher is what a county judge would become if there was no appeal from his decisions."[9]

Pepper believed that a lot of time was wasted discussing the merits and demerits of the case system. He said that was a false issue because the true choice was between doctrine and self-development. "If the teacher's objective is to stimulate the student's self-development he certainly will not do it by talking at him or by injecting textbook doctrine into him. The teacher will say no more than necessary to make the student discover the problem and isolate it for study."[10]

Stone, writing in 1918, said the profession at that time was better prepared than at any other time over the previous sixty years. That was because of the established practice of the better law schools to search for the underlying reasons for legal rules. That, plus the constant habit of examining legal doctrine in light of what Burke held to be the "two and only two fundamentals of the law—equity and utility." These values were giving to the bar an increasing number of lawyers whose respect for the law was not any the less because it was intelligent and discriminating. "Their influence is undoubtedly increasing in the profession."[11]

Stone further observed that the press for reform of the bar was almost entirely from the law schools with little push from the profession or the various bar associations. No state at that time required the study of law at a law school as a prerequisite to practice law, and no state required a preliminary education beyond that of high school to prospective members of the bar. Stone believed that the lawyer class more than any other preserves unbroken the continuity of the past with the present and formulates his rules of conduct on the basis of what has been done in the past. Stone said, however, that conservative mind is subject to two great dangers—the dangers of intolerance and the dangers of becoming closed-mined. "I find almost as much intolerance among those who pride themselves on their liberal opinion. The most precious heritage which the bar brought from the mother country were our notions of personal liberty and our belief that the function of law is to deal with and regulate conduct and not the freedom of opinion and speech when it does not incite to unlawful acts."[12]

In 1915 there were approximately two thousand lawyers listed as practicing law in Philadelphia. That was an increase of about four hundred from twenty years earlier. The increase in the number of lawyers was brought about because of greater popularity in entering law and because it was much easier to do so. The legal profession had become an American "growth" industry. The profession had changed from being able to practice law without law books to an almost entire dependence on prior cases. That led to the need for law libraries, which in turn encouraged the increased development of the bar associations. The main function of the bar associations was to provide their members with the reference tools needed to practice law. Furthermore, the dominant theme in the practice of law was coming to be more defensive than expansive. The major sources for legal defense were found in the law libraries.

The corporation lawyer continued to increase in importance and power. The large corporations when confronted with new legal problems turned to those counsels most familiar with their affairs and relied on them to find any necessary additional or specialized assistance. Such was the case, for example, in 1913 with the federal income tax amendment. This greatly increased the need for lawyers. To the common law and equity that constituted the whole law school curriculum in early twentieth century was added during the first forty years of the twentieth century a mass of federal and state regulatory legislation. These were interpreted and enforced by many boards, bureaus, commissions, and departments. The federal government was providing an increasing impetus for more lawyers.

The importance of the corporation to law was reflected in the fact that seventeen of twenty odd texts, published from 1869 to 1905, dealt with phases of corporate activity. The assertion and excesses of the new corporation and the impotence of the states to regulate them because of adverse decisions of the United States Supreme Court striking down various state regulatory statutes led to the vast increase of federal powers. The lawyer who started practice at the beginning of the post–Civil War era as the intellectual architect of the newly expanding corporation found himself at the end of the period as also the interpreter and a repulser of restriction exposed by the federal government.

It had become impossible for one human mind to encompass sufficiently all the statutes, regulations, and rulings of the Interstate Commerce Committee, the Bureau of Internal Revenue, the Securities and Exchange Commission, and the National Labor Relations Board—not to mention all the other federal and state administrative agencies. Specialization became inevitable for adequate legal service to business. Big business had led to big government and the big law firm. By 1920 there was in New York City a score or more of law firms with staffs of at least twenty lawyers, and many corporations had set up their own legal departments.[13]

Lippincott wrote that the work of the Law Academy consisted in the preparation and argument of cases by students and young members of the bar before the judges of the Philadelphia courts. "It is of the greatest practical help to these struggling young men not only in encouraging habits of thought along well-directed lines but in facility of expression and delivery."[14]

In Philadelphia almost all lawyers had sole practices, although during the early decades in the first quarter of the nineteenth century there were some partnerships. There were no real law firms, however, until near the end of the nineteenth century. The typical partnership in the city had been a two-men affair, usually with one the "office" member and the other the "court" member, and they commonly operated without a formal agreement of partnership. At the beginning of the century the law firms that did exist were small, usually two partners, a few law clerks, and one or two stenographers.

In 1911 in Philadelphia, according to listings in *Hubbell*,[15] there were thirteen firms with three or more lawyers. The largest had ten lawyers. A. J. and L. J. Bamberger, had three partners and five associates, and Joseph S. Clark, listed one partner and six associates. J. Levering Johns, had five partners and one associate. Morgan Lewis & Bockius listed six partners, but their associates were not listed. Simpson, Brown & Williams had three partners and seven associates.

In the first two decades of the twentieth century there was clearly developing the two worlds of law: civil and criminal. In the civil law there was a wide range of lawyers. At one extreme was the sole practitioner struggling to make a living through the writing of wills and small real estate matters. At the other extreme were the highly successful corporate lawyers who earned a great deal of money and enjoyed high prestige. The civil-oriented lawyers were characterized by office work and little contact with the courts, and when they did enter the courtroom it was a civil or federal court. The second world of law was the criminal division. That was the world of the criminal court and mostly attracted the least talented and least successful lawyers. Those who joined the district attorney's office often used it as a stepping stone to something else, often into politics. There were a few famous or infamous defense attorneys who received a great amount of press publicity and sometimes made a great amount of money. Most of the criminal lawyers were "hangers on" around the court, however, looking for a courtroom handout on which to survive.

Those two worlds of law generally had little contact with each other. The lawyers typically came from different social backgrounds, went to different law schools, and even had their offices in different parts of the city. The general public, because of the publicity, had little knowledge of lawyers' work other than in the more sensationally described criminal cases. One lawyer in 1916 appears to have had a strong feeling of conscience about that matter. In a letter written 27 April 1916 in a Philadelphia newspaper Samuel F. Wheeler said, "After 15 years of general practice at the Philadelphia bar, I have decided to specialize in criminal law because only on the rarest occasions now will you find reputable and capable attorneys attending the Criminal Courts. They have permitted themselves to be lured to the civil practice, by the lucrative returns to be derived from representing commercial and corporate clients, and by a desire to avoid even business contacts with the poor, ignorant and unkempt masses, who chiefly comprise the criminal class." He continued "their example has led the lesser 'legal lights' of reputable tendencies, to do otherwise. I cannot believe, that it is less honorable to represent the men or women, wrongfully charged with an offense, or to aid the human wrecks who have committed crimes by reason of meager education, bad environment or deficient moral make-up, than to be the tool in civil affairs of some wealthy individual, or some corrupt combination in showing them how to avoid the law or how to ruin the less powerful opponent."[16]

In 1916 there were disbarment proceedings against Edwin K. Adams, a Philadelphia attorney. He had made two attempts to obtain the admission of C. C. A. Baldi, Jr., to the local bar by impersonating Baldi before the State Board of Law Examiners. Baldi was a member of common council and a candidate for the state legislature. His father was a wealthy banker and leader in the Italian colony. He had made several unsuccessful attempts to pass the bar, and twice Adams failed to pass for Baldi.

In 1910, in the United States there had been 558 women lawyers, or 1.1 percent of the total. In 1920 the number was 1,738 women lawyers, which made up 1.4 percent of the total. When compared with women in medicine those in law legged behind. In comparison with the 558 women lawyers in 1910 there were more than nine thousand women medical doctors. A major reason for the difference was the greater difficulty for women being able to enter the bar. English common law had prohibited women from being called to the bar and in America the law had to be changed in each state before an application could even be made to state licensing boards. Also the practice of medicine was often seen as an extension of woman's nurturing role, whereas the practice of law saw women intruding in men's public sphere. The reactionary males contended that only a woman of dubious virtue would want to know about cases of rape, adultery, and prostitution that were the matters of daily adjudication in the courts. The supporters of women lawyers argued, however, that many of the defendants in these cases were women and had the right to female counsel.

In the law directory for Philadelphia in 1920 there were only four women lawyers listed: Cecelia P. Bass, Helena Haines, Margaret P. Klingelsmith, and Caroline K. Kenworthy. Bass had started the practice of law at the age of twenty-one and was hailed as the "nation's youngest Portia" and a year later was admitted to practice in the federal courts. She had been educated in the public schools of New York and received her preliminary education in law while working as a stenographer in a lawyer's office. Bass was born in 1896 and was Jewish. Margaret Klingelsmith was a member of the Philadelphia bar and librarian of Biddle Law Library at the University of Pennsylvania. She had graduated from that law school in 1898 and was the second woman admitted to the Pennsylvania bar. She was one of the top students in her law school class, receiving honors during the course and honorable mention for her essay on the common law. She was also a descendent of one of the Mayflower families in Boston. She was the only woman found in Pennsylvania law before World War II to have been from the upper class, but she was from Boston and not from Pennsylvania. It would appear that Boston was more tolerant and encouraging of women going into law. Compared with the four women lawyers in Philadelphia in 1920, there were fifty-six women lawyers listed in that same year in Boston.

There were a wide variety of sexist stereotypes directed at women's inabilities to be lawyers. They were charged with being by gender incapable of rational thinking, competitiveness, aggressiveness, strength, and seriousness. They were also accused of not being industrious enough, and that they would waste the courts' time with endless arguments off the point. Furthermoe, they could not be shining lights at the bar because they were too kind. That meant that they could not be good corporation lawyers because they were not cold and ruthless enough. They could not go into law firms because they would alienate the clients, and the client's wives if they heard about them. Furthermore there were no toilets for them. At best they were capable of doing a paralegal's work and at worse their work would be unacceptable law.

The stereotypes had a stifling effect. Those few woman who got over the hurdles and were admitted to the bar found themselves doing quasi-office work, collecting claims and preparing probate papers. One early study found that 90 percent of the lawyers wishing to employ a law clerk refused even to interview women, and such openings as there were often called for the additional skill of stenography. Most of the law schools recommended that women seek employment in government positions requiring legal training, in probate and tax practice, in legal aid work, or in some professional capacity for either trust or insurance companies. Absence of client contact marked the work of women at the bar.[17]

Coxe in his book written in 1908 about Philadelphia lawyers said there was no good reason why women should not become lawyers. He said that although there was the view that a sense of delicacy might restrain her from appearing in certain cases that it should be recognized that women physicians have fully overcome opposition by their achievements at no sacrifice of their delicacy or decorum. Coxe, however, saw women as "naturally" meant for specified legal work. "As general counsellors, as Orphan's Court practitioners, and in the conduct of equity cases, there can be no doubt that properly trained women lawyers could be, and, in fact are, as legitimately successful, and in the same proportion, as their brethren." He said women were obliged to fight, literally, as with men in this vocation, in a survival of the fittest. "More is apparently demanded of a woman at this stage of the experiment. She is still a novelty as a lawyer, and is expected to prove that her calling is sure." Coxe writes about Mary F. Lathrop in Denver, Colorado. "In the essentials of femininity, grace of manner and cultured community; and the very successful career effectively negates the theory that practicing law has a tendency to unsex a woman. We can believe that a woman's intellectual powers applied to legal practice will not interfere with the attention which domestic affairs demand; nor give a one-sided aspect to her existence." For Coxe the lawyer role was fine for the woman so long as the traditional feminine role was not damaged.[18]

Coxe also observed that several years before, a few Philadelphia courts refused, on technical grounds, to recognize women's right to practice. By 1908, however, the principal barriers were removed, and the doors were opened to women in law. They had been given an extended period of welcome as students at the Law School at the University of Pennsylvania. Coxe believed there was no good reason why women should not become lawyers. "Upon the whole, the ancient aversion to the higher education of women no longer prevails. Bryn Mawr turns out as thoroughly acceptable samples of perfect womanhood as could be desired. Some of the fair sex, it is true, are only born to 'suckle foals,' but, so too, a considerable part of mankind are destined from birth to be but drones and triflers"[19] Coxe's views were considerably more liberal toward women than most of his colleagues in law.

Efforts to exclude women from criminal law and courtroom practice often began in law school. There was a concern that the subject matter might shock their maidenly modesty. No matter how ably they represented their clients, women trial attorneys were greeted with suspicion and scorn. Clarice Baright, a woman with considerable courtroom experience, was asked by a New York reporter in 1916, "Wasn't it true that women lawyers were flirtatious in court, unfairly hoping to win verdicts on their sex alone?"[20]

An article in the New York *Evening Post* in 1913 noted that several women lawyers had developed areas of expertise that were of interest to the large law firms. When those firms wanted such specialists to assist them in their cases, however, they hired them as researchers but never as associates. In 1917 a well-known firm of law publishers refused to give credit to a brilliant woman lawyer for the work she had done in connection with a valuable law book, which she was writing with a distinguished male professor. The excuse offered was that it would detract from the success of the book to have a woman's name appear on the cover.[21]

According to the 1910 United States Census there were only 798 black lawyers in the country. The main difficulty was in attaining a legal education. During the last half of the nineteenth century there were nineteenth black law schools founded, but only one survived. That was at Howard University, and between 1877 to 1935 it was the only substantial source of legal education for blacks in America. In 1912, racism was so rampant within the legal community that there was great opposition over the "inadvertent" election of the first three black attorneys to the American Bar Association by its executive committee. After the committee unknowingly elected the three black lawyers they rescinded their action, stating that "the settled practice of the Association has been to elect only white men to membership."[22]

In 1925, twelve black lawyers organized the National Bar Association. The 1910 census reported there were thirteen black lawyers in Philadelphia. There is a record of the admission of one black lawyer in 1908, then none until 1920. During that twelve-year span no record exists of any black lawyers being admitted to the Philadelphia bar.[23]

In Philadelphia in 1920 there were approximately 2,400 lawyers and of that number 410 (17 percent) were in the *Social Register*. The upper class lawyers continued to dominate the Philadelphia Bar Association. During this decade, with the emergence of partnerships, that was more typical of the upper class lawyer. For example, although 22 percent of the *Social Register* lawyers were in a partnership of two or more lawyers, this was true of only 8 percent of the non–*Social Register* lawyers.

As previously discussed law was a more common profession of the upper class of Philadelphia than medicine. As compared with the 17 percent of all Philadelphia lawyers being in the *Social Register*, this was true of only 6 percent of all medical doctors in 1920. Also in 1920, 53 percent of the Philadelphia lawyers belonged to the Philadelphia Club, the Rittenhouse Club, or the Union League as compared with 28 percent of the doctors in the city.

In 1915 in the Philadelphia Law Association there were listed about half of all Philadelphia lawyers. Of the membership 26 percent were in the *Social Register*. Of the twenty-seven officers in the association, however, eleven (41 percent) were in the *Social Register*. Also during that year of thirty-two members of the judiciary 18 (56 percent) were in the *Social Register*. It was clear that the upper class lawyer of Philadelphia was maintaining his dominance in the most successful law practices, the judiciary, the law school, and the professional associations.

The decade of World War I saw little change in Philadelphia law. Probably the most important was the increasing number of immigrants and generally economically poorer students entering law. For most of them success was at best very difficult, however, and economic failure was very common. There was still almost no impact by women and blacks on the law profession.

Boies Penrose, 1860–1921. Courtesy of the Historical Society of Pennsylvania.

Profile 10: Boies Penrose (1860–1921)

Penrose's father was a prominent Philadelphia physician and a descendent of a Pennsylvania family of old wealth with many cultural achievements. Boies Penrose was prepared for college by private tutors, and then he went on to Harvard College, graduating magna cum laude in 1881. He graduated second in his class. First in the class was his brother Charles who went on to become a prominent Philadelphia physician.

After graduating from Harvard Penrose spent two years reading law under two distinguished Philadelphia lawyers, Wayne MacVeagh and George Tucker Bispham. He entered the bar in 1883 and became a member of the law firm of Page Wallinson & Penrose. Even as a student his interests were more in public administration than in private practice, however, and in 1887 he published a scholarly treatise, *The City Government of Philadelphia*. The later chapters contained a sympathetic appraisal of the Bullitt reform charter of Philadelphia. That appears to have been the last time he showed any sympathy for reform or for most forms of good government, however.

He began to pay decreasing attention to his clients to develop his contacts with the important Republican politicians in the eighth district where he lived. He was successful and became in 1884 the district's representative in the lower house of the state legislature. After serving only one term in the house he moved up to the state senate, and there he served from 1887 to 1897. From the time he left Harvard he had often stated that his main ambition was to become mayor of Philadelphia. He was assured of the Republican nomination in 1895 but was forced to withdraw from the race when the Democrats got hold of a photo showing him coming out of a house of prostitution at three in the morning.[1] Two years later with the support of Matthew Quay, the state Republican leader, he defeated John Wanamaker for the nomination to the United States Senate, however. After his election he went on to serve in the Senate for the next twenty-four years. As a senator his interest was mainly in high tariffs, and with time he became chairman of the Senate Finance Committee, which gave him a great deal of influence. He also became famous for his many negative positions. He was an opponent of prohibition, woman's suffrage, and most other progressive policies.

Simon Cameron had built the Pennsylvania Republican machine beginning in the 1860s, and after him it ran until the 1920s under the successful operation of Matthew Quay and then Boies Penrose. It was seen by his enemies as the classically smooth-functioning American political machine. It was in fact a confederation of local party chieftains who generally followed, but sometimes opposed, the boss. "The Cameron-Quay-Penrose organization was so successful and long-lived that more than any other organization it deserved the title 'machine,' which expressed the mingled hatred, despair, and admiration of its enemies."[2] Penrose took over the leadership of the machine after Quay's death in 1904.

As an old Philadelphian Penrose boasted, "I can trace my ancestry clear back to the first Adam, and I wouldn't be surprised if I didn't inherit some of his original sin." Penrose's father was descended from the Biddles and his mother from Lord Baltimore, founder of Maryland. As a youth he was physically imposing and had incredible energy when interested in a project. He was described as brilliant, cynical, and taciturn, but he was also seen as an arrogant, aloof, irrelevant individual who indulged his appetites.[3]

Penrose had shown his political skills in the state legislature. After Quay went to the Senate, Penrose visited all sixty-seven counties to establish a personal relationship with the state's more than twenty thousand Republican political workers. He followed the formula of Cameron and Quay and dispensed contracts, patronage, and campaign funds. He was much more systematic, however. He was accurate, precise, and meticulous in attending to political matters and constantly stressed in every location the necessity of electing legislators who would be loyal to the organization. Penrose was very much in tune with the industrialists who dominated the state. Quay was content to make money with the state's funds on the stock market, but not Penrose. He said, "I decided to get far enough along to be able to control legislation that meant something to men with real money and let them foot the bills. Never commit yourself to, but always be in a position where you can if you choose. The men with money will look to you then and you don't have to worry about campaign expenses." Because he was independently wealthy Penrose could disapprove of making money from politics.[4]

Lukacs describes Penrose as a boss on the national scale and one of the very few Philadelphians who ever achieved national influence in politics. He was one of the most powerful and often feared figures in the United States Senate. However his power within the city of Philadelphia was limited. "The best response he could get from proper Philadelphians was a kind of reserved respect."[5] In part he was rejected because he violated the traditional view of the old Philadelphia lawyer that one did not enter politics and certainly not in the publicly disgraceful way that he had.

One of Penrose' classmates at Harvard had been Teddy Roosevelt for whom Penrose felt great contempt. From the very first days Penrose always referred to him a "cock-eyed little runt" and a "conceited ass." He also hated Woodrow Wilson because of his contempt of "all sniveling reformers and sanctimonious statesmen." Although Penrose had one of the finest libraries in the state he despised the trappings of culture and played the role of the hard-boiled and hard-drinking politician all his life. Penrose was a multimillionaire (his father had owned most of the beach front in Atlantic City before it became a famous resort). That made it a bit easier for him to have no respect for Boss Quay who made money out of politics. "Take it from me, Mr. Quay," he once warned," this petty thievery won't pay. You almost went to the pen over a measly hundred thousand—look at all the things these corporations can do, all the millions they can uncover, with a little encouragement from the legislature."[6]

In his prime Penrose was physically a giant. He stood six feet, four inches in height and was powerfully built. He greatly enjoyed vigorous outdoor sports, particularly big game hunting. As he grew older his weight kept increasing, however, and by the time of his death he weighed close to three hundred pounds. His eating and drinking habits were legendary. His favorite breakfast consisted of "one dozen fried eggs, one huge slice of ham, a half inch thick, a dozen hard rolls and a quart of black coffee."

He was first and last a political boss who cared nothing for statesmanship. Penrose was determined to cover his tracks for posterity, writing nothing and saying as little as possible about his personal life. He does not appear ever to have had a close friend. It was his dictum that friends were only maudlin sentimentalists who used their friendships as a cloak under which to ask favors. He once said that most friends were stupid anyway. His lack of compassion and sentimentality were reflected in an event when his mother died. At that time he wrote to her best friend who was in Europe, "You might be interested to know that our mother was buried yesterday." Not another word. He never married and turned to prostitutes when he so desired. Although two brothers and a total of nine Penroses had belonged to the Philadelphia Club, he had neither the time nor the friends there (he probably was not asked). When he chose to entertain he did so in the lonely Gatsby style, at lavish parties in hotels.[7]

Burt has written that like William Penn on top of City Hall, as an appropriate symbol of the city's upper class view toward politics, Penrose stood alone and aloof, his hand extended in benediction over the red-light district, paying no attention to the small delinquencies of the City Hall below. He was a rebel, in his own way, and an outcast. He was not active in the Philosophical Society as was his brother Charles, and he did not play cricket or sit on charitable boards. The nice people of the city were afraid of him, and he scorned them. "Ruthless, cynical, blind to any conception of an honorable commonwealth, he yet secured for the city, the state and the nation the kind of smoothly organized misgovernment they deserved. Nearly everybody was contented with it."[8]

Samuel Pennypacker was a contemporary as well as fellow Republican of Penrose. Pennypacker, who was governor at the time, writes that at the death of Matthew Quay he talked to Penrose and told him "in effect that circumstances had imposed a certain responsibility upon him and me and that he could depend on me to do all that properly could be done to maintain the control of the state by the Republican party."

At that time he described Penrose as a large man, tall and stout, dark in complexion, and with a heavy growth of hair. He also said Penrose was intelligent and able to make a clear and convincing speech, cynical in his philosophy, given to self-indulgence, and mentally slothful.

> I never knew him to indicate that he was looking further than the results of the next election. I never knew him to urge support of a man or a measure upon the ground that the man was the most capable for the position or that the measure was likely to produce beneficial results, but his thought seemed ever to be to ascertain what would tide over an existing emergency in some political combination. Had I followed his advice, I would, on one occasion, have appointed a judge who within two weeks thereafter was arrested upon charge of embezzlement.[9]

One biographer suggests that although Penrose was master of the Republican machine in his state for eighteen years, in reality he was dominated by it. He was absorbed by the minutiae of an organization with nearly five thousand election divisions, and from twenty to twenty-five thousand hungry and active workers. Although qualified by education and ambition, if not by values, he failed to achieve statesmanship; nevertheless, he was considerably more intelligent as well as less grasping than his associates. One reason he was not grasping was that he never had the need to be with his great wealth.[10]

Even with all his personal wealth, however, he does not appear to have been above some ill-gotten gains. At the time of the senator's death in 1921 more than $400,000 in cash was found in his safe-deposit box. The money was traced to payoffs made by several bootleggers for permits to withdraw alcohol from government warehouses. It was to be used ostensibly for legitimate purposes, such as in medicinal and industrial use.[11]

Penrose like many of the outstanding Philadelphia lawyers had the old family background, the sheer brilliance of mind, and the education. He, more than others, had little social conscience or human compassion, however. The old Philadelphia families saw him as a disgrace because of his public spectacles, and the legal establishment generally viewed him with fear and hatred. His claim to fame historically was as a political boss. Nothing in his career met the mark of the great Philadelphia lawyers. In fact, Penrose was in total opposition to the old values of the Philadelphia lawyer as a gentleman.

11
1920s

Lawyers, I suppose, were children once.

—Lamb

The decade of the 1920s was probably the most dramatic in American history in its range and degree of social change. Immediately following the World War I, American society was ready for many changes—especially in the areas of personal and social behavior. The war had provided new experiences and opened up new awareness for millions of Americans. The old patterns of social behavior were being questioned by many, and the decade came to be one of great social conflict. There was not only the young against the old but also the new against the traditional. It was also a period of great technological change that was especially dramatic with the new mass-produced inventions that greatly influenced life-styles—the automobile, radio, and moving pictures.

The center of Philadelphia consisted of about sixty blocks, from fifth to sixteenth streets and between Arch and Walnut Streets. Located there were the offices of the city's most successful bankers, businessmen, and lawyers. There, too, were found the law courts and the city government offices. Adding to the mix of Center City were hotels, restaurants, the great department stores, clothing stores, theaters, and the many new palatial movie theaters. It was also the center of the metropolitan transportation system with the public system of streetcars, subways, and commuter railroads. The Frankfort Elevated train to the Northeast Philadelphia was opened in 1922, and the Broad Street subway opened in 1928 providing for rapid and inexpensive transportation into the city.

The 1920s saw a continuing spread of corruption that contaminated many of Philadelphia's politicians. By the end of 1923 there were some public-spirited citizens, including one or two old Philadelphians, who persuaded Mayor Kendrick to make a sincere effort at more effective law enforcement. He turned to Major General Smedley Darlington Butler to be Philadelphia's director of public safety. Before the political machine was aware of what was going on Bulter had fired five police lieutenants, three sergeants, and closed the city's estimated thirteen hundred speakeasies for forty-eight hours. He started leading raids on houses of prostitution and arrested more than one thousand Philadelphians, not including the prostitutes. Butler saw himself as an urban Teddy Roosevelt, but his behavior was totally unacceptable to the powers in the city. He was ruining the pleasure of the powerful men of the city as well as cutting into the economic returns. Very quickly Butler was dumped and life quickly returned to normal.[1]

In August 1928 a grand jury probe of crime in Philadelphia began, and after seven months of investigation it was revealed that within the city there were thirteen hundred speakeasies and saloons in operation. One police inspector was able to save $193,533.22 in one year out of his annual salary of $2,800, and five captains amassed wealth ten to twenty-five times their yearly pay. A lieutenant could be bought for as little as $200 a month, and a sergeant or patrolman could be had for much less. One Philadelphia bank had on deposit $10 million in "alky ring" funds. A whiskey manufacturer paid $8,000 a month to the police and carried its distribution in open entries on the company's books. One distiller alone shipped out eighty-seven freight cars of illicit liquor in three months, and one small-time munitions magnate sold, in fewer than ten months, 450 Victors and Thompson machine guns and a countless number of shotguns, revolvers, and silencers.[2]

After the Civil War the corporation had become the accepted business entity in America. Even before 1900, two-thirds of all manufactured products in the United States were made by corporations, and by 1930 the figure was well over 90 percent. Corporations employed more than 90 percent of all persons employed in manufacturing. The corporation form was reaching into all corners of American life, not only in manufacturing, merchandising, and construction but more and more into personal services. The corporation was also affecting farming and placing the economic focus increasingly on the city. The cities were the places of the corporations, and those corporations needed workers to carry out the seemingly endless production of goods.

The corporation had created a whole new concept in property ownership. No longer were owners simply a few "capitalists," financiers, or bankers but increasing included millions of citizens. By 1929, shares of common stock were owned by about 1 million Americans, and the United States was becoming a nation of citizen stockholders. Owners of corporate stock could be found among Americans of all occupations, all levels of education, in the city and in rural areas. Increasingly the "owners" were not the managers. In 1929 the stockholder lists of the largest railroad, the Pennsylvania Railroad, had 196,119 stockholders; the largest public utility, the American Telephone & Telegraph Company, had 469,801 stockholders.

Property in this new form separated ownership from management and thereby acquired a new meaning as well as a new mystery. For the average American the symbols and products of wealthy—land, houses, gold, furs, precious stones—were no longer a mystery. Now there was a new metaphysics of property, however, and the very counters in the gambles of the powerful became "entities as abstract and nearly as baffling to the uninitiated as the Platonian quintessence of the Neoplatonists of the theological emanations of the Holy Ghost would have been to a medieval serf."[3] At the same time the ordinary citizen was invited to acquire those entities, however, and by the twentieth century had begun to enter the market for corporate securities.

The values of the 1920s strongly supported the idea that government should leave business alone. The dominant belief was that mass consumption would lead to mass prosperity, and the old beliefs in reform were largely rejected. The traditional values of thrift and saving had been replaced by the opposite idea that spending was a virtue. Spending came to be the highest of all economic virtues, and the argument was simple and to be followed by all patriotic Americans. In spending the person was not only enjoying the comforts and luxuries brought about through mass production but was also feeding the sources of prosperity by making use of the indefinite expansion of the production of goods. Through the 1920s the spiral continued to build on itself and expand ever upward.

Shortly after the end of World War I there were about 100,000 cars as well as forty thousand trucks on the streets of Philadelphia. The great boom of the 1920s saw the number rise to 250,000 cars and eighty thousand trucks by 1930. The 1920s saw for the first time incredible traffic jams and many automobile accidents. There were 368 automobile fatalities in the city in 1922, whereas in 1930 there were 17,000 accidents reported. That was a godsend to many lawyers in the city, especially those barely earning a living. The large increase in automobile accidents meant a large increase in legal actions, and that became an important source of income for many of the more marginal lawyers.

The population of the United States in 1920 was 105 million with a foreign-born population of 14 million. In Philadelphia the greatest Italian population growth came after 1910 and extended into the 1920s. Also by the end of the decade, the Russian-Jewish and Italian-born populations in Philadelphia each reached about 200,000. There were also large numbers of both gentiles and Jews from other parts of eastern and central Europe. By 1930, in Philadelphia, there were a million who had been born in Europe or who had foreign-born parents.

In the 1920s the earlier progressive attempts to bring about greater social responsibility in the law had mostly disappeared, and the decade saw little in the way of new social legislation. Instead, the conservative post–World War I politics brought a halt in the trend toward government control and the regulation of business. The dominant belief of the 1920s was that industry should be left free to direct its own development. There was strong opposition to any move that suggested any direct government intervention in the economic sphere. Antitrust laws were mostly suspended, and the government controlled fiscal policy primarily in the interests of industrial enterprises. There was little interest directed toward the general tax-paying public.

The Supreme Court came down strongly against organized labor and virtually nullified the provision of the Clayton Act that had exempted unions from prosecution under antitrust law. The court consistently upheld the use of injunctions against both strikes and labor boycotts. Public opinion and popular support were widespread for industry. In the law schools and the courts the idea of social jurisprudence had little impact because the conservative temper of the time was hostile to all kinds of social legislation. The great exponents of the pragmatic philosophy of law, Holmes and Brandeis, were largely "great dissenters" in the leading labor and welfare cases.

Between 1920 and 1929 the number of law students enrolled in American city law schools more than doubled. Most of the increase was accounted for by the night law schools, which increased 142 percent during the ten years. By contrast, the increase was 47 percent for full-time law schools. The year of peak law school enrollment before World War II was 1928, and in that year four out of five law students in cities with more than a half-million population were in night law schools. Most of those left law school to became sole practitioners and struggled for economic survival.

Harvard Law School was still recognized as the greatest in America and the model for all others. In the 1920s Harvard was educating more than one thousand law students a year drawn from all over the country. To get into Harvard Law School called for no outstanding levels of intellect. All that was required for admission was graduation from a recognized college. That was the era when in the undergraduate college the "gentlemen's C" was quite respectable. During the 1920s Harvard did attempt to keep down enrollment by tightening its requirements, but still in 1926 they had an entering class of 694.

Up until 1920 a law student could continue under "condition" even if he had failed two courses. Beginning in 1920–21 he could not remain if he failed more than one course. From 1925–26 on a student who failed in one course could remain only if he had an average 5 percent better than the passing grade or had at least two C's. Those somewhat more stringent requirements resulted in a 37 percent loss after the first year. What the 1925 policy actually meant was a comparatively open admissions. Once enrolled, however, there was no longer any guarantee of success. That was because the end of the first year saw a competitive examination that failed several students.

There continued to be complaints against the case method in legal education, but it still dominated most law schools. The complaints were that the case method was too narrow and that it ignored the lawyer's special skills. The argument was that a lawyer must draft documents and untangle complicated tangles of raw fact. He must weigh facts for the formulation of policy in counseling clients and must know how to choose and employ legal tools as positive instruments of policy. The argument was also that the student under the case method learned those skills only as a neglected by-product of reading the assigned opinions or from passing references drawn from his instructor's experience. The rebuttal was strong, however—namely, lawyers came out of the case method approach as successful and highly competent lawyers.

The law schools of the 1920s were usually anti-Semitic. Nevertheless, in Philadelphia the number of Jewish lawyers increased dramatically. The Philadelphia bar had grown by 21 percent from 1920 to 1930, whereas the number of foreign-born lawyers, mostly Jewish, had increased by 73 percent. "Overcrowding" became the euphemism to describe the "problem" as posed by the Protestant legal establishment. Henry S. Drinker, a partner in one of the city's leading firms and who chaired the Philadelphia Bar Association Grievance Committee described those who having come "up out of the gutter . . . were merely following the method their fathers had been using in selling shoe strings and other merchandise." The head of another patrician law firm, Robert McCracken, later president of the Philadelphia Bar Association, explained to New York lawyers how the state handled "the question of the social origin of the members." Before a character examination was instituted. 76 percent of the applicants were immigrants—predominantly Russian Jews. Within a few years, he added with satisfaction, the proportion had dropped to 60 percent.[4]

During the 1920s and 1930s there were several outstanding black lawyers. Charles Hamilton Houston, Harvard Law School, 1922, was well known for his successful litigation of many civil rights cases and for his role in the accreditation of Howard University Law School. There were twelve black lawyers who met in Des Moines, Iowa, in 1925 and organized the National Bar Association.[5]

One of most famous women lawyers in the United States was Sadie Tabber Massell Alexander. She was the first black woman graduate of the University of Pennsylvania Law School, the first black woman admitted to practice law in Pennsylvania, and the first black woman granted a Ph.D. in the United States. She received her Ph.D. from the Wharton School of the University of Pennsylvania in 1921 but could not find a job. In 1923 she entered law school, and after graduation she worked in the city solicitor's office of Philadelphia and practiced law with her husband who was also a lawyer. There she took over most of the work in family law and estates.

The top law schools were recognized as one of the great achievements of the American educational system. One commentator wrote "In Great Britain, where the case method has made relatively small headway, the British schools have produced no law journals which even approximate in critical power to at least a score of the law school periodicals in the United States." The admirable training in the grasp of legal principles that a student gains by his membership on an editorial board is confined to a small group of the ablest students.[6] To make the *Law Review* was an achievement for only the top students, and they increasingly became an elite. From their *Law Review* position they could get the top federal clerkships and became associates with the top law firms. That was also becoming increasingly important for the less prestigious law schools where only the top students had any real chance for good positions. If they were Jewish and editor in chief of their *Law Review*, however, they had almost no chance to be hired by the old upper class firms of Philadelphia.

Nochem Winnet writes that in 1923, with a letter of introduction to three large Philadelphia law firms written by Harvard Law School Dean Roscoe Pound, he sought a position. In the three interviews only one was frank enough to tell him he could not have a Jewish lawyer in his firm. "I remember his words exactly: 'I could not have your name on my door.' " He said the other two firms told him they had no vacanices.[7]

During the 1920s there was a significant increase in the requirement of some formal legal training before one could be admitted to the bar. By 1928, every jurisdiction except Indiana had a compulsory bar examination. At the 1921 meeting of the American Bar Association resolutions were adopted on standards for law schools and the admission of their students to practice law.

(1) The American Bar Association is of the opinion that every candidate for admission to the bar should give evidence of graduation from a law school complying with the following standards:
(a) It shall require as a condition of admission at least two years of study in a college.
(b) It shall require its students to pursue a course of three years' duration if they devote substantially all of their working time to their studies, and a longer course, equivalent to the number of working hours, if they devote only part of their working time to their studies.
(c) It shall provide an adequate library available for the use of the students.
(d) It shall have among its teachers a sufficient number giving their entire time to the school to ensure actual personal acquaintance and influence with the whole student body.
(2) The American Bar Association is of the opinion that graduation from a law school should not confer the right of admission to the bar, and that every candidate should be subjected to an examination by public authority to determine his fitness.

The resolutions were adopted against the opposition of a small but vigorous minority, which charged that the movement to secure their adoption was a conspiracy on the part of the Association of American Law Schools. "If this charge is well founded, it indicates a signal reversal of policy on the part of the American Bar Association, which in the recent past has treated the law teachers organization with scant courtesy."[8]

In 1929 to be admitted to the Philadelphia bar it was required that the applicant pass a college board entrance examination in subjects totaling fifteen units and also pass an oral examination in spoken English language, or present an academic degree. They also had to be of good moral character. After registration the applicant had to complete successfully three years of study in an approved law school, or must study law for three years in office of a practicing attorney and then pass the final examination.

Two major trends that continued for the lawyer in the 1920s was toward specialization and toward providing legal service as an adjunct to business. The lawyer was becoming more and more the technician, and increasingly as the specialist he looked at such areas as tax law, commercial law, and accident law. The attitude and the public image of the lawyer was also changing. Increasingly was the disappearance of the admiring crowd that had given many lawyers in the past their courtroom glory. The modern lawyer, except on rare occasions, became an actor playing before an empty house. Except for a few who specialized in murder, the lawyer came increasingly to look at any visits to court as an interruption to the real business of the law office.[9]

There were in the 1920s many lawyers who had become businessmen. One estimate suggests that in the 1920s about 13 percent of all business leaders were classed as professionals, and of that group most were lawyers. Whether running a business or advising businesses the greatest rewards were coming to those who ran or advised the corporations. Business opportunities were important to many lawyers who had no chance in the developing world of the big law firm. That was one reason why many Jewish lawyers became very successful in business.

The 1920s saw the further development of the corporation lawyer and the emergence of large law firms. George Wharton Pepper, in writing about the corporation lawyers of the period, said that when they deserved to be scolded, it was not because their offenses were in representing a corporation or in being disloyal to his client, but because he allowed his fidelity to the client to dim or black out entirely his sense of public duty. Pepper wrote, "those who are indifferent to public interest are relatively few and can readily be identified. Those seemingly incapable of grasping the conception of trusteeship are legion and they are the microbes, working in secret, who threaten the life of the bar. By 'trusteeship' I mean the fixed principle that there cannot be any conflict of interest between the trustee and his beneficiary. The instant a question arises between them the trustee must yield. The instant that the attorney's interest becomes inconsistent with the client's the attorney's interest must be forgotten." Pepper guessed "that most of the young men who come to the bar think of the client as the merchant does the customer. The two deal at arm's length and the young attorney proceeds on the vicious assumption that the client is quite able to take care of himself. Few realize that to admit young men to the bar with no other educational test is to give a respectable and intelligent young fox easy excess to the hen roost."[10]

Paul D. Cravath, speaking to Harvard Law School in the 1920s, listed the prerequisites for the work in the large firm that he had created. He said what they looked at in the young lawyer was "good health, ordinary honesty, a sound education and normal intelligence." Cravath was practicing law when interests were with mergers being accomplished mostly through power plays and stock-market raids, "when the important negotiations were with investment bankers who would be, on the whole partners in the final enterprize, when the lawyers most difficult and longest range challenge was the management of a bankruptcy or the reorganization of the business."[11]

In 1923, a group from the Association of American Law Schools formed a committee on the establishment of a Permanent Organization for the Improvement of the Law. The committee was created in response to the growing feeling that law had a distinct public function to perform in relation to the improvement of the law and its administration.

It was proposed that the organization should concern itself with such matters as the form in which public law should be expressed, the details of private law, and judicial organization. "It should not promote or obstruct political, social or economic changes." It was asserted that the two chief defects in American law were its uncertainty and complexity. Those defects were said to cause useless litigation, preventing resort to the courts to enforce just rights. That often made it impossible to advise persons of their rights, and when litigation began, created delay and expense.[12]

The organizers and founders were eminent attorneys from across the United States. The committee's eight members were chaired by Joseph H. Beale of the Harvard Law School. The secretary was William Draper Lewis from the Law School at the University of Pennsylvania. The report of the committee was drafted mainly by Lewis, and he became the first director of the American Institute of Law. It appears that because of Lewis the institute was located in Philadelphia and has remained there.[13]

Who's Who of American Lawyers was published in 1925. From Philadelphia there were listed 185 lawyers, and 51 percent of them were in the *Social Register*. About 65 percent of those lawyers had graduated from the University of Pennsylvania Law School, and among those who gave their political affiliation almost all were Republicans. By religion, when given, 32 of the *Social Register* and 10 of the non–*Social Register* lawyers were Episcopalians. There was 1 Catholic in the *Social Register* and 10 in the non–*Social Register* sample. There were no Jews in the *Social Register* sample and 5 in the non–*Social Register* sample. For those who gave their occupations as political or on the bench there were 8 in the *Social Register* and 13 in the non–*Social Register* sample. In general those from *Social Register* backgrounds wrote about their families in their biographies, and also several specifically wrote that they had declined political appointment. There were two women in the *Who's Who*. They were sisters, Caroline and Joan Kenworthy, and were in partnership together. Joan Kenworthy was one of the first two women to graduate from Temple University Law School in 1920.

In 1914, a New York firm hired probably the first woman associate. She was Catherine Nayes Lee who had graduated, magna cum laude, from New York University Law School. She was the daughter of United States Court of Appeals Judge Walter C. Nayes and was employed by the prestigious law firm of Cadwalader Wickersham & Taft. She specialized in estate and matrimonial cases, and became a partner in 1942. In 1927 Columbia University Law School admitted Ida Klaus, one of the first women. She wrote that "being one of the first meant being in a hostile atmosphere. There were days I raised my hand until it dropped, but professors didn't like the idea of women at the Law School. They pretended we didn't exist and wouldn't call on us."[14]

In 1925 there were twelve women listed as lawyers in Philadelphia, and by 1928 the number had increased to twenty. That was still less then 1 percent of all the lawyers, and none of the women were in the *Social Register*. Violet E. Fahnestock was the city's first woman magistrate and was sworn in January 1925 and heard her first case a week later. In 1928 appeared the first listing of a woman as an associate in a Philadelphia law firm. She was Marcy Feder as an associate with the firm of Ladner and Ladner.

In the listing of lawyers in Philadelphia in 1928 about 11 percent of the lawyers were in the *Social Register*. In 1924 there were more lawyers (12 percent) in the *Social Register* than doctors (5 percent). Of all the Philadelphia lawyers in the *Social Register* about 25 percent of them belonged to the Philadelphia Club, which compared to less than 10 percent of the doctors in the *Social Register*. This reflects the historical pattern of law being more the profession of upper class Philadelphians than medicine.

Comparing type of employment in 1928 for *Social Register* vs. non–*Social Register* lawyers, 70 percent of the former and 89 percent of the latter were in sole practice. In the large firms employing ten or more lawyers, 10 percent of all *Social Register* lawyers were found compared with only 2 percent of all non–*Social Register* lawyers. In 1928 there were eight old-family firms, and of the seventy-seven lawyers listed for them thirty-eight (49 percent) were from the *Social Register*. There were other large firms in the city that were not old family, however, and they appeared to be both gentile and Jewish firms. The large firms that existed at the end of the 1920s were for the most part the firms that would emerge as the leaders in the city after World War II.

In the 1920s there were several distinguished lawyers in the city who were leaders in creating their large law firms. Those would go on in the second half of the century to be the giant firms in Philadelphia. The three mentioned here were upper class firms. From each some information is presented that tells something about law in Philadelphia during the 1920s.

Henry S. Drinker was a major force in the 1920s in Drinker, Biddle & Reath, a firm that could trace its beginnings back to 1849. In 1928 Drinker served as chairman of the Committee of Censors of the Philadelphia Bar Association. The association passed a resolution and made a substantial appropriation for the investigation of abuses in connection with ambulance chasing. After an investigation it was decided not to initiate disbarment proceedings against lawyers merely for soliciting negligence cases, because that practice had long been known, and the judges had done nothing about it. "We confined our proceedings for suspension and disbarment to lawyers who, in addition to ambulance chasing, had been shown to mulch their clients. We disbarred nine lawyers for such abuses. The Courts, on our recommendation, also adopted rules designed to eliminate solicitation of negligence business."[15]

The firm Duane Morris & Heckscher goes back to 1904, although there are ancestors going back to before the American Revolution. Roland S. Morris, after World War II became professor of international law at the University of Pennsylvania. He fit that in with his full day's work as a lawyer and his evening involvements as a politician and leading citizen of the city. In his younger years, he became an enthusiastic supporter of William Jennings Bryan. He was such an enthusiastic Bryan supporter that at one point there was discussion that he should be asked to resign from the Philadelphia Club. "This fate worse than death was happily averted and he survived without such action." He was the head of the Morris family in Philadelphia, in the sense that he was the oldest son of the eldest son all the way back to Anthony, who came to Philadelphia in 1682.[16]

Morgan Lewis & Bockius began as a law firm in 1873. Morris Bockius was the driving force in the development of the firm through the 1920s. Bockius came from a very old Germantown family and graduated from the University of Pennsylvania Law School. He established a determined work pattern that carries down to the present. Regular hours were 8:30 A.M. to 6 P.M. for five days of the week and 8:30 A.M. to 1 P.M. on Saturday. A two-week vacation in the summer was the maximum for anyone including the seniors. It was expected that the lawyers work two or three evenings a week. Bockius decided the policies of the firm and ruled with a strong hand. His firm, his work, and his interest in promoting the welfare of his partners and juniors were the dominant interests in his life. He regarded Bar Association activity as a waste of time and simply another siren seducing lawyers from their appointed tasks. He never married and took a dim view of that institution because he thought it diluted and interfered with the professional efforts of the lawyers in the firm.[17]

In 1929 there were thirty-one judges on the court of common pleas, the orphan's court, and municipal court. Of that number eight (26 percent) were in the *Social Register*. There continued to be some involvement on the bench by the upper class, which was made possible for a few during the years by their wealth. To serve on the bench for some was meeting a sense of social responsibility, and those few had the financial means to do so. The number of judges (eight), however, was not a very significant part of the total legal profession from the upper class, about 3 per cent. The old-family Philadelphia lawyers for the most part continued to take a dim view of the judiciary for themselves.

Profile 11: George Wharton Pepper
(1867–1961)

The Pepper family is a respected old Philadelphia family with their professional fame especially in medicine. George Pepper's grandfather Pepper had been a professor at the medical school, and the family had long been involved in the running of the University of Pennsylvania. As George Pepper grew up there was never any question as to where he would go to college or where he would go to law school when he decided to pursue a career in law.

In 1887, after graduation from the University of Pennsylvania, Pepper registered with the firm of Biddle and Ward to prepare himself for the practice of law. At that time legal education in Philadelphia was somewhat haphazard. There was a combination of office work and law school education. For the first time, however, an increasing cooperation was developing between the offices of the bar and the law school. The Law School was starting to be staffed by full-time law professors. Until that time lectures were almost always given by practicing lawyers who did the teaching part-time. Pepper wrote that those members of the bar who did not teach sometimes affected an attitude of amiable contempt for those who did. In court often the older lawyer would refer to his adversary as "my learned friend the Professor," in a not very complimentary tone.

The law office of Biddle and Ward had ten registered students and was one of the largest law preparation offices in the city. Pepper wrote that they were assigned books to read and quizzed at regular intervals. "We were given some of the practical work of the office to do, such as filing papers in the court offices and reporting upon the state of the trial lists." They attended law lectures from four to six each afternoon at the University of Pennsylvania, and the course of study lasted two years. "Since we worked partly in the office and partly at school our training lacked symmetry. Some things we learned thoroughly, some superficially, and some important things not at all."[1]

Pepper writes that at age twenty when he entered the Biddle law office because of his mother's influence he had grown up as a Democrat. Soon, however, his political views underwent a change, and it was difficult for him to give an accurate account as to why those changes occurred. On the intellectual side, however, Judge Hare in the classroom powerfully influenced him by the exposition of his constitutional views. "In particular, his advocacy of 'sound

George Wharton Pepper, 1867–1961. Courtesy of the Historical Society of Pennsylvania.

money' proved convincing. In the domain of psychology I had the impression that the Republicans of my acquaintance were in general the Doers and the Democrats the talkers."[2]

Like the gentlemen lawyers of the past Pepper had little interest in the judiciary. He wrote that soon after his inauguration president Taft offered him an appointment as a judge of the United States Circuit Court of Appeals for the Third Circuit. At the time the offer came it was a great surprise, and he saw active practice at the bar or the life of judge and teacher as alternatives. He was urged to accept by both John G. Johnson and Dr. Weir Mitchell. He declined and later believed that may have been a mistake because he said his mind was essentially judicial. "Such success as I have had in Advocacy has resulted, I think, from always recognizing the strength of arguments on the other side. Later I was to find that the habit of mind which qualifies a man for the judicial office is a handicap to him in politics. Yet as I look back I think my decision was the right one. I have had a life of wider activity than would have been possible had I been garbed in a black gown."[3]

When he looked back at his early experience in politics he did not consider that to have been a very wise choice. When he recalled the period between 1890 and 1914 he concluded that his dabbling in politics was of small use to himself or any others. He says he did nothing effective and learned very little about political organization. "If I had enlisted as a regular party worker instead of serving as an amateurish volunteer I would have been far better prepared than I was later when the senatorship came my way."[4]

Pepper's rise in the world of the Philadelphia bar was slow and steady, and unlike John G. Johnson he did not take the city by storm. He wrote that in his first year of practice his fees were $2,000. During the next five years they rose to $3,000, $6,500, $9,000, $10,000, and $10,500. "I estimate that through the years about half of the whole amount of my activity has been gratuitous nonlegal service to the church, to the University, to the Profession, to the community and to individuals; and that of the other half, which represents my legal work, about a quarter has been done without charge."[5]

Pepper had approached politics very cautiously and in general felt great scorn regarding politicians. He had no use for bossism, which he saw as represented by the political disasters of Senator Penrose and the Vare brothers. In 1921 he was appointed by the Pennsylvania governor to fill the United States Senate vacancy brought about by the death of Boies Penrose. He was then elected to fill a term on his own.

During those corrupt years of the Harding and Coolidge administrations Pepper was never a part of the scandals. He approved and fought for the economic issues, however, and somehow managed to preserve his faith not only in Republicanism, but in Harding and Coolidge as well. Ultimately he was defeated by his own Republican political machine. The Vares not only squelched his nomination when he tried to run for a second term, but Vare got himself elected in Pepper's place. The Senate refused Vare his seat because of his overlavish campaign expenses, and he died unseated. Pepper, who felt it was his duty to take his licking like a man, never again ran for public office. As Burt observes, he remained, like Nicholas Biddle, a perfect warning to Philadelphia of what happens when an honest gentleman gets into politics. His political failure merely enhanced his reputation at home. He had been done in by the corrupt and contemptible world of politics. From that point on he was always referred to as "Senator" as a title of honor but with no political meaning.[6]

During the years Pepper continued to rise higher and higher in the esteem of the Philadelphia world of gentlemen and legal prominence. He was increasingly in demand to preside and make speeches at all kinds of community activities. By the 1930s he was without competition recognized as the leader of the Philadelphia bar. In the practice of law he was immensely persuasive. He could be eloquent or sarcastic, quietly frank, and disarming, "dismissing an argument with the breath of a well turned phrase, or calling on the heaven's to fall if his opponents contention was accepted. His memory was unfailing, he spoke without a note, he could quote long passages of a brief by heart, or from Gilbert and Sullivan if so disposed."[7] He was an active Episcopalian and conservative to the bone and accepted without question the philosophy of the successful men of his day.

In 1938 George Wharton Pepper became president of the American Law Institute. After the death of Thomas Gates, Philadelphia banker and president of the University of Pennsylvania through the 1930s, Pepper was by common consent seen as the grand old Philadelphian. His political loyalty to his party was reflected in his hatred of Democrats and especially of President Franklin D. Roosevelt. Pepper said the packing of the Supreme Court attempt by Roosevelt was "a measure conceived in hate, drafted with cunning and projected with reckless disregard of consequences. He was greatly concerned with the legal implications of the *New Deal* but seems to have been totally isolated from the terrible urgency" brought about by the depression of the 1930s. He found it difficult "to appreciate the anxieties of the so-called underprivileged and simply could not imagine what it what it is like to be an elevator boy or a sharecropper."[8] During World War II he was torn between his love for England and his anti-Roosevelt isolationism.

Despite his many feelings of bitterness his life was for the most part calm and orderly. Even in his seventies, Pepper continued to rise at 6:45 A.M., do his sitting-up exercises, and take the 7:57 A.M. train in from his country place in Devon on the Main Line to work in his office. Burt writes that a friend of Pepper's told him that he was to meet Pepper for lunch at the Midday Club, a large businessman's club in Philadelphia. When Senator Pepper walked in and was observed the entire body of lunchers stood up in respect.[9]

When he walked down Chestnut Street men would raise their hats to him. He was a tall man with a well-trimmed mustache, and he constantly had his pipe strongly clinched between his teeth as he would stride along the streets of Philadelphia. He gave forth a powerful image of strength and success of the gentleman in the best tradition.

In Philadelphia for many years he represented all that was just and right. He was a great believer in public service, and his notion of service was the epitome of the Protestant ethic. For him his beliefs in Americanism and Christianity were about the same. Pepper had only a limited interest in art, pictures, sculpture, and music; his taste in literature, music, and poetry were essentially late Victorian. He was a Gilbert and Sullivan aficionado, and his favorite poet was Kipling. His marriage was respectable and solid, although it was commonly known that he had a mistress. She was a large, good-looking woman whose ample charms were different from those of Mrs. Pepper. Though he was otherwise guarded and forever discreet he would take his woman friend with him to all kinds of respectable public functions. "He refused to think that other people among the proper Philadelphians knew of the nature of his relationship; he did not believe what he did not want to believe."

Burt writes that perhaps no man in modern times was so well thought of and so well represented the virtues of the old Philadelphia gentleman and lawyer. His rise in the law was slow and steady—not meteoric but solid. He certainly was not a successor to John Johnson and Horace Binney as a great legal mind and hero. Despite his open scorn of bossism, he filled the senate seat of Senator Penrose after his death through a political appointment. His brief political career was admirable but not outstanding. Compared with his political enemy and fellow old Philadelphia family lawyer, Francis Biddle, his legal career attained comparatively little national fame or notoriety. He did have great charm, when not influenced by his frequent animosities. In general he was old Philadelphia's idea of what a grand old man should be. "Senator Pepper probably ended up being a better Philadelphian than he was any other thing."[10]

12
Great Depression: 1930s

May you have a lawsuit in which you know you are in the right.
—Gypsy curse

No two decades in American history have been more dramatically different than the 1930s when compared with the 1920s. The 1920s was the decade of great economic optimism, and a time of extreme and dramatic changes in life-styles. The 1930s started with the Great Depression, however, and then spent the rest of the decade trying to recover from it. For most Americans life became such an economic struggle that there was little interest or energy left for any rebellious life-styles. The American economy through the 1930s slowly recovered because of Roosevelt's New Deal, and the resurgence of the economy was helped along by the coming of World War II.

The presidential election of 1932 saw a victory that brought about Roosevelt's New Deal. That political victory came as a result of a new coalition from the West and South, urban and rural sections, blacks, Catholics, and Jews; it set the shape of American political life for the next forty years. The New Deal was the result of a pragmatic movement that originated at the beginning of the twentieth century as a revolt against fixed principles and rules. No longer was the truth seen as based in absolutes nor in set and mechanical formulas. Instead truth was seen in the context of individual growth and social action. Cultural relativism replaced the absolutism of the past. No longer could one talk about any singular American morality because there were many moralities on any given question.

With President Roosevelt, there came in the years from 1933 to 1938, through the New Deal, a series of sweeping legislative changes. They were dramatic changes, and in their totality they carried the political and administrative thrust of the United States further from the conditions of 1914 than those in 1914 had been different from the conditions of 1880. The new concern was to get business on a footing that would enable to it provide jobs. Unlike the past, however, the main interest was not in breaking up the large economic units of American society. At the core of the New Deal was not a philosophy but a pragmatic attitude "suitable for practical politics, administrators, and technicians, but uncongenial to the moralism that the Progressives had for the most part shared with their opponents."[1]

With the New Deal, Catholics and Jews were also brought into the highest levels of government to a degree they had never been before. Of the 214 judges appointed during the administrations of Harding, Coolidge, and Hoover, only 8 had been Catholics and 8 Jews. By contrast, of the 196 appointments made by Roosevelt, 51 were Catholics and 8 Jews; he also named the first black and first Italian American to the federal bench. Those minority appointments contributed to the extremely irrational and acute hatred of Roosevelt. That hatred was common to many members of the upper class establishment including that of Philadelphia. "The real source of the venom was that Roosevelt challenged their feeling that they were superior people, occupying by right a privileged place in the world. And as the New Deal went on it chipped away more and more of their sense of superiority."[2] Adding to their hatred of Roosevelt was that he had come out of the old upper class background and was bitterly castigated as having sold out his heritage.

The depression, the emergence of the Democratic party, and World War 11 effectively changed the patterns of the city's ways. On the eve of the Wall street crash of 1929, Philadelphia banking and industry were firmly controlled by men from old families. But business ceased to be dominated by autocrats and came into the hands of corporate managers. "Instead of the man giving luster to the institution, it was the corporation which gave position to the man."

No where were the changes more clearly seen than in the legal profession, long the pride of Philadelphia and the reservoir from which many of the leaders came. George Wharton Pepper was clearly the dean of the bar, Morris Wolf was the force behind the fastest growing office and Robert T. McCracken the most influential lawyer in town. But it was the firms made up of specialists which emerged as important. "As the period drew to a close no Morgan, Lewis or Bockius was renowned as an individual, but the law firm was the biggest, richest and most active in the city."[3]

During the first half of the twentieth century no mayors or leading municipal officials came from the Philadelphia upper class. The local city government, however, was run by the Republican party to suit the business interests of the city's upper class. The proper Philadelphian avoided government service, but sometimes satisfied his sense of noblesse oblige by serving on charitable boards and giving support to various city hospitals and medical schools. Through the 1930s the Philadelphia upper class continued to live in the same isolated and segregated world it always had, and most of them were little affected by the depression. Even when they lost money most still had sufficient funds to maintain their life-style.

By the end of the 1930s more than half of the population of Philadelphia were immigrants from Europe, children of immigrants, or from the southern states. The city had residential clusterings where many lived in nearly self-contained communities. The foreign language press flourished and contributed to the separation of communities as well as the overall heterogeneity of the city. An increasing number of professional, white-collar workers and the higher-paid skilled industrial worker no longer lived near their jobs. They could afford to live in the new residential communities and commute to work by car, rail, and public transportation. Philadelphia was well into the modern residential pattern where those who could afford it left the city for the suburbs with Center City becoming increasingly for the poorer groups.

Jews were underrepresented throughout the 1920s as judges in the city; they were largely confined, through the 1930s, to what was sometimes referred to as the "Jewish Court," Common Pleas No. 2 in Philadelphia. Each court had a president judge and two associate judges. Of the fifteen positions (when there were only five courts) usually only one position was held by a Jew. It appeared that the Jewish seat was limited for a long time to Court No. 2 where Mayer Salzberger presided until 1916 and in 1920, Horace Stern became associate judge at Court No. 2. Until the end of 1930s, Jews had no representatives on the Orphan's court. One position where Jews for some time appeared to have had adequate representation was as assistant district attorney. From 1920 to 1924, they held three of the fourteen positions and by 1941 held about 25 percent. Friedman writes that Philadelphia Jews were far more conservative than New York Jews; radicalism, including socialism, communism, and anarchism, was never common to Philadelphia Jews.[4]

The changing immigration patterns swelled American cities resulting in a legal profession with many who themselves or whose children were foreign born. The native American lawyers were determined to halt the challenges they saw to their own secure professional lives as well as the economic institutions they served. They did this first by consolidating their profession within corporate law firms that became their private enclaves. Second, they developed associations to control entrance to the bar.[5]

By the 1930s the upper class of Philadelphia had lost much of the great social, political, and economic influence it had since early Colonial days. That was inevitable as society expanded in size and complexity, and many more persons came into positions of power who were not of the old upper class. Of course, many of those who over the years had attained wealth and power were admitted into the upper class and that contributed greatly to maintaining a high level of power. The biases and discriminations of the upper class, however, severely undercut many of its potential sources of power with the most obvious loss of power resulting from anti-Semitism. Also the blatant sexism of the upper class proved to be extremely costly and still is to this day. Among other social groups, especially Jews, women were given more opportunities and encouragement for educational and professional success, and those contributed significantly to the social and economic advancement of their ethnic group. For example, many of the early women lawyers in Philadelphia were Jewish, although there were none from the upper class. On the basis of a crude ethnic identification of surnames of the forty women lawyers in Philadelphia in

1940, it would appear that at least fifteen were of eastern European Jewish background.

The tasks of the law profession have greatly changed, and much of the important legal work existing at the time of World War II would not have been recognized in the 1870s. The legal institutions in the twentieth century, however, would not have seemed very different to a lawyer one hundred years before. That earlier lawyer would have found little very strange in Washington, the state capitals, or in the local courthouses. Few social institutions had changed as little as the American legislature, although there may have been some legislative improvements in the 1930s as compared with the Reconstruction period. As Schwartz writes, however, the level of legislative ability continued to be depressingly low, and the situation in state legislatures was often even worse. The dominant feature had come to be the control of leadership as determined by longevity of service.[6]

The corporation continued to have great influence, and until 1938 innumerable legal cases were decided on the unquestioned assumption that the corporation was entitled to full protection by the Constitution. By the beginning of the twentieth century the legality of the corporation had been fully established. During the next twenty years the law was concerned with seeing that the corporation would most effectively serve the needs of the business community. The predominant theme of the first third of the twentieth century was to ensure the fullest use of the corporate device, unhindered by any government restrictions that might interfere with such uses. By 1930, simultaneously by competitive chartering in states such as Delaware and New Jersey, a new type of law had become common, which offered incorporation on increasingly liberal terms. The corporation continued to be the dominant factor in business and industry.[7]

Through the first half of the twentieth century many corporations become national in both scope and character. Government at all levels, found itself increasingly engaged in many new areas of regulation and supervision. New laws gave rise to new rights and to novel legal principles. Zachariah Chaffee, Jr., of Harvard Law School, in 1950 described four changes in the legal structure he had observed during forty years: (1) the enactment of workmen's compensation laws in all states, (2) the advent of federal income and estate taxation, (3) the growth of administrative boards with wide discretionary powers, and (4) a changing attitude toward labor rights and regulation.[8]

Roosevelt's attempt to solve the depression clashed with the restricted view of government power that was held by the Supreme Court. With the Court being the final arbiter there were several decisions that invalidated most of the important early New Deal legislation. The limited interpretation of government power by the courts in their decisions eliminated manufacturing, mining, and agriculture from the effect of federal power. The result was that Congress was powerless to deal with the severe economic problems in those fields. Many came to believe that the choice was either federal action or social chaos.

There was a dramatic reversal in the Supreme Court attitude toward New Deal programs early in 1937, however. From 1934 to 1936 the Court had rendered twelve decisions that invalidated New Deal programs, but beginning in April 1937 the Court upheld every New Deal law on which they ruled. Probably the change was because of changes in legal values common to the entire legal profession in the 1930s. Also, the extreme individualistic philosophy of law that had been the tradition was strongly shaken. Before 1937, the desirability of a statute was determined as an objective fact in the Court's independent judgment. Rapidly, however, the Court came to supply a more subjective test: Could rational legislators have regarded the statute as a reasonable method for reaching the desired result?[9]

Big government also had a snowball effect because the greater the government involvement, the greater the cost and the more money that was needed; the bigger the government, the more men needed to run the show. To get the money needed for a vast federal government meant the development of a huge taxing agency. That in turn led the government to becoming a major employer. In part, big government became more and more powerful as a result of the aid it provided plus the many persons who were employed to provide that assistance.

A system of administrative law had to be developed to deal with the operation of all the new federal government agencies. The first task of the developing system was to make legitimate the vast delegation of power to administer federal agencies, especially during and after the New Deal period. The history of the developing system of administrative law came to be one of a constant expansion of administrative authority, and that was accompanied by the reduction of judicial power. One result was that the scope of judicial review of administrative decisions became increasingly narrow.

The mass of administrative regulations to come out of the New Deal years was amazing. The *Federal Register* for 1947 contained 8,902 pages. To check all the federal regulations, however, one had to search the code of federal regulations with its fifteen volumes totaling 17,193 pages. The cumulative supplements for 1943 to 1946 alone contained a total of 57,242 pages. Even greater was the mass of reported American judicial decisions. By 1950, the number stood at 2 million compared with about sixty thousand a century earlier. The number of decisions was increasing at a rate of twenty-two thousand a month. The reported decisions of only four federal agencies approximated in volume the reports of all the federal district courts and courts of appeal. The historical attempt to deal with such an unmanageable mass of lawn was through codification. Private codification in America was primarily the work of the American Law Institute, an organization founded in 1923 by a group of leading lawyers, law teachers, and judges. From 1923 to 1944, nine legal subjects were restated: agency, conflicts of law, contracts, judgements, property, restitution, security, torts, and trusts. Those summaries took up twenty-four volumes with a total of 17,000 pages. Although they had no legally binding force, they were an important guide to the mass of American law.[10]

Legal Education

During the 1920s the number of lawyers had increased twice as fast as had the general population, but the growth varied around the country. In 1930, the legal profession was defined as overcrowded in at least five states. Altogether there were ninety-three cities with populations of more than 100,000; although they had 29 percent of the total population, they had nearly 50 percent of all lawyers. An oversupply of lawyers plus the depression also meant low-average incomes. For example, in New York City in 1938 the average income of more than three thousand practicing lawyers was under $3,000. In 1935 about 10 percent of the members of the Manhattan bar were qualified for relief under the poor laws. The percentage of economically poor lawyers was probably even higher in Philadelphia.

In 1932, there were 185 law schools in the United States; of that number, less than half (82), were academically approved. There were a total of 37,389 law students, and less than half (17,705) were in the approved law schools. The main criteria for those law schools having approval was almost always because they were full-time day schools in contrast to part-time night schools. Of the full-time day schools 73 (87 percent) of the total of 84 were approved, whereas for the night schools only 9 (9 percent) of 101 were approved.

At the beginning of the twentieth century most lawyers had received no formal law school training before being admitted to the bar. By World War II, however, the apprentice-trained or self-read lawyer was no longer common. In 1928 about one-third of all law students were in American Bar Association–approved law schools, but by 1936 it was up to 55 percent. There was also a general uplifting of law school admission requirements, and by 1921 typically two years of college before law school was required. Shortly after World War II it increased to three years, and the better law schools were requiring a baccalaureate degree.

The established bar was not only concerned with setting higher standards for admission to the bar, but they were also concerned with the competition resulting from the "ambulance chasers" coming out of part-time law schools. Control by the established bar increased when Massachusetts, as did several other states, introduced oral bar examinations in addition to the written examinations. The oral examination meant a personal appearance by the applicant, and that allowed the examiners to decide on the candidate's "fitness to practice law." Lack of "fitness" could be more than just poor legal training. It could also be for reasons of racial, ethnic, social, and gender discrimination.

Along with tougher grading of written examinations for admission to the bar, those new procedures succeeded in slowing access to the bar during the period of decreasing legal business. The difficulty in passing the bar reached an all-time high, and in 1931 less than one-third passed the bar examinations. The rate of failing to pass the bar was much higher in the part-time law schools. There were some instances of classes of forty or fifty students where not a single candidate passed the bar examination. As the depression continued it was the part-time law schools that suffered the greatest losses in enrollment.

What was taught to law school students typically developed around two main areas. First were those courses directly aimed at helping the student pass the state bar examination. That came to be the main focus of the night school law programs. Second were those courses related to the new and important work of the large law firms—for example, teaching students in areas of business, finance, and tax. That was mostly the focus of the high-prestige law schools, however. Beginning in the early 1930s there was also an increased interest in providing classes in public law that were an important part of the many new agencies of the federal government. All in all, the level of education in the top law schools was excellent; as one British historian wrote in the 1930s, "the best students in the law schools of at least a dozen American universities seem to me, at the end of their training, to be far ahead of a really good student at Oxford or Cambridge or London who has taken a higher degree in law. They have a deeper grasp of principle; they have a wider range of interest; and they are more willing to attempt an independent valuation of judicial decisions that is true of most first-rate law students in Great Britain."[11] American law schools have long taught the practice of law, whereas the British legal system has often leaned more toward the philosophical and theoretical.

By the early 1940s the top American law schools had a clearly established method for the best possible placement of their graduates, and that pattern continued to dominate in those law schools after World War II. For the greatest success in law the pattern became very clear. First, of the greatest importance was to gain admission to the best possible law school. Through the 1930s admission mainly depended on having graduated from a high-status college, having the money and sometimes the proper social connections. To get into the top law schools in America was not very competitive or difficult because it was nothing like it would become by the 1970s after the advent of aptitude examinations. The various types of admission tests that came into use provided a much more objective means of choosing students and was much more democratic. Once one got into a good law school one was fairly certain of graduating, which continues to be true. Second, to graduate from a high-status law school would get them a top starting position. The highly prestigious positions such as federal court clerkships and partner-track positions in the top law firms of New York and other cities were going to the graduates of the high-prestige law schools. In Philadelphia that was clearly the pattern at the University of Pennsylvania Law School, with the better students, from the proper social background, going into the large Philadelphia firms. That was further helped along by those firms being controlled by partners who themselves had gone to the University of Pennsylvania Law School.

By contrast those who entered the less prestigious law schools found admission much easier and the cost much less expensive. After graduation, however, even the top students often found it difficult to get hired by the top law firms and nearly impossible to get federal law clerkships. Most of those graduates went into sole practice and frequently had to struggle to survive. That was the situation for Temple University Law School in Philadelphia in the 1930s. A few of the city's big law firms would take in one or two top *Law Review* students from Temple.

The large Philadelphia firms before World War II were anti-Semitic, although they occasionally hired a young Jewish lawyer. When they did it was typically because it was good business in terms of getting Jewish clients or because they had no intention of placing them on the partnership track.

By the 1930s the larger law firms were hiring lawyers out of law school and starting them as associates. In general the pattern developed that one could not become a partner in fewer than six or seven years, and sometimes even longer. The percentage of associates who would make partner varied, but in the large firms in Philadelphia the chances were rarely better than one in two, with the odds against making partner often far greater. There was then and is today, however, a great advantage for the beginning lawyer to start with the large firm even if that person never makes partner. From that firm one can move into good positions with smaller law firms and increasingly by the 1940s into corporate counsel positions.

In 1940, in the eight largest firms in Philadelphia, listed in *Martindale and Hubbell* there were ninety-eight partners and fifty-four associates. Of the partners, 62 percent had their law degree from the University of Pennsylvania, 19 percent from Harvard University, and 7 percent from Temple University. The percentages among the associates from the University of Pennsylvania and Harvard were about the same, but 15 percent of the associates came from Temple University. It would appear, although the numbers are small, that the Temple associate had less chance to make partner than did the associate from the University of Pennsylvania or Harvard.

One Philadelphia lawyer, Andrew Young, had graduated from Princeton University and then from Harvard Law school in 1931. He said in an interview that for him there had never been any thought but that he would go to Harvard Law. "But Michigan was just as good. Harvard was not number one, in fact it was probably about the fifth best in the country. If you wanted to go to Harvard law you arrived with your Princeton diploma and were admitted. They didn't look at grades. The entering class was about 600 with a loss of about one-third at the end of the first year. You had to be stupid not to graduate." He said he remembered two general rules in law school. "Don't quote hornbooks or Indiana law'' (Indiana Law was held in ill repute because that state had no bar examinations).

Between World Wars I and II the University of Pennsylvania Law School drew most of its students from Pennsylvania with a few from New Jersey and metropolitan New York. It was not at that time a national law school at the level of Harvard and Yale. Most of the law students were commuters, especially during the depression of the 1930s. Philip R. Hepburn graduated from Harvard College, and his preceptor was a professor in the Law School. When the professor found that Hepburn wanted to practice law in Philadelphia he strongly advised him to go to Penn instead of Harvard. Hepburn did and graduated in 1929. In our interview he said it was good because at Penn he became a member of Sharswood Club, which was made up of many Harvard undergraduates. From attending Penn Law School he made many close and valuable ties that lasted throughout his life as a Philadelphia lawyer.

Temple University Law School opened in 1895 as a part-time night school. It continued to be possible to enter Temple Law School into the 1930s without having any undergraduate education. Joseph S. Kleinbard said that he did not go to an undergraduate college, but entered Temple University Law School and graduated in 1927. He was responsible for setting up the first *Temple Law Review*. The dean opposed it because he believed night school students did not have time for such endeavors. Kleinbard persevered and was finally able to get support and became the first editor in chief. Kleinbard went on to be a founding partner of his own successful law firm in the city.

Another Philadelphia lawyer, Reuben E. Cohen, who started practice in 1928 told in an interview how he came to study law. Cohen had a friend who was preparing to take the bar examination, and he served as a sounding board for his friend when he was studying. At that time Cohen found he could take the preliminary bar examination without any college education. A candidate had to know some history, math, Greek, and Latin to pass the preliminary examination, and Cohen had taken a commercial program in high school. He quit his job, crammed for six weeks, and passed the preliminary examination. To be accepted as a law candidate one had to be of good repute. For example, if your father had gone into bankruptcy that finished you off. Cohen started at Temple Law School, which called for four years of night school, but he attended for only one year and had to leave because he had no money. He got a job working for a lawyer, studied on his own for two years, and passed the Pennsylvania bar. Cohen also went on to a very successful career and is a name partner in one the medium large firms in the city.

Josef Jaffe graduated from the University of Pennsylvania as an undergraduate. He was admitted to Penn Law School but could not afford it, and instead went to Temple University Law School and graduated in 1933. For excellent students to choose Temple Law School was common among those who were economically poor. Jaffe felt there were some disadvantages in going to Temple Law School instead of Penn Law School. For example, Jaffe said, Temple was much more statute oriented and too focused on Pennsylvania law, and did not provide as broad a legal education as Penn. He said that the local orientation of night schools was common in the cities where the primary concern of the night school was to get the student through the bar examination.

There had been a spectacular increase in lawyers, particularly from night schools, during the 1920s; in that decade the size of the bar in the ten largest cities increased by well over 50 percent. There was a dramatic shift in the ethnic composition of the bar, with far more eastern Europeans, especially Jews, becoming lawyers. There was also a great growth in automobile injury cases, and those cases were often the staple of the sole practitioner and became the most lucrative part of their practice. That was occurring at the time when the larger firms were taking over most of the best and profitable corporate business matters, and that further widened the gap between the practice of the elite lawyers in the large law firm and the lower-class members of the bar in sole practice.[12]

By the 1930s the types of law schools were clearly sorting out lawyers into different kinds of practices. In the big cities between 40 and 70 percent of the sole practitioners were products of night law schools. That was compared with less than 15 percent of the lawyers in firms with more than 20 lawyers in those same cities. The first position out of law school became of paramount importance because if one started as a sole practitioner it was almost impossible for him to ever become a member of a large law firm. Almost the only way to make it in the large firm, then as today, was to start there out of law school.

For the young lawyers coming out of law schools in the 1930s jobs were very scarce. George M. Brodhead, a graduate of the University of Pennsylvania Law School, said that when he interviewed for his first job in 1930 there were at least ten men being interviewed for the one position. He relates that he went in as one in a group of three to be interviewed, all at the same time. The occasion he said was one of only two times he ever wore his Phi Beta Kappa key, and it was noticed by the head of the firm who also wore one. He thinks the key may have been why he got the position. When he started he did everything; there was no office space available, and he had to use the library as his office. Brodhead went on to become a partner of a prestigious firm in the city.

Herbert S. Levin graduated from Penn Law School and passed the bar in 1932. He took his first job, which paid nothing for three years, but was allowed to find his own clients. Because he wanted to become better known in his neighborhood, Levin joined a political speakers' group in 1932 for Franklin Roosevelt, and that got him into local politics where he became a ward leader. He then had a variety of political jobs serving as assistant attorney general several times and later was a judge of the common pleas court. Local politics were often very important to the beginning lawyer. As Rueben E. Cohen commented, when starting in his neighborhood, a lawyer hung out a shingle but did not chase business because it was not considered ethical. The ward leader was most important because he could control a lawyer's business.

Louis Lipschitz says that when he finished Penn Law School in 1927 those who had the family and social contacts were the ones who quickly found the better jobs. He had to look around and finally got a job with Adrian Connelly who later become president judge of the family court. Lipschitz said, "I sat outside his office at a small desk. I came in at 8 and he came in at 10:30. I wanted to learn and I would often stay in the office over the weekend. In two years I tried many different kinds of cases besides chauffeuring him around. I was with him until 1934 and was making $175 a week." He said the only way you could get your own clients was through the political ward leaders and by joining everything. "You had to get around, be known and make contacts. And eventually some of the contacts paid off."

Another lawyer, William C. A. Henry, graduated from Penn Law School and started to practice law in 1928. His best offer was $50 a month to work a five-and-a-half-day week. Instead, he went into sole practice and opened an office in Center City. His early work was in writing wills for $5 each and doing negligence work. He also got some work representing bootleggers. Henry said he drifted into probate and property work, and that came to be his "bread-and-butter" work. His first office space was with a couple of elderly lawyers where he helped them out in exchange for his rent.

Robert Massey described the average day of a young lawyer in a large firm in Philadelphia in the early 1930s. It might include answering the call of a motion or trial list, arguing or trying a case, preparing mortgage foreclosure papers, pleadings, wills, agreements or tax returns, writing a brief, attending an orphan's court audit, a sheriff's sale or a bankruptcy hearing, or even taking part in an income tax conference. Massey went on to say that at that time the amount of reading required to keep abreast of the law was much less than it was only a few years later. There were advance reports consisting of opinions of Pennsylvania supreme and superior courts, the federal courts, and the county courts. "The laws of the New Deal grew out of the depression and changed the practice of law. The number of business failures, bankruptcy and foreclosures produced a disaster practice that in volume, complexity and duration had never been seen before. It brought in new fields that took lawyers more and more away from the courts."[13]

Young lawyers starting out in the 1930s, unless they had family and social class contacts, had to look hard to find a job. Almost all new lawyers started as sole practitioners and usually had to look first toward their relatives and friends in their neighborhood to get started. That was a very difficult way to build a practice because every neighborhood had several other struggling lawyers, and many had been around for several years. Most of those who became politically active did not do so out of any desire for a career in politics but rather in the hope it would bring them clients. In actual fact the potential clientele of the sole practitioner was very limited. It was usually restricted to persons of the same social class and ethnic background from which they came. For the beginner, however, there was not only competition from other lawyers but sometimes from nonlawyers. In the 1930s that was especially true in real estate and the will, probate, and estate fields. Typically, the sole practitioner was entirely on his own and rarely would he get any referral business from law firms of any size. In fact, the law firms were in a different world in so far as his career was concerned.

From a sample of the 1940 *Martindale and Hubbell* listing of lawyers in Philadelphia it is estimated that 73 percent were in sole practice, 9 percent in a partnership, 14 percent in firms of three or more lawyers, and 4 percent in other positions (mainly in government). In 1940 there were not many lawyers working for large business because the big business firms placed their work with the large law firms. Those in sole practice ran the range from lawyers who chose to be their own boss to the many who had no other option. Probably most of the sole practitioners had no other choice. For some lawyers to make a living it was necessary to pursue somewhat dubious means, and some chased ambulances or took on litigation on a contingency basis. Before World War I some lawyers could make a bare living in sole practice by getting enough defense money from the courts. Herbert S. Levin said in an interview that in 1991 possibly only twenty lawyers could make a good living in criminal law. That is because court appointments are much less important today with public defenders. They provide free service, and even if the court makes an appointment available the defendant knows he will generally get better representation from the public defender.

The expansion of government law contributed greatly to the expansion of the large law firm because the many federal acts, commissions, and regulations had legal meanings. Increasingly the government lawyers were applying those laws to persons and institutions and when they were applied to an individual or corporation, they had to have legal representation to respond or defend themselves. The kind of expertise needed to handle the complexity of the new federal legal applications could not be provided by the sole practitioner nor even by the small firm. As a result the big firms got even bigger. A law firm might conduct a negotiation in a tax case with the Internal Revenue Service or process a claim for excess railroad rates through the Interstate Commerce Commission. They might defend a case for workmen's compensation with the appropriate agency or seek a reduction of a franchise tax. Three-quarters of the work was not done before any court but in their own or government offices.[14]

The growth of the big law firm was to a large degree a product of the New Deal and the vast new areas of administrative law. By 1940 the Cravath firm of New York had twenty-two partners and seventy-two associates, with a clerical staff close to 150. That firm resembled the executive office of a large business corporation. It was departmentalized into as many branches of the law as were being practiced by the firm. This was the model that would be followed in many other cities including Philadelphia after World War II.

The corporation lawyer has sometimes been portrayed as a tedious and unglamorous paper shuffler, but that is often far from accurate. The jockeying for corporate control or the strategies of corporate consolidation, for example, can have a strong sense of drama, excitement, and challenge. "Our contemporary credit-industrial economy of abundance could not have been fashioned without the brilliant imagination of the daring corporation lawyer of the 19th century who forged one device after another to lead the way, pressing far beyond the existing law."[15]

Mayer suggests that wills and estate practices were a great convenience for the emerging law firms because they supplied a place where the firm could employ the client's brother, its own senile partner, and the socially prominent but not terribly bright lawyer who might be useful in getting business. Wills are the most ritualized document in the law. A bad job is not likely to be uncovered, because nobody could ask the deceased what his intention had been, and socially established people mostly dislike battles in the probate court.[16]

In general the specialized law of the big firm provided the client with the best law. Swaine, writing in 1949, said a profession fails in its duty to those it serves if it does not give them the most effective and convenient service possible. "Are the clients of our hospitals, at those such as Mayo, unprofessional because they give their patients, under one roof, expert diagnostic ability and care for all bodily ills?"[17] The big firm had generally the best talent, the widest range of legal specialties, the best support systems and the capital resources to provide the best legal services. Of course, the client paid a high premium for the best legal services and the high premiums allowed the firm to expand and extend its capabilities further.

Swaine further observed that the private nature of the corporate lawyer made him a much less newsworthy person than the advocate arguing before a jury or performing in an appellate court. The spotlight was almost never focused on the corporate lawyer. The lawyers in the old days were much more legalistic in their approach to their cases and gave greater attention to form than to substance. They prosecuted or defended to the best of their ability and did not regard as unethical the use of any and every available technicality. Advocates at the end of the nineteenth century who transferred to corporate practice saw it as their function to tell clients how they could lawfully do what they wanted to do, however, and that came to be a private relationship between clients and lawyers. Because it was private it was sometimes assumed that it must be unfair or even ethically questionable.[18]

Early in the century there had been a common criticism that the bar was too heavily oriented toward the problems of business. Expression of concern for the public interest, much less action for it, was almost totally absent, however. By the mid-1930s the total affort directed toward public needs was meager, "a little legal aid work, some defense of indigent defendants and some direct *pro bono* work for the 'deserving poor.' "[19]

In 1928, in Philadelphia there were twenty-nine law firms employing three or more lawyers, with the largest having 18 lawyers. Those twenty-nine firms employed a total of 194 lawyers, an average of almost 7 lawyers per firm. By 1940, there were fifty law firms with three or more partners, and the largest had 24 lawyers. That was a total of 427 lawyers, with an average of between 8 and 9 lawyers per firm. Of the twenty-nine firms in 1928, sixteen (55 percent) continued to be in operation in 1940, and eight of the older firms in 1940. Partnerships of two lawyers typically did not last. For example, in 1947, 78 percent of the partnerships listed in 1932 were gone.

Another result of the emergence of the large firms was the sharper distinction between the two worlds of law that have come to be common today. One world was that of the large law firm with its upper class heritage and legal participation primarily in the corporate and business world. That was where the profit and prestige of law was to be found; the prestige was not public, but remained private and select. It was no longer the law world of the advocate but rather the law of the office. In this world, the need to appear in court is generally at the federal level. The best practice of law was to not reach the court. Good law was preventive and not combative.

The second world of law continued to be what had long been common, that of the sole practitioner, the partnership, as well as involvement in city government and politics. Often the small legal practice was in family law, crime, and personal injury; the fees for these cases were not large, and making a living was tenuous. Typically in the first world the Philadelphia lawyers were coming out of high-status law schools, mainly from the University of Pennsylvania. In the second world the Philadelphia lawyers were coming from Temple University's night school of law. The latter were more likely to be poor and from recent immigrant families who dealt with the court of common pleas and municipal court.

Lawyers in the first world continued to do all they could to avoid publicity, whereas those in the second world often highly valued publicity because it was a means of getting new clients. That was reflected in the sensational cases of crime, divorce, and personal injury that the second world sought. In the first world, criminal and divorce cases were almost always avoided, unless the firm took them on as a favor to a valued client.

The Legal Aid Society was founded in 1901 in Philadelphia. From 1921 to 1932, Legal Aid Services were carried out by a tax-supported municipal bureau. The number of cases for that twelve-year period averaged 15,245 a year. In 1935 it was reorganized as a privately supported society. The average case load for the twelve-year period, 1935 to 1946, was 11,068 cases per year.[20]

In 1947, the cost per case was $4.02 in Philadelphia. That was less than in

Boston with an average cost of $5.80 per case and in Pittsburgh $5.58 per case. During the years about 75 percent of the problems that came to them required only consultation or in some cases a referral to some other community service. About 15 to 20 percent of the cases were resolved by negotiation, investigation, and office work. Only 5 to 10 percent of the cases involved court proceedings. Abrahams found that less than 5 percent of the Neighborhood Law office work in Philadelphia involved litigation.[21]

Brownell, writing about the 1940s, said the Voluntary Defenders Association of Philadelphia was an example of the independent private Legal Aid office and specialized in criminal cases. It employed a staff of three attorneys, five investigators, and three clerical workers. They provided service to the United States District Court and the county court. The proportionately large investigating staff was necessary because they were called on the make investigations for the courts. That was a function performed in most places by the probation department of the courts.[22]

In Philadelphia there had been for more than one hundred years a lack of interest in the bench by the top lawyers in city. The low legal skills and status of those going on the bench became even greater in the 1930s, especially on the state court level. The pattern continued with fewer outstanding, well-trained lawyers being interested in becoming judges. In fact the top lawyers in Philadelphia increasingly had less and less contact with the Common Pleas courts because more and more of their work was to keep their clients from having to go to court. The larger firms were coming to deal as little as possible with criminal cases or the kinds of civil cases handled by the Common Pleas courts.

The judges were increasingly coming from the lower social and professional strata of lawyers, and they were not usually chosen on the basis of success in law school or in law practice. Rather, the most important criteria was often whether they met the political requirements for their elected offices where the primary concern was to get the politically proper ethnic and neighborhood quotas as city judges. There were, of course, some good lawyers who became judges and for admirable reasons. For example, Joseph S. Kleinbard said that Lowenthal became a judge even though he had to give up an income of $60,000 a year for one of $10,000. He wanted to be a judge because his father had been the top Orthodox Rabbi in Philadelphia, and he saw that as a kind of judge role; in his view becoming a judge was a great honor. He increasingly came to be the exception, however.

As one lawyer said about the judges in the past, "it was incompetence rather than venality—but they were just as inept." That same lawyer made a telling comment as to why Philadelphia still has so many incompetent and dishonest judges. He observed "what do you think you will get when you have a lawyer in practice for fifteen years who sees a salary of $65,000 a year as a judge to be a significant increase?"

Through the 1930s there was a high degree of anti-Semitism coming from the elite of the Philadelphia bar. There was also discrimination against blacks and Irish Catholics, but the Jewish lawyer was in number and success far greater then any other minority group. As suggested earlier, the Philadelphia Bar Association had always been dominated by the old upper class, and that continued until 1951, when Bernard Segal was the first Jew elected the chancellor of the Philadelphia bar. In the 1920s and into the 1930s the most important leader of the Jewish bar was Morris Wolf who has been described as an autocrat in running his firm.

Herbert S. Levin relates that when he was interviewed for admission to the University of Pennsylvania Law School he was asked where his parents were born and whether they spoke with an accent. The interviewer also said, "I take it you are Jewish." Levin finally asked him if he had anything against him or his religion. "In return I asked him what his religion was and he told me he would ask the questions." Levin went to Dean Mitchell and told him the story. The dean asked the interviewer if the story was true, and he admitted that it was. "The Dean then asked for my file and took over and I was admitted to Penn." Levin said that in the 1930s there were no Jews in the big old Philadelphia firms.

In Philadelphia anti-Semitism was also linked to negative perceptions about Temple University Law School. In part that was because Temple was a night law school, and there were strong biases directed against those law schools. A night school drew many who could not afford full-time law school, and given their high motivation many Jewish students attended Temple because they had to work during the day. The anti-Semitism was reflected in a common old establishment view of Temple Law being the Jewish law school. Some of the Jewish students who went to Penn Law School said they were sometimes confronted with, "Why are you at Penn? You really should be at Temple." The combination of having Jewish background and attending Temple often meant the lawyer, regardless of how highly competent, had two strikes against him and could not even get an interview with the old-family firms in the city.

One difference between Penn Law School graduates and those from Temple Law School is reflected in differences in careers. In 1944 most lawyers were in sole practice. That was truer of Temple Law graduates (77 percent), however, than those from Penn Law (59 percent). Another more dramatic difference was in the eight largest firms in the city in 1944. Of all partners in those law firms 64 percent were from Penn Law School, 23 percent from Harvard Law School, and only 5 percent from Temple Law School. Among the associates in those eight law firms 60 percent were from Penn, 15 percent from Harvard, and 15 percent from Temple. Temple law firm associates had less chance of becoming a partner than those from Penn and Harvard.

Women in Law

The 1920s had seen women get the vote, gain access to all state bars, and begin to serve on juries. The social concern of educated women, and particularly their concern with women's rights, declined as their desire to enter the male-dominated professions increased, however. With the depression there was a severe slowing down in the few gains women had made in business and other professions, and women were often discriminated against because of the scarcity of jobs for men. During the 1930s there were serious suggestions that married women should be prohibited by statute from jobs if their husbands were employed.

Honors law school graduate Sadie Turak in recalling the 1930s said that the depression gave law firms still another excuse not to hire women lawyers. "At every interview I was asked how I could possibly expect to be considered when there were men out there with families to support. It was bad enough I wasn't going to get the job with any of the law firms—on top of that they insisted on making me feel guilty, too."[23]

As suggested in an earlier chapter the development of part-time law schools was of great importance to women and other minority groups. A large number of the women who went to law school had to also earn a living. Full-time training at law school usually cost three or four times as much as night school, so most women attended part-time schools. The early influx of women in law school peaked in the late 1920s, but the number of women who were full-time in the elite law schools was very small. The depression ended the earlier boom of female law students, even in the part-time law schools.

The Portia Law School (now Northeastern School of Law) in Boston was the only law school in the world founded exclusively for women. It was founded in 1908 and chartered to grant LL.B. degrees exclusively to women in 1919; Portia remained open only to women until 1938. It served mainly as a school for the children and grandchildren of immigrants. In 1924, 82 percent of the Portia graduates passed the bar, and in 1929 it was 65 percent. That compared with an overall pass rate of 40 percent, and it was certainly successful in getting women to pass the bar.[24]

In 1920 there had been 1,738 women lawyers in the United States, and they made up a fraction over 1 percent of all lawyers. By 1940 there were 4,447 women lawyers in the United States, and they made up only 2.4 percent of the total legal profession. In 1928 there were 20 women lawyers listed in Philadelphia, and by 1940 the number had only increased to 35 women. In the law class of 1930 at the University of Pennsylvania 3 women started, and 2 graduated and went on to practice in New Jersey. Of the 20 women lawyers listed in 1928 only 8 were still listed in 1940.

When compared with Boston the chances in law for Philadelphia women was significantly less. In 1932 there were 26 women lawyers in Philadelphia, or 1 in every 115 lawyers, whereas in Boston there were 118 women lawyers, or 1 in every 34 lawyers. Women lawyers in Philadelphia also trailed behind women doctors. In 1942 there were 196 women doctors, or 1 in every 19; however, there were only 40 women lawyers, or 1 in every 85. None of the women lawyers was listed in the *Social Register*, but 3 of the women physicians were. That reflected the somewhat greater acceptance of medicine than law as a profession appropriate to women.

There were differences in the education of women when compared with a matched sample of men who entered the Philadelphia bar by 1940. No law school was given for 38 percent of the women and 25 percent of the men, and most of those lawyers would have passed the bar without any formal law school education. A higher percentage of the women, 30 percent, had graduated from Penn Law School as compared with 20 percent of the men, however. By contrast, Temple University Law School accounted for 25 percent of the women and 40 percent of the men. Seven percent of the women and 15 percent of the men graduated from other law schools.

Of the 40 women lawyers listed in 1940, 95 percent of them were in sole practice, whereas the matched group of 40 men had 72 percent in sole practice. At that time it was impossible for a woman to get a position with a top Philadelphia law firm. Mary Groff, in an interview, said there were 8 women in her law class of 1933 from Penn Law School, but none of them was offered a job. She said that was true even though one of the women had achieved the highest law school grades ever recorded at that time in the history of the law school. That woman took a job with the federal government because it was the only offer she received.

Although the federal government offered some chances to women during the 1930s, they were far from being an equal opportunity employer. In the 1940s Cecelia Gratz, who had graduated at the top of her law school class, attempted to get a position with the government as a trial lawyer. The prejudice against women was there even in the department headed by well-known liberals. It was quite a blow to learn, for example, that no women or blacks were being hired for the Antitrust Division of the Justice Department. When Gratz tried to get a position as a prosecutor at the Nurenberg Trials her request was initially not taken seriously. "You're much too attractive," she was told—she was finally accepted but had to sign a "waiver of disability" form. Her disability was the fact that she was a woman.[25]

Helen S. Chait, who graduated from Columbia University Law School in 1938, related one of her experiences. She got a position with a large New York law firm, and when it split off to form a new firm she went with them. That firm went on to become one of the largest in the United States. After she was there five years some of the men who came with her as associates were made partners. Chait asked the senior partner, with whom she had joined the new firm, why she had not been promoted; he said that if Chait had been a man, she would have made partner. She resigned from the firm and said that "to this day the managing partner does not understand why I was so upset." Chait also offered the observation that although she was discriminated against as a woman she does not ever remember any discrimination as a Jew.

Judge Lois G. Forer graduated from Northwestern University Law School in 1938. In 1953 she won the American Bar Association prize—the only woman to do so—for an essay that was read blind. There was one man who wanted to put her up for membership on the executive board of the Bar Association, which he did, and she got one vote. She taught at Penn Law School as an adjunct for seven years and said it never occurred to the administration to offer her a permanent position. Yet, because she was well published they wanted her to help a young man get published so he could be promoted in the law school.

With so few women in law in the 1930s there were also very few women judges, and by 1930 only twelve states had at least one woman judge. By 1950 there was at least one woman judge in thirty-nine of the states, but it was not until 1949 that a woman was appointed to the federal district court. It took until 1965 before a woman was a chief justice of a state supreme court, and it was 1979 before every state had at least one woman serving in some judicial capacity. The first woman on the United States Supreme Court was not until 1981.

In 1940, 10 percent of all Philadelphia lawyers listed in the directory were in the *Social Register*. Of the approximately 4,800 men in the 1940 *Social Register* 6 percent were lawyers, and 5 percent were doctors. In 1940, 36 percent of the *Social Register* lawyers and 46 percent of the doctors had received their undergraduate degrees at the university of Pennsylvania. Forty-nine percent of the lawyers compared with 34 percent of the doctors, however, had received their undergraduate degrees from Harvard, Princeton, or Yale. That reflected the historical pattern of somewhat higher social status of the lawyers over physicians in the city.

Attending the University of Pennsylvania Law School was associated with being in the *Social Register* as well as being a partner in one of the city's top law firms. For those partners in the top law firms in 1940, where the information is given, 75 percent of those in the *Social Register* were from Penn Law School. That was in comparison with 54 percent of those partners not in the *Social Register*. Eleven percent of the non–*Social Register* partners were from Temple University Law School, but there were no *Social Register* partners who had attended Temple.

Being in the *Social Register* also had a significant relationship to the type of law practice in 1940. A comparison was made of all *Social Register* lawyers in 1940 with a matched sample admitted to the bar at the same time. Of the *Social Register* lawyers 44 percent were in sole practice compared with 79 percent of the non–*Social Register* lawyers. Twenty-eight percent of all *Social Register* lawyers in contrast to only 3 percent of the non–*Social Register* lawyers were with law firms of ten or more lawyers.

In 1940, there were thirteen law firms with 10 or more lawyers, and all of them had at least 4 lawyers in the *Social Register*. Those thirteen firms had a total of 205 lawyers of which 96 (47 percent) were in the *Social Register*.

Social Register membership was also linked to the success of law firms. From 1928 to 1940 there were eight law firms that increased significantly enough in size to be among the largest firms in Philadelphia. In 1940, in those eight firms there were 134 lawyers of which 68 (51 percent) were in the *Social Register*. The biggest firms were successful because they had the contacts with the wealth and the power of the city, and they had that contact because they were members of highly influential families. Those lawyers had access to a level and kind of clientele that non-upper class families could never reach and in that way the upper class lawyer was able to expand and perpetuate his position.

Through the previous historical periods discussed there was little interest among the Philadelphia upper class lawyers in politics or in the bench. Baltzell has noted that six lawyers from Pennsylvania and five from Massachusetts sat on the United States Supreme Court up to 1940. All five of the Massachusetts justices embodied upper class Bostonian dominance of the leadership of the state. By contrast, no upper class Philadelphia families sent any members to the Supreme Court. As previously pointed out several upper class Philadelphians were offered the position but declined. Owen J. Roberts was a graduate of the University of Pennsylvania and a native of Philadelphia but not of the old upper class. He accepted a seat on the Supreme Court in 1930 and was the first important Philadelphian to sit since James Wilson who served on the very first United States Supreme Court after the Revolution.[26]

In 1948 there were eighteen judges on the court of common pleas with two of them in the *Social Register*. There were six orphan's court judges and two of those were in the *Social Register*, but of the eleven municiple court judges none was in the *Social Register*. The orphans court always had a higher status and greater attraction for the upper class. That was probably because that court dealt with matters of trusts and estates, which were very important to the upper class.

Although the percentage of Philadelphia upper class lawyers decreased during the years, they still retained a high level of influence. From the beginning in Philadelphia it was the individual practitioner who made his name as an advocate, and he was typically from the upper class. As the courtroom orator became less and less important, and the law firm developed its practice based on preventing courtroom confrontations, the upper class still continued to dominate. World War II ended the dominance of the upper class in Philadelphia law, however. In the years after the war they dramatically fell off in number and in influence, and have come to be of decreasing significance.

Francis Biddle, 1886–1968. Courtesy of the Historical Society of Pennsylvania.

Profile 12: Francis Biddle (1886–1968)

The Biddle family line started in America with the arrival of William Biddle in 1681. The family was originally Quaker, but most members left the meeting during the early generations. From the days of the American Revolution Biddles served in the army, navy, and marines, and fought all over the world. Francis Biddle's grandfather, George Washington Biddle, was a leader of the Pennsylvania bar, and during his era was one of the foremost lawyers in America. George W. Biddle, along with his lawyer sons Algernon and George, provided the legal training for several outstanding Philadelphia lawyers (including George Wharton Pepper). Francis Biddle's grandfather appears to have influenced him in some of his nontraditional old Philadelphia values. His grandfather, George W. Biddle, has been described as an uncompromising libertarian, and he named Francis Biddle's father, Algernon Sydney, after an Englishman who had been convicted of treason and was beheaded in 1683.

Of all the old Philadelphia families, none has turned out more distinguished lawyers during the years than the Biddles. It is estimated that up until World War II there were at least twenty-five lawyers from the family, many of them very distinguished. Therefore a strong case can be made that the Biddles, during the years, have been Philadelphia's first family of law. It has certainly been one of the oldest and foremost families in social standing in the city. In his autobiography Francis Biddle tells how his father's friends in Philadelphia looked at him and his three brothers with great expectations after their father's death. His father and brothers were strongly reminded of the family's glorious past, when their father and his two brothers were outstanding leaders of the Philadelphia bar. Biddle wrote that his father's old friends compared the past to the present at that time when little was being accomplished by the other members of the Biddle family. Francis Biddle writes that when he was at college, Dr. Weir Mitchell, a part of that venerable past, "reminded me that for the first time in the history of Philadelphia there was not one of my name who was contributing anything of leadership or service to the community. It was true I thought. My Biddle relations were not doing anything, hardly even a lawyer or doctor among them, few who were even making a living."[1]

Francis Biddle wrote that sometimes being a Biddle had more drawbacks than any very tangible advantages. He said that in Philadelphia, the name Biddle often implied the amateur and dilettante, and suggested a man who was so wealthy he did not need to work. While rich men were admired the admiration was mixed with contempt if they did nothing but lead cotillions and cut up at Newport. "The result was that if a young Biddle studied law, or went into politics, or, like my brother George, chose the life of the painter, society did not take him quite seriously."[2]

Francis Biddle went to Groton, Harvard College, and then Harvard Law School. He enjoyed his years at Harvard as an undergraduate and described his initial reaction to Harvard Law School as a strange continent that spoke a foreign language. "After the lazy, easy life of the undergraduate, with the hard drinking, occasional wenching, and the irregular hours—the Law School was regular, rigid, concentrated and enormously stimulating. Everything outside of work was thrown aside" He wrote that for many years members of the bar considered it a complete waste of time for students to be taught theory by professors instead of learning the practice of law from successful lawyers. "When I went to Philadelphia to practice in 1912 I well remember Chief Justice James T. Mitchell of the Supreme Court of Pennsylvania expessing to me such an opinion—I thought him as undistinguished as he was unimaginative." Biddle went on to write "even John G. Johnson, in many ways the most remarkable lawyer this country has ever known, said that teaching law was a 'lot of hogwash.' "[3]

Biddle had one criticism of law school, and one still common today among the better law students, and that was the feeling that the last year of law school was a waste of time. "I was bored like a good many of my classmates by the long preparation which seemed to postpone coming to grips with reality. I have never had any touch of the scholar about me, and had no particular interest in the accumulation of knowledge once I had been taught to handle the tools of the trade."[4] After graduation, he and his brother George were admitted to practice law in Pennsylvania in 1911.

Biddle spent a year in Washington, D.C., as a law clerk to Justice Oliver Wendell Holmes and when he returned in 1912 he spent most of his time as chairman of the speaker's bureau of the Bull Moose Party in Philadelphia, working for the "cause." He said that in Philadelphia it was not respectable among the correct and the socially elite to favor Teddy Rossevelt's campaign, and any enthusiasm in that direction was greeted by great waves of disapproval. Biddle said his older brother Moncure wrote to him that he was sorry that "I was backing a man whom every sane citizen deprecates to the extent of using abusive language—a thoroughly unstable and dangerous demagogue."[5]

In 1912, when Biddle returned to Philadelphia he entered the law office of Biddle and Ward. At that time he found little employment interest in him as a young lawyer, and so his choices for his initial law position were not great. He found that the Philadelphia bar cared little for a Harvard degree cum laude, because they turned to the University of Philadelphia to fill their needs for their annual supply of young lawyers. "I knew that the firm I was about to join was antiquated if not moribund; but never mind, I would change that, and the same time 'reform' Philadelphia by inducing intelligent, progressive government into the city administration."[6]

The firm was one of the larger ones in Philadelphia at that time with three partners and three young lawyers. Biddle had a desk in a windowless passageway between two offices and received forty dollars a month. His salary increased over two years to fifty dollars while he continued to try to think of some legal work to do. During his three years with the firm he hardly ever went to court. He relates that once Mr. Jayne "let me argue an interlocutory motion before Judge Sulzberger, a learned dyspeptic on the Common Pleas Court, who eyed me with unfriendly curiosity and promptly ruled from the bench against my contention." Biddle said that every now and then he would spend an afternoon working for the Legal Aid Society, "parcelling out doubtful advice to unhappy clients."[7]

Biddle was attracted to "causes" and became active in the Public Education Society in reform politics in the Seventh Ward and in a prison improvement organization run by a group of Quakers. He found that the feeling of failure kept increasing, however, and he was beginning to worry that "perhaps I was not cut out to be a lawyer. I thought for the first time, for until then I had never considered any other career since I was a small boy. I began to hate the office, hate living at home, and hate Philadelphia."[8] He took a year off and traveled through the western United States, and when he returned to Philadelphia in 1917 he entered the law office of John Hampton Barnes. That was interrupted with time he spent in the army during World War I. After leaving the army he returned to Barnes law office, and there he spent twenty years with Barnes, Sharswood and Brinton, and three or four younger lawyers. Biddle describes them as good years because he was able to have "close professional ties, unmarried by any quarrels. There was no competition for place, no attempt to steal clients, no disloyalty, or misunderstanding. In those days no one really specialized, although he did most of the trial work."[9]

In 1922, Francis Biddle was appointed special assistant to the U.S. district attorny's office, and he served there for three years. At that time there was a great deal of corruption in most branches of government, both in Washington and in Philadelphia. The dishonesty of the federal prohibition agents had become commonplace and generally accepted. "Even United States Marshals shared in the easy loot. But convictions for violations of the *Prohibition Act* were very difficult to get, particulary when beer was involved." His three years as special assistant gave him valuable experience, however, especially in trying cases. "The trial work doubled and I was in and out of Court all day, and after the strain and excitement of trial, had to spend long afternoons at my uptown office." In those days the assistants were not only permitted but encouraged to build up their private practice, as it was impossible to live on government salaries; as Biddle wrote, "I got four thousand a year."[10]

At that stage in his life Biddle felt good about his profession. "There is no more pleasant feeling for a lawyer than the sense of being at home in his own profession, of handling the techniques of practice with confidence, and of knowing the bar's traditions and talking its shop. I began to look back with equanimity to those early years of failure, when I knew no one and was without recognition or place in the brotherhood. It was satisfying to walk into a courtroom crowded with lawyers on a Monday morning when the Judges were hearing motions, and feel I belonged, was respected, and was beginning to arrive." Biddle served on the Board of Governors and Committee of Censors of the Philadelphia Bar Association, and as the appointee of the Orphans' Court on the County Board of Law Examiners, which passed on applicants for practice before they registered for law school."[11]

In 1934 Biddle became chairman of the National Labor Board where he participated in the preparation of the National Relations Act. He served until the late summer of 1935 and then returned to his law practice in Philadelphia. In 1936 he was appointed counsel of the Special Committee of Congress investigating charges against the authority of its former chairman. He again returned to his Philadelphia firm in 1937. In the history of that firm, Dechert Price & Rhoads (which Barnes Biddle & Myers had merged with), Robert V. Massey wrote that the city's social "establishment" found President Roosevelt "a dangerous radical and they distrusted his actions almost as much as they disliked him." For someone of Biddle's background and associations to join the hated New Deal group was considered both foolhardly and traitorous. It seemed to mystify many of his friends and undoubtedly disenchanted some of the firm's valuable clients.[12]

In 1938, Biddle was appointed to the United States Court of Appeals for the Third Circuit, but he stayed for less than a year. In January 1940, he succeeded Jackson as solicitor general of the United States, and a year later became attorney general and remained in that office until 1945. Biddle next served as the American member of the International Military Tribunal to try the major German war criminals. After that he returned to his home in Washington where he died in 1968 at the age of eighty-two.

Biddle's father had died when he was only five years of age, and he wrote that the women in his family played a large part in his development. He married Katherine Chapin in 1918. Katherine, with her two sisters Marguerite and Cornelia "did things," although none of them went to college—a practice that at the end of the nineteenth century was still frowned on by the genteel society of the day. Marguerite wanted to be a singer, and at ninteeth years of age went to Paris. She married Roffredo Caetani who was a pupil of Liszt, and was also a friend of Wagner and Brahms. Their house in Versailles was a meeting place for writers, musicians, and painters. Biddle's other sister-in-law, Cornelia, studied sculpture in Paris for three years. Biddle went on to say that "Katherine and I have developed a long close intimacy with my brother

George and his wife Helene Sardeau, a sculptor of power and subtlety." She was of Polish Jewish origin. Francis Biddle's admiration and support for women and for the arts set him dramatically apart from the Philadelphia upper class. When his "radical" politics were added to those different values he became totally incomprehensible to most of his social class peers in Philadelphia.[13]

Although Biddle broke from the old upper class of Philadelphia in his politics and artistic values, he remained part of the old establishment in other ways. He had become a member of the Philadelphia Club as a young man, and during the years remained and enjoyed it. He wrote that the spirit of leisure and camaraderie pervaded the club. "I greatly enjoyed lunching there, dipping myself in that quiet stream where the ceremonial and sense of class is still preserved, a little stiff and a little conventional, yet with a friendly casual warmth running round the long table in refreshing contrast to the restless contemporary world washing about it." His loyalty to Philadelphia was far from total, however, and he said of himself that he was considered a bad Philadelphian. He never really came to care about Philadelphia as he later grew to love Washington. Biddle said that to the good Philadelphian, Washington was ephemeral and unreal. "I found little in Philadelphia that stirred the spirit—it was as if something had been finished and was dying—and it had the essence of the commonplace."[14]

Francis Biddle was in many ways the personification of the old Philadelphia upper class lawyer. His practice of law in the city and his refusal to serve on the bench was in the best tradition of the Philadelphia gentleman lawyer. Biddle broke sharply from the accepted pattern, however, when he accepted appointments with the federal government. Even far worse it was with the hated Democrats, led by the detested Franklin Delano Roosevelt. Francis Biddle and other members of his family, however, marched to their own drummer. In his older years he escaped much of the wrath of upper class Philadelphia society by no longer living in the city. He also appears to have been the end of the line of distinguished Biddle lawyers in Philadelphia.

Epilogue: Early 1990s

It has been almost fifty years since the end of the history of the Philadelphia lawyer covered in this book. The world of law and the lawyer changed more during the last fifty years than it had in the previous two hundred years. For example, the number of lawyers has more than tripled during the last half century. In 1944 there were approximately 3,200 lawyers in the city, whereas in 1991 there were over 10,000.

The national trend has been one of a rapid expansion in the number of lawyers. In 1959 there were 250,000 lawyers in the United States, and it is estimated that by 1992 the number will reach 1 million. One striking change during the past fifty years has been the great increase of women lawyers. In Philadelphia, in 1944, only about 1 percent of all lawyers were women, but by 1991 they constituted about 22 percent.

The most significant sociological pattern developed in this book has been the importance of the old upper class in producing the legal leadership in Philadelphia. Although during the two centuries covered the percentage of upper class lawyers decreased, they still remained highly influential, far beyond their numbers. In 1944 about 10 percent of all lawyers in the city were listed in the *Social Register*.[1] A measurement of their greater influence can be seen, however, in the eight largest firms in the city where they accounted for 37 percent of the partners and 23 percent of the associates. By 1991 they represented only about 2 percent of all lawyers in the city. In the eight largest law firms 12 percent of the partners were in the *Social Register* but only 1 percent of the associates. Only eight out of almost eight hundred associates were found in the *Social Register*, and three of those eight were women lawyers. That was unheard of in the past when the *Social Register* did not even list the education of women.

The old upper class has increasingly become irrelevant to Philadelphia law. Many of the *Social Register* partners in the eight largest firms are getting older and nearing retirement. Clearly there are few placements for them coming up out of the associate ranks because there are very few young upper class lawyers. The main reason for this change is meritocracy. In the last fifty years students could no longer be admitted to the top law schools simply by having graduated from a prestigious undergraduate school. Scores on the LSAT are the most significant factor in law school admission today. That is an objective test and rules out the subjective variables of the past. With the great opportunities for higher education that have come about since the end of World War II there

274

is no longer the significant edge in admission based on who your family was. In the past a common pattern in Philadelphia was for the upper class sons to go to the high-status colleges, expecially Princeton. They would then typically go to law school at the University of Pennsylvania. An examination of the *Social Register* in 1987, however, shows only a small number of young men attending Princeton or similar high-status colleges. Most are having to settle for middle-and low-rated colleges, the only ones to which they are admitted. The Scholastic Aptitute Test (SAT) has become a great leveler. This is not to suggest that the *Social Register* children do not still have some advantages in so far as getting into good undergraduate schools. In some colleges there is a "legacy" principle that gives special consideration to children of alumni. Another advantage is that many attend private secondary schools where they are taught the skills for doing well on SATs and with placement advisers who are experts on how the system works. It may say something about the ability level of those old upper class children that even with the edge they have not gotten into the very elite colleges.

Another factor is that many of the brightest and most able of the younger generation of upper class backgrounds leave Philadelphia. They often see opportunities elsewhere and may have the desire to make it on their own, away from the traditional family setting. There are also biases in who is listed in the *Social Register*. Up until recent years divorced women were dropped from the listings. Probably more important, however, is the unknown number of the young who choose not to have their names listed in the *Social Register*. It seems likely that many of those who are the most academically successful are likely to be the more intellectual and liberal. Those would often be the ones who see the *Social Register* as an anachronism and want nothing to do with it. It certainly appears safe to assume that by the beginning of the twenty-first century the old influence of the upper class on the legal profession of Philadelphia will be very little.

Lawyers in 1990s

During the past half century the practice of law has changed dramatically. In a survey in 1991 of law school graduates, 62 percent entered private practice, an increase of almost 10 percent from a survey done in 1974. In Philadelphia in 1990, about 75 percent of all lawyers were in private practice. The other side of the coin has been the decrease in new lawyers taking government and public-interest jobs. For example, in 1975, about 18 percent took government jobs, whereas in 1986 it had dropped to 12 percent.[2]

After the Civil War and well into the twentieth century the two-person partnership was a common legal working relationship. With the rise of the larger law firms, however, both the sole practice and the small partnership became less likely to be successful. In recent years the decrease has continued in Philadelphia. In 1980, there were about 145 two-person partnerships, which meant about 1 in every 24 lawyers was in that kind of working relationship. By 1990, the number of partnerships had dropped to about 130. With almost 3,000 more lawyers in the city that meant only 1 in every 38 was in a two-person partnership.

The survival rate of two-member partnerships has not been high in Philadelphia. Of those types of partnerships existing in 1980, only 38 percent remained eight years later. In 1980 about one-quarter of the partnerships were composed of family members, and they had a somewhat better chance (46 percent) of surviving than those with no family bonds (35 percent). Private practice increasingly refers to being in a law firm rather than being a sole practitioner. In Philadelphia, in 1991[3], over one-third of all lawyers were in medium (10 to 135 members) and large (135 or more members) law firms. Another 10 percent were in governmental and community activities.

The most dramatic change across the United States as well as in Philadelphia has been the growth of the large law firm. In 1944 in Philadelphia there were six firms with more than 20 members. In 1991, however, there were ten firms, each having more than 135 members in their Philadelphia offices. In those ten largest firms there were about 660 partners and 1,150 associates. About one-third are partners, and two-thirds are associates. That is generally defined as a fairly desirable ratio.

Partners in the top revenue-producing law firms of Philadelphia do well compared with other cities. Their average earnings of $290,000 (1988) a year are the same as those in Washington, D.C. The two cities with higher earnings are New York with $410,000 and Los Angeles with $320,000. The salaries for starting associates are not as good relative to other cities, however. A starting salary of $40,571 places them behind eight other cities.[4]

There is sometimes a supposition that there is a high rate of partners moving from one large law firm to another, but that does not appear to be the case in Philadelphia. An examination of about 700 partners in the ten largest law firms in the city was made in 1988. When looking back to 1980, 88 percent of those partners had been with the same firm. Less than 2 percent had come in from one of the other ten large firms in the city and about 3 percent from midsize law firms.

In the midsize Philadelphia law firms, with 10 to 135 members, there were about 2,500 lawyers. The percent of partners in those firms is about 40 percent, about the same as in the large firms. According to some experts the midsize firms are struggling to survive in an increasingly competitive field. In 1986 and 1987, sixty midsize firms, more than 10 percent of the total nationwide, had either dissolved or merged.[5] In attempting to attract major companies as clients the midsize firm often cannot provide the human and technological resources that the big corporations demand. One lawyer in a midsize firm in Philadelphia said that his firm had a good shot to land a large client, but lost out because they had no international offices and facilities.

Another example may be shown by the large law firm that can increase its income by virtue of experience generated by its size. To illustrate, suppose that firm does a first-time job for a large client, and that new work calls for an intensive and costly effort. They charge their client $100,000, a fair amount for the work done. Once they have developed that package, however, they can go to another client faced with a similar need. They can then piggyback the work done of client A and offer client B the package for $50,000, and still turn a substantial profit. They sometimes point out to client B why they are getting a good bargain.

Beginning in the 1970s there was a sharp increase in the number of lawyers hired by large corporations, banks, and insurance companies. Most of the lawyers serve as in-house counsel, although some lawyers work in a management or administrative capacity. In 1991, in Philadelphia there were at least nine corporations with at least 15 lawyers. There were two with about 50 lawyers, the size of a midsize law firm. Even though the large corporations have their in-house staffs, they often turn over work to the large law firms. The in-house counsel can handle many of the day-to-day legal questions, but they do not have the resources or expertise to handle many more complex problems.

Most large corporations will retain several law firms to handle pieces of their work. One advantage of that approach is that it precludes any of the retained law firms from acting against them at some future time. Once a firm represents a client, it does not act against the client without permission because of the conflict of interest.

A common pattern is for the corporate in-house counsel to come from the large law firms. Sometimes they move from the law firm to the corporation because they have been working with that corporation and have built a rapport in that fashion. That move is usually made with the blessing of the law firm because it usually cements a continued relationship between the law firm and the company. The ex-member of the law firm will turn back to the firm for future needs. Often at various social functions held by large law firms their "alumni" who have gone into the business world come back and renew their contacts.

Frequently, senior associates leave their law firm to become in-house counsel in business corporations. They may choose to leave because they want the greater control over their lives. Other associates, who are not going to be made partner, are helped to find these placements. This allows both the ex-associate and the law firm to maintain a cordial and generally good economic relationship.

The patterns of occupational mobility in the Philadelphia legal structure are quite rigid. Beginning lawyers who start in a large law firm can move into any career in law from there if they do not choose or are not chosen to stay in that firm. They can move laterally to another large firm, they can become in-house counsel, or they can join a midsize firm. The lawyer who starts out in a midsize firm, however, has much less chance of moving up to a large law firm. The person who starts out in sole practice has practically no chance of ever moving into a medium-size law firm.

Obviously, what is most crucial is where you start in the process, and that is determined almost entirely by your law school. If your law school is not high status then how well you perform during your first year is of overwhelming importance. The large law firms hire the top students from the top law schools at the top salaries. Not only are they highly rewarded, but they also have a chance to gain prestige among their peers and have the potential to become a partner.

Several Philadelphia lawyers contributed to the following general description of the legal status system. At the top are the partners in the largest law firms. Also placed there are federal judges and some smaller law firms that are highly regarded for their specialties. There may also be some of the law school professors, especially from Penn. The second level would be the midsize law firms. At that level would also be found a few sole practitioners and some small law firms that are successful in specialized ways. Also included at this level would be in-house counsel from some large institutions and some lawyers employed by the federal government. The third level would include most small law firms and sole practitioners. Also there would be most of those in the city positions connected with the courts and the criminal system. There is also a bottom level made up of those lawyers barely able to earn a living in the practice of law. Some hang around the courts looking for opportunities; others seek out negligence cases or wait for whatever may walk in their door.

Law Schools

Graduation from an accredited law school is the means of entrance in most states into the legal profession. Graduation allows a person to sit for the bar examination necessary to practice in that state (and sometimes other states). There were in 1991, 175 law schools offering the J.D. that were approved by the American Bar Association. There were 36,121 degrees awarded in 1986, about 20 percent more than were awarded in 1976. Through the mid-1980s there had been a decline in law school applications, but in 1988 there was a sharp increase. As of February 1988, there had been an increase of 18 percent over that of February 1987. That increase was especially true for the most prestigious law schools and was occurring at a time when medical school applications were declining. Explanations for the increase ranged from the 19 October stock market collapse tarnishing the allure of a career on Wall Street to the popular television show "L. A. Law."[6]

The law school that one is admitted to may be the single most important determinant in a person's entire legal career, because there are sharp differences in the status of law schools. For persons admitted to the most elite law schools, they can finish almost anywhere in their class and still have the choice of a top position when they graduate. For example, probably the most prestigious law school in the United States is Yale. There, to incoming law school students in 1990, it was made clear that if it was their choice they could count on entering a law firm when they graduated at a salary of at least $75,000. It did not matter where they finish in their class because a Yale law degree is so prestigious.

All accredited law schools call for LSAT scores for admission. Although they all say that other factors are just as important, such as grade-point average as an undergraduate, few top law schools are going to take students who have not scored very high on the LSAT, except under special circumstances. Once in any law school, students who make the effort and are of reasonable intelligence will graduate.

One women law student at Yale, who scored a 48 out of 48 on her LSAT, and who has taught in the Stanley Kaplan LSAT preparation course says that certain analytical skills are important to do well on the test—that is, the ability to define the limits of a propostion precisely. To illustrate she says suppose you have the statement, "That car will not run without gasoline." The student must recognize that the statement says nothing about cars in general or general conditions about cars that run. She says that what is crucial is not to read into a statement anything that is not there. Success on the LSAT appears to be a high level of intelligence plus specific analytical abilities.

In Philadelphia there are two law schools and in the immediate suburbs a third. The oldest and by far the most prestigious is the University of Pennsylvania Law School. As pointed out in earlier chapters there were various attempts to start a legal program at the university from the time of the Revolution. Penn Law School did not officially start until 1850, however. In general it has been rated during the years, up to the present, as one of the top ten law schools in America. In 1987 Penn had 3,564 applications of which it accepted 29 percent. Of those 1,024 that were accepted eventually 22 percent enrolled because many top students have been accepted and chose other high-prestige law schools. For example, Yale only admitted 216 of which 80 percent enrolled.[7]

The average LSAT score for the beginning Penn law student was 42, where the top score one can attain is 48. At Yale the average score was 44, probably the highest of any law school. Women constitute 40 percent of the Penn law student body, and Penn draws 29 percent of its students from Pennsylvania and another 51 percent from other northeastern states.

In the past, Penn Law School graduates have dominated the large firms in Philadelphia. In 1944, 64 percent of all partners in the eight largest firms were from Penn. That was also true for 60 percent of the associates. This has changed, however, and in 1988, 33 percent of all partners in the ten largest law firms were Penn graduates as were 20 percent of all associates. The main reason for this change is that Penn has become a national law school. In 1987, Robert Mundheim, dean of the Penn Law School, said that the previous year had been the first time that more of his graduates chose to work in New York than in Philadelphia.[8]

In 1987, 58 percent of the graduates from Penn Law School went with large firms, 10 percent with other law firms, and 11 percent as judicial clerks. It appears that students anywhere in the top half of their class at Penn will get offers from the top Philadelphia law firms if they want them. The law firms take the view that you had to be very good to get in, and therefore you were competing with other very good students. Among those Penn law students who stay in Philadelphia, about 25 percent of their class, more than three-quarters go with the largest firms.

Temple University Law School was founded in 1901 and was from the beginning geared to the economically poorer student. It has always had both a full-time day school and a part-time night school. Of all students who apply to Temple Law School 39 percent are accepted and of those who are accepted 39 percent enroll. The average LSAT score is 33. About half of the students are women. On the basis of their average LSAT scores Temple would be in the top 40 percent of the 171 accredited law schools. Temple draws three-fourths of its student from Pennsylvania, and most of the rest are from other northeast states.

Only about one-fourth of the Temple Law School graduates remain in Philadelphia. Of those who entered the Philadelphia bar in 1986 and 1987 from Temple Law School almost half entered medium and large law firms. More than 29 percent of those beginning lawyers in Philadelphia were in sole practice, however. Most of those who had taken positions with medium and large law firms were in the top 10 to 15 percent of their class. If they are not it is very unlikely they will even be interviewed.

Villanova Law School was founded in 1953. Forty-two percent of all applicants are accepted and of those accepted 29 percent actually enroll. Women make up about half of the class, and more than 60 percent of the students are from Pennsylvania. The average LSAT is 36, which places it in the top third of the 171 accredited law schools. About 27 percent of all graduates are listed as having been admitted to the Philadelphia bar in 1986 and 1987. Many Villanova graduates also taken positions in the suburbs, especially in Montgomery country where it is located. Sixty-eight percent of the Villanova graduates listed in the 1988 *Martindale-Hubbell* are in large- and medium-size Philadelphia law firms. At Villanova, like at Temple, one must be in the top 10 or 15 percent to even be considered by the large law firms.

In 1991, of the associates in Philadelphia's ten largest law firms, 20 percent were from Penn, 10 percent from Temple, and 10 percent from Villanova. Being a member of the *Law Review* is especially important at Temple and Villanova. These are for the most part the only students considered for employment by the top law firms. Students can get on the *Law Review* by grades, by writing, or a combination of the two. Those who successfully make *Law*

Review through writing alone are relatively few. Most make it based on grade-point average at the end of the first year of law school. Usually they must be in the top 10 percent of their class, which places great pressure on students for grades during the first year of law school.

There are some students who make a great effort in their first year. If they are successful they can have interviews during the fall of their second year to become summer associates during the next summer. Almost everyone who goes through the summer associate program receives a job offer to start when they graduate. Clearly the best way to work the situation if at Temple or Villanova is to be in the top 10 percent at the end of the first year. That will get the student interviews and a likely offer as a summer associate. After that the student does not have to do too much, because very little attention is directed at later grades.

It is possible for a student who was not in the top 10 or 15 percent of their class at the end of the first year to bring up their cumulative grade-point average and eventually get a good job offer, but that is clearly much more difficult. *Law Review* students also provide other evidence of the importance of Philadelphia to Temple and Villanova law students. Of members of the *Law Review* from 1974 to 1984, 56 percent from Temple stayed in Philadelphia, 57 percent from Villanova, but only 30 percent from Penn Law School. The Penn *Law Review* student would be among the elite of all American law students and could in effect write their own ticket.

Law students from the top law schools and the top law students at less prestigious law schools are in great demand. There is strong competition between the large law firms for them. If a law firm is interested in a student, he or she is brought in for interviews and typically made to feel important and valued. The law student accepts an offer and at the end of the second year of law school becomes a summer associate. There are a few students from the top law schools who are brought in at the end of the first year. What makes that highly desirable is that they are paid at a first-year associate's salary. They are presented with some experience in legal work, and are wined and dined. The law firm wants them so they create the illusion that they are highly valuable. They almost all receive offers to begin the fall following their graduation. In some big firms they are given a bonus before they start working that allows them to prepare to take the state bar. In 1991, the beginning salary for an associate in the top Philadelphia firms was about $65,000.

There appears to be a wide difference in how the law schools view themselves and their students and how their products are seen by the large law firms. It is rare to hear any lawyer suggest that students entering a law firm for the first time have any idea on how they should practice law. At best they have learned the language of law but in actually doing legal work it is the firm who must teach them. The lawyers agree that what is important is for the beginning lawyer to be willing to work hard and have the desire to learn. The law firm makes a big investment in them for the first few years because their work has to be carefully checked. It is unlikely that few beginning lawyers actually make the firm any money during those first few years. Those years really constitute on the job training provided by the large law firm.

Women in Law

One of the most dramatic changes in law has been the great increase in the number of women in recent years. In 1944, only 1 percent of all lawyers in Philadelphia were women. In 1990 women made up about 22 percent of all lawyers in the city. Approximately 900 lawyers were admitted to the Philadelphia bar in 1989 and 1990, and of that number about 380 (42 percent) were women. It was not until 1953 that the first women were admitted to Harvard Law School. By 1974 about 4 percent of the class were women. In 1940, however, the incoming class was 40 percent women.

The kinds of positions that women take have also changed. Of those admitted to the bar in the mid-1960s, 21 percent of the men but only 5 percent of the women entered large law firms. By 1988, however, there were slightly more women entering mid-size and large law firms, 36 percent verus 30 percent. Of all persons who entered the large law firms in 1982 and 1983 only 41 percent of the men and 31 percent of the women were still there in 1988.

According to women interviewed the somewhat higher dropout among women is for the most part voluntary. Women sometimes drop out to have children and sometimes take less demanding jobs to spend more time in the mother role. Having and caring for children affects a woman's career in a way that is rarely true for a man's. It appears, however, that women who are not mothers at the time they are moving through their associate years are just as likely as men to stay and become a partner.

The world of the law firm has always been masculine, and there continue to be some barriers. For example, the number of women who can serve as role models for younger women is small. That is because there are still very few women partners in large law firms. In 1991, 7 percent of the partners in the ten largest Philadelphia law firms were women. Some women have pointed out that some of the successful women lawyers are not too willing to help women on their way up. Unfortunately, some have an attitude that says, "I made it in the male world on my own, and you can too."

Another problem for women is they do not have the network of successful people they can tap for new business. In any large firm the role of the "rainmaker," bringing in business, is usually crucial to the success of a partner. There may be, as one woman lawyer said, something as simple as a conference that stops for a break, and the men go to the men's room. Those men, almost always the powers, continue their discussion, and the women are excluded. Often the beginning lawyer is treated by a client as a secretary. If she is not regarded as a secretary, she is almost always treated as a more junior associate holding a subservient position to the male partner. The lower status of her position sometimes contributes to the lower status assigned to her as a woman. One successful woman partner in a large Philadelphia firm said these problems can be overcome with time. ''With time and experience one gains a demeanor, a sense of presence, that receives respect and eliminates what was before some kind of sexism. Your presence conveys clearly that you are not a secretary nor even an associate.''

A striking sociological change in who practices law during the past fifty years has been the great impact of Jewish lawyers. Up to, and even for a while after World War II, some of the large Philadelphia law firms would not hire Jewish lawyers. Anti-Semitism for the most part broke down, probably not because of any great enlightenment among the old guard, but rather because it was bad business. Not only were there many outstanding Jewish lawyers, but they also had the contacts to bring in very wealthy clients.

Also of great importance after World War II was the rapid increase in a merit system for gaining admission to the high-prestige law schools. In the past the Jewish lawyer in Philadelphia was sometimes passed over because he went to Temple and therefore was seen as having an inferior legal education. With many Jewish law students entering the University of Pennsylvania as well as high-prestige law schools like Harvard and Yale, those old stereotype could no longer be used. In talking to Jewish lawyers in Philadelphia the view seems to be that there is still some levels of anti-Semitism. It is not often encountered in the world of law, however, but rather in some of the social worlds of which lawyers may be a part. The same may also be said of sexism. Although various institutions, such as law, may be relatively free of anti-semitism and sexism, that is not true of the overall cultural patterns and values in American society.

Black Lawyers

In 1987, about 20,000 American lawyers were black. That was about 3 percent of the total number of lawyers. Of those 20,000 black lawyers, possibly 30 percent were black women. It is estimated that in Philadelphia in 1990 there are about 700 practicing black lawyers, about 7 percent of the total. In 1987, Penn Law School had 17 percent minority students, whereas Temple and Villanova had 11 percent and 7 percent, respectively.

In a book published in 1986 on black law firms in the United States there were 105 black lawyers listed in Philadelphia.[9] In that group about one-third were identified as members of black law firms that ranged in size from 2 to 7 members. Not all the members were black, however. The next largest category were 20 percent who were Common Pleas judges. A white male clubbishness in the law firms has persisted through most of the first half of the century.

Today the Bar Association is given high marks for its openness to minorities. The late Raymond Pace Alexander, the city's first common pleas black judge, once praised the Philadelphia Bar Association as "the leader of all American bar associations in this respect."[10]

On the national level it has only been in recent years that blacks have been appointed to the federal courts. Of the fifty-three blacks serving on the district court of the appeals court, thirty-eight were appointed during the four year Carter administration. In the eight years of the Reagan administration only four black appointments were made.[11] In the United State Court of Appeals in Philadelphia there are three black judges, and they are a distinguished group. In fact, all three are graduates of Yale Law School.

Judiciary

Traditionally in Philadelphia the old upper class, who were most often the successful lawyers, had little interest in the judiciary. Although by 1990 the old upper class is irrelevant to the Philadelphia legal world it continues to be true that the most successful lawyers have little interest in judicial positions. The exception to this is in the federal courts, where the appointees are generally very highly regarded lawyers. Those judges sometimes come from the partnership ranks of the large law firms in the city. Listed in the 1988 *Martindale-Hubbell* for Philadelphia are 22 U.S. district and circuit judges. The law schools of those judges were 32 percent from Penn, 23 percent from Temple, and 18 percent from each Harvard and Yale.

There are sixty judicial districts in the commonwealth, and each has a court of common pleas. The first district is Philadelphia county, the same area as the city of Philadelphia.[12] In 1985 there were 102 elected judges, and of those judges 11 were women and 20 were blacks. The commonest career path is to start out in a political district and gain the support of a political party. It appears that more than half of all the judges started out as sole practitioners. The judges tend to be from local law schools, with about 25 percent from Penn and about 35 percent from Temple.

An examination of the law clerks employed by common pleas court judges suggest they are recruited from less prestigious law schools. Of about 40 listed in the 1988 *Martindale-Hubbell* there are none from Penn Law School or from any of the other high-status law schools. Temple provides about one-third, whereas Villanova accounts for only 7 percent. Most of the others are recruited from lower-rated law schools.

The process of electing common pleas judges has been around since 1850. There has been during the years strong agitation to change that. The Philadelphia Bar Association has long been on record as in favor of a "merit selection" of judges rather than through the politically partisan elections. Although the case for the selection of judges by appointment through the merit system has been frequently made, it has not yet been successful. The resistence has been due in part to the belief that merit selection would shift the power from the voter, or at least the political parties, into the hands of an elite few selected by the governor. The quest for judgeships in Philadelphia is rooted in politics from start to finish. To win an election, a candidate needs money— often thousands of dollars. At the core of any election bid both lawyers and judges explained in interviews to the *Philadelphia Inguirer* that an endorsement is needed from the Democratic or Republican city committee. "Once endorsed, a candidate is expected to make a significant contribution to help defray the party's campaign expenses."[13]

The cost of becoming a judge in Philadelphia has escalated since the mid-1980s. In the 1985 election the Democratic City Committee looked for $10,000 in contributions from each individual candidate. All that got them was a foot in the front door. There was nothing to keep the party from taking the money up front and then turning around and not endorsing the person. Senator Vince Fumo said people better be prepared to spend "upward of $65,000 to make a decent run at it—that isn't city wide, that's maybe 15 targeted wards that are strong."[14]

In 1988 the Pennsylvania Supreme Court removed 8 Philadelphia judges from the bench for accepting hundreds of dollars from the Roofer's Union. "Bar leaders immediately praised the decision as a strong resolution to the two-year scandal that has turned the city's courts upside down." According to the *Philadelphia Inquirer* story the records showed that candidates for judgeships in Philadelphia routinely accepted donations from lawyers and then allowed those lawyers to try cases in front of them a short time later.[15]

One of the problems in getting more able lawyers to become judges is their pay scale. In 1986 a common pleas court judge received $65,000. That was about what a third-year associate in a large law firm earned in 1986. That is why almost always judges come from small practices where that yearly income presents a significant increase.

The problems with the commonwealth court system has continued to plague the state. In March 1990, former Superior Court Judge Edmund B. Spaeth, Jr., who had been appointed chairman of the State Judicial Inquiry and Review Board the previous year resigned. He told the governor that the system was too flawed to allow the board to do its job. The board has long been criticized as ineffectual, as being top-heavy with judges who protect fellow judges, and as failing in its two decades of existence to root out judicial corruption.[16]

Future

There is very high agreement that the future of law in American and certainly in Philadelphia is toward the ever-increasingly large law firm. A few firms will probably become megafirms, international in their practice. Philadelphia has at least one such firm, Morgan Lewis & Bockius, an old Philadelphia law firm, that is the eighth largest in the United States and has offices in six other American cities and four foreign countries. The common wisdom is also that the boutique middle-and small-size firms will become increasingly important. Those firms specialize in a few select areas and often spring up when a small practice group leaves a large firm to concentrate on more specialized areas. One example has been asbestos litigation.

In the future there will be a wider range of law schools to contribute their graduates to the top law firms in the city. As mentioned earlier that is because the University of Pennsylvania Law School has become increasingly national and is therefore sending a smaller percentage of its graduates into the Philadelphia law firms. In 1988, 20 percent of the associates in the largest law firms came from Penn, and 10 percent each from Temple and Villanova. It does not seem likely that the contribution from Temple and Villanova will increase much because the large law firms are likely to continue to take only the top 10 to 15 percent of their graduates. The large law firms have for some time been recruiting more from other top law schools. An increasing number of associates are coming from such high-prestige law schools as the University of Virginia and Georgetown University.

Often when small law firms look for an associate they look at those who have had a few years of experience in a larger firm. Having that apprenticeship typically means this associate will have experience that will be of immediate value to the small law firm. One partner in a four-member firm said, "we can't afford to hire a new graduate because we don't have the money and the resources to teach them what they need to know to be of value to us." This contributes to why the sole practitioner, because of so few options, has a bleak future. Many drift along the edges of the legal communities and barely earn a living. There are some who leave law completely for another occupation.

The second group of sole practitioners are those who choose to be. They are typically persons who have come out of law school and have taken good positions, and then decided to go into their own practice and better control their own work world. One sole practitioner, who had been a partner in one of the city's largest firms, left it because he did not like the internal politics or the constant pressure to bring in new clients.

Often the successful sole practitioner, and there are some who earn $1 million or more each year, has some highly valued specialty. One example is the small-time lawyer who gets a negligence case that has the potential for a large economic return. If that lawyer does not have the expertise or resources, however, his likely success against the resources of a huge insurance company are not very good. What he may do is turn to a sole practitioner who is one of the superstars on those kinds of cases—that is, a lawyer with great success, a large staff, and the resources for success. By turning his case over the referring lawyer may retain a third of any settlement the specialist makes. A third of a case with a good probability of success is better than 50 percent of one he has little chance of winning.

Another example might be farming out some legal work to specialists in personal law. The large firms are not usually anxious to handle divorce cases but sometimes do so more as a courtesy to clients. Rather than their personal law section handling to divorce, however, they may turn those cases over to a highly skilled and successful divorce lawyer. Those divorce lawyers are trusted by the large law firms because they know that legal specialist will not attempt to take any other legal business from their client.

Areas of legal specialization have changed over time. In the late 1970s, energy law and administrative-regulatory practice were the hot areas. By 1985, the popular areas included health care, bankruptcy, and computer law. In the early 1990s increasing areas of interest included intellectual property, high technology, international trade, pensions, and tax. Regardless of the practice or industry focus, transactional business is likely to be the wave of the future. The hot areas during the 1990s are likely to continue to be communications law, intellectual property, employment-related issues including discrimination and wrongful discharge, pensions, environment law, and governmental relations and lobbying. As the economy has declined in the early 1990s there is less work in real estate development and venture capital financing, securities, and banking, and more in bankruptcy, corporate reorganization, and tax.[17] One new source of law firm income is with the Savings and Loans bailouts.

There may also be changes in courtroom practices. The average trial takes far too long and is too complex for the average citizen to expect to obtain justice through the system of civil jury trials. In the future, fewer cases will probably go to trial. Increasingly negotiation and settlement will take the place of trials— alternative systems include arbitration, mediation, administrative tribunals, and informed decision making by a trained jurist.[18] There is little reason to think that the quality of commonwealth judges will improve in the future. There is little likelihood that a general merit system of appointment will be brought about. There is also little reason to think that the salary of the state judiciary will become competitive with other legal earning possibilities. Add to this the very low reputation of the commonwealth courts in 1990s, and it is highly unlikely that many of the better-trained and experienced lawyers will want to become judges.

There is the possibility of some court changes in Pennsylvania. With the passage of the new Business Corporation Law in 1988 there has been an increased interest in the creation of a separate court system similar to that of Delaware. It would be a court of chancery to hear business cases. The judges would be selected by special merit and from outside the current court system.

The computer age is having a great influence on the practice of law. One writer says that computers and their capabilities may well be the most significant change to affect the legal profession in the 1990s. There will increasingly be personal computers on every attorney's desk. This is especially true as the younger generation of lawyers who are "computer wise" move into positions of power. Attornys will be able to reduce their dependency on administrative support with the computer technology making it easier for lawyers themselves to edit documents. Economically, although the cost of personnel continues to increase, the cost of technology continues to decrease. "Using automation is one way that firms can gain a quick advantage in productivity and profitability, while setting the stage for reducing administrative overhead."[19]

There is another potential gain to be made with greater computer sophistication, and that is the elimination of much administrative work. Lawyers in large law firms appear well aware of their need to make policy and other major administrative decisions. If they are not protective they may find administrators increasingly taking over their law firms. They suggest that is not likely because lawyers will not give up their own control. They should let many of the universities be an example of what not to let happen. In some universities administrators have proliferated and taken over all important policy making. The professors are left with little control over much of significance.

Lawyers can increasingly negotiate and settle disputes using electronic communications rather than having to travel to conferences. Video-taped depositions of witnesses and other taped materials are being introduced into evidence in courts. That reduces the need to travel, and increases the range and volume of work an attorney may handle. "The communications revolution, combined with the Supreme Court's decision that lawyers have a right to advertise, has greatly changed the way lawyers practice."[20]

Leonard Dubin, president of the Pennsylvania Bar Association and a Philadelphia lawyer, suggests that the most revolutionary technological advance may be the fax machine. He writes that the fax machine is both a boon and a bane to the lawyer's existence. The disadvantage to using the fax machine is that every message has the same urgency. The sender is under the impression that the receiver must respond immediately. In fact, often the sender demands an immediate response, and this takes away the chance for thoughtful consideration before responding.[21]

In the two years since the Epilogue was first written there have been some social changes that have affected the Philadelphia lawyer. The recession of 1990 and 1991 has brought about changes in the economic system in America. The high flying world of junk bonds and leveraged buy outs has been replaced with jail sentences and the savings and loans scandals. This has had an effect on the large law firms, particularly in their business and fiance work, especially in acquisitions and takeovers. The economic effects on other sections of the large law firms has probably been less. For example, litigation, labor, tax and personal law have been somewhat less effected.

In the large law firms there is less work and less revenue coming in and that means less need for personal. Some of the firms have laid off associates and in some cases even partners. The mid-size and small law firms are also feeling the squeeze and this significantly effects the over all job market. It cuts off much of the flow occupationally downward that has existed in the past when associates left the large firms for the smaller ones. There are also fewer opportunities for the associate to leave the large firm for inhouse jobs in the banking and business worlds because they too are feeling the recession and are much less likely than in the past to be adding to their staffs.

These economic effects are influencing a range of lawyers because it means that there are more highly qualified lawyers looking at positions they would not have considered in the past. And those who would have filled them are being forced downward into less rewarding and status giving legal areas. In fact, some are leaving the profession because there are so few opportunities. It also appears that associates in the large Philadelphia firms have less chance now of getting on the partnership track then only a couple of years ago.

The recruitment of top law school students is also undergoing change. One senior partner in a large firm said it was about time because the "wining and dining" of summer associates had become ridiculous. He said that when times were good the firms would do it to keep up with the competition. But it was totally artificial and led the incoming associate to have a distorted opinion of their worth to the firm. The summer associate came to believe they were stars and when they arrived discovered that few paid any attention to them and found that what they had learned in law school had very little practical application to the practice of law. If the economic problems continue the law student may find themselves coming into a situation where their future with the firm has fewer and fewer possibilities.

In the winter of 1992 it is hard to know what will happen with the recession. But certainly the position suggested by some leaders of the large law firms is that this economic crunch provides them with a chance to tighten up their policies and get rid of unwanted lawyers. Whether or not that happens remains to be seen, but changes are taking place and the large law firms are becoming leaner. It seems safe to assume that while there may be some tightening and reordering in the big law firms of Philadelphia that the same strong ones will continue to dominate in the future as they have in the past.

In the 1990s, the legal profession in Philadelphia is generally as healthy and providing a future as good as in any other profession. Certainly it can be argued that today the Philadelphia bar is far more democratic than it ever has been. Even with the criticism directed toward objective testing like the LSAT, it is difficult to imagine that many would want to return to the past—when it was who you were rather than what you knew that mattered.

Notes

Preface

1. E. Digby Baltzell, *Philadelphia Gentleman* (New York: Free Press, 1958).
2. *Social Register* (New York: Social Register Association, 1898).

Chapter 1. Early Colonies: 1682 to 1750

1. See Laurence M. Friedman, *A History of American Law* (New York: Simon & Shuster, 1973).
2. See Anton-Hermanns Chroust, *The Rise of the Legal Profession in America* (Oklahoma: University of Oklahoma Press, 1965).
3. Friedman, *American Law*, 24.
4. Ibid., 26.
5. Max Lerner, *America as a Civilization* (New York: Simon & Shuster, 1958), 426.
6. Edwin Wolf 2nd, *Philadelphia: Portrait of an American City* (Philadelphia: Stackpole Books, 1975), 255.
7. John Hill Martin, *Bench and Bar of Philadelphia* (Philadelphia: Rees Welsh & Co., 1883), iv.
8. Edward B. Bronner, *William Penn's "Holy Experiment"* (Philadelphia: Temple University Press, 1967), 38.
9. John F. Watson, *Annals of Philadelphia* (Philadelphia: Carey & Hart, 1830) 254.
10. Ibid., 256.
11. Chroust, *The Rise of the Legal Profession in America*, 208–9.
12. Robert N. C. Nix, Jr., *The Supreme Court of Pennsylvania* (Philadelphia: 1986), 3.
13. Edward D. Cheyney, *History of the University of Pennsylvania, 1740–1940* (Philadelphia: University of Pennsylvania Press, 1940), 9.
14. Laurence Lewis, Jr., "Edward Shippens, Chief Justice of Pennsylvania," *The Pennsylvania Magazine of History and Biography* 3 (April 1883): 148.
15. Friedman, *American Law*, 72.
16. Herbert William Keith Fitzroy, "Richard Crosby Goes to Court," *Pennsylvania Magazine of History and Biography* 48 (1938): 12.
17. Lewis, "Edward Shippens," 171.
18. Friedman, *American Law*, 72.
19. Lewis, "Edward Shippens," 171.
20. E. Digby Baltzell, *Puritan Boston and Quaker Philadelphia* (New York: Free Press, 1979), 164.
21. Martin, *Bench and Bar*, 243.
22. Horace Binney, *The Leaders of the Old Bar of Philadelphia* (Philadelphia: Henry R. Ashmead, 1866) 111.

23. Chroust, *Legal Profession*, 216.
24. Ibid., 65.
25. Ibid., 46.
26. Ibid., 47.
27. Ibid., 34.

Profile 1: Andrew Hamilton (1676–1741)

1. Joshua Francis Fisher, "Andrew Hamilton Esq. of Pennsylvania," reprinted in *Pennsylvania Magazine of History and Biography* 16 (1892): 4.
2. Bernard C. Steiner, "Andrew Hamilton and John Peter Zenger," *Pennsylvania Journal of History and Biography* 20 (1896): 406.
3. Fisher, "Andrew Hamilton," 15.
4. Burton Alva Konkle, *The Life of Andrew Hamilton: 1676–1741* (Philadelphia: National Publishing Company, 1941), 49.
5. Ibid., see: Hamilton's jury speech.
6. Fisher, "Andrew Hamilton," 26.
7. Ibid., 27.
8. Horace Binney, *The Leaders of the Old Bar of Philadelphia* (Philadelphia: Henry R. Ashmead, 1866), 15.
9. Konkle, *Andrew Hamilton*, 107.

Chapter 2. Colonial Period: 1750s

1. See Timothy Daniell, *Inns of Court* (London: Wiley & Sons, 1970).
2. Chroust, *Legal Profession*, 34.
3. Ibid., 36.
4. Sydney G. Turner, "The Middle Temple and the U.S.A.," *Quarterly Review* 23 (1958): 450.
5. C. E. A. Bedwell, "American Middle Templers," *American Historical Review* 28 (1920): 231.
6. Edward B. Bronner, *Penn's "Holy Experiment"*, 47.
7. Lewis, "Edward Shippens," 84.
8. Nathaniel Burt, *The Perennial Philadelphians* (Boston: Little, Brown, 1963), 203.
9. Chroust, *Legal Profession*, 52.
10. James Allen, "Diary of James Allen Esq., of Philadelphia Counsellor-at-Law, 1740–1778," *The Pennsylvania Magazine of History and Biography* 9 (1885): 192.
11. John F. Watson, *Annals of Philadelphia* (Philadelphia: Carey and Hart, 1830) 268.
12. Chroust, *Legal Profession*, 30.
13. Ibid., 32.
14. Charles Page Smith, *James Wilson: Founding Father* (Chapel Hill: University of North Carolina Press, 1956), 319.
15. Chroust, *Legal Profession*, 58.
16. Thomas R. Meehan, "Courts, Cases and Counselors in Revolutionary and Post-Revolutionary Pennsylvania," *The Pennsylvania Magazine of History and Biography* 91 (1967): 4.

Profile 2: John Dickinson (1732-1808)

1. Henry Flanders, "The Life and Times of John Dickinson, 1732-1808," *Pennsylvania Magazine of History and Biography*, 4 (1891): 5.
2. Ibid., 6.
3. Ibid., 6.
4. J. H. Powell, "John Dickinson and the Constitution," *Pennsylvania Magazine of History and Biography* 49 (1936): 2.
5. Flanders, "John Dickinson," 2.
6. Ibid., 2.
7. Ibid., 11.
8. Ibid., 13.
9. Ibid., 6.
10. Ibid., 2.
11. Ibid., 23.
12. Ibid., 9.
13. Ibid., 24.
14. Ibid., 25.

Chapter 3. Revolutionary War Era: 1770-1788

1. See Philip S. Klein and Ari Hoogenboom, *A History of Pennsylvania* (University Park: Penn State University Press, 1980).
2. Ibid., 106.
3. See Chroust, *Legal Profession*.
4. See William M. Meigs, *The Life of Charles Jared Ingersoll* (Philadelphia: Lippincott, 1897).
5. Friedman, *American Law*, 97.
6. John Hill Martin, *Bench and Bar of Philadelphia* (Philadelphia: Rees Welsh & Co., 1883) 224.
7. Carl Bridenbauch, *Cities in Revolt* (New York: Alfred A. Knopf, 1955). 289.
8. J. G. DeRoulhac, "Southern Members of the Inns of Court," *North Carolina Historical Review* 27 (1933): 281.
9. Friedman, *American Law*, 320.
10. See Chroust, *Legal Profession in America*.
11. Nix, *Supreme Court of Pennsylvania*, 3.
12. Chroust, *Legal Profession*.
13. Allen, "James Allen."
14. Chroust, *Legal Profession*.
15. Ibid., 15-16.

Profile 3: James Wilson (1742-1798)

1. Charles Page Smith, *James Wilson: Founding Father* (Chapel Hill: University of North Carolina Press, 1956), 205-6.
2. Ibid., 256.
3. Ibid., 269.
4. James Bryce, "James Wilson: An Appreciation," *Pennsylvania Magazine of History and Biography* 49 (1936): 359.

5. Smith, *James Wilson*, 208.

6. Ibid., 341.

7. Bryce, "James Wilson," 361.

8. Ibid.

9. Ibid.

10. Ibid., 357.

11. John F. Watson, *Annals of Philadelphia* (Philadelphia: Carey & Hart, 1830) 269.

Chapter 4. Philadelphia—Nation's Capital: 1788–1800

1. Edwin Wolf, 2nd, *Philadelphia: Portrait of an American City* (Philadelphia: Stackpole Books, 1975) 97.

2. E. Digby Baltzell, *Puritan Boston and Quaker Philadelphia* (New York: Free Press, 1979), 217.

3. Ibid., 195.

4. Linda K. Kerber, *Women of the Republic* (Chapel Hill: University of North Carolina Press, 1980), 35.

5. Smith, *James Wilson*, 318.

6. Friedman, *American Law*, 113.

7. Richard Hofstadter, *Anti-Intellectualism in American Life* (New York: Vintage Books, 1963), 151.

8. Randolf Shipley Klein, *Portrait of an Early American Family* (Philadelphia: University of Pennsylvania Press, 1975), 78.

9. Meehan, "Courts, Cases, and Counselors," 34.

10. Binney, *Leaders of Old Bar*, 52.

11. Friedman, *American Law*, 113.

12. Meehan, "Courts, Cases, and Counselors," 8.

13. Chroust, *Legal Profession*, 277.

14. See Smith, *James Wilson*.

Profile 4: William Lewis (1751–1819)

1. Binney, *Leaders of Old Bar*, 43.

2. Ibid., 31.

3. Ibid., 40.

4. Ibid., 42.

5. Penn, "Men and Things," *Philadelphia Evening Bulletin* 18, November 1903.

6. Binney, *Leaders of Old Bar*, 38.

7. Ibid., 41.

8. "Men and Things."

9. Binney, *Leaders of Old Bar*, 12–13.

Chapter 5. New Nation: 1800–1830

1. Edwin Wolf 2nd, *Philadelphia: Portrait of an American City* (Philadelphia: Stackpole Books, 1975) 127.

2. See Baltzell, *Philadelphia Gentleman*, 95.

3. E. Digby Baltzell, *Boston and Philadelphia*, 288.

4. Charles M. Haar, *The Golden Age of American Law* (New York: George Brazilles, 1965), 330.

5. Ibid., 312.

6. Perry Miller, *The Life of the Mind in America* (New York: Harcourt, Brace, 1965), 126–27.

7. Friedman, *American Law* (New York: Simon & Schuster, 1973), 153.

8. Miller, *Life of Mind*, 102.

9. Ibid., 143.

10. Meehan, "Courts, Cases and Counselors," 17–18.

11. Ibid., 18–19.

12. Glenn LeRoy Bushey, "William Duane, Crusader for Judicial Reform," *Pennsylvania History* (July 1938): 212.

13. Friedman, *American Law*, 132.

14. Binney, *Leaders of Old Bar*, 160.

15. Ibid., 163.

16. Friedman, *American Law*, 111.

17. Miller, *Life of Mind*, 171.

18. Ibid., 176.

19. Friedman, *American Law*, 180.

20. Haar, *Golden Age*, 338.

21. Martin Mayer, *The Lawyers* (New York: Harper & Bros., 1966), 312.

22. Miller, *Life of Mind*, 146.

23. Wolf, *Philadelphia*, 127.

24. Edwin Wolf and Maxwell Whiteman, *The History of Jews in Pennsylvania from Colonial Times* (Philadelphia: Jewish Publication Society, 1956), 293.

25. Ibid., 293–94.

26. Binney, *Leaders of Old Bar*, 112.

27. Gary B. Nash, "The Philadelphia Bench and Bar, 1800–1861," *Comparative Studies in Society and History* 36 (January 1965): 206.

28. Martin, *Bench and Bar* (Philadelphia: Rees Welsh, 1883) v.

29. Binney, *Leaders of Old Bar*, 112.

30. Ibid., 317.

Profile 5: Jared Ingersoll (1749–1822)

1. *Dictionary of American Biography*, vol. 4 (New York: Scribners, 1972), 469.

2. Binney, *Leaders of Old Bar*, 84.

3. Ibid., 86.

4. *Dictionary of American Biography*, 469.

5. Binney, *Leaders of Old Bar*, 88.

6. Ibid., 88.

7. Ibid., 90.

Chapter 6. Jacksonian Era: 1830–1850

1. See Klein and Hoogenboom, *History of Pennsylvania*, 20.

2. Haar, *Golden Age*, 435.

3. Miller, *Life of Mind*, 246.

4. Jonathan Lurie, *Law and the Nation, 1865–1912* (New York: Borzai, 1983), 128.

5. Ibid., 192.

6. Ibid., 193.

7. Gary B. Nash, "The Philadelphia Bench and Bar, 1800–1861" *Comparative Studies in Society and History* (January 1965): 205.

8. Ibid., 206.

9. Ibid., 219.

10. Charles Chauncy Binney, *The Life of Horace Binney* (Philadelphia: 1903), 152.

11. Miller, *Life of Mind*, 187.

12. George Wharton Pepper, *Philadelphia Lawyer: An Autobiography* (Philadelphia: Lippincott, 1944), 47–48.

13. Robert T. Swaine, "Impact of Big Business on the Profession: An Answer to the Critics of the Modern Bar," *American Bar Association Journal* (February 1949): 90–91.

14. Binney, *Life of Horace Binney*, 182.

15. Haar, *Golden Age*, 14–15.

16. Barnie Winkleman, *John G. Johnson* (Philadelphia: University of Pennsylvania Press, 1942), 27.

17. Nash, Philadelphia Bench and Bar, 205.

18. Ibid., 219.

19. Winkleman, *John G. Johnson*, 30.

20. Nickolas B. Wainright, *A Philadelphia Perspective: Diary of Fisher* (Philadelphia: Historical Society of Pennsylvania, 1967), 207.

21. Nash, "Philadelphia Bench and Bar," 220.

22. *Philadelphia Bulletin*, 11 September, 1908.

23. Haar, *Golden Age*, 11.

24. Nash, "Philadelphia Bench and Bar," 121.

25. Friedman, *American Law*, 318.

Profile 6: Sidney George Fisher (1809–1871)

All references are to Wainright's *Diary of Fisher*.

Chapter 7. Civil War Era: 1850–1870

1. Edwin Wolf 2nd, *Philadelphia: Portrait of an American City* (Philadelphia: Stackpole Books, 1975), 42.

2. Friedman, *American Law*, 342.

3. Haar, *Golden Age*, 383.

4. Wainright, *Diary of Fisher*, 259.

5. Miller, *Life of Mind*, 209.

6. Ibid., 133.

7. David Paul Brown, *The Forum of Forty Years Full Practice at the Philadelphia Bar* (Philadelphia: Robert H. Small, 1856), 16.

8. Ibid., 16.

9. Ibid., 17.

10. Barnie F. Winkleman, *John G. Johnson* (Philadelphia: University of Pennsylvania Press, 1942) 37.

11. Emanual Furth, *Wit of the Bench and Bar and a Century of Observation* (Philadelphia: Prudence Publishing, 1924), 16.

12. George W. Woodard, *Law and the Lawyer* (Philadelphia: Law Academy of Philadelphia, 1859), 30.

13. Ibid., 31.

14. Miller, *Life of Mind*, 205.

15. Maxwell Bloomfield, *American Lawyers in a Changing Society, 1776–1876* (Cambridge: Harvard University Press, 1976), 137.

16. Binney, *Life of Horace Binney.*

17. Wolf, *Philadelphia*, 186.

18. William R. Wister, "Some Recollections," *The Law Association of Philadelphia* (1902): 360.

19. Clement B. Penrose, "Reminiscences of the Bar," *The Law Association of Philadelphia* (1902): 380.

20. Wister, "Some Recollections," 362.

21. Furth, *Wit of Bench and Bar*, 18.

22. Henry S. Drinker, *Office History of Drinker Biddle & Reath* (Philadelphia: Private Printing, 1961), 2–3.

23. Barnie F. Winkleman, *John G. Johnson* (Philadelphia: University of Pennsylvania Press, 1961), 37.

24. Miller, *Life of Mind*, 216.

25. Nash, "Philadelphia Bench and Bar," 220.

26. Henry E. Busch, "George M. Wharton," *The Law Association of Philadelphia* (1902): 391.

27. Samuel Dickson, "Introductory Address," *The Law Association of Philadelphia* (1902): 10.

28. Robert D. Coxe, *Legal Philadelphia* (Philadelphia: Campbell, 1908), 32.

29. Drinker, *Office History*, 5.

30. Edward Potts Cheyney, *History of the University of Pennsylvania: 1740–1940* (Philadelphia: University of Pennsylvania Press, 1940), 234.

31. Haar, *Golden Age*, 106.

32. F. Carroll Brewster, "Rights and Duties of Lawyers," *The Law Academy of Philadelphia* (October 1861).

33. Nash, "Pennsylvania Bench and Bar," 215.

34. Ibid., 216.

35. *Legal Intelligencer*, 1855.

Profile 7: Horace Binney (1780–1875)

1. Binney, *Life of Horace Binney*, 29–30.

2. Ibid., 33.

3. Ibid., 40.

4. Ibid., 72–73.

5. Nathaniel Burt, *The Perennial Philadelphians* (Boston: Little, Brown, 1963), 126.

6. Binney, *Life of Horace Binney*, 215.

7. Ibid., 220.

8. Ibid., 227.

9. Ibid., 240.
10. Ibid., 242.
11. Miller, *Life of Mind*, 202.
12. Wainright, *Diary of Fisher*, 304.
13. Binney, *Life of Horace Binney*, 298.
14. Ibid., 300.
15. Ibid., 307.
16. Burt, *Perennial Philadelphians*, 126.

Chapter 8. Corporate Era: 1870–1890

1. Burt, *Perennial Philadelphians*, 132–33.
2. See Ray Ginger, *The Age of Excess: The U.S. from 1877 to 1914* (New York: Macmillan, 1965), 213.
3. Baltzell, *Boston and Philadelphia*, 399.
4. Friedman, *American Law*, 339.
5. Francis R. Aumann, *The Changing American Legal System: Some Selected Phases* (Columbus: Ohio State University Press, 1940), 197.
6. Friedman, *American Law*, 441.
7. Daniel J. Boorstin, *The Americans: The National Experience* (New York: Random House, 1966), 416.
8. John Marshall Gest, "Legal Education in Philadelphia 50 Years Ago," *The Law Academy of Philadelphia*, May 1929.
9. Robert D. Coxe, *Legal Philadelphia* (Philadelphia: Campbell, 1908), 123.
10. Ibid., 12–13.
11. *Boyd's Philadelphia City Business Directory* (Philadelphia: 1885).
12. Robert Stevens, *Law School: Legal Education in America from the 1850's to the 1980's* (Chapel Hill: University of North Carolina Press, 1983), 82.
13. Ibid., 83.
14. Karen Berger Morello, *The Invisible Bar: The Woman Lawyer in America: 1638 to the present* (New York: Random House, 1986).
15. Edward P. Cheyney, *History of the University of Pennsylvania, 1740–1940* (Philadelphia: University of Pennsylvania Press, 1940), 305.
16. Morello, *Invisible Bar*, 223.
17. Ibid., 76.
18. Walter J. Leonard, "The Development of the Black Bar," *Annals of the American Academy*, (May 1973): 136.
19. Geraldine R. Segal, *Blacks in the Law* (Philadelphia: University of Pennsylvania Press, 1983), 27.
20. Whitney North Seymour, "The Bar as Lawmaker" in *The Life of the Law*, ed. John Honnold (New York: Free Press, 1964), 410.
21. Gest, "Legal Education," 2.
22. *Law Association of Philadelphia, 1802–1902* (Philadelphia: Association of Philadelphia, 1906).
23. Gest, "Legal Education," 3.
24. Martin, *Bench and Bar*, 220.
25. Coxe, *Legal Philadelphia*, 27.
26. Friedman, *American Law*, 326.
27. Robert T. Swaine, "Impact of Big Business on the Profession: An Answer to

the Critics of the Modern Bar,'' *American Bar Association Journal* Vol. 23 (February 1949): 91.

28. Barnie F. Winkleman, *John G. Johnson* (Philadelphia: University of Pennsylvania Press, 1942), 111.

29. Ibid., 112.

30. Beryl H. Levy, *Corporation Lawyer: Saint or Sinner?* (Philadelphia: Chilton Company, 1961), 57.

31. Jerald S. Auerbach, ''Access to the Legal System in Historical Perspective,'' in *Lawyers Ethics: Contemporary Dilemmas* Allen Gerson, (New Brunswick: Transaction Books, 1980), 35.

32. Ferdinand Lundberg, ''The Legal Profession,'' *Harper's Magazine* December 1938, 10.

33. Levy, *Corporation Lawyer*, 45.

34. William J. Campbell, *The Bench and Bar of Philadelphia* (Philadelphia: Penate Printing, 1893), 47.

35. Ibid., 49.

36. Levy, *Corporation Lawyer*, 47.

37. Edward M. Paxson, ''The Road to Success: Practical Hints to the Junior Bar,'' *The Bar Association of Philadelphia*, (April 1888): 13.

38. J. Hay Brown, ''Some of the Conditions of a Lawyer's Success,'' *Law Academy of Philadelphia* (May 1901): 6.

39. Ibid.

40. William H. Ashman, ''The Profession of the Law,'' *The Law Association of Philadelphia* (March 1889).

41. Brown, ''Conditions of Lawyer's Success.''

42. Martin, *Bench and Bar*, 56.

43. Winkleman, *Johnson*, 115.

44. Coxe, *Legal Philadelphia*, 74.

45. Ibid., 75.

Profile 8: John Graver Johnson (1841–1917)

1. Winkleman, *Johnson*, 192.

2. Ibid., 71.

3. Ibid., 192.

4. Ibid., 193.

5. Ibid., 99.

6. Francis Biddle, *A Casual Past* (New York: Doubleday, 1961), 307.

7. Winkleman, *Johnson*, 214.

8. Ibid., 218.

9. Ibid., 219.

10. Ibid., 219.

11. Ibid., 220.

12. Ibid., 306–7.

13. Ibid., 225.

14. ''John G. Johnson,'' *The North American* (19 April, 1917).

15. Biddle, *Casual Past*, 309.

16. Winkleman, *Johnson*, 283.

17. *Public Ledger*, 21 June, 1917.

18. "Johnson As a Lawyer," *Literary Digest*, 5 May, 1917, 23.

19. George Wharton Pepper, *Philadelphia Lawyer: An Autobiography* (Philadelphia: Lippincott, 1944), 60.

Chapter 9. Progressive Era: 1890–1910

1. R. Sturgis Ingersoll, *Recollections of a Philadelphian at Eighty* (Philadelphia: Private Printing, 1971), 37.

2. Lincoln Steffens, *The Autobiography of Lincoln Steffens* (New York: Harcourt, 1931), 410.

3. Samual W. Pennypacker, *The Autobiography of a Pennsylvanian* (Philadelphia: John C. Winston, 1918), 301.

4. Edwin Wolf 2nd, *Philadelphia: Portrait of an American City* (Philadelphia: Stackpole Books, 1975), 244.

5. Robert T. Swaine, "Impact of Big Business on the Profession: An Answer to the Critics of the Modern Bar," *American Bar Association Journal*, (23 February 1949): 167.

6. Bernard Schwartz, *The Law in America* (New York: McGraw-Hill, 1974), 157.

7. Friedman, *American Law*, 471.

8. Schwartz, *Law in America*, 152.

9. Ibid., 159.

10. Ibid., 181.

11. Richard Hofstadter, *Anti-Intellectualism in American Life* (New York: Vintage Books, 1963), 171–72.

12. Ray Ginger, *Age of Excess: The U.S. from 1877 to 1914* (New York: Macmillan, 1965), 171–72.

13. David Starr Jordan, "Pettifogging Law Schools and the Untrained Bar," *The Forum*, April 1895, 351.

14. Ibid., 352.

15. Schwartz, *Law in America*, 229.

16. William W. Porter, "The Present Status of the Legal Profession," *Law Academy of Philadelphia* (September 1907).

17. Robert D. Coxe, *Legal Philadelphia* (Philadelphia: Campbell, 1908), 39.

18. Ibid., 40.

19. Robert V. Massey, Jr., *Dechert Price & Rhoads* (Lancaster: Private Printing, 1975).

20. John R. Dos Passos, *The American Lawyer* (New York: Banks Law Publishing, 1907), 79.

21. Swaine, "Big Business," 168.

22. Porter, "Legal Profession," 4.

23. Coxe, *Legal Philadelphia*, 41.

24. *The Philadelphia Bulletin*, 1903.

25. Friedman, *American Law*, 638.

26. Hofstadter, *Anti-Intellectualism*, 159.

27. *The Philadelphia Bulletin*, 1903.

28. Coxe, *Legal Philadelphia*, 182.

29. *The Philadelphia Bulletin*, 1912.

30. *The Philadelphia Bulletin*, 1903.

31. Morello, *Invisible Bar*, 198.

32. Martin Mayer, *The Lawyers* (New York: Harper & Row, 1966), 131.

Profile 9: Samuel Whitaker Pennypacker (1843–1916)

1. "Samuel Whitaker Pennypacker," *Dictionary of American Biography*, vol. 5 (New York: Scribner's, 1964), 447.
2. Ibid., 447.
3. Ibid., 448.
4. Samuel W. Pennypacker, *The Autobiography of a Pennsylvanian* (Philadelphia: John C. Winston, 1918).
5. Ibid., 107.
6. Ibid., 108.
7. Ibid., 111.
8. Ibid., 112.
9. Ibid., 113.
10. Ibid., 114.
11. Ibid., 117.
12. Ibid., 128–29.
13. Ibid., 131.
14. Ibid., 16.

Chapter 10. World War I Decade: 1910–1920

1. Fredric M. Miller, Morris J. Vogel, and Allen F. Davis, *Still Philadelphia* (Philadelphia: Temple University Press, 1983), 73.
2. Burt, *Perennial Philadelphians*, 69.
3. Schwartz, *Law in America*, 193.
4. Alfred Z. Reed, "Legal Education," *Carnegie Foundation for Advancement of Teaching Bulletin* 15 (Spring, 1921): 91.
5. Jonathan Lurie, *Law and the Nation, 1865–1912* (New York: Bonzai Books, 1983), 54.
6. Ibid., 231.
7. Biddle, *Casual Past*, 32.
8. Ibid., 37.
9. Pepper, *Philadelphia Lawyer*, 347.
10. Ibid., 186.
11. Harlan F. Stone, "The Lawyer and His Neighbor," *Cornell Law Quarterly* 4 (1918): 189.
12. Ibid., 186.
13. Swaine, "Big Business," 92.
14. Horace Mather Lippincott, *Early Philadelphia* (Philadelphia: J. B. Lippincott, 1917), 176.
15. *Hubbell's Legal Directory for Lawyers and Businessmen* (New York: Hubbell Publishing Co., 1911).
16. *The Philadelphia Inquirer*, 27 April, 1916.
17. Albert P. Blaustein and Charles O. Porter, *The American Lawyer* (Chicago: The University of Chicago Press, 1954), 31.
18. Coxe, *Legal Philadelphia*, 94.
19. Ibid., 98.
20. Morello, *Invisible Bar*, 179.
21. Ibid., 200.

22. Geraldine R. Segal, *Blacks in the Law* (Philadelphia: University of Pennsylvania Press, 1983), 17.

23. Ibid., 29.

Profile 10: Boies Penrose (1860–1921)

1. Baltzell, *Boston and Philadelphia*, 410.

2. Klein and Hoogenboom, *History of Pennsylvania*, 360.

3. Ibid., 413.

4. Ibid., 414.

5. John Lukacs, *Philadelphia: Patrician & Philistine, 1900–1950.* (Philadelphia: ISHI Publications, 1980), 50.

6. Baltzell, *Boston and Philadelphia*, 405.

7. Ibid., 410.

8. Burt, *Perennial Philadelphians*, 548.

9. Pennypacker, *Autobiography*, 355.

10. Klein and Hoogenbloom, *History of Pennsylvania*, 417.

11. Nochem S. Winnet, *Vignettes of a Lucky Life* (Philadelphia: Private Printing, 1989), 23.

Chapter 11. 1920s

1. Arthur S. Lewis, *The Worlds of Chippy Patterson* (New York: Harcourt, Brace, 1960), 240.

2. Ibid., 297.

3. Daniel Boorstin, *The Americans: The National Experience* (New York: Random House, 1966), 271.

4. Murray Friedman, *Jewish Life in Philadelphia, 1830–1940* (Philadelphia: ISHI Publishing, 1983), 17–18.

5. Walter J. Leonard, "The Development of the Black Bar," *Annals of the American Academy*, 34 (May 1973): 139.

6. Harold J. Laski, *The American Democracy* (New York: Viking, 1948), 584.

7. Winnet, *Vignettes*, 25.

8. Alfred Reed, "Legal Education," *Carnegie Foundation for Advancement of Teaching Bulletin* 15 (1921): 87–88.

9. Winkleman, *Johnson*, 102.

10. Pepper, *Philadelphia Lawyer*, 342–43.

11. Martin Mayer, *The Lawyers* (New York: Harper & Row, 1966), 308.

12. "American Law Institute," *The American Law Institute: 50th Anniversary* (Philadelphia: American Law Institute, 1973), 13.

13. Ibid., 15.

14. Morello, *Invisible Bar*, 201.

15. Drinker, *Office History*, 41.

16. Morris Duane, *Duane Morris & Heckscher* (Philadelphia: Private Printing, 1979), 23.

17. J. Tyson Stokes, *Morgan Lewis & Bockius* (Philadelphia: Private Printing, 1973), 20.

Profile 11: George Wharton Pepper (1867–1961)

 1. Pepper, *Philadelphia Lawyer*, 50.
 2. Ibid., 77.
 3. Ibid., 81–82.
 4. Ibid., 93.
 5. Ibid., 384.
 6. Burt, *Perennial Philadelphians*, 140.
 7. Biddle, *Casual Past*, 358.
 8. Burt, *Perennial Philadelphians*, 140.
 9. Biddle, *Casual Past*, 138.
10. Burt, *Perennial Philadelphians*, 140.

Chapter 12. Great Depression: 1930s

 1. Hofstadter, *Anti-Intellectualism*, 325.
 2. Baltzell, *Boston and Philadelphia*, 254.
 3. Edwin Wolf 2nd, *Philadelphia: Portrait of an American City* (Philadelphia: Stackpole Books, 1975), 299.
 4. Friedman, *Jewish Life*, 282.
 5. Jerald S. Auerbach, "Access to the Legal System in Historical Perspective," in *Lawyers Ethics: Contemporary Dilemmas*, ed. Allan Gerson (New Brunswick: Transaction Books, 1980), 32.
 6. Schwartz, *Law in America*, 249.
 7. Ibid., 246.
 8. Albert B. Blaustein and Charles O. Porter, *The American Lawyer* (Chicago: University of Chicago Press), 112–13.
 9. Ibid., 201.
10. Ibid., 256.
11. Ibid., 584–85.
12. Jerome E. Carlin, *Lawyers on Their Own* (New Jersey: Rutgers University Press, 1962), 23.
13. Massey, *Dechert Price & Rhoads*, 53.
14. Ibid., 260.
15. Levy, *Corporation Lawyers*, 26.
16. Mayer, *Lawyers*, 327.
17. Swaine, "Big Business," 169.
18. Ibid., 171.
19. F. Raymond Marks, *The Lawyer, The Public and Professional Responsibility* (Chicago: American Bar Foundation, 1972), 38.
20. Emery A Brownell, *Legal Aid in the United States* (Rochester, N.Y.: Lawyers Cooperative Publishing, 1951), 102.
21. Robert D. Abrahams, "The New Philadelphia Lawyer," *Atlantic Monthly* April 1950, 71.
22. Brownell, *Legal Aid*, 135.
23. Morello, *Invisible Bar*, 203.
24. Ronald Chester, *Unequal Access: Women Lawyers in a Changing America* (Boston: Bergin & Garvey, 1985), 127.
25. Morello, *Invisible Bar*, 184.
26. Baltzell, *Boston and Philadelphia*, 350.

Profile 12: Francis Biddle (1886–1968)

1. Biddle, *Casual Past* (New York: Doubleday, 1961), 76.
2. Ibid., 76.
3. Ibid., 249.
4. Ibid., 254.
5. Ibid., 267,
6. Ibid., 293.
7. Ibid., 299.
8. Ibid., 310.
9. Ibid., 355.
10. Ibid., 345.
11. Ibid., 249.
12. Massey, *Dechert Price & Rhoads*, 59.
13. Biddle, *Casual Past*, 327.
14. Ibid., 386.

Epilogue: Early 1990s

1. All references are to *Social Register*, 1987.
2. *New York Times*, 20 November, 1987.
3. *Martindale-Hubbell Law Directory: 1988*, vol. 6 (New Jersey: Martindale-Hubbell 1988).
4. Elliott M. Epstein, Jerome Shostak, and Laurence M. Troy, *Barron's Guide to Law Schools, 8th ed.* (New York: Barron's Educational Series, 1988), 35, 40–42.
5. *Wall Street Journal*, 19 October, 1988.
6. *New York Times*, 1 January, 1988.
7. Epstein, Shostak, and Troy, *Barron's Guide*, 243, 286.
8. *Philadelphia Inquirer*, 4 August, 1987.
9. Marshall L. Williams, *National Directory of Black Law Firms* (Philadelphia: M. L. Williams Printing, 1988).
10. *Philadelphia Inquirer*, 12 January, 1984.
11. "Elected and Appointed Judges in the U.S., 1986," in *The Joint Center for Political Studies and the Judicial Council of the National Bar Association* (Washington, D.C.: 1986).
12. *The Pennsylvania Legal Directory: 1984–1985* (Dallas: Legal Directories Publishing, 1985), 62.
13. *Philadelphia Inquirer*, 18 January, 1986.
14. Mike Mallowe, "Still Crooked after All These Years," *Philadelphia Magazine*, December 1987, 230.
15. *Philadelphia Inquirer*, 10 March, 1990.
16. *Philadelphia Inquirer*, 10 March, 1990.
17. Susan Raridon, "The Practice of Law: The Next Fifty Years," *The Shingle*, Fall 1988, 28.
18. Epstein, Shostack, and Troy, *Barron's Guide*, 38.
19. Raridon, "Practice of Law," 28.
20. Epstein, Shostak, and Troy, *Barron's Guide*, 38.
21. Leonard Dubin, "Sidebar," *The Pennsylvania Lawyer*, 18 January 1989, 2.

Select Bibliography

Books

Adams, Grace and Edward Hutter. *The Mad Forties*. New York: Harper and Brothers, 1942.

American Law Institute. *The American Law Institutes 50th Anniversary*. Philadelphia: American Law Institute, 1973.

Andrist, Ralph K. *American Century*. New York: American Heritage Press, 1972.

Association of American Law Schools. *Selected Readings in the Legal Profession*. St. Paul, Minn.: West Publishing, 1962.

Balch, Thomas W. *The Philadelphia Assemblies*. Philadelphia: Allen, Lane and Scott, 1916.

Baltzell, E. Digby. *Philadelphia Gentlemen*. New York: Free Press, 1958.

_____. *The Protestant Establishment*. New York: Random House, 1964.

_____. *Puritan Boston and Quaker Philadelphia*. New York: Free Press, 1979.

Bench and Bar of Pennsylvania, 1940-1941. San Francisco: C. W. Taylor, Jr., 1941.

Berthoff, Rowland Tappan. *British Immigrants In Industrial America, 1790-1950*. Cambridge: Harvard University Press, 1953.

Biddle, Gertrude B., and Sarah D. Lawrie. *Notable Women of Pennsylvania*. Philadelphia: University of Pennsylvania Press, 1942.

Biddle, Cordella Drexel. *My Philadelphia Father*. New York: Doubleday, 1955.

Biddle, Francis. *A Casual Past*. New York: Doubleday, 1961.

Bigelow, L. J. *Bench and Bar*. New York: Harper and Brothers, 1871.

Bigelow, Marybelle. *Fashion in History*. Minneapolis: Burgess, 1979.

Bingham, Katherine. *The Philadelphians*, Boston: L. C. Page And Co., 1902.

Binney, Horace. *The Leaders of the Old Bar of Philadelphia*. Philadelphia: Henry B. Ashmead 1866.

Binney, Charles Chauncey. *The Life of Horace Binney*. Philadelphia: J. B. Lippincott 1903.

Blaustein, Albert P., and Charles O. Porter. *The American Lawyer*. Chicago: University of Chicago Press, 1954.

Bloomfield, Maxwell. *American Lawyers in a Changing Society, 1776-1876*. Cambridge: Harvard University Press, 1976.

Bowen, Catherine Drinker. *Family Portrait*. Boston: Little, Brown And Co., 1970.

Boorstin, Daniel J. *The Americans: The Colonial Experience*. New York: Random House, 1958.

_____. *The Americans: The National Experience*. New York: Random House, 1966.

_____. *The Americans: The Democratic Experience*. New York: Random House, 1973.

Breakfast to the Justices of the Supreme Court of the United States. Philadelphia: Lippincott, 1888.

Bridenbaugh, Carl. *Cities In Revolt*. New York: Alfred & Knopf, 1955.

Bridenbaugh, Carl, and Jessica Bridenbaugh. *Rebels and Gentlemen: Philadelphia in the Age of Franklin*. New York: Oxford University Press, 1962.

Bronner, Edwin B. *William Penn "Holy Experiment."* Philadelphia: Temple University Press, 1962.

Brown, David Paul. *The Forum on Forty Years Full Practice at the Philadelphia Bar*. Philadelphia: Robert H. Small, 1856.

Brown, Dee. *The Year of the Century: 1876*. New York: Scribners, 1966.

Brown, Esther L. *Lawyers and the Promotion of Justice*. New York: Russell Sage, 1938.

Brownell, Emery. *Legal Aid in the United States*. New York: Lawyer's Co-operative Publishing, 1951.

Burt, Nathaniel. *The Perennial Philadelphians*. Boston: Little, Brown, 1963.

Burt, Nathaniel. *First Families: The Making Of An American Aristocracy*. Boston: Little, Brown And Co., 1970.

Calhoon, Robert M. *The Loyalists in Revolutionary America (1760–1781)*. New York: Harcourt, Brace, 1965.

Campbell, William J. *The Bench and Bar of Philadelphia*. Philadelphia: Private Printing, 1893.

Carlin, Jerome E. *Lawyers on Their Own*. New Jersey: Rutgers University Press, 1962.

Cashman, Sean Dennis. *American In The Gilded Age Second Edition*. New York: New York University Press, 1988.

Chester, Ronald. *Unequal Access: Women Lawyers in a Changing America*. Boston: Bergin & Garvey, 1985.

Chestnut Hill: An Architectural History. Philadelphia: Chestnut Hill Historical Society, 1969.

Cheyney, Edward P. *History of the University of Pennsylvania, 1740–1940*. Philadelphia: University of Pennsylvania Press, 1940.

Chroust, Anton-Hermann. *The Rise of the Legal Profession in America*. Vols. 1 and 2. Norman: University of Oklahoma Press, 1965.

Claitor, Diana. *100 Years Ago: The Glorious 1890s*. New York: Moore and Moore Publishing, 1990.

Cochran, Thomas C. *Pennsylvania: A Bicentennial History*. New York: Norton, 1978.

Collins, Herman LeRoy. *Philadelphia: A Story of Progress*. New York: Historical Publishing, 1941.

Comegys, Cornelius. *A Summer Sojourn among the Inns of Court*. New Jersey: Soney & Sage, 1933.

Countryman, Vern, and Ted Fineman. *The Lawyer in Modern Society*. Boston: Little, Brown, 1966.

Coxe, Robert D. *Legal Philadelphia*. Philadelphia: Campbell, 1908.

Coxe, Tench. *A View Of The United States Of America Between 1787 and 1794*. New York: Reprints of Economics Classics, 1965.

Curran, Barbara A. *The Lawyer Statistical Report: A Statistical Profile of the U.S. Legal Profession in the 1980s*. Chicago: American Bar Foundation, 1985.

Curti, Merle. *The Growth of American Thought*. 2d ed. New York: Harper, 1951.

Daniell, Timothy. *Inns of Court*. London: Wiley & Sons, 1971.

De Concourt, Edmond and Jules. *The Woman Of The Eighteenth Century*. New York: Minton, Balch And Co., 1927.

Dictionary of American Bibliography. New York: Charles Scribner's Sons, 1964.

Directory of the Legal Profession. New York: National Law Journal Publishing, 1984.

Dos Passos, John R. *The American Lawyer*. New York: Banks Law Publishing, 1907.

Drinker, Henry S. *Office History of Drinker Biddle & Reath*. Philadelphia: Private Printing, 1961.

Dusinberre, William. *Civil War Issues in Philadelphia, 1856–1865*. Philadelphia: University of Pennsylvania Press, 1965.

Epstein, Cynthia. *Women in Law*. New York: Doubleday, 1983.

Epstein, Elliott M., Jerome Shostak, and Laurence M. Tray. *Barron's Guide to Law Schools. 8th ed*. New York: Barron's Educational Series, 1988.

Ervin, Spencer. *The Magistrate Courts of Philadelphia*. Philadelphia: Thomas Shelton Harrison Foundation, 1931.

Evans, Frank. *Pennsylvania Politics, 1872–1877*. Harrisburg: Pennsylvania Historical Commission, 1966.

Farrow, Tiera. *Lawyer in Petticoats*. New York: Vantage Press, 1953.

Friedman, Lawrence M. *A History of American Law*. New York: Simon & Schuster, 1973.

Friedman, Murray. *Jewish Life in Philadelphia: 1830–1940*. Philadelphia, ISHI Publishing, 1983.

Furth, Emanuel. *Wit of Bench and Bar and a Century of Observation*. Philadelphia: Prudence Publishing, 1924.

Garvan, Beatrice. *Federal Philadelphia 1785–1825*. Philadelphia: Philadelphia Museum of Art, 1982.

Gerson, Allan. *Lawyer's Ethics: Contemporary Dilemmas*. New Brunswick, N.J.: Transaction Books, 1980.

Gibson, Jane Mork. *The Fairmount Waterworks*. Philadelphia: Philadelphia Museum of Art, 1988.

Gilbert, Michael. *The Oxford Book of Legal Antidotes*. New York: Oxford University Press, 1986.

Ginger, Ray. *Age of Excess: The U.S. from 1877 to 1914*. New York: Macmillan, 1965.

Goulden, Joseph C. *The Super Lawyers*. New York: Weyhight & Talley, 1972.

Haar, Charles M. *The Golden Age of American Law*. New York: George Brazilles, 1965.

Handler, Joel F. *The Lawyer and His Community: The Practicing Bar in a Middle-sized City*. Madison: University of Wisconsin Press, 1967.

Headlam, Cecil. *The Inns of Court*. London: Adam & Charles Black, 1909.

Herbert, A. P. *Uncommon Law*. London: Bibliophile Books, 1935.

Hershberg, Theodore. *Philadelphia: Work, Space, Family and Group Experience in the 19th Century*. New York: Oxford University Press, 1981.

Hofstadter, Richard. *America at 1750*. New York: Knopf, 1971.

_____. *Anti-Intellectualism in American Life*. New York: Vintage Books, 1963.

Honnold, John. *The Life of the Law*. New York: Free Press, 1964.

Hubbell's Legal Directory for Lawyers and Businessmen. New York: Hubbell Publishing, 1911.

Hurst, James W. *The Growth of American Law*. Boston: Little, Brown, 1950.

Independence Square Neighborhood. Philadelphia: Pennsylvania Mutual Life Insurance, 1926.

Ingersoll, R. Sturgis. *Recollections of a Philadelphian at Eighty*. Philadelphia: Private Printing, 1971.

Jackson, John W. *With the British Army in Philadelphia, 1777–1778*. California: Presidio Press, 1979.

James, Marquis. *The Life of Andrew Jackson*. Indianapolis: Bobbs-Merrill, 1938.

Jeaffreson, John Cordy. *A Book about Lawyers*. New York: Private Printing, 1867.

Johnstone, Quintin, and Dan Hopson, Jr. *Lawyers and Their Work*. Indianapolis: Bobbs-Merrill, 1967.

Jones, E. Alfred. *American Members of the Inns of Court*. London: The Saint Catherine Press, 1924.

Jones, Howard Mumford. *The Age of Energy*. New York: Viking, 1970.

Josephson, Matthew. *The Robber Barons*. New York: Harcourt, Brace, 1934.

Joyce, J. St. George. *Story of Philadelphia*. Philadelphia: Harry B. Joseph, 1919.

Kammen, Michael. *Colonial New York*. New York: Charles Scribner's Sons, 1975.

Kelley, Joseph J. *Life and Times of Colonial Philadelphia*. Harrisburg: Stackpole, 1974.

Kerber, Linda K. *Women of the Republic*. Chapel Hill: The University of North Carolina Press, 1980.

Klein, Philip S., and Ari Hoogenboom. *A History of Pennsylvania*. College Park: Penn State University Press, 1980.

Klein, Randolf Shipley. *Portrait of an Early American Family*. Philadelphia: University of Pennsylvania Press, 1975.

Konkle, Burton Alva. *The Life of Andrew Hamilton, 1676–1741*. Philadelphia: National Publishing, 1941.

Larkin, Jack. *The Reshaping Of Every Day Life: 1790–1840*. New York: Harper And Row, 1988.

Laski, Harold J. *The American Democracy*. New York: Viking, 1948.

Leonard, John William. *Who's Who in Jurisprudence (1925)*. New York: John W. Leonard, 1925.

Lerner, Max. *America As a Civilization*. New York: Simon & Schuster, 1958.

Levy, Beryl H. *Corporation Lawyer: Saint or Sinner?* Philadelphia: Chilton, 1961.

Lewis, Arthur M. *The Worlds of Chippy Patterson*. New York: Harcourt, Brace, 1960.

Lewis, John Frederick. *A History Of An Old Philadelphia Land Title*. Philadelphia: Patterson and White Co., 1934.

Lief, Aflred. *Family Business: A Century In The Life And Times Of Strawbridge And Clothier*. New York: McGraw-Hill, 1968.

Lippincott, Horace Mather. *Early Philadelphia*. Philadelphia: Lippincott, 1917.

_____. *A Narrative of Chestnut Hill*. Philadelphia: Old York Press, 1948.

_____. *A Story of the Philadelphia Cricket Club, 1854–1954*. Philadelphia: Private Printing, 1954.

Looney, Robert F. *Old Philadelphia: In Early Photographs 1839–1914*. New York: Dover Publishing Co., 1976.

Loyd, William H. *The Early Courts Of Pennsylvania*. Boston: Boston Book Company, 1910.

Lukacs, John. *Philadelphia: Patricians & Philistines, 1900–1950*. Philadelphia: ISHI Publications, 1981.

Lurie, Jonathan. *Law and the Nation: 1865–1912*. New York: Borzai Books, 1983.

Lyman, Susan Elizabeth. *The Story of New York*. New York: Crown Publishing, 1964.

MacElree, Wilmer W. *Side Lights On The Bench And Bar Of Chester County*. Westchester, Pa.: Private Printing, 1918.

MacLean, William. *The Law Academy and Early Legal Education in Philadelphia*. Philadelphia: City History, 1935.

Marks, F. Raymond. *The Lawyer, The Public, and Professional Responsibility*. Chicago: American Bar Foundation, 1972.

Martin, John Hill. *Bench and Bar Of Philadelphia*. Philadelphia: Welsh & Co., 1883.

Martindale-Hubbell Law Directory. Summit, N.J.: Martindale-Hubbell, published yearly.

Massey Jr., Robert V. *Dechert Price & Rhoads*. Lancaster: Private Printing, 1975.

May, Henry F. *The Enlightenment in America*. New York: Oxford University Press, 1976.

Mayer, Martin. *The Lawyers*. New York: Harper & Row, 1966.

McNamara, M. Francis. *2,000 Famous Legal Quotations*. New York: Aqueduck Books, 1967.

Megarry, Robert. *Inns Ancient and Modern*. London: Seldon Society, 1972.

Meigs, William M. *The Life of Charles Jared Ingersoll*. Philadelphia: Lippncott, 1897.

Miller, Fredric M., J. Morriss Vogel, and Allen F. Davis. *Still Philadelphia*. Philadelphia: Temple University Press, 1983.

Miller, Perry. *The Life of the Mind in America*. New York: Harcourt, Brace, 1965.

Morello, Karen Berger. *The Invisible Bar: The Woman Lawyer in America, 1638 to the Present*. New York: Random House, 1986.

Morley, Christopher. *Travels In Philadelphia*. Philadelphia: J. B. Lippincott, 1920.

Nye, Russel Blaine. *Society and Culture in America, 1830–1860*. New York: Harper & Row, 1974.

Oberholtzer, Ellis Paxson. *The Literary History of Philadelphia*. Philadelphia: Jacobs, 1906.

———. *Philadelphia: A History of the City and Its People*. Philadelphia: S. J. Clarke, ca., 1900.

Parrington, Vernon L. *Main Currents in American Thought, 1620–1800*. New York: Harcourt, Brace, 1930.

Patterson, L. Roy, and Elliott E. Cheatham. *The Profession of Law*. Mineola, N.Y.: Foundation Press, 1971.

Pennypacker, Samuel W. *The Autobiography of a Pennsylvanian*. Philadelphia: John C. Winston, 1918.

Pepper, George Wharton. *Philadelphia Lawyer: An Autobiography*. Philadelphia: Lippincott, 1944.

Philadelphia Bar: A Complete Catalogue of Members from 1776 to 1868. Philadelphia: Review Printing House, 1868.

Philadelphia Bar Association. *150th Anniversary, 1802–1952*. Philadelphia: George H. Buchanan Company, 1952.

Philadelphia Club, 1834–1934. Philadelphia: Private Printing, 1934.

Phillips, Orie L., and Philbrick McCoy. *Conduct of Judges and Lawyers*. Los Angeles: Packer and Co., 1952.

Rice, Kym S. *Early American Taverns*. Chicago: Regency Galeway, 1983.

Scheer, George F., and Hugh F. Rawkin. *Rebels and Redcoats*. New York: World, 1957.

Schlesinger, Arthur M. *The Birth of the Nation*. Boston: Houghton Mifflin, 1968.

Schwartz, Bernard. *The Law in America*. New York: McGraw-Hill, 1974.

Segal, Geraldine R. *Blacks in the Law*. Philadelphia: University of Pennsylvania Press, 1983.

Sewell, Darrel. *Thomas Eakins*. Philadelphia: Philadelphia Museum Of Art, 1982.

Shackleton, Robert. *The Book of Philadelphia*. Philadelphia: Penn Publishing, 1918.

Smith, Charles Page. *James Wilson: Founding Father*. Chapel Hill: University of North Carolina Press, 1956.

Social Register. New York: Social Register Association, published yearly.

Solmssen, Arthur R. G. *Alexander's Feast*. Boston: Little, Brown, 1971.

_____. *Rittenhouse Square*. Boston: Little, Brown, 1968.

Solomon, Barbara Miller. *In the Company of Educated Women*. New Haven: Yale University Press, 1985.

Stevens, Robert. *Law School: Legal Education in America from the 1850's to the 1980's*. Chapel Hill: University of North Carolina Press, 1983.

Stimson, Shannon C. *The American Revolution In The Law*. Princeton, N.J.: Princeton University Press, 1990.

Stokes, J. Tyson. *Morgan Lewis & Bockius: Memoirs of a Law Firm*. Philadelphia: Private Printing, 1973.

Sutherland, Arthur E. *The Law at Harvard*. Cambridge: Harvard University Press, 1967.

Sweet, David G., & Gary B. Nash. *Struggle and Survival in Colonial America*. Berkeley: University of California Press, 1981.

Taft, Henry W. *A Century And a Half At The New York Bar*. New York: Privately Printed, 1938.

Tayler, Frederick. *Law Courts, Lawyers, and Litigants*. London: Matthew & Co., 1926.

Taylor, Frank H. *Philadelphia in the Civil War*. Philadelphia: Published by the City, 1913.

Taver, Isabella. *Successful Women*. New York: Dutton, 1945.

Tolles, Frederick B. *Meeting House and Counting House*. New York: Norton, 1948.

Trades League of Philadelphia. *The City of Philadelphia, 1894*. Philadelphia: Geo. S. Harris & Sons, 1894.

Tryon, Warren S. *A Mirror For Americans*. Chicago: University of Chicago Press, 1952.

Van Tyne, Claude H. *The Loyalists in the American Revolution*. Gloucaster, Mass.: Peter Smith, 1959.

Wainright, Nicholas B. *A Philadelphia Perspective: Diary of Sidney George Fisher*. Philadelphia: Historical Society of Philadelphia, 1967.

Walker, R. J., and M. G. Walker. *The English Legal System*. London: Butterworth, 1972.

Watson, John F. *Annals of Philadelphia*. Philadelphia: Carey & Hart, 1830.

Wecter, Dixon. *The Sage of American Society*, New York: Scribner's, 1937.

Weigley, Russel P. *Philadelphia: A 300 Year History*. New York: Norton, 1982.

Welter, Rush. *The Mind of America: 1820–1860*. New York: Columbia University Press, 1975.

White, G. Edward. *Tort Law In America*. New York: Oxford University Press, 1980.

Williams, Marshall. *National Directory of Black Law Firms*. Philadelphia: M. L. Williams Publishing, 1988.

Winkleman, Barnie F. *John G. Johnson*. Philadelphia: University of Pennsylvania Press, 1942.

Winnet, Nochem S. *Vignettes of a Lucky Life*. Philadelphia: Private Printing, 1989.

Wit and Humor of the American Bar. Philadelphia: George W. Jacobs, 1905.

Wolf, Edwin, and Maxwell Whiteman. *The History of Jews in Pennsylvania from Colonial Times*. Philadelphia: Jewish Publication Society, 1956.

Wolf, Edwin. *Philadelphia: Portrait Of An American City* Philadelphia: Stackpole Books, 1975.

Wolf, Stephanie Grauman. *Urban Village*. Princeton N. J.: Princeton University Press, 1976.

Wurman, Richard Saul And John Andrew Gallery. *Man-Made Philadelphia*. Baltimore: MIT Press, 1972.

Young, Philip. *Revolutionary Ladies*. New York: Knopf, 1977.

Zinn, Howard. *A Peoples History Of The U.S.* New York Harpers, 1980.

Articles

Abrahams, Robert D. "The New Philadelphia Lawyer." *Atlantic Monthly* 51 (April 1950): 69–72.

Alderman, Ernest H. "The North Carolina Colonial Bar." *The James Sprout Historical Publication* no. 3 (1913) 5–31.

Allen, James. "Diary of James Allen Esq. of Philadelphia, Chancelor-at-law 1740-1778." *The Pennsylvania Magazine of History and Biography* no. 9 (1885): 176–96.

Andrews, J. Cutler. "The Gilded Age In Pennsylvania." *Pennsylvania History* 67 (January 1967): 1–24.

Arnold, Christine C. "Women in the Law: What It Takes to Get There." *The Pennsylvania Lawyer* 12 (15 January, 1986): 12–17.

Auerbach, Jerold S. "Access to the Legal System in Historical Perspective." In *Lawyer's Ethics: Contemporary Dilemmas*, edited by Allan Gerson, 29–37. New Brunswick, N.J.: Transaction Books, 1980.

Austin, Edwin C. "Some Comments on Large Law Firms." *Law Practice Forum* no. 13 (April 1959): 8–16.

Bedwell, C. E. A. "American Middle Templars." *American Historical Review* 28 (1920): 680–89.

Berkson, Larry. "Women on the Bench: A Brief History." *Judicature* 12 (December-January 1982): 186–93.

Berle, A. A. "The Modern Legal Profession." In *The Life of the Law*, edited by John Honnold, 398–403. New York: Free Press, 1964.

Beveridge, Albert J. "Philander Chase Knox, American Lawyer, Patriot and

Statesman." *Pennsylvania Magazine of History and Biography* no. 47 (1923): 89–114.

Bradbury, M. L. "Legal Privilege and the Bank of North America." *Pennsylvania Magazine of History and Biography* no. 96 (1972): 139–66.

Brown, Margaret L. "Mr. and Mrs. William Bingham of Philadelphia." *Pennsylvania Magazine of History and Biography* no. 13 (1889): 286–324.

Bryce, James. "James Wilson: An Appreciation." *Pennsylvania Magazine of History and Bibliography* no. 60 (1936): 358–61.

Bushey, Glenn Leroy. "William Duane, Crusader for Judicial Reform." *Pennsylvania History* 28 (July 1938): 141–56.

Carbon, Susan. "Women in the Judiciary: An Introduction." *Judicature* 12 (December-January 1982): 285.

Carbon, Susan, Pauline Houlden, and Larry Berkson. "Women on the State Bench." *Judicature* 12 (December-January 1982): 295–305.

Carson, Joseph. "Portrait of a Courtroom." *The Shingle* 11 (June 1941): 132–34.

Carter, Katherine D. "Isaac Norrisses Attack on Andrew Hamilton." *Pennsylvania Magazine of History and Biography* no. 104 (1980): 139–61.

Chroust, Anton-Hermann. "The Beginning, Flourishing and Decline of the Inns of Court: The Consolidation of the English Legal Profession After 1400." *Vanderbilt Law Review* no. 10 (1956): 79–123.

Cirucci, Daniel A., and Nancy L. Hebble. "Breaking Through: Conversations with Women Who Led the Way." *The Single* 53 (Fall 1983): 30–43.

Clark, Dennis, "Militants Of The 1860s: The Philadelphia Fenians," *The Pennsylvania Magazine Of History And Biography* No. 95 (1971): 98–108.

Cordato, Mary Frances. "Toward a New Century: Women and the Philadelphia Centennial Exhibition." *Pennsylvania Magazine of History and Biography* no. 107 (January 1983): 113–35.

Eaton, Clement. "A Mirror of the Southern Colonial Lawyer." *William and Mary Quarterly* 42 (1951): 520–34.

Elected and Appointed Black Judges In The U.S., 1986. The Joint Center For Political Studies And The Judicial Council Of The National Bar Association, Washington D.C., 1986.

Fisher, Joshua Francis. "Andrew Hamilton Esq. of Pennsylvania." *Pennsylvania Magazine of History and Bibliography* no. 16 (1892): 1–27.

Fitzroy, Herbert William Keith. "Richard Crosby Goes to Court, 1683–1697: Some Realities of Colonial Litigation." *Pennsylvania Magazine of History and Bibliography* no. 72 (1938): 12–19.

Flanders, Henry. "The Life and Times of John Dickinson, 1732–1808." *Pennsylvania Magazine of History and Bibliography* no. 15 (1891): 1–25.

Fossum, Donna. "Women in the Legal Profession: A Progress Report." *ABA Journal* 28 (1981): 578–81.

Gibbons, Walter B. "Integration of the Bar," *The Shingle* 8 (May 1938): 98–99.

Greenberg, Irwin F. "Charles Ingersoll: Aristocrat as Copperhead." *Pennsylvania Magazine of History and Bibliography* no. 93 (1969): 190–217.

Groff, Mary E. "Judge Hazel Hemphill Brown." 32 *The Shingle* (June 1952): 147–50.

_____. "Of Women Lawyers." *The Shingle* 8 (February 1938): 30–31.

Hamilton, J. G. DeRoughac. "Southern Members of the Inns of Court." *North Carolina Historical Review* 18 (1933): 273–86.

Hanna, Meredith. "The Organized Bar in Philadelphia." 24 *Temple Law Quarterly* (1951): 301–13.

Heinz, John P., and Edward O. Lauman. "The Legal Profession: Client Interests, Professional Roles and Social Hierarchies." *Michigan Law Review* 43 (1978): 1111–42.

Henderson, Elizabeth K. "The Attack on the Judiciary in Pennsylvania, 1800–1810." *Pennsylvania Magazine of History and Bibliography* no. 61 (1937): 113–36.

"Johnson As a Lawyer." *Literary Digest* (5 May, 1917).

Jordan, David Starr. "Pettifogging Law Schools and An Untrained Bar." *The Forum* (April 1895): 350–55.

Klaw, Spencer. "The Wall Street Lawyers." *Fortune* (February 1958): 140–44.

Leonard, Walter J. "The Development of the Black Bar." *Annals of the American Academy* 34 (May 1973): 134–43.

Lewis, Lawrence. "The Courts of Pennsylvania in the 17th Century." *Pennsylvania Magazine of History and Biography* no. 5 (1881): 141–90.

_____. "Edward Shippen, Chief Justice of Pennsylvania." *Pennsylvania Magazine of History and Bibliography*. no. 7 (1883): 11–84.

Livingston's Law Register, April 1851. *New York Monthly Law Magazine.* (1851). 27–32.

Lortie, Danc. "Laymen to Lawmen: Law School, Careers and Professional Socialization." *Harvard Educational Review* 33 (Fall 1959): 352–69.

Lundberg, Ferdinand. "The Legal Profession." *Harpers Magazine* (December 1938): 1–12.

Mackey, Philip English. "Law and Order, 1877: Philadelphia's Response to the Railroad Riots." *Pennsylvania Magazine of History and Bibliography* no. 96 (1972): 183–202.

MacKay, Winnifred K. "Philadelphia during the Civil War, 1861–1865." *Pennsylvania Magazine of History and Bibliography* no. 70 (1946): 3–51.

Mallowe, Mike. "Still Crooked after All These Years." *Philadelphia Magazine* (December 1987): 151–55; 222; 224–30.

Martin, Elaine. "Women on the Federal Bench: A Comparative Profile." *Judicature* 12 (December-January 1982): 306–12.

Mayer, Cynthia. "The Irrepressible Bernie Segal." *The American Lawyer* 3 (March 1984): 11–14.

Meehan, Thomas R. "Courts, Cases and Counselors in Revolutionary and Post-Revolutionary Pennsylvania." *Pennsylvania Magazine of History and Bibliography* no. 91 (1967): 3–34.

Nash, Gary B. "The Philadelphia Bench and Bar, 1800–1861." *Comparative Studies in Society and History* 13 (January 1965).

Nix Jr., Robert N. C. "The Supreme Court of Pennsylvania." (1986).

Parker, Kellis E., and Betty J. Stebman, "Legal Education for Blacks." *The Annals of the American Academy* 39 (May 1973): 144–55.

Pessen, Edward. "The Egalitarian Myth and the American Social Reality." *American Historical Review* 41 (October 1971): 989–1034.

Pollock, Herman I. "The Voluntary Defender as Counsel for the Defense." *Journal of the American Judicature Society* no. 32 (1949).

Powell, J. H. "John Dickinson and the Constitution." *Pennsylvania Magazine of History and Bibliography* no. 60 (1936): 1–14.

Raridon, Susan. "The Practice of Law: The Next 50 Years." *The Shingle* 58 (Fall 1988): 24–30, 34–35.

Reed, Alfred. "Legal Education." *Carnegie Foundation for Advance of Teaching Bulletin* no. 15 (1921): 86–111.

Richards, Louis. "Honorable Jacob Rush, of the Pennsylvania Judiciary." *Pennsylvania Magazine of History and Bibliography* no. 69 (1945): 53–68.

Riley, Edward M. "Philadelphia, The Nation's Capital, 1790–1800." *Pennsylvania History* 53 (October 1953): 358–79.

Sack, Saul. "The Higher Education of Women in Pennsylvania." *Pennsylvania Magazine of History and Bibliogrpahy* no. 83 (1959): 29–73.

Steiner, Bernard C. "Andrew Hamilton and John Peter Zenger." *Pennsylvania Magazine of History and Bibliography* no. 20 (1896): 405–8.

Stone, Harlan F. "The Lawyer and His Neighbor." *Cornell Law Review* no. 4 (1918): 175–89.

Strong, William. "Discourse Illustrating the Life and Character of Honorable Horace Binney." *Law Association of Philadelphia*. (1902): 204–39.

Swaine, Robert T. "Impact of Big Business on the Profession: An Answer to Critics of the Modern Bar." *American Bar Association Journal* (Fall 1949): 89–92, 168–71.

Turner, Sydney G. "The Middle Temple and the USA." *Quarterly Review* 12 (October 1958): 447–53.

Wharton, T. I. "A Memoir of William Rawle LLD." *The Law Association of Philadelphia, 1802–1902* (1902): 240–77.

Wister, William Rotch. "Some Reflections." *The Law Association of Philadelphia* (1902): 354–65.

Wolf, Edwin. "The Library of a Philadelphia Judge, 1708." *Pennsylvania Magazine of History and Biography* no. 83 (1959): 180–91.

Zackary, Alan M. "Social Disorder and the Philadelphia Elite Before Jackson." *Pennsylvania Magazine of History and Biography*. no. 99 (1975): 288–308.

Speeches, Papers, and Newspaper Reports

Arnold, Michael. "Law Reform" (address). *Law Academy of Philadelphia* (4 January, 1887).

Ashhurst, R. L. "William Morris Meridith." *The Law Association of Philadelphia* (1902): 278–327.

Ashman, William N. "The Profession of the Law." *The Law Association of Philadelphia* (23 March, 1889).

Binney, Horace. "Death of Hon, John Sergeant: Memorial Address." *The Law Association of Philadelphia* (1852): 185–203.

Brewster, F. Carroll. "Rights and Duties of Lawyers." *The Law Academy of Philadelphia* (30 October, 1861).

Brown, J. Hay. "Some of the Conditions of the Lawyer's Success." *Law Academy of Philadelphia* (28 May, 1901).

Bullitt, John C. "Some Recollections of the Bar Fifty Years Ago." *The Law Association of Philadelphia* (1902): 328-53.

Busch, Henry E. "George M. Wharton." *The Law Association of Philadelphia* (1902): 390-92.

"Charter, Constitution and By-Laws of the Law Academy of Philadelphia" (1867).

Dickson, Samuel. "Introductory Address." *The Law Association of Philadelphia* (1902): 1-12.

Gest, Hon. John Marshall. "Legal Education in Philadelphia 50 Years Ago." *The Law Academy of Philadelphia* (22 May, 1929).

"John G. Johnson." *The North American* (19 April, 1917).

"Johnson as a Lawyer." *Literary Digest* (5 May, 1917).

Konkle, Burton Alva. "Background and Beginnings of the Law Academy of Philadelphia." *The Law Academy of Philadelphia* (10 October, 1928).

Leaming, Thomas. "A Philadelphia Lawyer in the London Court." *The Law Academy of Philadelphia* (14 March, 1906).

MacLean, Jr., William. "The Law Academy and the Growth of Legal Education in Philadelphia." *The Law Academy of Philadelphia* (7 March, 1900).

McPherson, John B. "Proposed Changes in Pennsylvania Practice." *The Law Academy of Philadelphia* (30 April, 1895).

Mitchell, James T. "Historical Address: The Law Association of Philadelphia, 1802-1902." *The Law Association of Philadelphia* (1902): 13-78.

Paxson, Edward M. "The Road to Success: Practical Hints to the Junior Bar." *The Bar Association of Philadelphia* (14 April, 1888).

Peirce, William S. "Reminiscences of the Bar." *The Law Academy of Philadelphia* (17 April, 1883).

Penn. "Men and Things." *Philadelphia Evening Bulletin* (18 November, 1903).

Penrose, Clement B. "Reminiscences of the Bar." *The Law Association of Philadelphia* (1902): 375-89.

Porter, William W. "The Present Status of the Legal Profession." *The Law Academy of Philadelphia* (September 1907).

Samuel, John. "Address." *The Law Association of Philadelphia* (1902): 393-405.

_____. "John Cadwalader's Office." *The Law Association of Philadelphia.* (1902): 366-74.

Strong, William. "Discourse Illustrations of the Life and Character of Honorable Horace Binney." *The Law Association of Philadelphia* (1902): 204-39.

Sulzberger, Mayer. "Special Issues and General Issues." *The Law Academy of Philadelphia* (28 April, 1898).

Wister, William Rotch. "Some Recollections." *The Law Association of Philadelphia* (1902): 354-65.

Woods, Catherine. "John G. Johnson, Giant at the Bar, Shuns Notoriety." *Public Ledger* (21 June, 1914).

Woodward, George W. "Law and Lawyers." *The Law Academy of Philadelphia* (28 September, 1859).

Name Index

Abrahams, Robert D., 262
Adams, Abigail, 72, 73
Adams, Edwin K., 223
Adams, John, 52, 61, 67, 68, 72, 73, 74, 88, 130, 149, 155
Adams, John Quincey, 155
Alexander, James, 27, 30, 40
Alexander, Sadie Tabber Massell, 237
Allen, James, 44, 62, 79
Allison, John, 172, 175
Aquinas, Thomas, 160
Arlett, William, 25

Bache, Richard, 106, 141
Bacon, Francis, 38
Baker, George H., 96
Baldi, C. C. A., 223, 224
Baldwin, Matthias W., 106
Ball, Joseph, 38
Baltzell, E. Digby, 9, 267
Bamberger, A. J., 222
Bamberger, L. J., 222
Baright, Clarice, 226
Barkaloo, Lemma, 163
Barns, John Hampton, 271
Bass, Cecelia, 224
Batter, Edmont, 25
Beale, Joseph H., 240
Biddle, Algernon, 267
Biddle, Charles, 73, 141
Biddle, Charles J., 135
Biddle, Craig, 135
Biddle, Edward, 73
Biddle, Francis, 185, 219, 220, 247
Biddle, George, 237, 273
Biddle, George W., 128, 157, 167, 172, 175, 180, 210, 215, 269
Biddle, Moncure, 270
Biddle, Nicholas, 88, 96, 106, 118, 130, 141, 246
Biddle, William, 269

Bigelow, L. J., 137
Bingham, William, 73, 106
Binney, Horace, 23, 78, 83, 84, 87, 88, 93, 94, 96, 98, 100, 104, 105, 108, 111, 113, 114, 118, 124, 130, 131, 134, 137, 142, 167, 215, 247
Blackstone, William, 15, 19, 38, 39, 40, 41, 61, 81, 90, 94, 95, 98, 139, 159
Bland, John, 25
Bland, Sarah, 25
Bland, Theodore, 25
Blankenberg, Rudolph, 194
Blizzard, Adeline, 158
Blount, William, 103
Bockius, Morris, 205, 242
Boswell, James, 38
Bradford, William, 27, 44, 73, 76, 79
Bradley, Joseph, 163
Bradley, Richard, 31
Bradwell, Myra, 163
Brahams, Johannes, 272
Brent, Margaret, 26
Brewster, Benjamin Harris, 132
Brewster, F. Carroll, 140
Brewster, Francis E., 137
Brewster, Harris, 194
Briggs, Amos, 170
Broadhead, George M., 257
Brouwer, Adriaen, 190
Brown, Anne, 29
Brown, Charles, 111
Brown, David Paul, 114, 115, 168, 174
Brown, J. Hay, 131, 173
Brownell, Emery, 262
Bryan, William Jennings, 242
Bryce, James, 70, 112
Bullitt, John C., 136, 138, 139, 168, 170
Burke, Edmund, 38, 40, 112, 221
Burt, Nathaniel, 149, 156, 231, 246, 247
Busch, Henry E., 137
Butler, Smedley Darlington, 233, 234

Subject Index